Tracings

Tracings
Writing Art, 1975–2020

Ian Carr-Harris

Concordia University Press
Montreal

Cover and original template design: IN-FO.CO
Design and typesetting: Garet Markvoort, zijn digital
Copy editing: Bryne McLaughlin and Saelan Twerdy
Proofreading: Saelan Twerdy
Index: Lin Gibson

The body text of *Tracings* is set in Kis Antiqua Now. Released in 2006 by Elsner+Flake and designed by Leipzig type designers Erhard Kaiser and Hildegard Korger, Kis Antiqua Now pays tribute to the original Antiqua typeface cut in 1686 by Hungarian punchcutter Miklós (Nicholas) Tótfalusi Kis (1650–1702).

Printed and bound in Canada by Marquis Book Printing, Montreal

This book is printed on Forest Stewardship Council certified paper and meets the permanence of paper requirements of ANSI/NISO Z39.48-1992.

Concordia University Press's books are available for free on several digital platforms.
Visit www.concordia.ca/press

First English edition published in 2024
10 9 8 7 6 5 4 3 2 1

978-1-988111-51-3 | Paper
978-1-988111-52-0 | E-book

Library and Archives Canada Cataloguing in Publication

Title: Tracings : writing art, 1975–2020 / Ian Carr-Harris.
Names: Carr-Harris, Ian, author
Series: Text/context (Montréal, Québec)
Description: Series statement: Text/context: writings by Canadian artists |
   Includes bibliographical references and index.
Identifiers: Canadiana (print) 20240437985 | Canadiana (ebook) 20240437993 |
   ISBN 9781988111513 (softcover) | ISBN 9781988111520 (EPUB)
Subjects: LCSH: Art, Canadian—20th century. | LCSH: Art, Canadian—21st century. | LCGFT:
   Art criticism.
Classification: LCC N6549.C37 A35 2024 | DDC 700.411 | 709.2—dc23

Concordia University Press
1455 de Maisonneuve Blvd. W.
Montreal, Quebec, H3G 1M8
CANADA

Concordia University Press gratefully acknowledges the generous support of the
Birks Family Foundation and the Estate of Tanneke De Zwart

For Roddy, my brother and first best friend
1944–2022

Contents

List of Illustrations

A Note on Acknowledgements

The writer Jorge Luis Borges once wrote a short story about the problem of mapping and in his story it transpired that, for the Emperor's geographers to adequately map his domain, they had no option in the end but to produce a map the exact same size as the empire. Some such challenge arises in adequately acknowledging the sources and influences that cloak a life, a challenge rendered increasingly difficult the longer that life persists. Avoiding the trap into which the geographers fell, I must limit my map of acknowledgements to just a few of the landmarks that have had the most profound and lasting impression on my journey as an artist drawn to writing.

I need first to credit the warmth and imagination of Rosamond Green, my mother, who showed me how to draw a horse when I was very small (they're more difficult than you might think), and the analytical demands of my father who taught me how to draw a locomotive (tricky as well). To Professor Sydney Wise in the History Department at Queen's University, I owe the life-changing decision in 1963 to study library science, as it was then known, and launch a career as both artist and librarian. In continuation of this, I also want to credit the Ontario College of Art from 1967 to 1971 for a laissez-faire approach to learning that allowed me to spend several years practicing various approaches to making art, and for constructing the conditions that led to my becoming the college librarian.

For this latter I must credit OCA's first professional librarian, Ketha McLaren, who hired me to catalogue the collection and handed me the job when she left in 1971. I spent a considerable amount of my time over the next several years as the college librarian, a role I enjoyed and which I came to view as providing a service to humanity in general, and possibly to certain students in particular. I also read a lot of books and magazines.

However, in 1988, with the support of David Hall-Humpherson, then President of the college, and Michael Harmes, the Academic Coordinator, I traded my library job for faculty teaching appointments and administrative positions that enabled me to restructure the study of sculpture as a program devoted to an inquiry into what that study might mean, and to develop a new program in criticism and curatorial studies. To both David and Michael, I owe the honour of being able to assist to some degree in advancing the idea of an art college as a legitimate alternative to a multi-disciplinary university. I discovered in the process that some ideas advance, and others don't.

I owe a great debt as well to Chris Youngs, who in 1969 invited myself and Stephen Cruise, while still at OCA, to show together in his new Nightingale Gallery on Saint Joseph Street, and then subsequently in his *Concept 70* exhibition. The gallery later transformed into A Space at 85 Nicholas Street as an artist-run space, and I briefly served on its inaugural Board. In retrospect, these experiences introduced me to the realities of being an artist within the contemporary world of art.

In 1960s Toronto, that world came to be dominated by two commercial ventures on Yonge Street, the Isaacs and Carmen Lamanna galleries, and I owe a special debt of gratitude to Robin Collyer for encouraging Carmen Lamanna in 1972 to take an interest in my work. From this point on, Carmen became central to my work as an artist, but also as a writer since he provided through his gallery what mattered most to me—a place through which I could experiment with the idea of art. It was through Carmen that I met the writer and curator Philip Monk, to whom I owe an equivalent debt—not only for taking the work seriously and giving it an audience that I respected, but also for providing a model by which to practice an examination of what art is or can be. After Carmen passed away in 1992, I was again fortunate in that Susan Hobbs invited me to join her newly established gallery. That I continue to have an audience for the work I owe to Susan and her unswerving support and encouragement.

I am further indebted to Russell Keziere at *Vanguard* for supporting my writing, as I am as well to Chantal Pontbriand at *Parachute*, Sarah Milroy at *Canadian Art*, and Rick Rhodes at *C Magazine*. That debt includes two wonderful editors—Elke Town and Susan Harrison—both of whom ensured that my writing remained readable. I want also to add the many engaging hours of discussion and exchange that I have had with Philip Monk, Marc Mayer, Sarah Milroy, Jeanne Randolph, Gary Michael Dault, Barbara Fischer, and Louise Dompierre, simply to name a few. And I want especially to credit the many years of dialogue with colleagues and students at OCAD University with honing my sense of criticality as well as ensuring my admiration and respect for their commitment to testing the idea of art. That commitment in the seminar or the studio critique inevitably embraced the wider world of critical inquiry and the excitement of contributing to a conversation where definition is redefined.

Perhaps acknowledgement is the wrong word, or at least an inadequate one, for speaking of the partners who have shared my life in its several versions. I'm not sure what the right word would be, and possibly there isn't one that could account for the intimacy of connection that provides immeasurable guidance through decisions that are never secured by clarity. In any case, I owe more than I can say to Janis Higginson, my first love, wife, and mother of our wonderful and talented daughter Lisa; to Janis Hoogstraten, my partner of almost twenty years and a sensitive and lyrically engaging painter; and to Judith Schwartz, whose life I was privileged to share for seven years and an amazing artist whose work always seemed to me to epitomize the sublime in the beautiful.

But there are no words to adequately frame the significance in my life of my current and final partner as well as frequent collaborator, my lovely and brilliant Yvonne Lammerich—an artist for whom I have unbounded respect and whose acute critical perception is as evident in the arresting intelligence of her work as it is in our daily discussions with one another.

Finally, I want to return to my title for these acknowledgements, and the word has several uses. I have approached it as an opportunity to record a journey through the landscape of my attachments, the better to read the map that is embedded in the writing. Those attachments include a lifetime of readings and other sources that are impossible to adequately name, though it no doubt becomes clear that along with Borges they include Roland Barthes, Dave Hickey, Terry Eagleton, the theorists Derrida, Lacan, Kristeva, Foucault, and, by implication, Hegel and Marx.

An acknowledgement can, however, also be an opportunity to note an aporia or absence, and as I look back on these writings it is clear to me that they reflect a particular way of seeing that privileged my own history and its struggles with the viewpoints that motivated my ideas about art and how to write it. While I can regret that my sources seem now to be limited by that history, I realize also that we live in history and are inevitably therefore its children, studying attentively and often with misgivings the stories we've told ourselves over the years.

And like a story, these acknowledgements have an end, which is that there is this record. Of what, exactly? Well, certainly my engagement with the idea of art, and for that it enables a perspective on what I thought I was saying and doing, not always comfortable but always enlightening. For the reader, however, this book may be seen as a single snapshot marking a passage in time, the mid-1970s through the early 2000s, that in retrospect I think represents an awakening of ideas and ambitions in Canada's circumstances as a contender in the international realm of art.

I am therefore truly indebted to Geoffrey Little at Concordia University Press for approaching me with the idea of publishing this anthology and for his thoughtful comments on what should be included, to Dan Adler for his support and engagingly provocative introduction to my work as both artist and writer, as well as to Ryan Van Huijstee and Saelan Twerdy for their incredible support and encouragement in taking this anthology to completion. While over the years I had from time to time thought of publishing some of these texts myself, it never seemed a real possibility. This book is consequently a gift, and I cannot express more deeply the value it holds for me.

Preface

Why write? And why write about art? I was once asked at the university what I thought I was doing. In reply I wrote:

> I enjoy commentary, and it has become increasingly clear to me that this is why I enjoy the things I do. What I do is invent artworks—which is a little like writing instructions for a better mousetrap. For some time I have worked with students so that they could make better mousetraps too, and from time to time I write reviews and essays that theorize what a mousetrap might be.

Like all children, as a child I made something we could call art. But Art was the National Gallery of Canada in downtown Ottawa, and History seemed more attainable. So ultimately a degree in history as well as one in library science enabled me to spend several pleasant years working first in the catalogue department of the University of Toronto Library system and later at the Ontario College of Art. My studies at Queen's University had been analytical in nature, and I credit this experience with a conviction that if something is worthwhile, it deserves to be articulated clearly and emphatically, examined for its strengths and its possible shortcomings as I might understand them. Noting that Duchamp had worked in a library, I honed my ability to negotiate institutions and write a good memo. Writing memos is a good exercise in discrete analysis and balanced summation, qualities that in the course of time I have tried to apply in my writings on art.

An interesting question of course is just when and under what conditions did it occur to me to write, and I want to elaborate on this for a moment. I had graduated from OCA in 1971, and in the course of a conversation during a visit to my studio in 1974, the artist Vincent Tangredi challenged me with the suggestion that given my visceral commitment to the practices and theoretical constructs of artmaking, I should apply myself to writing on what I was seeing. The opportunity to write for a publication came the next year when *Parachute* asked me to write a short piece on three photographs I had exhibited at the Carmen Lamanna Gallery. As the anthology notes, I began to write more generally on art around 1978. I had never really imagined this, but a group of artists, unhappy with the lack of attention in the mainstream media, started *Artists Review*, a small-circulation publication of a few pages stapled together. I was encouraged to submit, and so began my career as an art writer that later grew to include *Vanguard* in Vancouver, *Parachute* in Montreal, and *Canadian Art* and *C Magazine* in Toronto, as well as essay contributions to catalogues and so on.

Originally, I thought I would return to the writings included in this anthology to retrace my views on what they had addressed, to see what I had said and perhaps cohere what I had thought over a period of almost forty-five years. A true preface in other words, a discussion of my intentions, my methodologies, and the scope of my ambition.

But retrieving intentions is famously slippery. I can re-read a text I've written, but all I have is the text before me; what I don't have is the text-in-its-context and in its time, what I was thinking when I wrote it. I would be left with only one alternative—to surreptitiously invent an intentionality for the writing, drawing on my context in the present.

It is nonetheless precisely the nature of the Present that is the problem, since its reach extends back into the past and forward into the future. The Present is ever-present, a series of presents, of which this is simply the latest version. Each present has its own dynamic, which is why chronology matters when it comes to reading what has been written. As I now read these texts in this present, it is clear that the concerns currently dominating our attention, for instance and most clearly questions of racialized identity and the politics of inclusion, have been for me channelled through issues of meaning-construction and their inconsistencies, consequent on hegemonic or traditional ways of seeing. The issues, based to some extent on my own experience, lay less in historical events and rather more in the implicit structures that could lead to delusional ambitions. Here, the issues closest to me lay in my experience of the gender relations that I observed growing up in mid-twentieth-century Canadian society, overwhelmingly white, male, and Eurocentric in orientation. Gender and social inequities seemed both central and available to critique, guided largely by theoretical constructs available in Marxist, feminist, and poststructuralist thought.

Yet, I have to ask, was this a framed intention or simply a reverse bias, an applied discomfort with middle-class assumptions that a good dose of Lacan or Derrida could unravel? I feel it would be inauthentic to post facto elevate this to an intention, something generated by a graduate seminar, for instance. Not only would I have to note that my investment in writing has primarily been propelled by personal interest in specific artists and their work, but that it has also been driven to a great extent by commissions and requests rather than by any intention to cover the scene or construct a narrative.

A recent case for an apparent intention might be found in the *Voices: artists on art* interview project conducted by Yvonne Lammerich and myself

0.1   Yvonne Lammerich and Ian Carr-Harris, *Voices: artists on art*, project and exhibition, 2017; exhibition catalogue and book, 2020; hardcover, 309 pp., col. illus., 26 × 26 cm.

between 2015 and 2017, and in the subsequent publication of the book that coheres those interviews. Conceived as an artwork, the project was itself a document based on another document, the exhibition catalogue for the National Gallery of Canada's *Sculpture '67* exhibition from fifty years before. That exhibition selected fifty-one artists across Canada, but predictably reflected the largely white, male art world of the time—there were, for example, only four women included—a situation that persisted more or less up to the early 2000s. Our project sought, within its limitations, to embrace the more diverse range of cultural, racial, and gender identities that characterize artists' practices in Canada today, including the recent rise to prominence of several generations of Indigenous voices. But while such a project might normally be considered the basis for a critical review or survey, we were instead simply dedicated to listening to what artists have to say, and how they say it. All this perhaps suggests that, rather than a gen-eralized intention, I could legitimately claim that a leitmotif in my work and thinking has certainly been the feeling that without critical attention, artists and the art they produce simply disappear.

Methodologies, on the other hand, such as those I mentioned above, are precisely and shamelessly inventions—fascinating, mesmerizing in their possibilities and illuminating in their ability to explore the dimen-sions of a subject. One could imagine that a methodology might be a clear delineation, a route map as it were. But methodologies are, it seems to me, a many-headed Hydra as every system divides into versions of itself, while all the while they each invite a seductive *pas de deux* with their alternative selves. Methodologies are exhilarating, and it is utterly impossible for me to single out or convincingly identify an overarching attachment. They remain instead invitations to a dance with many partners.

And what is to be said about ambitions? I could say I began with the idea of a public forum into which I hoped to insert a critical position that seemed to me lacking in the community I shared. I could also say that as an artist writing criticism or commentary, I imagined that I would be contrib-uting a useful voice, one which in some sense represented a more intimately engaged perspective on the act of making and its reception. And I could say, further, that the evolution of that ambition shifted over the years from a position critical of the project to be addressed to one more invested in the value that can be anticipated or coalesced in the individual practices under review.

However...

> The little girl had the making of a poet in her who,
> being told to be sure of her meaning before she spoke, said,
> **"How can I know what I think till I see what I say?**
> —Graham Wallas[1]

To say something clearly requires that there is something to be said, an observation about the world and what it means to assert one's place in it. The world pre-exists our entry into it, and perhaps my ambition in writing art was simply summarized by Wallas's allegorical reference to that little girl: to see what I might have to say about art-in-the-world in order to know how I could think about the idea of art. An ambition rooted not primarily in contributing something to the public forum, but instead and more urgently to find in the public forum catalysts to my own curiosity concerning the scope and function of artworks, and then to share that curiosity with others. I find evidence of this in an insistence that appears in many of the texts that the concept of the artist as authentically insular, separated and somehow

1   Graham Wallas, *The Art of Thought* (New York: Harcourt, Brace and Company, 1926), 106.

2   First published in Spanish in 1939, the first English translation of this story appeared in 1962. See Jorge Luis Borges, "Pierre Menard, Author of *Don Quixote*," *Ficciones*, ed. Anthony Kerrigan, trans. Anthony Bonner (New York: Grove Weidenfeld, 1963), 54. Note that this edition renders the title of the story as "Pierre Menard, Author of *Don Quixote*," whereas many other English translations use "Pierre Menard, Author of the *Quixote*."

detached from lived realities, was a false assumption that impoverished both the artist and the art itself—an insistence instead that artworks form part of a conversation that originates in a responsive network inherent in their social fabric.

So, while to write in order to think might seem itself insular in its purpose, writing comes with a responsibility to the reader as much as it does to the writer. Writing without implicitly taking into account the reader would be as vacant as saying something to no one, speaking in a vacuum. Moreover, to note the point of the girl's response, in the act of speaking or writing there is no guarantee that what has been said is immutable. Pauline Kael once remarked that criticism is meant to prompt discussion, not to suggest objective judgment, and what is thought in the present may very well contribute to a very differently stated position in the future. Thinking— and writing—is an activity, an action, for which there is no beginning and no conclusion.

What, then, could a useful preface look like?

...to read Le jardin du Centaure by Madame Henri
Bachelier as if it were by Madame Henri Bachelier.
—Jorge Luis Borges, "Pierre Menard, Author of Don Quixote"[2]

A small thought experiment: I write a sentence on a piece of paper. If I try then to trace over the letters, to retrace faithfully the lines of that sentence, I will find the task impossible. My lines will never correspond.

In his story "Pierre Menard, Author of the *Quixote*," Jorge Luis Borges assumes the role of a friend to a deceased author, Pierre Menard, whose life's work was to write *Don Quixote*, not as a new or reworked version of Cervantes's classic novel, but as a faithful word-for-word revisiting of Cervantes's text, exact in every way. Introduced as a letter to one Silvina Ocampo but resembling an extended preface to Menard's *Don Quixote*, Borges treats Cervantes's text as one would a photograph, original yet capable of infinite permutations of the meanings inherent in its capacity for reproduction and reception. For Borges, the meaning within a text is suspended in advance of a retracing that will never take the same path but will inevitably guide the reader to another. "To read *Le jardin du Centaure* by Madame Henri Bachelier as if it were by Madame Henri Bachelier" would require us to apprehend through the text the infinitely scattered drafts and musings, the imaginings and experiences, in fact the very body of the author, in order to read the book as if it were written by her. For Pierre Menard writing *Don Quixote*, the impossibility of such a retracing is further complicated by Time itself—words written by Cervantes in the seventeenth century are not the same words rewritten in the twentieth. We do indeed read a text through our experiences in the present.

To cite Borges's story here is to suggest an allegorical function to a preface. If I approach Borges's story as a preface to his own body of work, it seems clear that he intends the reader to be aware that to read is not a simple matter of absorption, but rather to be confronted with a palimpsest that is the reader's own invention. Reading the one through the other, the allegory begins with the first word read.

> …la parole humaine est comme un chaudron fêlé où nous battons des mélodies à faire danser les ours, quand on voudrait attendrir les étoiles.
> (…human speech is like a cracked kettle on which we beat out tunes for bears to dance to, when we long to inspire pity in the stars).
> —Gustave Flaubert, *Madame Bovary*[3]

Stepping back, perhaps it's too easy to dismiss intention as being beyond recuperation, or ambition as circumstantial. When I see what I say, I'm seeing not simply the content of what I say, but also the manner in which I say it. When I write a sentence, a paragraph, or an entire text, I am writing to convince, to seduce even, to enroll the reader in the enterprise of reading. There is more to writing than the intention to say something. There is in fact the ambition, as Roland Barthes puts it, to enter into the pleasure of the text: "If it were possible to imagine an aesthetic of textual pleasure, it would have to include: *writing aloud*."[4] So there you have it—an ambition consistent in my approach to writing that remains, beyond any doubt in my mind even now, that the writing should sound somehow *present* for the reader. Perhaps this persuasion was honed by years of seminar and studio discussions; perhaps it reached further back into reading the comics section in the *Ottawa Citizen* as a child. I remember quite clearly that my brother read them too, in a flash, and wondered at how slow I was to absorb them. While I was slightly abashed by this, I know what I was reading was not the content—though the content followed—but the sounds of the words. I was, in effect, writing aloud in my mind.

Of course, an intention is not always fulfilled, and I'm prepared to admit that the writing may not always have traded on the ambition behind the intention. This may lead to a paradox involved in the shifts that occur between the practice of artmaking and the practice of commentary on artmaking. Simply put, as it often is, a question almost inevitably arises as to why an artist, any artist, would want to enter into commentaries on art. Are they not, these two, separated by a gulf of intention—the one to picture,

3   Gustave Flaubert, *Madame Bovary*, Part 2, Ch. 12., trans. Lydia Davis (New York: Penguin Books, 2010), 167. The first French publication was in 1857. Author's note: While the Lydia Davis translation of Flaubert's famous line is perfectly fine, I prefer the variant translation I've used in the past for its cadence, but for which I cannot locate a firm reference: "Language is like a cracked kettle on which we beat out tunes for bears to dance to, while all the time we long to move the stars to pity."

4   Roland Barthes, *The Pleasure of the Text*, trans. Richard Miller (New York: Hill and Wang, 1975), 66.

5   Michael Fried, "Art and Objecthood," in *Minimal Art: A Critical Anthology*, ed. Gregory Battcock (New York: Dutton, 1968), 146.

6   Susan Sontag, "Writing Itself: On Roland Barthes," in *A Barthes Reader*, ed. Susan Sontag (1982; repr. New York: Hill and Wang, 1987), xvii.

7   Rosalind E. Krauss, *Passages in Modern Sculpture* (New York: Viking, 1977).

the other to parse. The paradox, however, is not one that exists between disciplines so much as it exists within each of those practices. As an artist engaged in the discipline of art, I must be aware of the dimensions that the artwork embodies—it is both picture and commentary. Conversely, as an artist engaged in the discipline of commentary, I have to be aware that inquiry without persuasion is simply sterile. Each side of the coin is conjoined with its other.

There is another question that follows from inquiry, whether generated by the artwork or through writing: for whom is it intended? In either case, artwork or commentary, there is an imagined public, and every artist or commentator answers to that demand. The writings in this anthology were directed to what one might call a community of interest—not necessarily professionally committed but engaged nonetheless in an adventure.

As an artist who works with objects to elicit meaning, normally but erroneously called sculpture, I have a particular interest in how such work is to be experienced: whether as simply a discursive collection of objects in a room, or instead as a collectivity of those objects whose affect could be described, as Michael Fried insists in discussing Anthony Caro's sculpture, "as a kind of instantaneousness."[5] Similarly, is one's experience of a piece of writing, an article or a review, to be seen as a string of conceptually directed words in a grammatical and syntactical arrangement, or are those words to be understood also as a gestalt, an arrangement whose purpose is, as Susan Sontag suggested in writing about Barthes, "to make us bold, agile, subtle, intelligent, detached…and to give us pleasure"?[6] I would argue that both the artwork and the text share a project: to enable the viewer and the reader to reach through the work or the text to imagine that within an apparent incommensurability between artwork and text there lies a common critical reality.

To better appreciate how this works, I was interested some years ago to read Rosalind Krauss writing in *Passages in Modern Sculpture*[7] about Rodin's *The Three Shades* that surmount his *Gates of Hell* (1880–1917). Modelled on, and perhaps critiquing, the classical trope of the Three Graces, Rodin's male is a three-fold repetition of the same figure posed to present the body from three different points of view. That the figure is a repetition sets it apart from the classical tradition of sculpture that Baudelaire dismissed as "vague and elusive," yet at the same time it trades on precisely that elusive quality. Now as a repetition of a figure that has become an object, it eludes the narrative search for meaning that establishes the normal order of things. Neither a single figure set in an imaginary landscape, nor a grouping of figures, like the *Burghers of Calais* (1884–1889) on their intended plaza, *The Three Shades* are suspended, in fact they suspend us, in an instantaneous yet incommensurate reality.

Ceci n'est pas une pipe
—Rene Magritte / Michel Foucault

8   First published in French in 1973. See Michel Foucault, *This is Not a Pipe*, trans. James Harkness (Berkeley: University of California Press, 1983).

If, as Susan Sontag says, the point of writing is to make us bold and subtle rather than simply leave us with a cracked kettle, then the language of writing on art must include an awareness, extended to the reader, of how image and text intersect. Magritte's "Ceci n'est pas une pipe" is the classic case study for an interrogation of these relations, or more specifically, the relations between resemblance and representation. So much so that the series became the subject of an extended essay by Michel Foucault, titled also "Ceci n'est pas une pipe," or "This Is Not a Pipe" in the English translation.[8]

Foucault treats Magritte's examination of the respective roles played by the image of the pipe and its textual negation as the construction of an "after-image," an unravelling of a previous symbolic unity of image and text, where a resemblance—a drawing of a pipe, for instance—is locked into a representation through the text as title: "a Pipe." One can, for instance, imagine this as the title for a traditional painting of an old man smoking a pipe. For Foucault, in Magritte's work the pipe drawing and its negating text drawing are in fact self-identical, a doubling of one to the other, refuting the opposition that normatively separates seeing and saying, a refutation Magritte most clearly rendered in *Les Deux mystères* (1966). In this painting from 1966, the large image of a pipe seems suspended, like an apparition, over a classroom containing, on an easel, his 1929 painting *Le trahison des images*. This apparition is, in Magritte's frame of reference, the originating image of the pipe in the painting below, what we can call its referent. It is here that we can most closely apprehend that which cannot be represented, and which consequently lies beyond the scope of signification. To write, or to paint, is to confront the limits of representation, to find ourselves suspended in the act.

So what do we have here? "Ceci n'est pas une pipe," both Magritte's painting and Foucault's essay, articulate that suspension I mentioned previously in discussing Rodin's *The Three Shades*. If in Magritte's painting we are suspended between seeing and saying, in Foucault's text we are suspended between saying and seeing. To write within this suspension is to write in an attempt to move the stars, if not to pity, then perhaps to wonder.

Or at any rate one might discern in this suspension an overriding purpose connecting my work as an artist with my practice as a writer. And not simply as a writer, but also as a teacher during my years in studios and seminars with students, who themselves hoped to provoke a sense of wonder in others through their pursuit of that better mousetrap.

Still, it's one thing to have an intention or an ambition, and quite something else for others to find it in the evidence. If the reader writes the

9   Walter Benjamin, "Theses on the Philosophy of History," *Illuminations*, trans. Harry Zohn (New York: Schocken Books, 1968), 256.

text, as Barthes insisted, this preface nevertheless suggests some qualities I hope the reader will find echoed in the writings collected here. As for how I think the writing may have contributed in some way to a progressive agenda, the writing reveals, as I have noted earlier, that gender identity and the social tensions involved have been a primary lens through which I have viewed political issues in art production and reception and, at this most elemental level, the possibilities for cultural change.

Of course, gender identity is not the only tension lacing through the production and reception of art, and if I were to retrace my steps to the beginning of my career as an artist, I could note that certain works suggest the potential for a more focused examination of class and racial bias. An instance of this would be a photo-text work from 1973 that presented two pages of illustration from an anthropology journal, with the title, *Mussurongo Types / Girl from Huila*, simply lifted from the journal's captions. The work sought to reveal the way Western modes of depiction and classification de-humanized peoples beyond the white European sphere. Or to state it more broadly, as Walter Benjamin did, "there is no document of civilization which is not at the same time a document of barbarism."[9] But while these issues were familiar to me from my university studies in the history of European expansionism, I became cautious about allowing my art practice to become an illustration of historical wrongs. Even more problematic it seemed in retrospect, was the thought that from another point of view such a venture could only pour salt into the wounds of those who had been demeaned. This led me to reconsider the foundation of my art practice, including my writings, within the inherently complex nature of identity as it is performed in language and in the intimate relations that underwrite human desire.

In any event, sometimes openly a critique, and more often a veiled investigation into value, the writings collected here reflect the layered and evolving nature to be found in four decades of reflection on what it is to look—and somehow look to see what to say.

Debate and Difference: An Introduction to the Writings of Ian Carr-Harris

Dan Adler

Initially trained as a historian and a professional librarian, Ian Carr-Harris has explored what it means to speak in both visual and verbal registers over the fifty years of his practice. For anyone familiar with his work, it is clear that throughout his career a primary concern has been with how identities are formed through language, and consistently in his art and criticism he has investigated how this formation occurs as we each come to terms with the social codes imposed upon us.

From the beginning, Ian Carr-Harris has occupied multiple roles within the cultural community. While shifting between the roles of professor, critic, editor, librarian, and archivist, his career creates an image of an artist whose discursive approach casts an extraordinarily expansive semantic net. In terms of his writing, these multiple roles are reflected in a longstanding tendency to question and probe the systems in which, to some extent, he is always a participant: for example, he frequently offers institutional observations that reach far beyond a relatively solitary, studio-based perspective. This probing informs the questions that Carr-Harris has persistently posed: What do, or should, the ideas of "community," of "communication," of "difference," of the "social" mean for artists? In this sense, Carr-Harris became a pivotal part of a conceptualist community of "artists who write" within an array of milieus, both locally in Toronto and elsewhere within Canada, the US, and abroad.[1] Indeed, while helping to build a burgeoning artist-run culture in Toronto as an exhibiting artist, he has also consistently sought to support the strategy of writing *as an artist*—both through his own published contributions and through his initiatives in establishing programs in criticism and curating at the Ontario College of Art, now OCAD University. Consequently, Carr-Harris's writings seem all the more relevant to an understanding of both his own studio practice and those of others who share his interest in a written discourse running parallel to, and intersecting with, the making of artworks. Indeed, Canada has had very few artists able

1   The literature on conceptualism in Canada is vast. One crucial source is Grant Arnold and Karen Henry, eds., *Traffic: Conceptual Art in Canada, 1965–1980* (Vancouver: Vancouver Art Gallery and Douglas & McIntyre, 2012). There has been much valuable work done in recent years in terms of offering narratives of conceptualism within more diversified local contexts and communities, inspired in part by groundbreaking exhibitions (and accompanying publications) such as *Global Conceptualism: Points of Origin, 1950s–1980s* at the Queens Museum of Art (1999). For a detailed look at the relationship between Black activism and conceptual art within the context of Halifax, see Krys Verrall, "Beyond Parochialism: Telling Tales about Black Activism and Conceptual Art," in Charmaine Nelson, ed., *Towards an African Canadian Art History: Art, Memory, and Resistance* (Concord, ON: Captus Press, 2018), 295–346.

2   While there is a diversity of reference points—in terms of identities and social groups within multiple social and psychological contexts—there are, of course, artistic communities that are not directly addressed by Carr-Harris's writings. For other perspectives, see for example Monika Kin Gagnon's Introduction to the compilation of her essays, reviews, and other writings from the 1980s and 1990s, *Other Conundrums: Race, Culture, and Canadian Art* (Vancouver: Arsenal Pulp Press, 2000), 21–30; Gagnon and Richard Fung, eds., *13 Conversations about Art and Cultural Race Politics* (Montreal: Artexte Editions, 2002) includes reflections by artists, critics, and curators on issues of ethnicity and racialized difference within the contexts of Toronto and other Canadian cities during the 1980s and 1990s.

3   Other writers and artists, of course, have interrogated and engaged with issues of identity, semiotics, and self-representation more directly within the context of the cumulative effects of colonization (and efforts to decolonize) in recent decades, including those performed by First Nations, Métis, and Inuit individuals. See, for instance, Nancy Marie Mithlo, "The First Wave …This Time Around," in Mithlo, ed., *Manifestations: New Native Art Criticism* (Santa Fe: Museum of Contemporary Native Arts, 2011), 18; Heather Igloliorte, ed., *Decolonize Me / Décolonisez-moi* (Oshawa and Ottawa: Robert McLaughlin Gallery and Ottawa Art Gallery, 2012), 18–37. In a similar vein, Frances Henry and Carol Taylor's *Discourses of Domination: Racial*

to offer such sustained, broad-ranging, and insightful commentary on their own artistic milieu.

An introduction can be many things. It can offer a biographical overview into the subject's career and place it in a broadly historical context. Or it can attempt to suggest the signal importance of that career to the reader and insist on what needs to be learned from an exploration of its trajectory. Less ambitiously perhaps, it can offer a close reading of the content of that career that would suggest the tone and purpose at play in the moment of production.

In this Introduction, I emphasize the latter approach. I am convinced that close readings—attention paid to particular works—provide a chance to investigate the tenor of each and every document without contaminating the record through an overarching judgment. With an anthology of writing that represents nearly half a century of production, it is best left to the reader, now or in the future, to determine how these texts respond in time to the inevitable flux of contexts and conditions.

That said, there are certain features clearly relevant today that I want to focus on in Carr-Harris's work as both an artist and a writer. Of particular interest is his use of language and social constructs as determinants of identity, and their importance in making and reading artworks. I will explore how his work as a writer relates to his art practice, as well as to the individual artists and groups he has supported and with whom he has identified. And I will discuss how the operations of difference and debate come to bear upon these relationships, since I believe that it is difference, employed as an interpretive tool—in art and writing—that, more than any other concept, has grounded his practice of cultural critique. Difference is the means by which subjects negotiate and renegotiate positions in the context of communities, which Carr-Harris has defined diversely in terms of gender, sexuality, social class, cities, and national culture.[2] The importance of Carr-Harris's conceptions of difference lies with the imperative of striving and struggling—sometimes contentiously—to acquire an appreciation of what it can mean to critically relate to the social sphere. His careful explorations of how we (mis)identify with others consistently yields such understanding, offering up those moments of awareness that occur as we rub up against what is expected of us through issues of presence and absence, gain and loss, success and failure, pride and shame, certainty and doubt.

Carr-Harris developed his approach to art and to critical writing in an arena dominated by first-generation conceptualists and minimalists such as Joseph Kosuth and Lawrence Weiner or Carl Andre and Donald Judd. Influential though they were, their concerns were restricted in their social scope. While questioning preconceptions about the artist, the artwork, and the museum, they did so in relatively reductivist ways that left little room for the more detailed sociological, semiotic, and psychological subject matter that Carr-Harris sought to assess.[3] Distinct from industrially fabricated abstract sculpture or from radically dematerialized practices, Carr-Harris's art has been rooted resolutely in the realm of lived, everyday experience. As Jessica Bradley once observed, Carr-Harris's art "proposes that reality is a mental construct which is redefined with each successive experience and is therefore the product of memory, expectation, and socially learned patterns of interaction." While exploring the social codes that govern behaviour, he crafted "tableaux or ensembles whose various elements—still or moving images, language, light, sound, and seemingly familiar objects—combine to reveal the discontinuous but cumulative nature of our relationship to the world."[4] Accordingly, the reader, like the viewer, is called upon to make decisions or to imagine being a self-conscious participant rather than a passive observer. Indeed, his earliest artworks incorporated staging devices and prop-like elements: *On Stage* (1970), for instance, featured a platform just large enough for someone to stand on, surrounded on three sides by rows of tilted lights which resembled stage footlights. A visitor stepping onto the platform activated the lights, hence becoming the performer as the "subject" of the work and the "object" on display.

Similarly, Carr-Harris's writings often may be read as theatrical-type tableaux, as they project the idea of being on stage, of performing for others. Writing in *Parachute* on "Sentences on Art," part of a larger lecture series held at the Rivoli Tavern in Toronto in 1982, Carr-Harris describes the well-attended lecture by the curator and critic Philip Monk.[5] Referring to the speaker as "Philip," Carr-Harris conveys a personal affinity, and yet quickly makes it clear that their views diverge, portraying himself having a beer at the bar while Monk delivers an on-stage talk, one that assesses Toronto's art scene.[6] While sympathetic to many of Monk's views—and impressed by the speaker's willingness to offer frank remarks in a public and performative manner—Carr-Harris engages in a bit of sly satire. Comparing Monk's persona to a Presbyterian minister—while observing how his leather jacket, with a rose in its lapel, marks him as a member of the group he was critiquing—Carr-Harris reflects on Monk's philosophical foray into how truth and judgment bear upon art's social basis. Carr-Harris hones in on a quality of uncertainty arising from Monk's take on the already-prominent collaborative trio General Idea: that it is not clear whether they can achieve critical distance from that which they were ironically appropriating. Allowing his beverage to take effect, Carr-Harris uses this performance by a respected colleague—with whom he frequently collaborated—to speculate about existential issues affecting the artistic community in Toronto. The literal presence of many members of the local community in that tavern allows Carr-Harris to develop a self-critical aesthetic outlook, one with a

Bias in the Canadian English-Language Press (Toronto: University of Toronto Press, 2002) reflects on how the fields of cultural studies and semiotics have led to a relatively specific process of questioning how meaning is created and for whom; how signs are perceived and understood by certain communities and social groups; and how inequalities are (re)engrained or (re)enforced by visual and textual systems of representation.

4   See Jessica Bradley, "Ian Carr-Harris," in Bradley, ed., *Ian Carr-Harris/Liz Magor: Canada XLI Biennale di Venezia 1984* (Ottawa: National Gallery of Canada, 1984), 5–6, 8.

5   "Sentences on Art" was the title of Philip Monk's lecture in the larger lecture series "A Critical Structure(ing)," organized throughout November 1982 by YYZ Artists' Outlet.

6   For discussion, see the groundbreaking study by Philip Monk, *Is Toronto Burning? Three Years in the Making (and Unmaking) of the Toronto Art Scene* (Toronto and London: Art Gallery of York University and Black Dog, 2016). More recently, see Luis Jacob, "When Fictions Become Form," in Jacob, *Form Follows Fiction: Art and Artists in Toronto* (London and Toronto: Black Dog and the Art Museum at the University of Toronto, 2020), 12–19. Jacob's groundbreaking show and catalogue—which featured two of Carr-Harris's works from the 1970s—makes the case that "Toronto" demands "further articulation of its intricacies, and requiring a practice of interpretive synthesis that avoids smoothing over the ways in which these

discourses corroborate but also question one another" (15). The book also includes a quote from Carr-Harris: "Toronto has begun to see itself historically. I'm not sure whether we are ready to meet History just yet but perhaps that's always the way it happens, when you're not ready" (89). Also relevant and useful in this regard are Wanda Nanibush and Georgiana Uhlyarik, eds., *Toronto: Tributes + Tributaries, 1971–1989 = Gchi-oodenaang: ezhi-mina-waajimong eni-naabiis-chigeng* (Toronto: Art Gallery of Ontario, 2018) and Julie Crooks, Silvia Forni, and Dominique Fontaine, eds., *Making History: Visual Arts & Blackness in Canada* (Vancouver: On Point Press, 2023).

relatively independent ideological influence—a renewed, ever-changing, and shared sense of difference that must be formed to some extent in opposition to the then-dominant French and American mythologies and values. Carr-Harris's critical take reflects a consistent and crucial assumption: that a shared artistic identity may only be forged within a context of friendly debate, in which artists feel comfortable with critiquing each other—sometimes negatively—in constructive ways.

Published in *Vanguard*, "Winging It: Noel Harding" (April 1984) is not an exhibition review in the conventional sense, nor is it meant to be, since it covers several years of the artist's practice. Harding's artistic approach is of interest to Carr-Harris for the fact that they both used theatrical or prop-like everyday objects in their work. So to set the stage, Carr-Harris provides a close look at several works in the form of well-crafted descriptive accounts, along with some anthropomorphic associations. But while sharing affinities with Harding, Carr-Harris sees such similarities as a vehicle for expressing difference from his own position, most crucially the importance Harding places on creating a certain sense of disjunction between artwork and audience. Carr-Harris envisions Harding's practice as a case of a capable artist who is charting a path that falls prey to myths of heroic individualism that divide the artist from the audience: "I am disillusioned by his apparent lack of sophistication, and his grasp of what artmaking involves. The disappointment is that his essentially romantic transcendentalism simply ends up by isolating its adherents in the emptiness and banality of the oldest convention of all: the lonely individual as misunderstood prophet amongst the philistines. Such a position is meaningful neither for Harding, nor for me." As I have noted, such frankness is meant in the spirit of a shared social context—one that includes artists who are prepared to offer critical analysis—in which debate is the currency of thought. In my view, such a context should not be forgotten during our present moment, in which constructive criticism—for example, "mixed" reviews or more detailed texts that advance an argument against particular tendencies—is often avoided in favour of promotional language.

The combative tone that Carr-Harris has frequently adopted in his criticism clearly signals his view that the art community, particularly his own, should be prepared to embrace rather than evade an identity freed from nostalgic fantasies, and this is evident in his contribution to the catalogue for the opening exhibition of the Power Plant. In "Toronto, Art, and History" (1987), Carr-Harris reflects on the roots of Toronto's cultural identity, proposing that the city's history is tied to conditions of absence and a hesitancy associated with a vein of colonialist insecurity. Referring indirectly to his own practice, he holds up installation art as an aesthetic model especially suited to Toronto "with its detachment from specific limitation and its earnest theatrical promotion of critical discourse." For Carr-Harris, Toronto's identity, an issue of perennial discussion in the city, should properly be envisioned in terms of a layering of absences, resulting in an ever-changing complexity supported by its history of attracting ambitious and talented individuals from beyond itself. This identity is founded on an accumulation of othernesses.

It is the propensity among peers to deny these complexities and ambiguities in the search for a "coherent" identity that Carr-Harris has sought to argue against most polemically. "Serious Art in Toronto: Tracing Curatorial Imperatives" was presented in the pages of *Canadian Art* (Spring 1988) as a review of two shows organized by Bruce Grenville at the S.L. Simpson Gallery and the Power Plant. Carr-Harris sets forth a combative perspective on what it means to be a serious artist and critic within the Toronto context, insisting on the significance of a fragmented identity. While acknowledging the selection of impressive works—by artists with whom Carr-Harris was closely associated and aligned—he takes the view that the curatorship of the exhibitions in question failed "to recognize the ways in which we construct ourselves." For Carr-Harris, the issue stems from a patronizing (and commercializing) need to deny the "complexities of interaction between a viewer and an artwork," thereby missing the opportunity to challenge viewers by crafting shows as a medium for our real social experience.

Similarly, Carr-Harris's *Parachute* review of *New City of Sculpture*—an exhibition co-sponsored by YYZ and Mercer Union and held at six Toronto venues in 1984—includes no detailed treatment of exhibited works but rather an in-depth argument against what he sees as a lack of complexity and complication, both in the show and in the essay by Bruce Grenville accompanying it. While identifying with the pragmatic approaches expressed by sculptural statements included in the extensive show—as well as with the intentions of David Clarkson and Robert Wiens, his fellow Toronto artists co-curating it—Carr-Harris criticizes the project's general lack of substance as reflecting a subservience to mythologies and uncritical self-involvement. The show, he states, was "grounded in the romantic ennui of the historical avant-garde and its nihilistic—wilfully ignorant—impatience with history and process...their New City has nowhere to go, nothing to do, except to fuss about in the fragments of old art and old history. Their nihilism, founded on superficial appearance as an alternative to historical dialectic, ensures this. The New City is simply another failure to realize that nihilism is not deconstructive, but simply narcissistic. And narcissism reconstructs the emptiest of formalisms."

7   On the history and culture
of ARCs in Toronto, Canada,
and elsewhere see, for example,
Gabriele Detterer and Maurizio
Nannucci, eds., *Artist-Run
Spaces* (Zurich and New York:
JRP Ringier and D.A.P.,
2012); AA Bronson et al., eds.,
*Decentre: Concerning Artist-
Run Culture* (Toronto: YYZ
Books, 2008); and Luis Jacob,
ed., *Golden Streams: Artists'
Collaboration and Exchange in
the 1970s* (Toronto: Blackwood
Gallery, 2002).

Carr-Harris's disappointment reflects his own direct participation and dedicated belief in the radical roles that artist-run centres (ARCs) and publications could play within Canada's cultural scene.[7] In Toronto especially—as an urban centre in which corporatist and consumerist ideologies were becoming more and more naturalized—these platforms had the capacity to shape a city's cultural history and identity in terms of non-commercial tendencies that could challenge audiences *differently* from public museums and for-profit galleries. In "Museums in the '80s," published in *Vanguard* (March 1983), Carr-Harris portrays A Space—an ARC of which he was a founding member—as a vehicle to "redefine the social context of art-making in Toronto." But just as essential to A Space's identity, he argues, is an ongoing expression of difference, not only from more traditional institutions, but from other artist-run organizations, locally and nationally. While YYZ, Art Metropole, *Fuse*, and *FILE*, among others, featured practices and points of view that certainly aligned with those of A Space, their social identities tended to differ and change in ways that made the cultural landscape diverse and that resisted being categorized, packaged, and marketed in terms of more mainstream systems that thrive upon relatively static and stable institutional forces.

Attachment to this critical condition of ambiguity and elusiveness runs through much of Carr-Harris's writing. Another case in point is his contribution to the projected catalogue (never published) for the exhibition *Small Villages: The Isaacs Gallery in Toronto, 1956–1991*, curated by Ihor Holubizky and held in 1992 at the Art Gallery of Hamilton. While this text is appropriately appreciative of a commercial venue's pivotal significance to Toronto's art history, Carr-Harris nonetheless takes issue with the gallery's agenda. While acknowledging that the Isaacs Gallery (which opened in 1956) was devoted to challenging conventional tendencies in contemporary art, Carr-Harris suggests that it found itself too much in the service of a conveniently static or reified cultural identity, one that cohered in ways which were overly receptive to market forces. He singles out the gallery's support of painting practices clinging to "abstract heroics" and male-oriented mythologies rooted in the reception of retrograde visions of avant-garde individualism. In his view, this not only compromised the venue's criticality, but was unnecessary when compared to the alternative, also for-profit Carmen Lamanna Gallery, which represented Carr-Harris himself. Lamanna's gallery had from its outset in 1966 searched out and supported a diversity of practices that defied an easily defined theoretical base. In other words, at the core of Carr-Harris's discontent are organizations that presented a progressive stance while at the same time associating with a "strong belief in the presence of the artist as lightning rod to a lost cohesion," a condition of unity which we, as a community, should no longer strive uncritically to regain.

While as an artist Carr-Harris did not adopt painting as a primary medium, he never believed—as many conceptualists did—that it was hopelessly compromised and corrupted. In the *Vanguard* article "Standing on the Mezzanine: Ewen, Wiitasalo, Monk and the AGO" (December 1988–January 1989), Carr-Harris looks to the paintings of Patterson Ewen, an exemplar of an avant-garde and essentially modernist tendency to advance a universalizing outlook. Ewen's version of the self is akin to Edmund Husserl's philosophy, which addresses knowable phenomena "secured at the cost of enclosing that world within the centrality of a universal subject unmarked by difference." Accordingly, in Ewen's work there is a sense of certainty that Carr-Harris admits to finding attractive. And yet Carr-Harris makes the case that it is Shirley Wiitasalo's approach to painting that allows for encounters with incompleteness and unknowing, or the "implausibility of direct perception," that are more faithful to our sense of the Real. In fittingly diverse ways, her paintings signify difference by throwing a range of wrenches into the workings of the universal subject, as she "turns to the maskings, or surfaces, which separate us from each other and screen even this interpreted reality from view." Compared to Ewen, Wiitasalo expresses a more detailed social self, with imagery that "depicts the interruptions and distortions that intercept our desire to view directly and establish secured conditions." Hence, the presence of these complications cannot "magically eliminate or settle difference."

Drawing this comparison between Ewen and Wiitasalo in a critical and explicitly evaluative manner makes this another instance of Carr-Harris's willingness to engage in public debate within his own immediate institutional milieu, and with respected colleagues. Sixteen years his senior and eight years his junior, respectively, Ewen and Wiitasalo were represented, like Carr-Harris, by Carmen Lamanna, and all three had been recognized with solo shows at the Art Gallery of Ontario around the same time. And yet, implicitly siding with the artist-run community, Carr-Harris does not hesitate, in the same text, to offer a pointed critique of the museum's function as uncritical outlet for the middle-classes—one that operates in the service of market forces and of a romanticized mythology of the avant-garde that too often "settles for a validation from elsewhere." By dwelling on the differences between Wiitasalo and Ewen's AGO exhibitions, both organized by Philip Monk, Carr-Harris imagines, while standing on the gallery's mezzanine, as it were, that this mainstream museum could be the means for setting the stage for a renewed culture of painting. For Carr-Harris, this culture strives to represent the conditions of mediating signs and the construction of consciousness, by coming to terms with the "distortions and *mirages* that characterize the surfaces which, in *effect*, constitute our sole knowable reality."

Carr-Harris's art and writing have worked in tandem to critique a culture of institutional investment in modernist notions of originality, with its ties to monographic modes of thought and marketing, including tropes of the heroic artist who offers a unifying and singular vision. For Carr-Harris, the questioning of *singularity* has a deeply personal history. In his unpublished lecture "Tracing Reading Writing" (2002), Carr-Harris reflects on an episode from his childhood, when at the age of seven he traced a comic book image against a sunlit window in his Victorian home. Admonished at the time for copying rather than making something of his own, in retrospect this event represented a liberating realization: "no amount of making 'something new' had ever touched me so deeply, excited me as much, as that discovery of the 'trace.'" For Carr-Harris, this submission to the image suggested a practice that can develop a context that is collective and fluid, in which there is "a logic of momentum or mobility which draws us, we could say, to trace that which we anticipate having revealed not once, but a thousand times—an insistence that is even infinite in its proportions or quantifiability—as completely invested in the necessity of repetition as it is dis-invested in the possibility of singularity."

In staging such an act of metonymic submission, Carr-Harris has frequently invited a sense of comedic structure into his art practice as well as into his writing. In doing so, he has challenged submission to conditions of conformity that rest on authority and authorization. This questioning may be located within a feminist context in which performativity enacts parodic deconstruction. His treatment of paintings by the British painter Torie Begg in *Contemporary* (Summer 2002), for example, dwells upon her dialogue with modernist mythologies: Begg self-consciously dramatizes acts of mimicry while mocking the idea of heroic and authentically expressive gestures, and Carr-Harris focuses on defining her repetitive actions of accumulation. In these paintings, the "assumption and separation of painting's mechanics—on the one hand paint, layer upon layer of paint, and on the other any support, from canvas to bedsprings, that can hold the paint— converge as a cover story borrowed from the conventions of modern art for a body whose embodiment has been 'flayed,' unstretched from its frame, re-ordered for us into parody like bones in the Paris catacombs." In this regard, Carr-Harris makes use of Sandra Gilbert and Susan Gubar's literary theory, which posits an ambivalent combination of acts of emulation and singular expressiveness within a two-level signification: while Begg offers up accessible surface conventions—which mimetically imitate what we see—she ironically hints at a "deeper," obscured meaning whose existence threatens to disrupt the very surface that provides our vantage point. It is this dialectical quality that allows Begg's pictures to *provisionally* converge as mimicry in ways that deconstruct tradition without wholly dismissing it.[8]

In another instance of Carr-Harris's interest in performance, his contribution to the anthology *Caught in the Act: An Anthology of Performance Art by Canadian Women* (2006), focuses on performance works by Johanna Householder, a longstanding participant in Toronto's artist-run culture. Crucially, Carr-Harris stresses the collaborative context of Householder's practice as the means by which she "could undercut the inherent trap of narcissism at the heart of modern art's ambition 'to astonish.'" In particular, he points to her need—alongside others—to perform, or re-perform, everyday tasks rather than simply appear within the extended context of a play with protagonists following an instructive and linear narrative arc. Householder explores a shared social context—rather than a protagonistic one—providing performances that rely on pronounced repetition, allowing for ironic or parodic critiques of conformist and other coded behaviours. As with Begg's pictures, Householder's emphasis on reiteration is intended not only to misplace but also displace those "proper" gestures as static and complete understandings of who we thought we were, and who we were taught to be. For Carr-Harris, the importance of such work lies, in part, with its ability to unexpectedly offer subversive insight into how social groups can be marginalized according to hegemonic (and historically male-dominated) cultural frameworks.

Consistently, Carr-Harris has offered close readings of practices by his colleagues—such as Householder, a fellow faculty member at OCAD—who shared his particular priority of offering performative provocations in the form of ideological and institutional critique, both within and without the Toronto setting. This interest in taking a stand within one's own community was expressed in the recent conference "This is Paradise: Art and Artists in Toronto," held in 2015 at the University of Toronto. Presented in the panel "Toronto's 'Absence' of History," Carr-Harris's paper reflects on *Toronto: A Play of History*, the inaugural show held at the Power Plant in 1987 in which chief curator Louise Dompierre and her team attempted to address the previous decade of art production in the city. While not commenting in much detail about the show itself, Carr-Harris dwells upon a symposium that was held at the time in which several speakers alleged that this then-new institution was compromised by exclusionary ethos and/or coopted by corporate interests. Carr-Harris cites a series of scathing reviews of the show, including curator and writer Elke Town's discussion of how starved local audiences were for more challenging recent Canadian art, and Bruce Grenville's lament about a widespread "deep distrust of any attempts to represent the current scene." As a founding member of the Power Plant,

8   See Sandra M. Gilbert and Susan Gubar, *The Madwoman in the Attic: The Woman Writer and the Nineteenth-Century Literary Imagination*, 2nd ed. (1979; repr., New Haven: Yale University Press, 2000).

9   Cited in *Ian Carr-Harris: 1971–1977*, ed. Philip Monk (Toronto: Art Gallery of Ontario, 1988), 23.

10   See Philip Monk, "Deaccessionings: Fallen Knowledge and Memory Traces in the Work of Ian Carr-Harris," in *Ian Carr-Harris: Works 1992–2002*, ed. Monk (Toronto: The Power Plant, 2002), 23. See also Monk, "Ian Carr-Harris: Lessons in the Pleasure of Pedagogy," *Sketch* (Fall 2002): 6–7.

11   See Elke Town, "Ian Carr-Harris," in *Fiction: An Exhibition of Recent Works by Ian Carr Harris, General Idea, Mary Janitch, Shirley Wiitasalo*, ed. Town (Toronto: Art Gallery of Ontario, 1982).

Carr-Harris chooses in his paper to focus on a community-based context of debate, implying that his version of "paradise" is rooted in an institution's contentiousness and capacity to provoke arguments about what constitutes "criticality" within the current visual culture. And, significantly, Carr-Harris emphasizes the words of others as contributors to a fragmentary narrative that includes an exhibition occurring more than three decades ago. Carr-Harris's contribution casts a *positive* light on the condition of absence for those seeking to reconstruct Toronto's cultural history—as opposed to the complaint about a lack of exhaustive examination—one that recognizes an ongoing sense of incompleteness while maintaining the paramount import-ance of striving to recall such moments, albeit in ways that are always partial and subjective. He once reflected that he "saw artmaking as a kind of writing of history, as a kind of extension of the project of history using a different set of vocabulary, a different grammar, but a syntax that really seemed iden-tical—the syntax of thinking historically."[9] As Philip Monk has pointed out, a main concern of his has been with the "little histories of everyday experi-ence, 'stories' shot through, all the same, with a social sense that embodied a historical period."[10]

Of course, it is this ongoing process of questioning what constitutes "historical knowledge" and "learning"—within a variety of institutional contexts, including museums and (art) schools—that has motivated much of Carr-Harris's own art practice over the years. For the group show *Fiction*, curated in 1982 by Elke Town at the AGO, Carr-Harris's work ... *across town* ... (1981) staged a "knowledgeable deceit," through a combina-tion of language and visible illusion, intended to trigger memories tinged with anxiety—of a fragmentary story within a story about a wolf and a crane, remembered during an evening at a nightclub. As Town comments in the catalogue, Carr-Harris sought to consider the fictional nature of historic reconstruction and to suggest the possibility of intervening with information not generally preserved within narratives supplied by main-stream museums, lecture halls, or library stacks—all-too-familiar sites for Carr-Harris.[11] Casual observations, snippets of overheard conversation, or flashes of erotic suggestion: such minor moments may be incorporated as means to critique the ways that we struggle with difference while our social identities are shaped.

Employing standardized institutional means for conveying historical information as truth—such as tables, framed photos, and framed segments of sentences—some of Carr-Harris's installations go further to critique museological knowledge especially. *After Dürer* (1989), for example, features cabinetry and audio-video equipment, including a speaker, projector, and screen, all custom fitted by the artist. The cabinet houses a copy of a print by Albrecht Dürer of an Indian rhino. A button on the cabinet, when pushed by the viewer, starts a film of an actual rhino, photographed by the artist at the Toronto Zoo. With furniture and "interactive" features that seem sourced from a historical archive or museum, Carr-Harris's presentation strikes notes of absurdity and satire aimed at questioning what it means to be a civilized, cultured, or acculturated self.[12] For Carr-Harris, such critique is framed within a performative format that plays with the notions of display and demonstration, posing and imposing. In this regard, Carr-Harris has stated that his art operates as "static theatre, occupying a position between art object and public performance in order to see more closely what seeing is."[13]

As an artist and writer, of particular interest for Carr-Harris are the ways in which images and objects, anchored by verbal messages, naturalize ideology, while leaving in their wake a trail of loss and absence, along with memorializing or melancholic effects.[14] He suggests that his project "centres on acts of re-tracing—we could call it 're-touching'—conceived as forms of demonstration. Events rather than objects, they require that we look at something we already 'know,' and in that looking to discover—not quickly, not entirely grasped—something we took for granted."[15] For the work *On TV* (1986), first exhibited at the Vancouver artist-run centre Western Front, Carr-Harris sets the stage by considering Édouard Manet's motivations when conceiving his paintings *Le Déjeuner sur l'herbe* and *Olympia* in 1863, a time and place of institutional importance for the avant-garde. Carr-Harris provides a projected image of a field without figures, in front of which is placed a table strewn with a rumpled tablecloth or bed sheet—a two-pronged reference to incidental backdrops (or props) within both of Manet's pictures. While recognizing the absence of naked female figures within this voided venue, viewers listen to an audio lecturer who claims that Manet sought both confrontation and complicity with the male gaze, while referring to a female gaze within the context of the Parisian Salon of his day. And the voice encourages us to muse about our voyeuristic relationship to screens, as we may envision television and paintings in the same manner. In his text "On TV" (1986), Carr-Harris explains how the installation—as a "retracing" of appropriated imagery in photographic form, with accompanying props—was meant, in part, to raise awareness, *within theatrical and conceptual contexts*, about how such an artwork "constructs through its imagery an implied location of the viewer, an attachment. That location carries ambiguities which the work's audio text proceeds to ground in a set of clear intentions, intentions that become at once a demonstration and a reminder of the work's status, and the viewer's position."

Indeed, Carr-Harris has often been drawn to canonical objects—in this case two precious commodities housed at the Musée d'Orsay in Paris—as means to deconstruct how such works are instrumentalized as sources of

12 See Carr-Harris's "Notes for *a demonstration* (1981)," in *Ian Carr-Harris: Recent Works* (Dalhousie Art Gallery, 1982).

13 Ian Carr-Harris, "An Approach to Criticism," *Parachute* 1 (October 1975), page 185 in this volume.

14 For excellent commentary, see Monk, "Deaccessionings," 11.

15 See Carr-Harris, "Notes on Work" (1997).

16   See, for example, Hans
Haacke, *Working Conditions:
The Writings of Hans Haacke*, ed.
Alexander Alberro (Cambridge,
MA: MIT Press, 2016), 70–74,
for further reflection on *Manet-
PROJECT '74*.

knowledge in necessarily incomplete ways, and always infused with social
and gender-based biases. While never discounting the avant-garde importance of Manet's profoundly subversive project, Carr-Harris plays with the
presiding and authoritative voice of the lecturing scholar. Such strategies
are comparable, to some extent, with those conceptualists operating in the
mode of classic institutional critique, who seek to offer other perspectives
that stray from officially sanctioned stories. Hans Haacke's *Manet-PROJEKT
'74* (1974), for example, detailed the provenance of Manet's *Bunch of
Asparagus* (1880), offering a black-and-white reproduction of the painting
along with framed "explanatory" pictures of text, revealing the Nazi-era
career of patron and Deutsche Bank chairman Hermann Josef Abs, who
had given the painting to the Museum Ludwig in Cologne as a permanent
loan. As such, Haacke's work was rejected by the institution since it had
the potential of souring relations with powerful individuals important
to the museum. As with Haacke, the role of writing for Carr-Harris—as
treated both within his artworks and through his parallel practice as a writer
and critic—plays multivalent roles as a means of exploring how ideologies operate.[16]

While at times Carr-Harris's discourse has addressed specific institutions, compared to Haacke he has tended to be less focused on targeted
attacks—upon individual patrons or corporations—in favour of broader
social, sociological, and semiotic issues bearing upon questions of identity. Indeed, in contrast with Haacke's reliance on the rhetoric of factual
evidence and a "coldly" rendered administrative aesthetic, there lies a sort
of spirited openness in Carr-Harris's art and writing, allowing the reader
or viewer to subjectively experience the artist's articulation of difference
while confronting the staging of an educational (or some other institutional) premise, often in the form of historical episodes that possess both
textual and tangible traits. Carr-Harris has exhibited a deep commitment to
forms of conceptualism which resist hierarchical orders of art, along with
genres such as portraiture and statuary, as historical means of transmitting
truth and exercising Eurocentric and masculinist regimes of knowledge,
including its requisite standards of skill, iconography, and expressive individuality.

Taking on grand themes from a modest, and sometimes mocking,
perspective that is capable of incorporating contradiction, Carr-Harris
has sought to complicate conventional aesthetic pleasures. His two-part
photo-conceptualist work *Two men confirming* (1973), for example, critiques
categories of the art historical canon, as expressed by exemplars of Roman
Imperial and French Baroque styles—a sculpture of Augustus Caesar and
a painting of Louis XIV, offered up as photographic reproductions of

the sort found in survey textbooks. Carr-Harris supplies captions which confirm, tongue-in-cheek, that these men of power "shaped events, rose above the common herd" and that they "shaped events, found love & affection." Adopting a black-and-white, text-image format that employs found imagery, the approach compares with those of other pioneering photo-conceptualists, contemporaries who subverted romanticized mythologies of photography in terms of its evidentiary power, by exposing its historical function as support for claims of truth. The British artist John Hilliard's *Cause of Death? (study)* (1974), for instance, features four images of a corpse, cropped and captioned differently to demonstrate how they signify in remarkably diverse ways. Like Hilliard, Carr-Harris draws on Roland Barthes's studies of the rhetorical force of photos and texts in tandem, including the relationship of captions to images within educational contexts.[17]

Carr-Harris's sculptural tableau *A section of Julius Caesar's left thigh* (1973) combines an alleged plaster cast of Julius Caesar's thigh, complete with body hair, displayed upon a table as material evidence of the great general's existence, along with a framed statement that mimics a patiently pedantic museum label. In this case, he playfully deconstructs the viewer's desire to know through simple deduction, and critically (as well as comically) demonstrates the process by which a supposition may become truth, sometimes through the fetishistic mythology of the relic accompanied by words with definitive explanatory power. Carr-Harris's art criticism reflects a similar critique of such fetishizing and pedantic tendencies. His reviews and other essays operate in tension with our conditioning, with our need to compulsively cling to a comfortable and coherent reference point, to follow a deductive logic of reference. Carr-Harris invites us to confront the possibility that there may be *no reference point* that will instill a sense of interpretive closure that is comfortable.

While more "orthodox" conceptualists in the 1960s and early '70s had dramatically expanded the field of what was possible artistically—by dematerializing the aesthetic object into the realm of pure idea or linguistic proposition—Carr-Harris sought to explore the sea of images supplied by media cultures of advertising and consumerism. As such, Carr-Harris's project as a writer and artist is comparable to that of the so-called Pictures Generation. Sharing their interest in the writings of Barthes, Michel Foucault, and Julia Kristeva, among others, Carr-Harris worked to short-circuit the mechanisms of seduction and desire, investigating how identity is not organic and innate, but manufactured and learned through constructions of gender, race, sexuality, and citizenship. Barthes had famously questioned the very possibility of authenticity in his 1967

17 See Barthes, "The Rhetoric of the Image" (1964), in Barthes, *Image, Music, Text*, ed. and trans. Stephen Heath (New York: Hill and Wang, 1977), 32–51. The educational dimensions of Carr-Harris's project are relatively understudied, as they relate to issues of social identity and community within the context of art schools, including the one most familiar to him, OCAD. For helpful commentary on the educational contexts of conceptualist practices, see Steven Henry Madoff, ed., *Art School: Propositions for the 21st Century* (Cambridge, MA: MIT Press, 2009) and Garry Neill Kennedy, *The Last Art College: Nova Scotia College of Art and Design, 1968–1978* (Cambridge, MA: MIT Press, 2012).

18   For insightful discussion, see Douglas Eklund, ed., *The Pictures Generation, 1974–1984* (New York: Metropolitan Museum of Art, 2009). Still one of the best treatments of Pictures Generation conceptualism is offered by Douglas Fogle, ed., *The Last Picture Show: Artists Using Photography, 1960–1982* (Minneapolis: Walker Art Center, 2003).

19   See Kruger's compilation of writings *Remote Control: Power, Cultures, and the World of Appearances* (Cambridge, MA: MIT Press, 1993).

20   For discussion, see Ann Pollock, ed., *Confrontations: Ian Carr-Harris, John McEwen, John Massey* (Vancouver: Vancouver Art Gallery, 1979), n.p.

manifesto "The Death of the Author," in which he stated that any text (or image), rather than emitting a fixed meaning from a singular voice, was but a tissue of quotations that were themselves references to yet other texts, and so on.[18]

It is worthwhile to compare Carr-Harris's *A section of Julius Caesar's left thigh* to works by Barbara Kruger, such as *Untitled (Your gaze hits the side of my face)* (1981). Both can be envisioned as exploring how difference is reinforced through media presentation. Kruger's approach to critique—which included a series of polemical published writings—has similarly played on clichés and cultural stereotypes to underscore, and undermine, the persuasive power of representation.[19] And yet Kruger was relatively focused on developing a "signature style" intended to visually compete with the advertising cultures she sought to subvert—using cropped, large-scale, black-and-white photographic images juxtaposed with raucous, and often ironic, aphorisms, with prominent, red-painted wooden frames. As is the case with Carr-Harris, her works are meant to signify *undoubtedly as objects*, rather than as dematerialized images. Her inclusion of personal pronouns in works like *Untitled (I shop therefore I am)* (1987) implicates viewers in the here and now by confounding any clear notion of who is speaking. However, artists such as Kruger or Richard Prince practiced an in-your-face sort of critique of the ways in which identity, desire, and public opinion are manipulated and perpetuated. While certainly sympathetic to such literal and remarkably accessible modes of address, as a critic and artist Carr-Harris has been relatively indirect in approach, preferring to occupy a metonymical mode that approximates a fine mist or a subtle prodding rather than a sledgehammer of verbal and visual messaging.

I would suggest that Carr-Harris's consistent concern has been with the finer intricacies of how identity is socially defined—and the power that group demands can have over individual choice. His installation *If you know what I mean* (1977), for example, features a framed photo of two women sharing an amusing thought, and a third woman isolated from them with her back to the viewer. The latter figure is displayed as a visual equivalent of verbal signage, set upon a department store sales counter containing a dress whose sensuous material is arranged in soft folds. Notions of erotic and commercial seduction are expressed as being mutually dependent. The work's title signifies an implied distance between the represented figures, which in turn is carried over into the relationship between the work and its beholder, one that exudes ironic detachment and that wavers between reality and fantasy.[20] Carr-Harris here explores the predicament of being plagued with doubt about whether one is measuring up to societal standards of behaviour and how such insecurity may be channelled into consumer desire.

Similarly, Carr-Harris's text on Susan Schelle's work, "A History of Manners" (1993), focuses on subtle—and sometimes abstract—strategies of material and verbal manipulation which, in his words, "de-cloaks the investments of authority—the common-sense assumptions negotiated by generations before us on our behalf." Carr-Harris portrays aspects of Schelle's project as a remarkably complex critique of bourgeois taste, of manners and social obligation, expressed with everyday means—from furniture to fashion statements—as vehicles for considering our complicity with gender-based constraints and other controls upon our behaviours.

Carr-Harris's feature article on installations by Mark Gomes, which appeared in *C Magazine* (Summer 1992), allows for another excursus into how language variably reconstructs memory. Gomes's works offer up terms that define each other through their contrasts, but they do so within "a funhouse of alternative differences and any definition arising from their interrelationships must be transitory, always in the process of being overwritten by another." In the end there is no fixed meaning, just as there is no fixed end to meaning: there is only a "constant flickering of presence and absence together."[21] Applied to the artworks of Gomes and many other members of his community, Carr-Harris's critical position is, of course, further expressed in statements accompanying his own exhibitions, such as one at the Montreal artist-run centre Optica in 1993. While stating that his exhibition is meant to encourage an awareness that the structures "we use to identify ourselves are themselves contingent and fluid," it is the strategic use of subtle suggestion—to relook at something we already know—which is uniquely capable of "disturb[ing] our field of knowledge while leaving it also apparently intact. Nothing has factually changed, nothing has been invented or promoted: it is simply that some insertion—perhaps a footnote or repetition, maybe an archaism, or just an object in a room—has complicated the linear flow of the narrative, and we realize, with an atavistic pleasure, that we never are where we thought we were."

As a writer and artist—as well as an eminent educator—Carr-Harris's half-century story features a compelling need to recognize, and sometimes to dispute, how qualities of ambiguity and ambivalence are present in the work of others. He has consistently sought to ground the practice of ideological critique within a context of community, and to continually reconceive a sense of local identity. And it is that level of interpretive complexity and renewal that Carr-Harris has continued to fulfill and express as an unwavering critical awareness which informs all of his discourse. His career serves as an inspiring example of how and why we should create spaces for meaningful dialogue and debate, through varied means which flow between the gallery, the written word, and the broader social world.

21   Carr-Harris's approach in this text is indebted to the Marxist literary critic Terry Eagleton. See Eagleton, *Literary Theory: An Introduction* (London: Blackwell, 1983), 128.

Debates, 1983-2015

Museums in the '80s: The London Regional and A Space (1983)

Published as "Museums in the '80s: The London Regional and A Space," *Vanguard* (March 1983).

In recent months, internal stresses at two prominent Ontario art institutions have come to a head. The situations behind the election of a controversial Board of Directors (Carol Condé, Tanya Mars, Norman Richmond, Clive Robertson, Lisa Steele, Kim Tomczak, Jane Wright) at Toronto's A Space and the temporary closure of the London Regional Art Gallery soon after its opening have been the subjects of rumour, speculation, and misinformation. As clarification and, by extension, instruction for other Canadian parallel and public galleries, *Vanguard* is publishing commentaries by Ian Carr-Harris, founding member (1970) and Board member (1981/2) of A Space, and Goldie Rans, the London art critic.

Ian Carr-Harris on A Space

I have been asked to comment on A Space as it has functioned over the last two years or so. I accepted because I wanted to make certain points about the gallery which I feel are important; for the most part, however, this commentary will be a broad historical perspective rather than an attempt at investigative journalism, and I think it is necessary to start at the beginning.

Why A Space at all? In 1970, Toronto lacked the options open to young artists that we are familiar with now. Indeed, there were few serious options for anyone: Lamanna and Isaacs both had solid continuing commitments and could only take on new artists infrequently. Yet Toronto in the late '60s was experiencing the pressure of the post-war generation; it is clear that in 1970 fresh options had to be found which were independent of the conservative imperatives of the small Canadian art market.

In fact, A Space was forged out of the collapse of an attempt to establish an option that did depend on the market. Chris Youngs opened his Nightingale Gallery in 1968 as a commercial attempt to show different work in Toronto, largely American painting, but very quickly expanded to include experimental work from both Toronto and the US. By 1970 it faced financial collapse; in an attempt to save the gallery, Chris turned for support to a circle of artist friends who recognized the importance of the venture; it was agreed to fold Nightingale as a commercial concern, and re-open as a public corporation—the Nightingale Arts Council—dependent not on the art market but on a charitable status through which it could appeal for private donations and most especially for public funds. The gallery became an aspect of the new charitable foundation and was called simply: A Space.

In making this transformation, the founders of A Space stumbled upon an option which provided a solution to a structural hole in Canada's post-war efforts to construct through the Canada Council (created in the late fifties) a national visual arts culture in Canada. By providing competitive grants to artists and operational funds to public galleries, the Canada Council established a need for serious exhibition space which in 1970 neither the commercial galleries nor the public museums were in a position to keep pace with. A Space, or more correctly the Nightingale Arts Council, posed a relatively inexpensive solution, since it combined the do-it-yourself-as-you-starve economics of artists' cooperatives with a legal structure for the protection of public money. The rest is history, as they say, and the parallel network was born.

The rest is also a curious and continuing mixture of structure and mandate. A charitable foundation legally requires a Board of Directors, a President, and so on. In its early version, A Space's Board was simply that: a requirement; the operation of the Gallery fell to a rather fluid assortment of artists and others who, while theoretically a Board, were also an undefined management and caretaking staff responsible for everything from programming to renovations.

The inherent contradictions between a publicly funded corporation and the highly personal and focused dynamics of artists' cooperatives which A Space represented finally brought trouble. Following complaints that A Space's purpose to offer disinterested service to its community was not being met, the Canada Council suspended funding in March of 1978, providing a $10,000 grant for the specific formation of a consultative committee to redefine A Space's structure and mandate. That committee reported to the September annual meeting; its report was never adopted. Instead, AA Bronson of General Idea and Art Metropole proposed that A Space change its name and find a new space from which it would operate as a "museum without walls": an office for managing projects throughout the community at large. It would, in other words, "inhabit" or "appropriate" the continuing structures of the community, rather than echo the dubious validity of the art museum, and its mandate would clearly reflect that ideology. The proposal was accepted, though not with a change of name, and A Space re-opened in its current location in an office building at 299 Queen St. West. The Canada Council, satisfied that the original charges of mismanagement had been dealt with, reinstated funding; but the question of service to the community was more difficult.

Accompanying this new mandate, two important structural changes were made as well. The Board of Directors was transformed from a legal fiction into an accountable reality by opening up its membership to a vote of the majority of members at the annual meeting. This very accountability, a basic requirement for establishing A Space's new mandate, presented also a basic weakness: with a membership as small and potentially as ad hoc as A Space's, the vulnerability of the Boards to complete changes of membership and direction at the whim of the annual meetings was, and is, obvious. Correspondingly, the lag in programming options arising from the commitments to programming established by the previous Board introduces a further frustration to any sense of direction.

The other important structural change concerned the responsibilities of the new democratized Board for the day-to-day management of the Gallery, particularly significant now that it functioned in the capacity of a control and planning office. Peggy Gale moved from Art Metropole to A Space to act as the new manager. This in itself caused some concern to those in the community who felt that the structural and ideological relationships between A Space and Art Metropole were in danger of becoming uncomfortably symbiotic. Frictions developed within A Space itself over the lack of a defined role for the managerial position with respect to programming decisions. In 1980 the situation became acute following difficulties between the guest curators selected by the Board to programme the year's events on the one hand, and A Space's manager on the other. It was finally agreed that the role of the manager would be that of an executive director with administrative responsibilities and powers in the operation of the gallery, but that programming choice and decision-making would remain with the Board. This clarification reflects the management conditions under which A Space has operated since 1980, although the resignation of Peggy Gale in 1981 and the appointment of a dual executive directorship complicated the picture in 1982.

The last two months of the 1982 Board were dominated internally by the breakdown of the dual executive directorship, and externally through political interference by Toronto Metro Council in voting to deny municipal grant support on the grounds that its programming was offensive to the community at large. While these issues have some interest, particularly the issue of service to the community, which in one way or another has been a constant question for A Space, their particular nature rendered them more or less irrelevant to A Space's existence or purpose, and I will not go into them here.

What is of significance, it seems to me, are the issues of A Space's mandate to serve its professional community, and the related question of control over how that mandate is exercised by the annual general membership meetings.

The radical inhabitation of the community implicit in the concept of a "museum without walls" was never totally adhered to. A Space has continued to provide a gallery space as well as site-specific programming, and one can find the reasons for this in the relative lack of interest in political ideology that Toronto artists, and indeed artists elsewhere in North America, have expressed. Site specificity in itself is difficult in a country which experiences great seasonal changes and in a city which has almost no art press and only a nascent critical establishment. The programming just was not there. Co-sponsorship of events with other galleries has had greater potential, and A Space has at its disposal enough funding to make its joint sponsorship of events with other artist-run galleries an important aspect of its programming, but this role as a kind of middleman between the funding Councils and the smaller parallel galleries is not ultimately satisfactory, or even self-sustaining. As the 1982 Board discovered, the modified mandate to pursue the notion of a museum with *some* walls, a mandate adhered to despite a disappointingly anaemic response to its call for programming submissions from the community, had lost its sense of purpose. The Board, had it evolved through the annual meeting, was prepared to tackle this problem by more aggressively canvassing potential curators; in fact, however, it did not get the chance.

At the annual membership meeting in November 1982, the tensions and vulnerabilities in A Space's fading mandate and democratic structure produced a new Board elected as a slate for the express purpose of opening up A Space to certain defined communities, among them women, Blacks, and what one gathers would be grass-roots artists. What this represents is a bit early to say; there are those who see it as an exchange of *FILE Magazine* for *Fuse*. Perhaps so, but in a curious way the concept of a "museum without walls" may find a new purpose, and "inhabitation" a new dimension

The new Board, however, returns me to the issue of coherent and committed direction. It seems clear to me that as long as A Space is subject to the vagaries of those who can bring the most supporters to the annual meeting, its presence will be ambivalent. At the last annual meeting, there were in fact three different contending factions; the new Board represents the faction which most successfully understood its political nature. One assumes that as long as it continues to understand it, the current Board may remain indefinitely; it must simply ensure that its supporters show up next

November. Alternatively, it will lose to a new and different ideology. In either case, what A Space as an entity will be, is in fact, difficult to engage; it is as distant from the professional community as a whole as is the Art Gallery of Ontario.

What, then, is A Space? There is no final answer; it changes as particular pressures reform it. At the moment A Space has been appropriated by a number of committed and energetic members who wish to use it to redefine the social context for artmaking in Toronto. I am curious to see how long this particular appropriation will last, and what it can deliver.

Goldie Rans on The London Regional Art Gallery

The London Regional Art Gallery closed its doors to the public December 31, 1982, and is scheduled to re-open on March 1, 1983, with renovated exhibition areas on the first and second storeys of the three-storey vaulted building it occupies. The top storey, which contains the prime exhibition space, some 1,536 square metres of it—more than half the total area—will be shut down until 1985, unless the Board of Directors comes up with the $200,000 it costs to keep it open, over and above the $800,000 it needs to run the gallery even in its severely trimmed-down state. The original staff of twenty-one full-time and eleven part-time has been dropped to eight full-time and one part-time, just one more than the seven Clare Bice had with him in the old gallery on Queen's Avenue before he retired. Most of the staff will be called back; inevitably, some will not return. Hopes for professional curators of historical and contemporary art (performance, video, film), increased acquisitions and an endowment for purchases of works of art, and more exhibitions for London and region artists have vanished into thin air. The Director, Brenda Wallace, who, at the time of her arrival had to cut the number of shows per annum in half, has had to reduce her exhibitions schedule for 1983 by five shows, but other programming will resume where it left off last December. Governments and Councils are continuing to support the programming temporarily; the private sector, however, is not coming up with its share.

It is ironic to look back to the day of the official opening of the $5.5 million building on May 3, 1980. Dennis Kucheraway wrote in the *London Free Press* how at last "the splendour of this latest gem in London's cultural crown" would be revealed. He was, of course, referring to the newly renovated Theatre London, and the Centennial Hall, a concert-cum-banquet hall badly in need of renovation, which together with the new gallery would form London's "arts centre." While the general public, and London's quality who kicked in $1,750,000 of tax-deductible dollars showed their interest by watching the fun rather than taking part in it, the event was greeted with sceptical curiosity by the art public (C.A.R. had been opposed to it all along), and enthusiasm by the then current Board of Directors, Women's Committees, members, and staff. Visiting dignitaries included the Lieut. Governor of Ontario, Pauline McGibbon, other gallery and museum directors, and officials from the three levels of funding bodies, who kicked in the rest, $3,750,000. (It is frequently said in these parts that the gallery didn't cost the citizens of London a cent: and this is true if you paid no taxes of any kind to anyone.) In any case, the board handed itself and the city a debt-free, mortgageless structure in one of the most beautiful and historic locations in the city. What it did *not* do was provide for its future, a flaw of such seriousness that financial difficulties were experienced within three months of the opening ceremonies.

Whatever people may have thought and felt that day, it was common knowledge to nearly everyone that the gallery was needed, for up to that point it had been housed in the second storey of the Elsie Perrin Williams Memorial Library and Art Gallery. With around 1,000 square metres of exhibition space (not much less than is currently available), and inadequate room for storage of a not unsubstantial collection, the gallery wasn't even able to receive major travelling exhibitions from the National Gallery of Canada. Film and slide lectures, children's classes, painting groups, special services, and so on were endured in cramped quarters. Its permanent holdings had never been shown in their entirety, and for a long time the quality of art on view there had been middling at best, if not downright disappointing, in view of the considerable size of the city (over a quarter million people) and the reputation it had as an art centre.

In 1972 Clare Bice and his staff submitted a proposal for a new art gallery that finally caught fire after a few earlier attempts in the 1960s had fizzled. Other proposals were presented, and parties gathered behind one or other of them; steps were taken to make the gallery an autonomous institution, a new Board was created, and consultants were called in. The choice of site, architect, a new director, curators, and personnel—all these became highly publicized, controversial issues exacerbated by the predilection of the Board for *in camera* meetings instead of public debate, a situation that rankles to this day. How the public will respond to the temporary closure and accompanying modification of their expectations is related to the decade of wrangling that accompanied the planning, construction, opening, and subsequent financial difficulties. A member has already written a request for the refund of a sum of money paid for a membership card to take account of the two-month shutdown.

However, the gallery's basic needs were not, I suspect, the only motives for the proposal's acceptance. An important catalyst was the John H. Moore Gift, 454 works of art from Moore's private collection which were offered to the London Art Gallery through the Ontario Heritage Foundation between 1974 and 1976. While it may not be the brightest star among Canadian collections, the Moore Gift contains some sparkling older paintings—six L.L. Fitzgeralds and eleven David Milnes, a significant number of drawings, watercolours, and paintings by Jack Chambers and Greg Curnoe, as well as a wide range of art from nearly every major centre in this country. The international part includes mainly twentieth-century artists who seem to be represented more for the value of their signatures than the intrinsic quality of their work. At the same time, there are some exceptional things such as a cubist drawing by Léger and several works on paper by Matisse. Moore also donated $200,000 to the building fund. Nothing toward upkeep was suggested or promised.

London was now in need of a good museum as well as an art gallery—and it was about to get it. Raymond Moriyama, the architect, who ultimately made do with a design modelled after the Kimball Art Museum in Fort Worth, Texas, acceded to suggestions from a by then megalomaniacal Director (William Forsey) and Board of Directors to increase the size of the gallery by more than a third. Fund-raising targets included the new needs which were quickly met—but, again, the figures did not include an operating endowment. Pressure from the *London Free Press*, and from succeeding Board members reveals that nothing had been promised by London nobs and worse, nothing had been *demanded* by either the Board or the funding agencies. The sod was turned without any binding commitment to posterity.

The situation stands. A new Board (which includes a good number of old members) was recently voted in. If they care about art, they will take the initiative in implementing a vigorous fund-raising campaign that will establish an endowment for the maintenance of the gallery in a manner worthy of the city. The former Board seemed paralyzed, as if waiting for some outside agency to shut the gallery down completely or some single benefactor to rescue the maiden. Meanwhile art at LRAG limps. Soon, no one will remember to care.

Under the Gaze of Criticism? (1985)

Published as "Under the Gaze of Criticism?," in *Artists/Critics*, proceedings from a conference held at the Ontario College of Art in Toronto on May 12, 1985 (Toronto: YYZ, 1985).

1.1   Andre Jodoin, ed., *Artist/Critics* (Toronto: YYZ Artists' Outlet, 1985). Symposium publication of two panels, "Under the Gaze of Criticism" and "Representation of the New Now," coordinated by Bruce Grenville and Jeanne Randolph for YYZ Artists' Outlet; 41 pp., 28 x 21.5 cm.

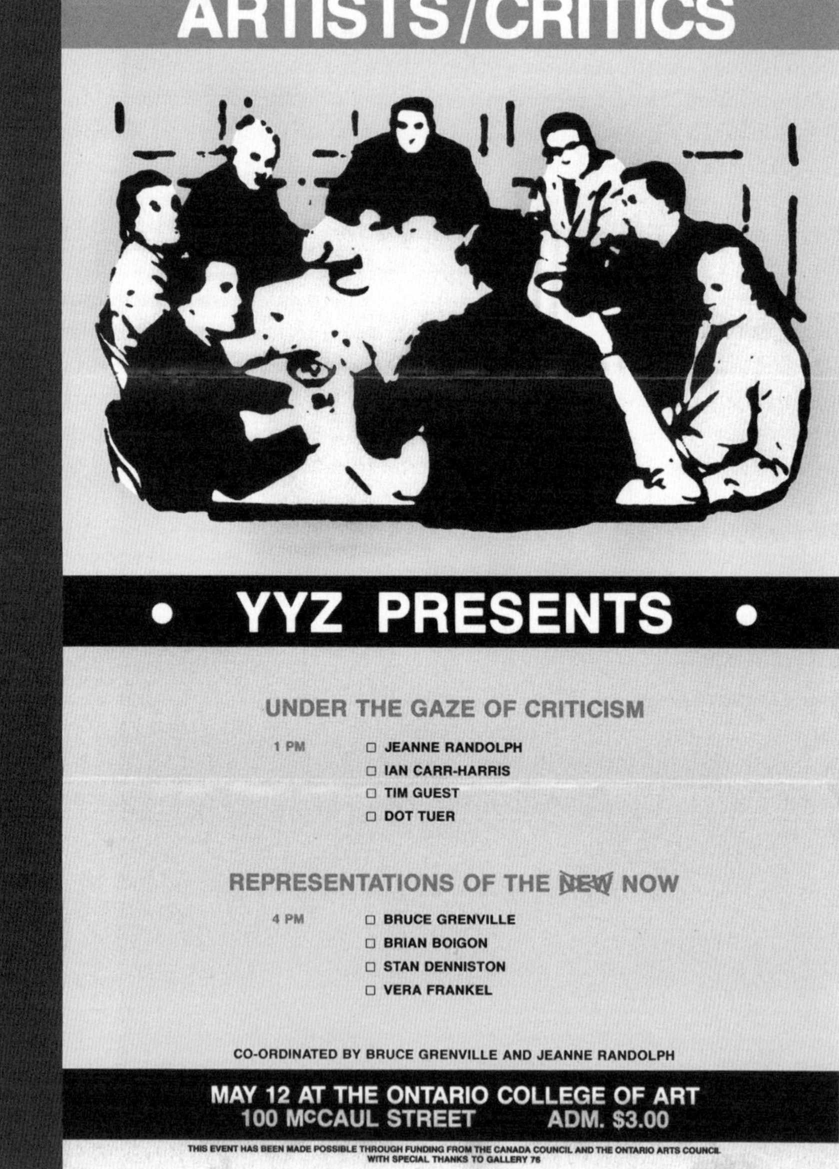

What is criticism, how does it proceed, and what use is it?

This is what I want to talk about. But first I want to be clear about three things:

> Gazing is complicated;
> Understanding is productive;
> I'm glad I'm not a critic.

You might legitimately wonder, if I am placing myself at a distance from criticism, what contribution I am likely to make to a discussion which attempts to clarify my own critical position. The question is fundamental, but I want to leave it alone for now and consider the complications of gazing and the productivity of understanding.

I could say that criticism is the process of examination and evaluation of this or that, that it proceeds by analysis, and that it enlarges our understanding of something. But I would have said nothing; or rather, I would have addressed only a question founded in a particular kind of innocence. Because beyond this disguise of objective query lurks a decisive question: what do we want? what do we want from criticism? That question is directed to the very process of understanding that criticism is supposed to enlarge, and because it renders that understanding contingent, we cannot usefully consider criticism to be by its nature disinterested.

Instead, then, I will say that criticism is not in fact analytical, evaluatory, or objective. It is not about "enlarging" understanding through these processes. I will say, rather, that it is about wanting, and about what purpose our understanding is meant to serve. I could even say that criticism is the process of imposing what we want to understand, of imposing what we want to have understood.

If criticism is not disinterested, if it is impositional and self-interested, if it is wilful; if it is rude, that is to say, we can say that criticism is an act not of observation, but of gazing. When we gaze, we do not simply observe: we project longing—an act of aggressive possession.

How does this act work? Directed towards us, we view it as an affront, an implicit invasion of our being and our will, of our independent status. We react to protect ourselves from it. But this reaction is countered and denied by what we know about ourselves as perpetrators of the gaze. When we in turn direct that gaze, we do so knowing already this protective response as recipients. Yet we defy that protective response and in doing so create a contradictory one out of our perpetrations—a response of abandonment to the gaze. As we who gaze, we do so longingly, desirously, voraciously, shamelessly, in complicity—provocatively. We wish to provoke: what? Anger or shame? Rebellion or obedience? Perhaps. And who do we wish to provoke? The object of our gaze is always a person, or a personification, never a thing. Do we wish to provoke ourselves, or another person perhaps? Probably neither. In fact, no. We wish to provoke an assault on the act itself, on the gaze, on the relations constructed by that gaze. The gaze is directed not at an object, but at the conflicting relations it constructs with that object, at its responses, we might say. Its possessiveness, or its nihilism, its longing, is a longing for its own extension, for what it does not, or more precisely cannot, possess. And for its own annihilation.

If it can be said, however, that criticism is an act of gazing as I have described it, it must also be admitted that if it were simply this act—an imposition of will upon the subject of the gaze defined by its own relations— we would be in trouble. Would it be appropriate to call a peculiarly intimate self-referential voyeurism an act of criticism? It would seem, more likely, to be a primitive self-indulgence, an irrelevant solipsism, and understanding to be purposeless, if not inconceivable. While we gaze, and submit to the gaze of others with more or less abandon within an inescapable vortex, we do not seem to be operating critically. Something is missing.

What is missing is the mechanism of displacement and the necessity of production. Terry Eagleton has a useful phrase when he remarks that "all understanding is productive: it is always 'understanding otherwise,' realizing new potential for the text, making a contribution to it." I want to apply this idea of "otherwise."

In fact, in the act of gazing, there is a displacement. It is language. Language is itself an "otherwise": otherwise to the primitive directed intuition of needing or wanting. It is a construction of codes which names our needs and wants, and in naming them and ordering them places them in relationships, and therefore subject to the organization of priorities. Language arises out of the social impossibility of the gaze: it is not just a displacement requirement, but the mechanism itself. Its attributes are precisely those required to socialize the gaze. If language didn't exist, we could say, we would have had to have invented it—to stay alive. So much so, in fact, that we can call the effects of language "culture" and it is culture which, being a coherent placing of things in value, displaces the voracious solipsism of the unmediated gaze. We can call the tension resulting from this displacement of the unmediated gaze a "critical condition." And this critical condition represents a return of the gaze from its focus on the subject's relations back towards the object of those relations.

If the mediated gaze, the displaced gaze, is a return to the object of the gaze, and differs from its unmediated state in being critical, what do we mean by that, or—we could say—what use is it?

The first important consequence is that this displaced gaze is essential to understanding. Understanding is a concept that is completed only in culture. As much as it requires the self-reference of the primitive gaze, it requires as well the recognition of the object of that gaze. Language, the mechanism of displacement, in constructing the tension inherent in the mediated gaze, constructs, or reclaims, the object of the gaze; and with it, the attachment necessary for understanding.

The second important consequence of the displacement is memory, or history. It is easy to equate the consequence of history with the consequence of displacement as a form of parallax. Parallax is familiar to us: it is how we determine distance. That is, how we distinguish an object rather than simply a flat plane. We could say it is how we observe rather than merely see. History enables us to observe. The displaced gaze, as it operates through language and culture to construct history, enables us to make observations. Critical understanding is historical observation.

What use, then, is historical observation? One could call it a meta-gaze, if one were given to that terminology. Or we could call it what we usually do—historical perspective. What it is, is the gaze focused both on its own relations and on its object, and able consequently to observe, to make observations, to "understand otherwise." Its use *is* emphatically to understand otherwise. This is what it is to be critical. What is essential to realize about this process, and why I have so laboriously attempted to detail it, is that the term "to be critical" is not referenced to the object of the gaze, nor does it refer to relations to that object. It refers to the entire process involved—the back-and-forth displacement, the fundamental contradiction—and includes recognition of the voracious self-referential voyeurism of the unmediated gaze synchronically, or in the same moment, with intellectual recognition of the object of that voyeurism through the abstractions of language and culture. To be critical is to be in this state of recognition, and inevitably as well to be caught in an act of development within it. We are not critical of the object of our gaze. We are critical of its meaning. And meaning is exactly the state of "being recognized." It is the sound of the tree falling in the forest: it exists when we recognize it; it flourishes when we develop it.

It flourishes when we develop it. Earlier, when I remarked that "something was missing" in the unmediated gaze, I suggested that this "something" comprised both the mechanism of displacement, and the necessity of production. I have been concentrating on the matter of displacement since it induces understanding and history, induces "being critical," and I have said that being critical is a state of recognition arising from that "otherwise"; that "meaning" is the term we use to describe the locus of criticism, the place where being critical, or "critical understanding," occurs. I have also said that being critical is also to be forced into an act, an act of development; that is, an act of production. I want now to address this act of production as a necessity, or necessary condition, of critical understanding.

It is not particularly complicated. When we are in a state of recognition, we act. We act to determine the characteristics of the "object" around which this recognition occurs. This action is no longer a gaze in the primitive, unmediated sense, but an observing through the gaze. In observing, we can picture ourselves rotating the focus of our recognition, to see it from all sides. In the process we construct an understanding around it. That is, we produce understanding in association with that focus. Our understanding is a production, and we interpret that production—or hold it to have meaning—as an act of critical understanding; criticism, for short. As we all know, that interpretation can be structured in a number of ways, often sharply different in their perspective. Terry Eagleton would hold that that part of the production which is the responsibility of the reader, or viewer, is the most significant focus of meaning for a given text, artwork, or by extension, I assume, any other focus of a state of critical recognition and production. Others hold that the production which is identifiably the responsibility of the author, artist, or initiator is the most significant focus. This is the arena of conflicting interpretation within the common state of "being critical."

It is also the cause for so many to feel that criticism is capricious, contingent, contradictory, obscure, or just plain wrong; or that it is, at least, elitist and unnecessary. It is easy to forget that being critical, as we have seen, is a given condition, and that it is not a question of making a case for criticism, of whether it is useful, but of what use it is being put to. Or what it is, we could say, that we want from criticism.

You'll remember that I began with this question, and I have attempted to clarify that it is an inherent property of understanding. That is, that criticism is inherently ideological, concerned with value, and by its very nature neither dispassionate nor evaluatory. Not disinterested, but interested. Criticism, functioning critically, is the function of being interested.

If criticism is an act of interest, not disinterest, then we come to address my own particular critical position. I said I was not a critic, and I said this was fundamental to my position. I am in fact an artist. But what does this entail? What is the connection between art and criticism? I'm sure you have already recognized that what I have described as critical understanding is the basis not only for criticism but for artmaking as well. It is a common structure. What distinguishes them would seem to be a different relationship to the qualities of the displaced gaze. This displacement, after all, cannot be seen as a stable phenomenon; it is an alternating gaze, one which seeks constantly to "maintain its balance," one could say—although this would be a metaphor—between its own relations and its object. The distinctions between the dual functions we call art and criticism in effect reflect this instability, and operate as an institutionalization of the duality of the gaze in its unmediated and mediated phases. Criticism is our response to the demands of the mediated gaze—its requirement that the object be observed. Artmaking is our response to the demands of the unmediated gaze—and its requirement that the relations formed by the subject be paramount. In practical, or formal terms, this requires that criticism, to be criticism, proceed in such a way as to reveal the object, for instance the artwork, in the gaze of the subject for the viewer. To describe and analyze, we often say, and this is true of all criticism, not simply so-called formalist criticism. It is to proceed towards closure, by which we mean implied closure. Artwork, to be artwork, requires that it proceed to reveal our relations; it uses the familiar tactics of implication, gesture, suggestion, or allusion—flirtation, if you like—towards a strategy of entrapment concerned not with closure, but with what in French is called *jouissance*,_what we might, with our Anglo-Canadian gift for subtlety, call "presence."

I'm glad I'm not a critic, then, because in "being critical" I have a choice—I have to choose: closure or *jouissance*, and I prefer the second. What is fundamental to my position towards criticism, and why from time to time I appear to operate as a "critic," to whatever effect, is that not only is the model and theory I employ portable from artmaking to criticism as a result of their being common functions of critical understanding, but that both functions exhibit the instability of the displaced gaze: they both proceed out of contradiction as much as committed purpose. It is this instability that makes either of them possible, and both of them desirable.

I have been attempting so far to make a useful construction for discussing criticism as I see it. It is now important to address certain specific questions about my views on the practice of criticism, and I want to do so "under" five investigations suggested by the panel discussion itself.

Firstly: what is my view on the title of this seminar?
Clearly, as I said at the beginning, the gaze of criticism is a complex one. It is easy to view it as deterministic and repressive, as placing the field of its vision under that gaze. It is harder, but I feel more correctly the case, to view it as essentially productive and expansion through a particular kind of "repression" which is the concomitant of focusing on the object of the gaze. The repression serves to recuperate the object, to rescue its independence from the cannibalism of the unmediated gaze. Criticism, that is, critical understanding as "criticism," is more compassionate than critical understanding as artwork.

Moreover, because critical understanding is unstable and dualistic, and carries its dualism into both criticism and artwork, it is also not correct to see criticism as a repression in which those characteristics we associate with artwork are placed under, or hidden *below*, a necessarily bowdlerized gaze. Criticism is a condition of emphasis, not repression.

If "under" implies a number of misconceptions about criticism, perhaps another term should be substituted: *through* the gaze of criticism, for instance. Yet critical understanding is, after all, rude—even while it is compassionate—and it is striking how much the complexity of our response to the word "under" echoes the complexity of our displaced gaze.

There is the word "gaze," as well. Gazing is generally understood as a concept related to vision—to ocular experience. It is obvious that that experience of the world is only one of many that we have. Its pre-eminence in this discussion, indeed in general discussion, can be challenged as itself surreptitiously ideological; it has been convincingly argued that the focused and abstract representation nature of ocular experience establishes certain preferred or prejudiced concerns when compared, for example, with our more direct and disturbingly physical experience of the world through smell. However, the pre-eminence is so strongly entrenched that it is practical to continue use of the dominant experience as a forum for conducting the totality of the experience within which visual experience is privileged. It is debatable whether we would be prepared to redefine our dominant experience in the world; visual experience and its prejudices are deeply rooted in language and culture. What must be realized is that even as we see, we smell, we touch, we feel, we hear, we listen; and our gazing is, finally, not merely seeing, but an imploding of all our experience.

Secondly: what critical model do I favour? That is, what methodology do I favour?

As you might suspect, I find the processes of argumentation and demonstration most useful. Developed by a serious critic, they offer a coherent clarity of purpose accessible to any intelligent person. Indeed, I find them essential in making art as well. We have a natural commitment to them, and their shortcomings are usually an aspect of their development. Arguments can be rendered vertically as well as horizontally; demonstrations secure them to our experience. Together they present a seductively multidimensional capability to tell us what we are.

Thirdly: what theoretical base do I assume? What, in fact, are my assumptions?

As I mentioned when I started, understanding is productive. What we generate in the course of being critical is rendered public. It is an aspect of knowledge, and knowledge is never without value. It situates, and in situating it produces validations and dilemmas. Criticism, then, I assume to be a moral investigation into those validations and dilemmas. So is art.

Fourthly: what correspondence exists between criticism and the process of interpretation. What does it mean, to interpret a work?
Quite simply, I consider the focal points of criticism, whether artworks or anything else, as departures for the elaboration of speculation; speculation being understood as the application of methodology and assumption; speculation being also understood as another word for gaze. It is vitally important, as I think I've made clear, that speculation therefore respects the conditions of its focal point to the extent that those can be identified. Speculation is, by definition, not irresponsible gossiping.

Fifthly: what attaches my critical procedures to the intentionality of artists, the receptivity of audiences, or the credibility of other critics?
Artistic intention and its place in the production of meaning is always a moot point. I look for it, and reconstruct it within my relations with the work, and because I enjoy argumentation and like to have things demonstrated to me, I expect intention to manifest itself fairly clearly. It is possible that, lacking such clarity of purpose, I may not just misunderstand a work, which is always possible and to a degree desirable, but distrust it as well. I view intention as important not only for valuing a work's critical statement of experience, but for the dialectic it consequently constructs with my own intention. Since intention is always present in work, clear or not, I will inevitably assign it one. It is more interesting if my experience of the work is based on something more than an assigned intention. Ultimately, however, an artist's intention is one issue of many raised by an artwork.

Audience receptivity is equally problematic. Criticism, it seems to me, must—within the particular differences in articulation between itself and artwork—deliver what it shares with them and other phenomena-in-the-world: the experience of the displaced gaze. Argumentation and demonstration are useful tools for elaborating the complexities of that gaze into as many of its separations as it is possible, or at least digestible, to communicate. But audiences are diverse and both culturally and historically bound to the point of being for all intents and purposes non-existent as a general entity. Audiences exist only as an abstraction of ourselves.

And finally, my credibility on the part of other critics is not my problem. I never said I was a critic. I'm glad I'm not. It's hard work.

Patronage or Subsidy? Government Funding of Canadian Artists (1985)

Published as "Patronage or Subsidy: A Position Paper," *Artviews* (Summer 1985).

The argument is that artists should receive public funds. It is not—and I want to be very clear about this—that artists have a right to public funds, or that certain artists should always receive public funds, or that artists should be salaried employees of the government, or a host of other arguments which in their several ways fail to correlate the activity of being an artist with other socially productive activities. The argument in favour of government funding of artists must be approached on the basis of our society's historic necessities, and secured on the basis of our response to those necessities.

We have been forced by history and geography to construct a complex and sophisticated culture for a handful of people spread across a vast, near-virgin continental landmass within a period of little more than a single lifetime. Moreover, our very reason for national existence was founded, not on cultural or geographical isolation, but on political and philosophical difference. What does this mean? On the one hand, that only the full support of the state could afford the immense risks and expenditures necessary to pool the slender financial and human resources available for the task of building such a nation; and on the other hand, that inherent in Canada's political philosophy is the premise that the state is the embodiment of the people, not the servant of an ideological laissez-faire. Public funding in Canada is not a witness to charity and self-interest, but the articulation of national purpose.

What do we have, then? We have the necessity and a tradition of government as architect and facilitator, with public funding the application of that role—whether in business, in social welfare or, more recently, in culture. To object in principle to government funding of artists in Canada is to misunderstand the nature of Canada.

Since the Renaissance, it has been assumed that art performs a critical function. Can artists who receive public funds also be critical? The question is meaningless in Canada; it is an established assumption of parliamentary democracy that a strong society supports dissent, and that individuals receive funds to help make that dissent more pointed. To refuse public funds is to refute that basic principle.

It can also be argued that with public funding available, artists do not have to work so hard and become lazy and cloistered. That is, that however good in principle public funding may be, it is detrimental to a spirit of marketplace survival and to clarity of perception. There are lots of lazy or polite or cloistered artists. Some of them receive public funds some of the time. Public money has nothing to do with it. Laziness and politeness, and disregard for popular appeal, are not functions of minimal government aid, but of personal desire and public opportunity. If there is concern that artists in Canada are not ambitious enough, or perceptive enough, or critical enough—a dubious hypothesis in my opinion—that concern has to do with the marketplace options facing artists, the nature of the public, and the values hidden in the hypothesis.

In fact, I suspect that the problem within this criticism of giving public funds to artists relates not at all to the corruption of artists, but to the very success that funding has had in helping to construct a context for culture in Canada. When Canadian artists stay in their country rather than emigrate, it is the fragile condition of their context which becomes clear. Artists no longer want that context to consist of the paternalism of their peers or the demographic neutrality of "the officers." What we want is not *disinterest*, but *interest*—interest from the society at large, interest from abroad; interest that will confirm the human necessity for art, not simply institutional necessity. It is misapplied habit to see public funding as the origin of this frustration. The problem is that public funding of artists cannot create an audience.

What can create an audience? This, it seems to me, is the real question facing us. What remains to be seen is whether, having helped to convince a great number of energetic and powerful artists to stay in their own country, the commitment of our government will be supported by equally energetic and powerful individuals in the "society-at-large." The real question, one to a great extent constructed by three decades of government funding of individual working artists, remains: is Canada finally ready for its artists?

Toronto, Art, and History (1987)

Published as "Toronto, Art and History," in *Toronto: A Play of History*, exh. cat. (Toronto: The Power Plant, 1987).

This will sound ridiculous, but as a small boy growing up in what we could call a trans-Atlantic attachment I was, well, mortified to discover that I was Canadian. It seemed a cruel twist of fate to be something which had no significance—to be, in an excruciating sense (at least for a child of eight or ten), merely an absence of something.

Later, I came to turn this absence into a positive virtue. To be honest, I expect that is how I still see the act of being Canadian. I say "act" because I think for many of us the assumption of this identity is a conscious decision, or at least a conscious rationalization. It's hard work, being Canadian, though this has little or nothing to do with being poor, or hungry, or even miserable. It has to do with choice. Hunger is shared with all living things; choice is what describes being human. A choice of absence may seem a curious choice to make, but it has its merits. I'll get back to this later.

While all of this may also sound ridiculous, at least to Canadians, it is a fact in the world that we carry our national attachments around with us like Marley's ghost. So they bear some investigation. The question that therefore concerns us, whether we like it or not, is how we write our own story, how we write our History. History is slightly different from fiction or fantasy, although it does have certain relationships. History is a bit like the tar-baby: stuff sticks to it. I want to talk a bit about some of this stuff that sticks to us, and most particularly about the part Toronto plays in this engagement. This brings me roughly to the circumstances of this exhibition, and the opening of the new gallery.

What seems to me most significant about the last decade in this city has not been that many good artists have made important work, which is true, nor that the issues they have dealt with have altered and continue to alter our assumptions about what is significant, which is also true. Rather, it is the context within which we have come to deal with all of this that is significant. Our notion of the context has changed. Until, say, 1976 or thereabouts, the context was seen as frontier. Hog Town. The artists of the '50s drank themselves into a stupor at the thought. Ab Ex Toronto was an Ab Sense indeed. No longer. Toronto has recently begun to construct an archaeology of itself. That is, it has begun to see itself historically. I'm not sure whether we are ready to meet History just yet but perhaps that's always the way it happens, when you're not ready. In any case, Toronto has glimpsed History in the mirror, and like the Medusa, History demands respect. But what kind of respect? What is the character and significance of this intersection of Toronto's current "Will to History" and our national "absence"?

One thing is sure. Nobody likes Toronto. Commentaries on the city become allegations, of which there seem to be three. The most significant charge is that art in Canada over the last decade has been dominated by Toronto. The second is that the art which has established this dominance has been installation art. Installation art may be thought of as sculpture which kicked off its pedestal, and then kicked off any other annoying formal limitations. And finally, art in Toronto, whether installation or not, is widely criticized as both intellectually disembodied and morally aggressive—or, Not Much Fun. This is revealing. Because as we all know, Toronto used to be known as Toronto the Good. Or as they say in Montreal, full of *têtes carrées*. Not Very Much Fun. As the guy said: the more things change…? Let's look at this more closely. I'm going to try some history.

Central Canada—Ontario and Quebec—still dictates what Canada is. There are only two cities: Montreal and Toronto. The rest are characters. In 1976 the Parti Québecois took power in Quebec, and for the next ten years Montreal was transformed from Canada's pre-eminent international centre into the capital of French Canada. Nineteen seventy-six was therefore a watershed year in Canadian cultural history. Toronto found itself during a critical decade unchallenged as the capital of national Canada. What is worth noting here, I feel, is not only the collapse of Montreal as Canada's cultural capital, but the destruction of the Franco-Scottish Canadian culture which Montreal represented. This destruction eliminated a century-old distinctive Canadian accommodation. It is not a matter of being sentimental; the accommodation had many inequalities and undeniable cultural tension. But both had two things in common: neither liked the English, and neither had any illusions about the "old country." Both French and Scots shared an attachment to a sense of transferred place, an attachment to where they found themselves. The French Normans left a France they despised almost four hundred years ago. The Scots left Scotland when the English overran it. Even when their interests collided, the Scots and French of Montreal knew they were Montrealers.

Not so Toronto. Toronto was an English city. It was built for United Empire Loyalists, to secure the Empire in what was left of British North America, not that the British even cared much about what was left: masts for ships, and some feeling that they owed the UEL's a debt. Disraeli came to see us as a millstone around his neck. The Family Compact which governed the city for so long—until just the other day, some would say—represented a culture located not in Toronto, but in London. For the Toronto establishment, home was England, and Toronto merely a local inconvenience. Toronto in 1956 was still a local inconvenience. Home was an England that few of the Toronto elite really knew or would have cared for, but one they constructed securely in their Past/Future, a place they would one day be, as one imagines one day being "grown up." This curious displacement could not help but construct an attitude of mind which ignored substantial reality for projected reality, a projection whose central characteristics were abstract idealism and confused identity. England and the dream of a United Empire had vanished, and Toronto was not London.

Now, in the Toronto of 1986, it is true that this seems ancient history. But beginnings are important; they never really go away. On this city of absence has been layered a series of other absences. As one of the two great cities in Canada, Toronto has attracted the displaced from other regions and from other countries for a century, and has done so with a vengeance in the last ten or fifteen years. Since 1976, it has become the natural cultural magnet for anyone in Canada who wanted to be seen. This is a process which works exponentially. In 1986, Toronto is no longer English, and arguably no longer even Central Canadian. It is a city of old and imported idealisms, of fantasies and desires. It remains a city of absences. Absence, they say, makes the heart grow fonder. It turns its focus into a moral foundation. The absences which give Toronto its essential character, absences inherited from its past and exacerbated by its immigrants, have ensured that Toronto is still Good. The focus may no longer be Imperial Unity. It is perhaps more usefully employed in critical theory and social radicalism. But it is Good nonetheless. And as any Montrealer will tell you, Not Really Much Fun.

And this, boys and girls, is what is therefore so significant about the first allegation I mentioned, that Toronto dominates Canadian art. If it is true, then the character it extends to that art is significantly idealist, "intellectually disembodied and morally aggressive." And installation art, with its detachment from specific limitation and its earnest theatrical promotion of critical discourse, seems quintessentially suited to Toronto. While it is true that painting is undeniably important here, it comes as no surprise that it is installation art, with its cousin video art, which strikes so many as a characteristic expression of this city. It may well be an amusing and perhaps appropriate irony that Canada's least Canadian city has become its most concerned identifier. But there is a risk.

I said at the beginning of these speculations that a choice of absence has its merits. It ensures a position of apartness that views things critically and is quick to engage what is wrong and what should be right. Its virtue is its freedom, its risk is its detachment. And this, I think, is what is so annoying for others about Toronto and about its dominance of Canadian art, namely, its attempt to be Good without being Bad. To be morally engaged without complicity, without politics. But dominated by a city of absent longings, what location can be found for Badness in Canadian art? The very character of intellectual disembodiment paradoxically reduces the idea of evil to a travesty. Evil, after all, is physical, and Toronto has always known that it could only be found down river in Montreal. Unfortunately for us all, Montreal just now is not in the crap game.

The tantalizing dualism of this problem is an intellectual dilemma which, I suspect, would cease to exist as soon as conditions ceased to privilege intellectual dilemmas. No doubt this is why so many Canadians unconsciously imagine they will be Americans when they grow up—Americans are not very intellectual, and their conditions reflect it. Still, in the City of the Intellect on Lake Ontario, the CBC provides valuable insights into the dilemma. Driving home the other night, I was listening to a radio play which restaged a debate held over fifty years ago between G.K. Chesterton and George Bernard Shaw. Rising on an accusation made by Shaw, Chesterton replied:

> Mr. Shaw here will only say what he can defend. That makes him a rationalist, and a Puritan. I, on the other hand, feel entirely free to say what I cannot possibly defend. That makes me a humourist, and a Catholic.

Counter-Narrative (1988)

Panel address given at "The Liberal Arts Seminar: Panels on Representation," moderated by Bruce Grenville, at the Ontario College of Art, March 9, 1988. The panel title was "Counter-Narrative." The other speakers were Anna Gronau and Elizabeth MacKenzie.

The purpose of this panel is described as an attempt "to indicate the effects on representation that are determined within a counter-narrative practice." Bruce Grenville has defined counter-narrative practice as a critique of the traditional relationship between representation and the "Real," a relationship in which representations act as transparent windows through which we can "see" reality laid out before us.

I will try here tonight first of all to add my own clarifications onto what these statements might mean theoretically and historically, and second of all to speak briefly about my own working practice in light of these clarifications.

Let's look first at the term itself. Since I am not personally familiar with it, and may not understand the nuances of usage placed upon it in whatever critical context it inhabits, I must speculate on its usefulness for me. It seems harmless enough. Counter-narrative suggests analogies in terms like counterculture, counter-argument and so on; as such, it implies a position not against narrative as such, but against certain narratives. This is important and appropriate, as we will see later perhaps. But it is worth emphasizing at the beginning. Bruce Grenville has suggested that for most people the narrative is assumed to be the Real—that the story is True, a literal reflection of reality. Centuries of intense controversy, and bloodshed, surrounding interpretation of the Bible bear him out. It is therefore tempting to think that if we could dispense with narrative, we could dispense with the assumption, and somehow set things right. But as Bruce Grenville points out in quoting the French critic Lyotard, narrative is more complicated than a few popular mythic stories. All general assumptions, or we could better say "propositions" that operate to express directed meaning can be seen to operate as narratives—they provide "the story" of meaning for us. They are, in Lyotard's phrase, master narratives. The New Testament, with its story of transcendental salvation is certainly the dominant Western narrative; but we can name other significant narratives as well: classical science, with its story of mechanistic determinism; patriarchy, with its genealogies of linear male inheritance, property, and order;

even space travel, with its Wild West frontier exchange of the present for
the future, a kind of techno-linear amnesia closely fitted to the American
dream. With master narratives, as we can see from these examples, we enter
into the realm of ideology; and as we therefore see that a counter-narrative
practice is a practice which is alerted to the play of ideologies, we must see
also that it does not seek to stand outside their attendant representations,
but to inhabit them "contingently"—one could say ironically, but perhaps
suspiciously catches the flavour better.

Let's therefore look now at the definition of this term "counter-
narrative" as positing a contingent Real, one in which we are conscious
of its production. It is important to distinguish how this contingency and
this consciousness operate within this practice. The "father" we're playing
to here is constituted by the modernist and avant-garde traditions which
have dominated artmaking and critical language in this century. Taking
the key issue of production, certainly Modernism and the historical avant-
garde were fully conscious—indeed painfully self-conscious—of their own
production. One could argue that for modernists, all meaning was provided
within the character of the production itself, a character sharply separable
from the Real and from historical process, a character caught, for better
or worse (depending upon which modernist you are), in the epiphany of
the frozen gesture. As for the avant-garde, one could argue that they were
not only extremely conscious of the processes of production, but vocal
about the contingencies behind cultural determination. After all, they had
read their Marx. But perhaps Marx was a bum steer. If Modernism can be
accused of complacency, if not disinterest, with respect to the social fabric
of society; and further, of a dangerous belief in the immense benefits of
technology and an effortless assumption of infinite progress, it is also true
that the avant-garde can be accused of simply applying a remarkably similar
belief in technology's benefits towards a badly misconstrued utopian notion
of classless society. In either case, the impulse for both concerning notions of
production and contingency was to "totalize" the equation and attempt the
dissolution of those contingencies and productions in order to construct a
seamless transparency, an elimination of difference, we could say, between
representations and the Real. Finally, to quote Voltaire's ironic commentary, all will be for the best in the best of all possible worlds.

From a position within a counter-narrative practice, both the avant-
garde and Modernism obviously missed the point. The thrust of both
these great revolutionary movements is clearly teleological—that is, intent
on a specific over-riding conclusion to their immense narratives. This is
not what I am sponsoring within the definition of contingency and production here. Rather, I am concerned with definition that attempts no
such reductive project, one which is prepared to accept instead a dialectic

of inconsistency and contradiction, a dialectic whose basic purpose is to suggest the problematic relationship between representations and Reality, and construct a recognition of differences in place of a "repetition of the Same," to borrow from Bruce Grenville's recent catalogues. The purpose is to accept the role of Devil's Advocate to what we represent ourselves to be, rather than to suggest our Mastery over the Real. The purpose, in other words, is to recognize the complexity of the Subject's construction, the construction of our identity and its inevitable contingencies, however determined we must also be to speak with our voice. Indeed, it is only by speaking with our own voice that we can begin the processes of argumentation which ultimately prevent us from falling into the fatal error of reading narratives as absolute or monolithic structures of meaning, the error, to refer again to Lyotard's lexicon, of turning perfectly good local narratives into master narratives which will brook no argument. Within argumentation we can recognize politics and position, and the immense range of specific narratives useful for the elaboration of contingent meaning. Out of this recognition we can begin to detect their interplay, an interplay that may construct grand narratives—such as the Bible, which whatever else it may be is most certainly, at least in its fullest form, a magnificent narrative—but an interplay which always calls into question the unifying and exclusionary impulse which transforms narrative curiosity into narrative oppression. The Bible is exhilarating, provided it is understood within the context of its complicated histories; provided, that is, that it be approached dialectically.

So, you might ask, how does all this clarification make for any art? Since I am an artist, I want now to speak about my own development within these general terms so that, hopefully, I can establish for you how questions of counter-narrative practice have determined, or can be read against, my own work.

Before I discovered that my commitment was to making art, I initially studied modern history at Queen's. It was and has remained crucial to my views about artmaking. The experience of reading History clarified for me that History is written, not simply made. It is written by real historians, or real textbook writers even, attempting to construct, let us be frank, master narratives, but sometimes grand narratives, to explain what real people find themselves doing, or believing.

Turning subsequently to making art, I realized that the master narratives of the avant-garde and modernist texts seemed unsatisfactory. Avant-garde gestures against middle-class norms seemed quaintly exciting, but somehow irrelevant within the complex dynamics of the historical narratives with which I was familiar; even worse, from the perspective of the 1970s and late '60s it had a depressingly adolescent quality I associated with the more histrionic aspects of the early and mid-sixties. On the other hand,

Modernist disregard for anything tainted by the impurities of content and the messier contingencies and vulnerabilities of irresolute intentions and ignoble actions seemed downright superficial and irresponsible. However much Greenberg might talk up his notions of absolute engagement, or Michael Fried might defend ineffable presentness, it seemed necessary to redefine a sense of purpose. Like many others, I felt that this must involve the situational relations established between individuals and their conceptualizations of Reality, or the Real. Vital to understand here is the notion that this question of "the conceptualization of the Real" is not divorceable from the relations acted out—day by day, year by year—between individuals who, after all, are also simultaneously conceiving this Real. That, in other words, History is pervasive—it is not merely one among many philosophical options, but is in fact our inevitable inscription, whether or not we like how we write it as we go. With History, the name of the game is the Re-Write.

Given this central importance of the historical process, with its historiographical acceptance of contingency, and its structural dependence on witnesses and artifacts, I came very quickly to see artmaking as a form of historiography, or to borrow a slightly more elegant term from Foucault, archaeology. I saw this archaeology as implicitly grounded in questions of memory, paradox, contradictory progressions, complicated purposes, futile but brave intentions, and above all in ethical dilemma.

In short, I saw artmaking as grounded in the dialectical and circumstantial situation of the Real. If this sounds complicated, let's turn now to consider two actual works. Both constructions had as their general purpose the exhibition, description, and demonstration of those productions and contingencies which construct the narratives we spin in order to place ourselves within meaning. The piece *Julius Caesar's left thigh as it appeared when he mounted his horse to cross the Rubicon* dates from 1973. I wanted to take an element from a particular narrative of power which has entered into Western mythology, and invest it with a countering, but equally significant, narrative concerned with the physicality of the individual and the individual's movements in the world. The one "subverts" the other, but also more importantly it "fleshes out" the "real" conditions of the "Other," understood as a Subject in their own right.

The second work is from 1984 and is simply titled *5 explanations*. It includes five carefully spaced voice-over "explanations," local narratives if you will, each directed at the central representation of the hands (executed as a sculptural trompe l'oeil in partial three dimensions). Each explanation carries a different set of purposes, and together they counter one another, or we could say play with one another, suggesting the contingencies of our viewing, and the complex reading that all representations invite in attempting to reach out and grasp reality. What I want to insist on, however, is that this playfulness must not be interpreted as disengagement from the necessity to establish ethical and relational position. In one way or another, all five of these texts were conceived as explorations of possible approaches to the question "how should I live?"

What do we have here, then? We have a responsibility as artists and as viewers to counter the narratives we find oppressive, to construct a critical perspective. While this is hardly news, our reading of countering may be. Some years ago, I gave a lecture on my work at the Emily Carr College of Art, and I was challenged by a member of the audience on the reading I placed upon my theory and practice. She suggested, quite correctly, that I was "reading backwards," inscribing into the work purposes she called into question and which she identified as simply an attempt to appropriate fashionable and perhaps flattering forms of critique. My defence fell into two categories. On the one hand, I agreed that I was prepared to adopt terms of critique which I felt were useful and apply them post facto to particular works. While it is only honest to examine where this may radically alter the original purpose, if indeed one can really be sure of the dimensions of that original purpose, it is also important to note that works will be read very differently as different perspectives are brought to bear on them, including perspectives brought by the artist responsible for the works' existence. This is, after all, central to the contingent nature of our relationship with the Real, and consequently our countering of narratives must be seen in more fluid and pervasive terms than perhaps it has been.

My second defence was directed at the anger and passion with which she made the charges. It wasn't, of course, a personal attack; it was an outrage that matters of importance could be rationalized and fitted neatly into an apparently seamless fabric of explanations. While I feel that the seamlessness which angered her was a misreading arising out of the problematics associated with panel discussions and lectures, I nonetheless appreciated the outrage. My problem with it is connected to the question of how we should proceed in countering oppression. There's no easy answer to that one, and anger is obviously important and inevitable in pursuing particular actions. My response to it, therefore, was not to dismiss it as inappropriate, but to argue that outrage can be directed and expressed through a process of quiet but direct speech, a process—that is—of insistent and determined curiosity informed by a relentlessly dialectical rationality. While this process may seem sometimes seamless, its nature is difficult to absorb into coherent master narratives, as the immense commentary that we blithely label Marxism illustrates. This is, in any case, despite all its possibilities for distortion, how I have proceeded in my own work to counter the oppressions of certain overweening narratives.

Note: The term "dialectic" has a number of nuances. I am well aware that it is inevitably inflected and can legitimately be seen as limited by its methodology. I must therefore admit to some complicity with that inflection, but as inflections go it seems nevertheless one I can generally subscribe to. It is used here to suggest a process of inquiry which recognizes the play of reasoning from difference but does not seek to end that difference in closure, or to perpetuate difference that is inappropriate. For a dictionary definition, the two possibilities below may help to clarify something of its intent:

Any method of argument or exposition that systematically weighs contradictory facts or ideas with a view to the resolution of their real or apparent contradictions.

The contradiction between two conflicting forces viewed as the determining factor in their continuing interaction.

Made in Canada/Fait au Canada: Situating the Canadian Art Identity (1989)

Presented as part of "Made in Canada/Fait au Canada: Situating the Canadian Art Identity—a symposium," 1989 Riddell Lectureship, Saturday, March 18, 1989, at the University of Regina's Department of Visual Arts.

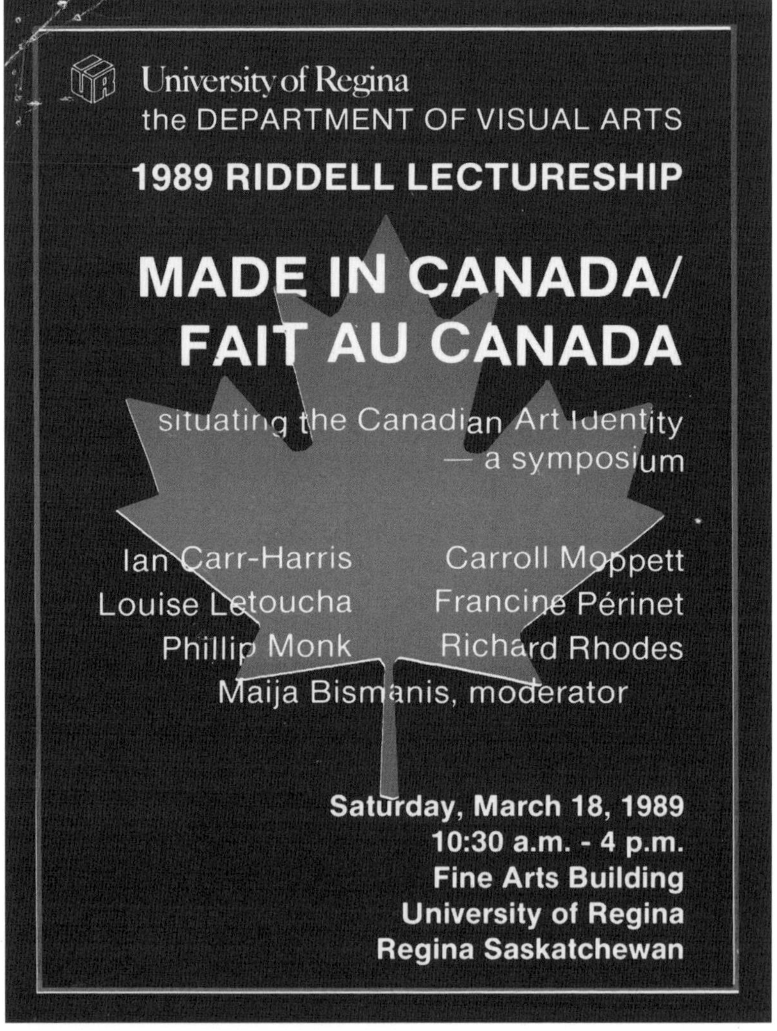

1.2   Riddell Lectures, *Made in Canada/Fait au Canada*, Department of Visual Arts, University of Regina, 1989. Symposium flyer

This paper will begin my brief to the Symposium followed by answers to all the questions posed by the panel. I will finish with some concluding remarks.

Brief to the Symposium:
It is important to examine first just what are the main assumptions currently operative in Canadian culture—and consequently in Canadian art and criticism, and then to consider what direction implied by these assumptions would best serve our interests.

We are North American. Despite serious misassumptions we hold, we are not like America, or even Western Europe. We are not economically and politically powerful, nor have we—like the major powers—mythologized our identities into totalizing presumptions. This allows us a predisposition to appreciate historical context, individual construction, and political intervention as more than novelties on the one hand, or national emergencies on the other. Our curiosity about our own identity is a manifestation of this general condition. The direction this should take us in, I believe, is towards a strengthening of our terms of inquiry both within our national cultures and outside of them. Ultimately, Canada's identity, and the identity significant to Canadian art and criticism, should involve a sophisticated recognition of how identity works, and what responsibilities it entails.

1. What activities promote a Canadian consciousness?
It seems to me that any consciousness, Canadian or otherwise, is promoted by an investigation of historical circumstance—political, social, economic, and ideological. Being Canadian or American, or being female or male, or being Roman Catholic or Atheist, these are no different. A distinction must be drawn between a genuine consciousness—that is, an arguable one—and a false consciousness based upon myth and indulgence. The American Dream, for instance, is one such myth, and while it is undeniable that it is a potent force in constructing a sense of "being American" it is a dangerously insular and destructive force in both American and world affairs. Promoting similar totalizing myths in Canada may promote some kind of Canadian consciousness, but I would argue that this is neither appropriate to our circumstance, nor desirable as an option. The purpose of having a consciousness is not to impose power, or to suggest superiority, but to recognize differences, to discern values, and to derive a practicable theory from them.

As to activities associated with such an investigation into a Canadian consciousness, these must include a re-evaluation of how we have defined the intersecting cultures we have. I think we actually have no clear notion currently about these intersections; instead we have regional biases based largely upon ethnic and colonial heritages dominant in one region or another. While these are significant aspects of our culture, they are also destructively isolationist in their mutually hostile claims. Their territoriality is not particularly interesting and tends to prevent the promotion of an identity rich in contradiction and "dialectical" play. Regionalism easily becomes a kind of cultural apartheid—certainly easier to administrate (which is perhaps why the federal government seems to favour "multiculturalism"), and certainly more accessible for regional audiences. This is not, however, to promote a Canadian sense of significant identity. Instead of entrenched regionalisms, we need to have a climate of argumentation, a programme of intersecting discussions that would involve artists, critics, and historians in a continual examination of our individual histories. It's amazing to me, after at least two decades of extensive post-graduate education in this country, how little consideration has gone into these histories.

2. Does our geographical location in any way affect the work being done?
I can interpret this question in two ways.

I assume it is meant to address Canada's geographic location at the "top of the world" along with Greenland, Scandinavia, the USSR—at any rate somewhere north of the 49th parallel. I'm not sure to what an extent artists working out of a local geography differ nationally or internationally— except for the obvious fact that the light in Provence, say, or in Frankfurt, differs from the light in Winnipeg or Toronto, or that prairie horizons differ from those in California suburbs. It is more likely that the work will be influenced by whatever metaphysical tradition or influence the artist has found persuasive.

The question of marginality is perhaps bound up with the adoption of influence. While I am certain that all artists working in this country are conscious of being marginal—as Canadians, and as professionals within an international arena dominated (at least currently) by the US, Germany, Italy, and to a lesser extent France and Britain—I don't know that this affects per se their working practice, except to the extent that international indifference can tend to result in either self-indulgence or in a decline of productivity. Most obviously problematic, of course, is our proximity—wherever we may be in Canada—to the United States. While this is a recurring theme in our history, I'm not sure that this proximity exerts more than a vague anxiety. This anxiety over the dominating influence of American culture, most especially popular American culture, is shared by many cultures around the world. We do have a special problem in that from the vantage point of Europe or Asia we seem to be indistinguishable from

Americans, but we share this problem with a host of other nations situated next to powerful neighbours. If an assumption here is that this is a unique problem, well it isn't. Much more to the point perhaps is that Canadians, especially Canadians who have never lived in the US, think that we are like Americans. But this is largely separate, I think, from what we actually do. It affects our general assumption of context, and confuses us when it comes to planning and policy, but I'm not sure it affects our work much. What affects work is the play of theory, and because American theory—for instance Greenberg's modernism or Judd's Minimalism—was a dominating influence internationally during the fifties and sixties, we were affected by US models. Currently, we are probably influenced far more by European models, digested for obvious linguistic and publishing reasons through British, French, or American interpretations.

My second interpretation of this question would be to distinguish between the geographical locations individual artists find themselves working in within Canada. I think regional influences are a factor in the development of a practice: like everyone else, artists react to significant aspects of their personal landscape. Regional influences may include regional geography, but they are certainly not merely geographic. It is difficult for me to evaluate how strong a factor geographic location might be because Toronto—the location I am familiar with—is not truly a location; rather, it is a meeting place for an extremely diverse array of artists and potential artists from across the country. It is very rare to find anyone who is actually "from" Toronto, and even difficult to find a lot of people from southern Ontario. I suspect that while Toronto may currently be the largest case in point, Canada's rapid shift towards urban centres with little inherent tradition may signal a watershed in Canadian identity. Urban issues cut across regional and inherited definitions, and for the practicing artist pose problems of validity that beg larger questions of cultural identity than may be necessary within the more stable traditional regionalisms.

3. Does the physical geography of Canada affect the work produced?
To some extent, my remarks on geographic location relate to this question. Perhaps I could add, however, that the sheer vastness of Canada, taken together with a relatively small population limited by the nature of the north to a shallow band of settlement,[1] poses both a problem in communication and an issue of metaphysics. This is partly overcome through agencies like the Canada Council, and university venues such as this, but communication remains difficult for most artists and critics. As to the metaphysical dimension, this is a subtle affair difficult to track at the level of production: Canada's physical geography is diverse, like many other countries. Clearly, this always affects artists, everywhere, somehow.

1   Author's note: That "shallow band of settlement" has more recently been expanded to include communities in the north, though the problem of communication remains a serious obstacle to engagement despite social media platforms like Instagram.

4. How is Canadian art received by the international community?
The question undoubtedly is: how is Canadian art received by that international system of power-brokering which chooses to support certain artists for political and economic purposes related to the authenticity of particular institutions—including national cultures? As one might suppose, with a great deal of indifference. Power-brokering is a complex affair, requiring great skill and sensitivity to the exercise of advantage. Like chess, perhaps. Canadian art, qua Canadian art, has no cachet. For Canadian art to have cachet would require that Canada, as a national culture, would have to have an *aura*, however constructed, which would become a factor in the exercise of advantage. Certain Canadian artists, recognizing this, have been careful to insert themselves as individuals into the fabric of international advantage. But they do this quite separately from any notion of Canadian art identity. I believe it might be a mistake to take this question too much to heart; if we are to consider the recent resurgence of interest in German art, for instance, we must remember that the question raised concerns not so much about general notions of "German" identity, but a particular set of issues concerning German historical and cultural experience in the last few decades. If Canada has anything to learn from this, it is that the international community becomes "interested" when there is a crisis of consciousness that has general political dimension, and when that crisis is carefully orchestrated by the national culture for specific purposes in its own national interest. It would be the height of naiveté to think that power-brokering is interested in anything but the brokerage of power.

There is, however, another international community, and that is simply other artists, and critics, working away in other countries. My experience is that on this level there is immense curiosity and interest in what is done here, whether as art or as criticism. Unfortunately, of course, this does not translate into so-called international venues, though it may very easily translate into local venues—as long as the Canada Council or External Affairs will pay the shipping.

5. Are there motifs, themes, structures, and media which are signals of Canadian work?
I would say no, for two reasons. On the one hand, Canadian artists are fully integrated into an international Euro-American consciousness, and are concerned with the same issues as artists elsewhere in Western culture. On the other hand, Canadian artists have no strong national traditions which would empower them with such motifs, themes, or structures. Canadian artists work very much from personal constructions of significance within the dominant themes prevalent in transatlantic culture.

6. Do we have, can we have, or should we have a unified visual language given the reality of a French-speaking and English-speaking Canada?
I don't know what a unified visual language is.

7. Are we merely a scaled-down version of the American art scene? Or do we have our own flavour?
I am not sure that there is an American art scene. There is an international system, in which New York has taken on the role of central art market. Certainly, the US is well-suited to this role, since American mythology supports market-driven institutions. Europe has its own private economies, as we know, but it has in addition, and in contrast to the Americans, a clear recognition of the part that public support mechanisms can play in the construction of a national culture. Of course, apart from rhetorical flourishes, the Americans know how to use the state apparatus to further cultural goals; it is simply that the separation of private and public spheres in American culture is sometimes difficult to distinguish because Americans prefer to pretend that the public sphere is simply an innocent extension of the individual. While it is probably possible to talk of an American art scene as constructed by the art magazines, as one can also in Canada, I remain unclear as to what extent this is a reality for more than a very few critics and artists for whom these magazines are a venue. Perhaps I'm unclear about just what constitutes a scene. There are, of course, a number of American art scenes, and they do tend to have in common with New York a set of assumptions derived from private enterprise support. I don't know about flavour, but in Canada we do not really have the basis for any such set of assumptions. We do, however, have an extensive system of public support necessary to the existence of a scene in this country. Canada is a mixed economy, in which public and private initiatives have been vital to the development of a mature culture within the evolving complexity of this century. The Canadian art scene represents an extension of the same necessity, and this does set us apart from American experience.

8. Does the Canadian marketplace put different and/or special demands on its artists?
The Canadian marketplace has never placed any demands on me. Partly this is the case because I have never thought about the marketplace—I've always had another job. Maybe that's the clue: the marketplace in Canada is largely a factor of absence, and the demand it "places" on artists is simply to learn to have a separate source of income. It has been suggested that Canadian artists have consequently had the unavoidable option of being more intellectual than artists elsewhere—if you aren't concerned about the client, you

can afford to be more concerned about ideas. There may be something to it, but I don't know how much.

9. Are Canadian artists being allowed to speak independently and define what is being made, or is their production framed by the critical community? What is the source of that criticism and is it inhibiting authentic Canadian production? Speaking independently and being framed by the critical community are not mutually exclusive states, unless an artist has no ideas of their own. They are also inevitably co-existent states: all artworks are framed by criticism— this is what criticism is for, and this is why we both want and need it. If criticism didn't exist, artists, let alone everyone else, would have to make it exist.

The source of that criticism, however, is a more interesting question. It is not that international critical concerns inhibit an authentic Canadian production, but that they can certainly do so if misapplied. Critical theories are developed in response to problems which develop in practice; that is, theory operates as a model, or paradigm, to solve certain problems which arise as we detect contradictions. Misunderstanding contradictions, or not detecting them, clearly carries implications for the application of a given theory. To import theory from one circumstance to another is therefore somewhat fraught. Modernism, for example, was forged within the conditions of a Europe for whom nationalism and inherited culture had become synonymous with regressive regimes and conservative repression. For the Europe of the early twentieth century, it became a liberating force, particularly in its alter ego, the avant-garde. But for marginal cultures such as Canada's at the time, and arguably even now, modernism's critical edge is blunted on the sheer pathos involved in struggling to find a voice. Sure, much of that voice carries colonial yearnings and unexamined assumptions. But the circumstances within which they were being played out were totally different, and required then, and now, a close examination of the role a theory such as modernism could play within those circumstances. Without such examination, the theory becomes just another repressive force.

10. Is there an identifiable mode or look to the Canadian work which gets shown both in Canada and beyond our borders? How are curatorial decisions affecting development? What is the mandate of the 49th Parallel in New York? And is it being fulfilled?
Possibly there is an identifiable mode, if not a look, to work shown by a few influential venues. I suspect that behind this question lies an anxiety that these venues are the official state-supported institutions, like the 49th Parallel, or the National Gallery, or the Canada Council, and so on, which

have a strong voice in selection of work "where it counts." This mode is probably definable as critical and historically self-conscious, less concerned with expressing fundamental human concerns (though by no means necessarily dismissive of them) and more concerned with how a representation of those concerns may proceed within current contexts of theory and practice. This does not in itself produce satisfying work, though it probably produces a great deal of correct work. It would be nice to think that it also allows a venue for a great deal of intelligent work, and broadly speaking I think it does. Intelligence, however, also is not in itself exciting, or stimulating, and I think that a lot of work that is exciting and stimulating fails to get shown because it does not seem to address an identifiable critical mode. I think this is a failure of criticism, and by extension, curation. In fairness, I think one of the problems is that Canada occupies such a tenuous cultural position both at home and abroad that there is a kind of desperation, an immense pressure, placed on those who must make the choices to show what and who we are. It is understandable that the choices often end up more correct than risky, more intelligent than exciting. I remember how much dissension was caused when the US gave over their pavilion at the 1984 Venice Biennial to the New Museum, who then chose a raft of completely unknown mid-western painters to represent the US. If the Americans can get that upset over risk, it isn't hard to imagine how difficult it is for Canadian curators to attempt it. It is harder for me to say how all of this affects our development. Of course we are all influenced by watching choices, and this may cause some to emulate apparent success; it likely causes many to simply acknowledge the choices and hunker down. Some may become disillusioned and quit or leave. I don't know how this works out. I do know, however, that a healthy critical climate—one in which there are a multiplicity of voices—sooner or later gets around to confronting distortions. Perhaps we need to ensure a healthy critical climate.

11. Are certain regions of Canada represented more often than others, and if so, does this impact on the Canadian art identity? What regional voices are not being heard?
I don't know the statistics on this, but I would expect that artists from Central Canada are exhibited more consistently than those in other regions. On the other hand, Toronto, the area I am familiar with, itself represents artists from across the country. Not simply because artists in Toronto come from across Canada, but because places like Mercer Union, YYZ, the Power Plant, A Space, and so on regularly schedule such exhibitions. If representation includes representation in the press, it seems to me that *C Magazine*, *Vanguard*, *Canadian Art*, and even *Parachute* approach a balanced

representation of voices. Certainly, being an artist in Toronto has little
bearing on whether you get to be shown or heard.

*12. What role does the Canada Council play in establishing a Canadian
art identity?*
The Council's role is central to the existence of a national culture. Through
its jury system, it undoubtedly establishes a base level of competence and
intellectual strength which has made good Canadian art comparable with
anything practiced anywhere. Some are afraid that it establishes as well an
upper level of competence by encouraging intelligence over transgression.
I'm prepared to believe this is a potential within the system, and certain of
its strategies, such as initial screening through slides, very much risks such
a failure of nerve. But it must be remembered that the Jury system operates
through peers of artists and critics, and consequently it is not the Council as
such, but artists and critics who establish identity.

13. How is Canadian art viewed by the international community?
It isn't. It may be received, and I've discussed that previously, but effectively no one looks at Canada from abroad apart from consideration for
exhibitions in foreign venues. This may be regrettable, and reflect rampant
parochialism, but it is not particularly surprising. For it to be any different, Canada would need to be a sexy culture—like Berlin, or New York,
or Milan, or perhaps Tokyo. Sexy cultures have their problems, and most
people spend a lot of time making sure they remain unsexy. It takes a long
time, or devastating failure, to get sexy.

*14. Can we predict the future direction of Canadian art production? How will
international political and economic relations affect Canadian art?*
I assume this means: will Free Trade affect Canadian art? I don't know. I
think it depends upon how Canadians react to the implications free trade
has for access to their own voices. I tend to suspect that we could hardly
be much worse off than we are already. One thing about free trade is that
it has changed the context within which discussion of identity has traditionally occurred by actually entering the lion's den. We can't any longer
indulge ourselves with an illusion of Canadian independence: Canadians
will have to put up or shut up. If central institutions of independence—like
the Canada Council—are threatened, the threat will be not to this or that
cultural policy, but to the sheer existence of our culture. Perhaps this will
make Canadians discuss their identity in more substantial terms than as
a kind of national hobby for liberals and intellectuals. Perhaps not. As
far as making art is concerned, loss of independence, on whatever scale,
represents a loss of context, not a loss of opportunity, or freedom. Since

our context as it stands seems highly dubious anyway, I'm not sure just what it is we will be losing. Potential, perhaps. The world will someday say: "What a pity that Canadians, the 'other' North Americans, could not imagine a way in which to merge consumer desire with a determination to speak for themselves, to offer the world a different voice at a time when the Western democracies—and most particularly the United States—had clearly exhausted their imagination."

15. Does Canadian art reflect the political culture of our country, or does it ride on the coat-tails of world market values?
I think that it is possible to say that art made in Canada does reflect our political culture to the extent that it is bound together, that is definable as Canadian, by its freedom to explore meaning without the constraints of a seductive and destructive market economy. Our political culture is also an odd amalgam of local interest within a national debate. Canada is a confederation of interests, not a centralized state. This is different from many countries, including the USA, which—despite its name—has evolved into a strongly centralist and unified entity. Canadian artists, I think, reflect at once a local emphasis—and I use the term free of any pejorative inflection—and a national consciousness. I'm not sure that this necessarily translates into a "look," but I believe it constructs a context within which artists across the country can work with a degree of self-worth. Of course, absence of a strong market brings other problems—especially if artists accept the notion that a market economy gives meaning to art. Speaking for myself, I find this notion inadequate, though not entirely unjustified.

On the other hand, I don't see how Canadian art could be seen as "riding on the coat-tails of world market values." Canadian art is incredibly cheap. If this another way of suggesting that artists here make work just to mimic successful trends elsewhere, well, I suppose that is always a factor in certain decisions by certain artists—here and elsewhere. To suggest that this is typical of Canadian artists is, I think, to suggest that Canadians are irredeemably shallow and lacking in integrity, and I for one have rarely encountered this. A distinction must always be drawn between legitimate curiosity and cynical laziness.

16. Should the notion of a Canadian art identity be an issue?
Yes. I just spent 8 pages on it.

Concluding remarks:
On Radio St. Lucia there is a daily program of fifteen minutes called *The Children's Broadcast to Schools* or some such thing. A man leads the children in singing the national anthem and every morning he begins by asking: "And

what is culture, boys and girls?" To which the children respond in chorus: "It's what we do and how we do it."

The internationalist culture of our century has had on its agenda—for some excellent historical and progressive reasons—a determination to sponsor similarities between human experiences and to marginalize difference. Yet it has become increasingly clear—and on a level of theory this constitutes the crucial re-evaluation of cultural modernism—that we marginalize difference at great cost, and ultimately to no avail.

Some years ago, Pierre Vallières wrote a devastating book about the Québecois experience in Canada. The thesis concerned how difference is perceived, and what to do about it. It is arguable that Canada has come to play out a traditional female identity to America's—and perhaps Europe's—male. If we are to have a sophisticated recognition of how our various identities work, and what responsibilities they entail, we could undoubtedly learn a lot from current feminist critiques. If "what we do and how we do it" fails to include a critical awareness to support and sponsor our own dignities—if instead we accept a traditional role constructed for us elsewhere—our culture is merely stillborn.

Report from Toronto (2005)

Presented at the Comox Valley Art Gallery Conference, "Reports from Canada: Practice and Place," Courtenay, BC, August 2005.

Closeted within the Conference title "Practice and Place" lies the scary question of authentic production: "how can I know the necessity of what I register?"

Authenticity is one of those big words. If a significant element in the idea of authenticity involves clarifying what one knows to be true, the concept of place offers itself both as a good place to start, and as an impossible problem: where exactly is a place? The concept of "a place" is now no longer isolatable geographically speaking, and though it continues as a concept of specificity, that specificity is mediated by our near-simultaneous experience of other places—through constant travel and such daily exposures as the news and advertising, let alone films. The concepts of here and there remain linguistic indicators of proximity, but no longer offer guidance as to identity. A place, for instance Toronto—and perhaps especially Toronto due to its historical inability to see itself as a destination—must now be seen in quotation marks. Destination cities like London or New York have long been manufactured signs, but to anyone in the developed West, the lowliest village is merely quotable, a conflation of any number of other places. Identity—that is, so-called authentic identity, is now "lost in translation," to employ a further quote, and the task when it comes to discussing place and practice is to acknowledge that the specificity of place is lodged within the intertextuality—the interconnectivity and consequent displacement— of transmission.

On the question of conflation, it occurred to me that a story of Jorge Luis Borges offers a possible route by which to examine a particular thread of necessity—and let me say that necessity seems still critical, given that the concept of choice remains the defining core of our Western cultural inheritance—inherent in the practices of artists working from Toronto.

In the story titled "Pierre Menard, Author of *Don Quixote*," Borges begins with a detailed listing of all the supposed writer's published works, the last of which is delightfully described as verses which owe their efficacy to their punctuation.

1 Jorge Luis Borges, "Pierre Menard, Author of *Don Quixote*," *Ficciones*, ed. Anthony Kerrigan, trans. Anthony Bonner (New York: Grove Weidenfeld, 1963), 48.

> This work, possibly the most significant of our time, consists of the ninth and thirty-eighth chapters of Part One of *Don Quixote* and a fragment of the twenty- second chapter…
> He did not want to compose another *Don Quixote*—which would be easy—but *the Don Quixote*. It is unnecessary to add that his aim was never to produce a mechanical transcription of the original; he did not propose to copy it. His admirable ambition was to produce pages which would coincide – word for word and line for line – with those of Miguel de Cervantes.
> —Borges, "Pierre Menard, Author of *Don Quixote*"[1]

Embedded within Borges' portrait of this fictional writer—but we could also say the artist—are at least three possible mechanisms by which the artwork may be secured.

> The first mechanism is the lever of authenticity.
> The second mechanism is irony, or we could say improbability. Currently we have been calling it appropriation.
> The third mechanism is disengagement, or as we might normally say, commentary, reportage or simply that supplement called by lawyers a "rider."

I would add that embedded within these three mechanisms there is another mechanism: the dialectical relationship between fact and fiction, or we could say between the tragic and the comedic.

Let's consider the lever of authenticity.
Authenticity, as I just suggested, is complicated. What is authentic? And how does it separate from nostalgia—the idea that everything was better before. What is authentic can be as difficult to untangle as trying to determine what is art. Not so long ago it was considered that truth lay in the formal or objective, quasi-scientifically provable qualities of materials or structure—formal truth. Alternatively, authenticity was considered to be adherence to historical truth—as in Marxist or Hegelian notions of history as an inevitable progress towards a set goal. Another avenue to authenticity has been that of the voice: either the personal voice of the "I" who enunciates myself, or the cultural voice of the "I" who belongs to and speaks for a given community. All of these have their complications. So many, in fact, that currently I have the impression generally in Toronto that while all of these continue to exert some pull, authenticity for most artists lies largely in the act of quotation and reference—if indeed many have not in fact given up on authenticity as a test altogether.

Next, we have irony, improbability, or appropriation.
The problem of authenticity tends to lead to irony, parody, and the like, including a renewed interest in paradox. If authenticity can be linked to an allegorical search for the *punctum* of truth, versions of improbability or appropriation can be linked to a metonymic chain of interconnecting possibilities, none of which need to be defended as such. In a combative and multi-layered cultural environment like Toronto, this can be the safer way to go. Toronto is also a major entertainment centre, and one mark of entertainment is that it needs no defence—it just is. Good or bad, who knows? Maybe it will work. Maybe it won't. In any case, it's over almost as soon as it starts. Maybe sooner. The important thing is to get the name spelled right.

Thirdly there is disengagement, commentary, reportage, or simply supplement.
The somewhat tenuous hold on purpose that marks the nature of working as an artist in Toronto as I have outlined it—rather theatrically to be sure— is offset, I think, by the widespread conviction that none of us are actually artists. I mean this in the sense that the concept of the artist is itself now historical, and consequently naive as a claim to production. Of course we still call ourselves artists—and why not? It's a useful term of ironic distance, if you know what I mean, and for those who don't, it serves to shorten the conversation, helpfully. Installed within the shell of this term artist, artists in Toronto function in many respects as commentators, reporters, even curators and critics, providing a cultural service for others. Within their own practices, the idea of art is an idea of, as Camus put it half a century ago, reportage—a supplemental notation within the discourse of art.

And finally *the dialectical relationship between fact and fiction, between the tragic and the comedic.*
If the focus I've trotted out above seems a tad dystopic in picturing the practice of art in Toronto, I want to correct the focal length and end by allowing for a greater depth to the field. There is nothing bloodless about living and working in Toronto. The antinomies I've addressed are just that—contradictions that work together to press an advantage that we can call working against the grain, constantly aware of the enterprise of art as a work in progress, a work of anticipation without false privileges. Perhaps that's Toronto's route to authenticity.

Relevant to this discussion, and especially to make the point concerning the interconnectivity of place today, I want to try out some thoughts on developments I've noticed in current art practices generally. The basis for these came from my reflections on the Berlin Art Fair (Art Forum Berlin) in the fall of 2003, but which I've also drawn from recently visiting London's

Frieze Art Fair, Madrid's ARCO, and the alternative art fair in Toronto. I've also discussed it in reference to a comparison between Janet Cardiff and Robin Collyer at the Venice Biennale.

Briefly, there were three what we might call "implosions" that stood out for me. They seemed to be implosions because they all suggested a diminishment of certain positive elements (the word should probably be "positivist" in the general dictionary sense of "dogmatic certainty") associated with normal or normative assumptions about our average perceptual experience. I thought of this diminishment as a kind of collapse. As in "a collapse of faith."

The first of these collapses, let's say, is the collapse of a concept of **Time**. By this I mean an erasure of process, of getting from here to there. This seemed to be expressed as either an illusory sense of immortality—a fantasy of cybernetic immortality—or a utopian anticipation of absolute perfection. I put this down to the spread of cell phones, Photoshop, and other forms of digital technology.

My references here included forms of narcissism in a return to childhood and adolescence in images of anger (detached from any particular issue) and sexual innuendo. The walks of Janet Cardiff represent another version—one in which we experience time past and time present as a palimpsest.

The second is the collapse of **Identity**. By this I mean the emergence variously of the prankster, the clown, and the idol—call them caricatures—all of which constitute a reinvigorated "camp" or "kitsch" substitute for an abandoned concept of a moral or responsible—*accountable*—subject. A contemporary version of Oscar Wilde's Dorian Gray. I put this down to a culture of irony, itself a consequence of widespread disenchantment with the evolution of the secular utopia promised by eighteenth-century rationalism, and its imminent eclipse in a world retreating into borders defined from without rather than within. If this casts doubt over certainty, its formal fulcrum lies in the several versions of paradox.

My references in this respect included a reliance on cartoons—think Disney or Japanese manga and anime—and computer manipulations of form (shape-changing).

The third collapse is that of **Reality**. And by this I mean the substitution of either fantasy or artificiality—in both cases untestable experiences—for experiences that require contact and equivalency. The sign detached from its symptom. A dis-location. I put this down to an increasingly prevalent and creative advertising industry, and to the iPod's siren call into solipsism.

The references here include a fascination with the miniature, models and modeling (in both the sense of miniature and of glamour), and toys—of whatever kind, including the iPod. We should note also the resurgence of a cinema of fantasy, magic, and mystery—incorporating a nostalgic enterprise of myth—with the *Lord of the Rings* and *Harry Potter*.

To summarize, we have a complex nexus of considerations to entertain when coming to the work we see in Toronto, and of course no single work can be successfully decoded by assuming that all of them operate simultaneously, or equally, in that particular instance. This is the fun of approaching artworks and investing time in pursuing the credible possibilities.

All of these attributes relate to purpose or content. The issue of formal means is less easy to ascribe. That is, many of these artists do not restrict themselves to painting, which raises the problem: how do we define painting today? What are its boundaries? And when do we not include an artist as a "painter"? Is a painter necessarily involved in "painting"?

Painting could be described as a discourse. A discourse is always historical. So a particular work, a painting, cannot be classified as "in the present" or "contemporary," because it is locatable only with respect to an antecedent which has already been classified. The "new" work is only supplemental to that classification. I do not speak to a painting; I speak to how that painting has been introduced or advertised. Moreover, to borrow from Lyotard if I understand him, any address in this present—that is actually a past—is contingent on what will have been addressed in the future. Consequently, any current or "contemporary" work, such as a painting, insofar as we address it, is always already merely a half-forgotten trace or vestige of the past.

300 Words on Art Outside Institutions (2008)

Published in *decentre: Concerning Artist-Run Culture/propos de centres d'artistes*, ed. Elaine Chang, Andrea Lalonde, Chris Lloyd, Steve Loft, Jonathan Middleton, Daniel Roy, and Haema Sivanesan (Toronto: YYZ Books, 2008).

Proposition: over coffee, an artist tells me that he dislikes institutions, and intends to work outside them.

I think I've heard this before. I note that he is male.

Thought: why would an artist work outside an institution?
A second thought: how could an artist work outside an institution?

Such apparently simple, looping thoughts inevitably lead back to definition—and here the ground gets tricky. Let's say that an artist is only an artist because a sufficiently knowledgeable group has consistently applied the term to them in reviewing the relevance of their work to the history of art practices. We can, for brevity's sake, call this group an institution, though it can, and will, take many descriptive forms—artists, curators, critics, art historians, dealers, and so on.

Of course there are many to whom the term is loosely applied, meaning they have made something that looks like art, or is claimed to be art. They may very well merit the definition of artist, but that must remain contingent on the test of consistency.

The issue that need not be addressed here—whether the work reviewed is of any consequence, artist or not—is another matter.

Let's say, then, that an artist, meriting the term, wishes to work outside an institutional structure—to self-organize, one might say. But why would they, when, by definition, they cannot—since they are defined as artists only through the intervention of the institution? Leave aside the fact that artists are also people, and do the various things people do—renovate, collect stamps, whatever. As artists, in their role as artists, they must work—whether they like it or not—only through the institution. And this fact will not change.

The Power Plant and the Play of History (2015)

Presented at the conference "This Is Paradise: Art and Artists in Toronto," University of Toronto/Justina M. Barnicke Gallery, May 2015.

> In the future, everyone will be world-famous for fifteen minutes.
> —Andy Warhol[1]

I'm looking back almost thirty years to the controversial opening exhibition of the Power Plant on May 1, 1987, titled *Toronto: A Play of History (Jeu d'histoire)*. And I want to situate this within the question before us as to whether there is a history of art in Toronto or not, and either way, what are we to make of it.

History is very appealing, rather like Paradise in a fuzzy sort of way. We all want to be there, in fact we all *expect* to be there, some day. It is a fundamental objective, an object of desire. But how to get there, exactly, how to have it? And will it be only for fifteen minutes?

It's tempting to argue that the problem is that most of us are not very well organized. Desire tends to be like that. But perhaps it isn't so much that we aren't organized; quite the contrary, perhaps the problem is that *there are so many of us* being very organized. I hear all the time that Toronto is a great city with a vibrant and multifaceted art scene. I hear as well that it seems difficult to understand it, to define it. Which brings us back to the issue of organization. If you can't organize it, if you can't define it, everything remains somehow vague, like Paradise. For many, Toronto remains vague.

In an effort to be less vague it would seem to come down to organization. Rather like that other Toronto desire, to de-clutter, and believe it or not, you can hire someone to de-clutter your life. In Toronto. Aside from happily living with clutter, there are two ways to think about de-cluttering. One is to be overwhelmed by panic and get rid of everything as just too overwhelming, to downsize and live in a 300 square foot condo. People do. Amnesia is bliss. The other is to analyze the constituents of the clutter, to look carefully at what is there, to realize that within the clutter lie potential histories and that there are stories to be told as long as they—whatever they

1   Often attributed to Warhol, the first printed use of this quotation was in the program for a 1968 exhibition of Warhol's work at the Moderna Museet in Stockholm, Sweden. See Jeff Guinn and Douglas Perry, *The Sixteenth Minute: Life In the Aftermath of Fame* (New York: Jeremy F. Tarcher/Penguin, 2005), 4.

are—can be organized and made accessible. It's not complicated. It's a question of *which* stories you want to tell. That, however, *is* complicated.

If organization is the key to recognizing what history is, it's obvious that someone has to do the organizing. The complication lies in just *who* is doing the organizing, *who* to trust—one might even say *how* to trust. With this little parable to go on, let's look at Louise Dompierre's attempt to do some organizing back in May 1987, and the reception to that attempt.

Briefly, in taking stock of Toronto's art scene at the time, Dompierre had assembled a curatorial team consisting of Alvin Balkind, Bruce Ferguson, and Blaine Allan that, while clearly credible from the perspective of contemporary artistic practices, was intentionally structured to work from outside Toronto's own artistic/curatorial community. The following quotes from her lead essay in the catalogue hopefully catch the gist of her team's positioning:

> Exhibitions are, of course, an act of choice…. The selection process on which they are based expresses support and recognizes the importance of a certain kind of art activity. Selecting means concentrating on certain artworks at the expense of others…. On another level, exhibitions are also a system of meaning, a discourse between the [artist's expressed intentions], [the curator's text] and the exhibition's premise or theme.
>
> The history of art activity in Toronto in the past ten years has already been explored, at least in part…. Such awareness enables us to isolate some of the issues that were discussed. Of central importance here are the artists themselves, their artworks and their various relationships to the events of the period. Though most of the artists included in this exhibition took an active part in shaping the events of the last ten years, it by no means includes all the artists who were notably active in the years between 1977 and now. This approach was deliberate, chosen not simply because space did not permit, but more fundamentally as a means to avoid closure and the implication that it would be unnecessary to "review" this period from other perspectives.
>
> The relationship between the artists included here and the artist-run spaces is clear. Not only has the current mainstream been identified and fostered by these institutions…here "mainstream" is closely associated with specialists within the art world.
>
> Toronto art is often described as being serious, solemn, even moralistic. While it is undoubtedly serious—thoughtful and thought-provoking—it avoids solemnity by relying on irony, principally ironic reversal, in which the intended implication is served by an opposition to what we see and hear. It seems typical that these artists,

aware of the forces that shape ideology, have resolutely undertaken (while knowing fully the futility of the task) to undermine them.

We hope the present approach will encourage other studies of different periods from different perspectives.

A few weeks after the exhibition opened, a panel discussion titled "Re/Viewing: Reflections in the Mirror" was struck by the Power Plant with Jeanne Randolph as moderator, Lisa Steele (whose work was included in the exhibition), David Clarkson (whose work was not), Michael Cartmell, representing film, and Dot Tuer, writer. The original panel was to address the question "When is art contemporary?" and its purpose was to "discuss the questions which arise when 'contemporary' artworks are contextualized in historical shows, and will seek to evaluate the distortions and reflections inherent in 'looking back.'" The panel, however, changed the topic to consider not contemporary art as such, but the relationship between the Power Plant and its exhibition, and the artists, writers, and curators who were not represented in the formation of that exhibition. In her preface to the panel, Jeanne Randolph posed three "predicaments" posed by the *Play of History* that needed to be addressed. One was the promotion and publicity surrounding it; a second was the curation itself and its distanced position from, as Jeanne put it "an awful lot of us here [who] have actually lived our day-to-day lives through the past ten years of Toronto artmaking. You might say that the history is pretty well us."

I can only summarize quickly the various positions on the panel, but in view of Jeanne's remarks, I want to quote from David Clarkson and a recent letter in which he elaborated—perhaps with a hint of that Toronto irony Louise mentioned—on his original call for an encyclopaedic rather than targeted approach to the exhibition:

Though discouraged at the time—I remain unrepentant and naïvely idealistic; I still think curators should be bold intellectual cultural provocateurs. I think they should make sweeping pronouncements, invent new artistic movements based on narrow aesthetic parameters of their own devising. They should explicitly exclude—nay, viciously attack—all artists they deem unworthy and promote only the handpicked geniuses they certify and anoint before the entire world. Curation is glorious business! Stakes are high! History is up for grabs! Surely, curators are brave purveyors of unseen truths—true seers, risk takers, fearless explorers of the unknown, leaders, and pioneers of the New Frontier! Curators are not supplicants of some status quo. They speak from the heart—and let the chips fall. Let one thousand arguments bloom! Like artists, curators embrace the possibility of failure—court it, to learn from it. And if need be—after an appropriate *mea culpa*, of course—they also may be forgiven for changing their minds.

On the panel, Michael Cartmell put his finger on the "institutionaliza-tion of art. How best contend with the ideological contradictions and pitfalls of mounting an exhibition like this, or any exhibition in a place like this." And further: "How can we address…a curatorial strategy that continually signals the extent to which its efforts are massively fraught with ideological constraint, lateral inversion, distortion, and contradiction?"

Dot Tuer focused on the context for the exhibition constructed by the promotion and ubiquitous corporate presence. I'm tempted to quote Dot's colourful presentation at length, but the main points she made are developed in the following: "the 'new' Power Plant gallery…is not for artists, nor for a Toronto art community, nor for the people of Toronto.… Rather, its agenda is to legitimize corporations as the benefactors of cul-ture and luxury development as a public service.… What are we, then, as artists and writers, as the producers of culture, to make of this deliberate co-option of our work.… Are we as a community still interested in challen-ging, in questioning the issues of colonialism, exploitation, racism, sexism? Or has a challenge become a rhetoric which can be defused by Dompierre's plea for a vision where we are all equal as individuals?"

Lisa Steele, in a somewhat similar vein, asked whether "we're just another quiet meal on the ever-changing banquet table of a cultural indus-try." Questioning Louise's insistence that the exhibition was intended to avoid closure on the period, Lisa suggested that:

Not having or exercising "closure" means that art can once again be considered to be universal.… A truly contemporary exhibition about the last ten years of Toronto art would have been inclusive, not exclusive; it would have allowed the public to see influences, schools of thought, random interventions, truly unique works and works that are referenced and inter-woven, until it becomes hard to tell who made what until you see the name. We could have seen contradictions and controversy—maybe some of that infamous Toronto "bitchiness" would have surfaced…here finally we get to see the power behind the faceless name of "private market." Here at the Power Plant we are forced to be in the presence of these "new Medicis," forced to see our work used to bolster corporate images.

As well as the panel, there was a level of published critical reception that would be the envy of our current situation. The very next day Adele

Freedman and John Bentley Mays wrote substantial reviews in the *Globe
& Mail*, Elke Town covered the exhibition for *Vanguard*, Gary Dault for
Canadian Art, and Bruce Grenville for, I believe, *C Magazine*.

Freedman pointed out that the on-going negativity surrounding the
role of developers at Harbourfront risked contaminating the Power Plant
as well.

Gary Dault dismissed the artists as mere A-list.

Mays dismissed the gallery and the exhibition as entertainment,
and dismissed as well the Power Plant's progenitor, the Art Gallery at
Harbourfront, as "never [having] maintained the sort of assertive programming that influences the course of contemporary art history."

He went on to say that, "The list of artists is lazy, almost automatic,
without risk and apparently based on famous names, not actual works" and
that the survey exhibitions cited in the catalogue as significant territory for
further examination—for instance the 1982 encyclopedic show *Monumenta*,
developed by artists David Clarkson, Stan Denniston, and Bernie Miller,
as well as *New City of Sculpture*, developed by David Clarkson and Robert
Wiens, "came after the much smaller, but far more significant parallel-
gallery shows by Philip Monk, Richard Rhodes and others...."

Elke Town agreed with much of this criticism: "For those not in the
know," she wrote, "it might have seemed that this was to be the opening of a
show about the history of Roots [the clothing company]," and was similarly disappointed by the catalogue's failure to reference "Philip Monk's
attempts at establishing a position from which to construct contemporary
Canadian art history." Elke quotes from Philip on the difference between
being *put* into history—"a history of autonomous objects, of individualistic
expression, etc., and being *given* a history. If it were given a history then we
might learn of its conditions of production as well as the conditions of its
reception of influences."

Elke finished her review by reminding the reader that the National
Gallery's *Songs of Experience* exhibition the previous year also received hostile criticism "born of the fact," she says, "that the National Gallery—and so
many other public galleries across Canada—has produced so few exhibitions
of contemporary Canadian art in the past few years. When they do, the
artists' work and genuine critical response are jeopardized by the politics of
the exhibition itself."

Bruce Grenville echoed Elke's remarks, and went on to say that,
"Certainly the critical reaction to the recent *Songs of Experience* exhibition
[curated by Jessica Bradley and Diana Nemiroff]...revealed a deep seated
distrust of any attempt to represent the current scene." In fact, Bruce
opened his review with an interesting question: "Why," he asked "are we

2   In 2018, the Museum of Contemporary Canadian Art (MOCCA) changed its name to Museum of Contemporary Art (MOCA) Toronto.

drawn to condemn every attempt that is made to address the history of contemporary art in Canada? Are we so conscious of the strategies of representation that we find all representations unacceptable?"

In his closing paragraph, Grenville targets Louise's insistence that *The Play of History* should be seen as only the first of many different approaches to the history of art in Toronto. All very well and good, he says, but the reality of exhibitions is the requirement that they be funded. "It is clear," he writes, "that no other exhibitions will have access to the same funding and resources as those in this inaugural exhibition....Thus it remains that...this history will be the dominant and authentic history and all other histories will be seen as nothing more than isolated and inauthentic reinterpretations of that dominant history."

This presentation today can from necessity only be a sketch of what it is to write a history, and it has taken seriously the idea that history proceeds from its documents.

I suggested earlier that history is about organizing something. Research into Louise Dompierre's exhibition as a case study suggests some of the complexities, the complications, involved in that organizing. What we learn from it is up for grabs. But I'll finish with Sholem Krishtalka's quotation in an essay from 2012, "Toronto Curating Itself: An Unhistory," of David Liss and Camilla Singh's curatorial statement for the MOCCA[2] exhibition *LoVe/HaTe: new crowned glory in the GTA*:

> Traditionally it is the role of museums to sort through a particular theme, idea or art scene or movement and arrive at a proposition that will distill an idea down to a palatable, life-force-sucking antiseptic theory that assumes an audience's need for clean, easily definable and consumable product. But that approach is, like, sooooo last century and naturally compels MOCCA to peel off in the completely opposite direction...It's a big, contentious, eclectic, messy and confusing scene.

> And here you have it. The more things change...well, you know the rest. And I think my fifteen minutes are up.

Artists, 1978-2018

Joseph Kosuth: Text/Context (Toronto) (1978)

Originally published as "JOSEPH KOSUTH: Text/Context (Toronto)—Part One," *Artists Review* 2, no. 6 (1978). The exhibition under review was presented at Carmen Lamanna Gallery, November 18 to December 7, 1978. Carr-Harris's text was preceded by a contrasting review of the same exhibition by Karl Beveridge.

> For you to see this (discourse) you must see beyond this (text/ gallery); for you to see this (text/ gallery) you must see through this discourse.
>
> —quoted from the work under discussion

1　Joseph Kosuth, "Introductory Note by the American Editor," *Art-Language* 1, no. 2 (February 1970): 1–4.

> At its most strict and radical extreme, the art I call conceptual is such because it is based on an inquiry into the nature of art. Thus, it is not just the activity of constructing art propositions, but a working out, a thinking out, of all the implications of all aspects of the concept "art." The audience of conceptual art is composed primarily of artists—which is to say that an audience separate from the participants doesn't exist. In a sense, then, art becomes as "serious" as science or philosophy, which don't have audiences either. It is interesting or isn't, just as one is informed or isn't.
>
> —Joseph Kosuth[1]

It is a comment, I suppose, on our capacity for confusion that Joseph Kosuth's work and position are important to current art.

Let me rephrase that.

The Kosuth work at Carmen Lamanna Gallery consists of a text, of which the first quote above forms the final sentence and summation. This text is set neatly and appropriately in the large window at the front of the gallery so as to cause that window to read as we would read a page from a magazine; in this case, however, a transparent page which in turn causes the gallery space beyond to read as we would read an illustration; turns it, in other words, into a material subject of discussion rather than the normally passive container of objects a gallery generally operates as. We are presented, then, with a discussion on the nature of the gallery itself—and by extension therefore art and society and our relationship to them.

Now, so far as this takes us, so good, and let us therefore rest here a moment. (Indeed, it is tempting to conclude that we are meant to rest here for quite a while, since K. has chosen to describe this work as Part One.)

We have been forced to accept the gallery itself as a material proposition, and to accept a discourse on this proposition through our normal channel of communication—the printed page in a "real" space or three-dimensional context.

I find this interesting. It eliminates a lot of extraneous problems and with a crisp logic channels our entire apparatus of perception and cognition directly at the subject of consideration.

To anyone accustomed to, let us say, more conventional use of gallery space, this work must come as either exhilarating or incomprehensible.

There is, however, a nascent problem. Since we have now rested, let us pursue the matter further, ignoring for the time being the fact that we have only Part One to deal with.

The problem concerns the matter of the viewer. I wish immediately to say that K's position appears to me to be unassailable. In fact, it is this very quality which I find most dissatisfying. I feel, in fact, that I haven't been taken very far. And I suspect that K., if he limits art to the concept "art" has succeeded only in limiting the possibilities of discussion as severely as Clement Greenberg. I suspect, in fact, that the concept "art," in itself, is of very little interest in a discursive sense.

There are at this point two directions.

If K. is concerned with our consciousness, and with the concept of "art" as a lever in that direction, he is telling me little that I didn't already know. This is not to criticize, however; it is only to point out that art as a lever of consciousness is a concept which one either understands or doesn't understand. The sound of one hand clapping is learnt by self-examination. It is not, by itself, more than a platitude.

If K. is concerned, on the other hand, with developing terms of discussion involving concepts in a relationship to art—as he appears to hint at in his text and in the title of the work—I do criticize, because no such terms emerge. I have not come away with "a working out…of all the implications of all aspects of the concept 'art,'" except insofar as such generalities presume there to be a working out. I haven't, in fact, come away with a single such working out. I require a bit more dialogue with which to agree or disagree and form consequent propositions. What is Part Two of this work?

Let us turn to K's comments on the audience for art. I confess that I disagree with him on the matter, not out of romantic delusions concerning art for the millions, but because I detect here a mistaken assumption. (As a matter of fact, I detect here several mistaken assumptions or certainly oversimplifications on the nature of "audiences," but that is something else). If only artists are to be concerned with K's propositions, and since artists—or at least those worthy of the name—would be equally aware of the concept "art" as consisting of propositions relative to enhanced awareness,

K's generalities on this matter, while certainly acceptable and in their presentation entertaining, are too familiar for interest. Yet there is no one else who can legitimately be considered. We are all left with the boatman in Siddhartha, and K. is of interest only to himself, a patently absurd position to occupy in any context. I do not believe this is K's position.

If, however, K's equation is reversed, I believe we are somewhat nearer a more acceptable truth. In this case, K. is of primary interest only to the uninitiated, or at least to those of the uninitiated who have an interest in such matters, and K. is a good teacher and an enlightened artist.

I do not believe that this view of the audience for art does justice to the facts or to an appreciation of K's work, but it is K's context and forms the basis for assumptions on which much of K's work rests, and to a great extent defines its limitations.

I have avoided making comparisons of this work to K's previous work, since I am more concerned here with considering reaction to a particular experience. I will point out, however, that K. appears to have retreated somewhat from the tendency in his recent work to present complicated logical involutions which (whatever his intentions) constructed needlessly inaccessible paradigms whose significance consequently became hermetic. I find this present work much more in the spirit of his early definition pieces which, as far as I am concerned, set out K's basic proposition that art is by nature linguistic with more clarity and conviction.

To rephrase my initial comment, then, K. occupies a central and unassailable position in art today, and this position is a vital one. K. understands, and more importantly for any artist concerned about the relationship between artist and society, he radically confronts the potential for confusion inherent in the complex relationship that exists between art as thing and art as understanding. Whether he confronts this successfully as art requires the kind of agility in formulation that I admired in his definition pieces, and which I find less evidenced—so far—in the particular work at hand. I remain curious about Part Two.

John McEwen: Recent Work (1979)

Published in *Real Sculpture: John McEwen*, exh. cat. (Lethbridge: Southern Alberta Art Gallery, 1979). The exhibition was curated by Alan Mckay and presented at the Southern Alberta Art Gallery, Lethbridge, September 2 to 30, 1979.

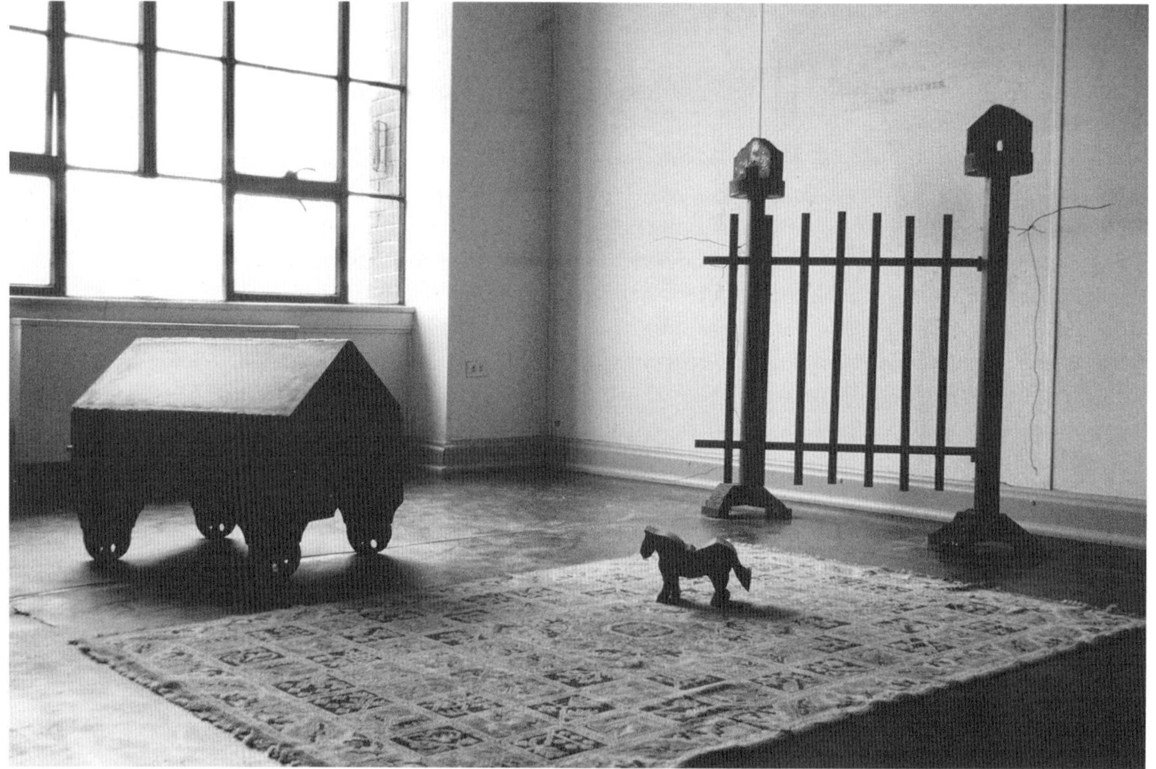

2.1   John McEwen, *Now Standing in His Own Yard, Health and Weather Permitting*, 1978. Steel horse with rug, steel barn (½ in. plate) on wheels, functioning steel gate. Dimensions variable. Collection Ydessa Hendeles, courtesy the artist.

It is the duality of the context which is important.

I enjoy John McEwen's work, and I believe I enjoy it for two very simple reasons: John makes art in an attempt to understand why he makes it; and he makes this attempt with great caution and developing humour. But it is the contextual framework within which he works, and his relationship to it, which gives him an interesting significance among current Toronto artists.

McEwen grew up in Toronto. As we all know, metropolitan Toronto is a sprawling, complex entity that, like all large cities, fosters that sense of urban frustration which finds solace and virtue in alienation. And yet Toronto is the heart of southern Ontario, a pleasant land of gently rolling countryside dotted with agricultural and industrial affluence that has produced one of Canada's most enduring traditional societies.

McEwen is unusual for knowing and understanding both these worlds with equal respect, and it is his examination of the personal implications of this duality which forms the basis of his work.

Now, making art as a process of self-examination is of course shared by all thoughtful artists. It is the degree to which McEwen relies on the relationship between artist and work that is striking. In constructing this reliance he is taking risks of accessibility, and his chance of developing work which is independently compelling depends on ensuring that it does not become merely private or self-indulgent. It doesn't, and the successful avoidance of this trap is a mark of the artist's maturity in applying a cautious intellect to a sturdy intuitive materiality. This combination, I believe, arises naturally out of McEwen's involvement in the two cultures he inhabits, and the components of this combination deserve some elaboration.

Ideas are the building blocks that form the structure of existence. The problem for McEwen lies in the nature of ideas. Their insubstantial facility and their easy manipulation is a familiar dilemma, and one which the artist came to view with considerable suspicion as a result of his own involvement in the Conceptual art movement of the early 1970s. But if he is consequently unwilling to allow ideas the freedom to fabricate art, at the same time he sees art as a search for knowledge about experience, a search that inevitably must be based on ideas. Borrowing from the concept of "models" used in logic and scientific research—for example in studying DNA molecular construction—McEwen resolves the dilemma by enhancing the status of the work as a tangible model of reality in order to restrain the more mercurial tendencies of ideas and provide a solid vantage point from which to consider their validity. The work must operate, in other words, not so much as structured idea but as restrained ideas, and artmaking for McEwen becomes a means of considering what he doesn't know from the basis of what he does know. The model is manageable if the ideas are not.

While the model's function is to restrain the facility of conceptual invention, the larger purpose it serves is to construct a personal space which will provide the artist with an opportunity to relate structural ideas to the pragmatic circumstances of a physical environment. The environment chosen is not Toronto's urban complexity, but Ontario's nineteenth century solidity. The contrast is at the heart of McEwen's work. The conceptual sophistication which formulates the model is placed in a context based on rural conceptions of time and place, with their attendant familiar physicality and natural pacing. The result is a tension of known and unknown, familiar and unfamiliar, and the uneasy balance of materiality and abstraction.

This tension in fact led McEwen for a time to separate his interest in model construction from the structure of art entirely. This is a simple enough operation if you view art as an alternative structure paralleling other functions. The artist adopted as an alternative model the blacksmith in Hillsdale. Far from being simply an investment in real estate or a retreat from Toronto, he proceeded to invest the processes of existence in this situation with the same status he had hitherto placed on artmaking. As he remarked to a friend, the only functioning difference lay in the audience. It was only when he began to realize that the shop as a model had become too complicated for clear reflection, had itself become too unmanageable, too time consuming, that he turned back to the structure of art as the preferred solution to model-formulation.

The experience, however, is interesting, and for the artist it was important. The flexibility McEwen showed in experimenting seriously with the contingency of art as a process of understanding is impressive evidence of his concern for reality over performance. And the effect of the experience on his perception of relationships and acceptance of ideas went a long way towards enabling him to develop the sense of humility and humour which has begun to soften the truculent anxiety of his earlier work and replace it with a personal tension more appropriate to a proper understanding of the realities he is attempting to face.

There are many artists who create highly personal work, and it is unfortunately the case that the idiosyncratic characteristics they exhibit often have little or no interest beyond their visual display. In so far as the work is concerned, McEwen is one of the few who have risked revealing their personal, even private, concerns while maintaining a toughness of physical presence unmarred by visual irrelevance.

In attempting to confront intention he has examined the basis of trust, and insofar as we are concerned, this confrontation places the process of artmaking where it must always ultimately begin: as an honest inquiry into personal elegance and values.

Vincent Tangredi (1983)

Published as "Vincent Tangredi," *Parachute* 30 (March–April–May 1983). The exhibition under review was presented at Carmen Lamanna Gallery, Toronto, November 20 to December 16, 1982.

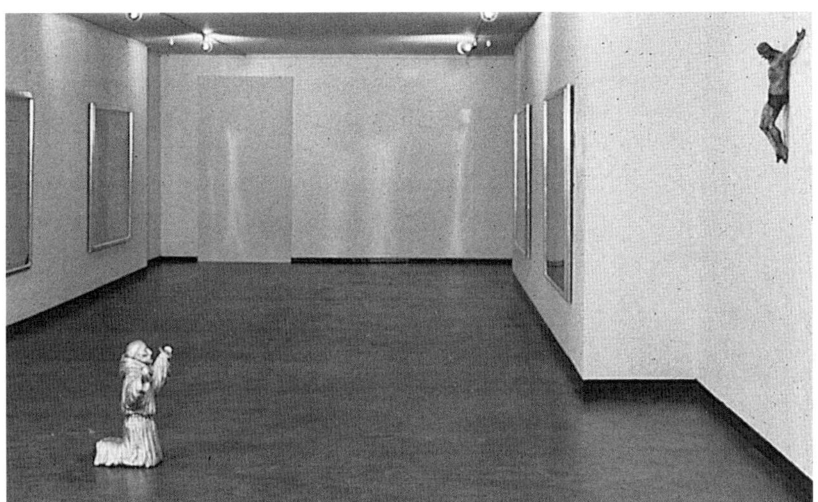
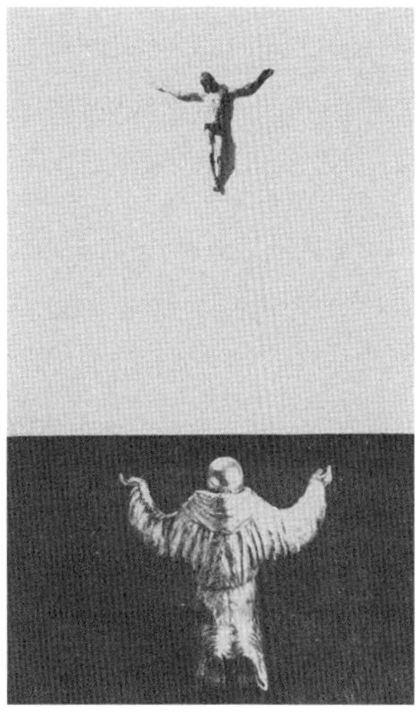

2.2/2.3   Vincent Tangredi, *Of the Four Considerations (in six units)*, 1981– 82. Framed texts, each 1.30 × 1.63 m; St. Francis, carved wood gilded with gold leaf, 67 × 69 × 20 cm; Christ, carved wood, polychrome & cloth, 55 × 60 × 13 cm. Courtesy the artist. Photos: Henk Visser.

With elegant coherence, Vincent Tangredi's new installation, *Of the Four Considerations*, constructs a complex experience out of very simple elements. I do not say this lightly; varying strategies of reductivism have been central to artmaking in recent years, perhaps because reduction is linked to clarity, perhaps because fashion dictated it. The fashion has changed, however, which makes it useful to consider simplicity again quite carefully; and because Tangredi's work touched me to a degree that other works around have not, I want to examine it and perhaps demonstrate what constitutes an act of imagination.

The installation itself is in five parts, of which four are large (1.3 × 1.63 m) framed texts and the other an opposition of two figures. The work is approached through these figures: the one an immaculately gilded saint, about half life-size, kneeling on the floor in the middle of the gallery with arms open and gaze lifted in an act of embrace facing the second figure—

a battered wooden effigy of the crucified Christ suspended just above eye level on the north wall. In forcing us physically to intercept, or choose not to intercept, the relation between them, Tangredi manipulates us into an immediate awareness of the power these symbols have over us. The four texts face one another, two to a wall, on both sides of the gallery space beyond the figures in such a way that the entire work becomes a kind of circular "reading" from right to left, counterclockwise, with the viewer starting in a position facing the saint. It is an oddly unstable position, at once too intimate and too incongruous: our difference in scale to the saint renders us ponderous and absurdly physical. We are drawn back, clumsy voyeurs, into that other relationship defined by the saint's fixed gaze towards his god.

We are, however, voyeurs invested with an understanding modified by the texts. They are in a way "stations," or stanzas in a poem whose full expression can only be felt as theatre, a physical presence in which the viewer's institution—soul and body, to use an older term—completes the meaning of the work. The four texts reflect this theatre: they are identically constructed in the manner of a Renaissance painting, with wooden frames in a classical style finished to resemble burnished silver. Within this inflected frame of reference each unit houses two large sheets of rag paper held loosely against the backing, making them fragments preserved rather than statements projected. The narrower left hand sheets, grey-brown, carry the subheadings—a device Tangredi has used consistently in previous work, and one deriving from an archaic publishing format in which the text carried a running annotation in the margins; Bibles often still use it. The larger right hand sheets, a warmer brown, carry the narrative, and each is titled in succession: *Of the First Consideration* to *Of the Fourth Consideration*. The size ratio of the left and right hand sheets to each other approximates the golden section. And most insistently, the text *Of the First Consideration* is dominated by a large drawing of Saint Francis as a nude woman in the position of the she-wolf giving suck to Romulus and Remus, the founding heroes of the Eternal City.

The installation is spare, and these resemblances, references, and mergings of identity are very quickly established for us. What struck me was the simplicity of the question which first came into my mind: "Who was St. Francis?" I wanted to know. This question naturally embraces another: not "who was?" but "what is St. Francis?" Because *Of the Four Considerations* impels us to shift between these two questions, it demonstrates—it lays bare—the historical nature of our identity, an identity characterized by Roland Barthes as a "tissue of quotations." In Tangredi's complex examination of St. Francis we begin to realize, actually to taste, the necessity that reality merge with myth in a supra-historical modality whose purpose—a purpose we impose—is to establish a personal equivalence with the world;

a bond which includes us in a synchronous past, present and future, and removes us from the abhorrence of isolation. We remove ourselves through this history: we are not so much human beings as historical beings, and everything we say or do flows from this consciousness.

In an interestingly austere structural examination, "Arresting Figures" (*Vanguard*, March 1982), Philip Monk critiques a previous work of Tangredi's—*1902* (1979/80)—through a formal analysis of the relations set up between the work and the viewer. As a grammatical paradigm it is worth consulting, particularly since the physical conditions for the viewer have strong similarities in both works, and Monk's final paragraph is penetrating and powerfully evocative. What is specifically interesting is that Monk chose Tangredi's work as the occasion for an essay on semiotic criticism. Both *1902* and *Of the Four Considerations* provide a clear arena in which the representational and linguistic biases inherent in such an approach can be seen to have a positive reality. The formal construction of his installations—the use of effigy, of typographic style as reference and allusion, the Renaissance characterization in *Of the Four Considerations* as a whole, with its strong implication that the viewer's space is a museum and the viewer thereby institutionally obliged to read their own presence—combines with the physical manipulation of our engagement with the work to induce in us a very material understanding of the degree to which we structure desire. Tangredi's work is, quite evidently, about the reality these structures have for us, the manner in which they emanate from us. Monk's essay, however, concentrates on how the grammatical relations between the viewer and the work construct meaning. I am less prepared to accept this emphasis, at least to the almost exclusive and subliminal extent that the essay suggests Monk's own relation has a peculiar detachment to it, a detachment arising from the demand he makes that the viewer occupy a position of critical self-witness on a very literal and measurable level—as though the linguistic mechanics by which we arrive at meaning were the only relations possible. The result is an alarming refusal to engage the presence of the artist within the work (a first-order scientific requirement, one would think), or even to engage the obvious complexities surrounding the viewers' understanding of their own identity in relation to the particular nature of the representations through which Tangredi has constructed the work. In *1902* and in *Of the Four Considerations*, Tangredi's presence and the corresponding challenges he makes to the viewer's own personal sense of presence is critical.

It is this presence and this challenge that constitute the meaning of the piece. Central to *Of the Four Considerations*, and discernable throughout Tangredi's work, is his peculiar fascination and obsession with virtue and decay and its sexual roots. As I have said, the key to this work lies in the relationship between the two figures. That the figure of the saint is rendered in a style which refers more to the humble condition of garden sculpture than to high idealism, and yet is clothed in real gold leaf, and that the Christ-figure—an actual antiquity invested with generations of worship—is worm-eaten and broken are immediately curious attributes. Gold is an incorruptible element usually associated with gods; the saint is St. Francis, known for his humility. The inversion and ambiguities Tangredi employs dissolve the religious cliché, and the god becomes as much victim to the saint as the saint a witness to his god. It is an ambiguity latent in many religions, including Christianity. Perhaps it is latent because we instinctively realize its potentially destructive power; we have made humility the greatest virtue. In Tangredi, we sense a searing comprehension of the awesome control we are compelled to exercise over our physical embodiment. In the figures he invests the god with our own mortality; in the texts, his drawing of St. Francis with its merged and ambivalent identities re-invents for us the layers of an identity we both desire and fear. The she-wolf, the devil, and the hollow rock, the elaborate Basilica and the inevitable ruins; finally the vision of the god and the mystical material transference of the stigmata from the god to the saint—a witness or pact signalling inextricably merged identities—all these are inventions of our own devising. "What is there in these ruins?" It is our pride, our lust and our eternal determination to go on constructing the disembodiments we require to protect ourselves against our own desires.

This, then, is Tangredi's *Of the Four Considerations*. It is a work which reeks of the sexual fragrance of our formalized containments for birth, collapse, and death. Its controlled passion speaks of individual frailty and collective power.

I began with a reference to simplicity. We are going through a period in which a long twentieth-century tradition of engaging moral values through an abstracted and often even Calvinist purity of material conception is disintegrating in favour of an older tradition of direct imagery and often morally prescriptive action. Against this background, Tangredi's piece fulfills the broader purposes of both traditions: to address our being in the world in order to better understand something of our dimension. *Of the Four Considerations* does this with simple and direct purpose.

A.R. Penck (1983)

Published as "A.R. Penck," *Parachute* 31 (June–July–August 1983). The exhibition under review was presented at Yarlow/Salzman Gallery, Toronto, March 23 to April 16, 1983.

> Before thinking in pictures I think in abstract motions. The content of such motions is abstract gesture. Such abstract gestures are what interests me.
> —A.R. Penck, quoted in the catalogue for Waddington Galleries, London, England, April 1982

It is precisely because Penck restricts himself to abstract gesture that his work fails to penetrate surface and reveal the condition of things. Under the guise of a stark simplicity, A.R. Penck is a stylist of a very particular kind, and I want to suggest that seductive though his adopted style may be, he simply perpetuates a middle-European expressionist existentialism whose Wagnerian banality has become predictable.

I think this is unfortunate. Not because the tradition is banal—the tradition will continue and is interesting for that fact alone—but because Winkler may be a good artist. And this leads me to a particular proposition which adheres to the exhibition at Yarlow/Salzman: that artworks may not allow themselves to become artifacts. It is the extensions of this proposition as they related to the Penck works in the exhibition that I wish to explore, and most especially those which seem to place the works in greatest tension.

Before continuing, I should clarify that we have here Penck at his most radically coded, with 300 × 200 cm paintings from two series: *Standart West* (KR 6, 8, 9, 10) and *Wird Zeichen Realität?* (#3, #4) as well as seven untitled drawings which do not need to concern us here.

The *Standart West* paintings are in vertical axis, each conforming to the limits of a single central figure facing the observer. This figure, while unmistakable (and male), is represented to us through a linear graphic symbol as though drawn with quick expressive brush strokes on a chalk-white prepared ground. The obvious references are to primitive, or prehistoric, symbolizing on the one hand, and to infantile attempts to objectify the self and non-self on the other. As in all Penck's work in both these series, the white ground surrounding the figure is the arena for a complicated symbolic text whose vocabulary is accessible as much through the emotional power of its presence in the ground as through its identification with a formal hierarchy of objectified or semi-recognizable coded signs such as letters, numbers, and primary geometric figures.

The series titled *Wird Zeichen Realität?* (perhaps translatable as *Do symbols become reality?*) is in horizontal axis and allows more narrative in its structure, at least in that each painting contains two central identifiable figures. In *#4* a slightly smaller left-hand figure juxtaposes the larger right hand one, with the familiar ground symbols occupying the central space between them rather like an elaborate conversation—or lecture. In *#5*, the right-hand figure, now red, is opposed to (or is divorced from) a red-brown eagle figure on the upper left, with the generally black ground symbols carrying the "text" between and around them. The relations between the red and the black can easily be read as part of this text.

Do symbols, or signs, become reality? In a certain obvious way, of course they do; if common sense didn't tell us that, contemporary linguistic studies would. But this is not a class in linguistics, and the question cannot be innocent. There are two options: the question is ironic, or it is rhetorical. I do not believe it is ironic. Or more correctly, I cannot believe on the evidence that Penck would construct so painstakingly such a complex gestural vocabulary of signs as an ironic tactic for the discouragement of symbolic conversion. The work refutes the notion that this is Dada. If it includes irony, it is the passionate irony of despair directed not at symbol but at reality. We are being addressed rhetorically, and the answer to this challenge has already been formulated in the title of the other series included in this exhibition: *Standart West*.

Standart appears to be an invented hybrid term, one Penck has used generally to refer to his work. It has connections to both German and English, most revealingly with the term Standard; not so much the standard of "normalcy" though that may be included, but the standard of mobilized exhortation. The meaning of the full term *Standart West* thus becomes clear. It is no accident that in the presence of these paintings at Yarlow/Salzman one is awed. These are paintings as para-military symbols, rallying banners alerting us to the imperatives of morality and discipline; their size, structure and warrior references shout relentlessly at the viewer the perils of failure and the ethics of power.

Does Symbol become Reality? Yes, when despair and determination meet, as they frequently have in German history. But the reality that Symbol pre-figures is a dream reality of concentrated and idealized desire which has little to do with the reality of intimacy, compassion, and "presentness." Like religious icons with their false humility, these paintings with their expressive sense of demoralized man simply demand all the more eloquently the substitution of Nietzsche's *Ubermensch*. Whether they are intended diaristically or not does not change this.

I said these paintings shout at the viewer. Standards are moral signifiers; but they quickly become artifacts. By artifacts I mean witnesses to
circumstance. Artworks also certainly bear witness to circumstance, but
as artworks they internalize circumstance and deflect it through a personal understanding of history. Artifacts are social witness; art is personal
witness. Confronted by Penck I remain nonetheless a viewer; at most,
a voyeur.

Penck's work, then, exists as sociology, and it derives its significance
from that condition. The specific circumstance is—quite appropriately—
divided Germany and the incredible pressure of ideology. Penck has
suffered this experience in a very personal way, and I do not begrudge him
the need to concern himself with these circumstances in the work. I do not
believe that Canadians of my generation can imagine coherently the social
context within which these paintings arise. To us that context is bound to
have the distant and mythic aura of literature, Le Carré or *Funeral in Berlin*
perhaps. So be it. My quarrel is that Penck fails to correct this romanticism.
Indeed, he presents us with another, one in fact which seems predictably German rather than even personal. He presents us with a kind of
Ursprungsehnsucht as a call to arms, with Spengler and noble savages among
the dramatis personae, and the *Götterdämmerung* as a script. If I appear to
trivialize the greatness of German culture and the complexity of German
thought, I do so intentionally to convey the dangers that arise when results
parody intention, or when intention parodies circumstance. There are a
thousand ingenious ways that middle-European culture manages narcissis-
tically to express simultaneously both self-contempt and self-glorification.
It amounts to a mythic religion, and it produces an amazing array of artifacts
whose subject is the very dialectic that Penck offers us here: the decadence
of the sophisticated Present contrasted with the power of the simple Past. It
is the kitsch of German thought.

If we are to take the exhibition at Yarlow/Salzman seriously, and I for
one welcome it and take it very seriously, Penck's symbols have indeed
become his reality for coherent and easily understood historic reasons.
What I am not convinced about is the necessity of this, and I am very suspicious of the social existentialism it embodies. I am, however, convinced by
the work that Canadians cannot—as yet—be mobilized by Symbol. Perhaps
we are not—as yet—sufficiently sophisticated and decadent. Perhaps we
still want to be. Perhaps that is better. Perhaps, on the other hand, there
is no need for a middle-European to allow himself the mock-humility of
becoming just another "worker in a Coalmine of Culture," as Penck has
suggestively described himself.

I am conscious that in writing this review I have given short shrift to
the hypothesis that Penck occupies that other strand of German intellectual

history represented by the famous illustrated weekly *Simplicissimus*. The Yarlow/Salzman exhibition does not contain any hint of this possibility for me. Certainly it is tempting to contextualize the work against the obviously horrendous results for Germany, and for the world, of such symbolizing and to derive from that a position of intellectual irony for Penck. I would then argue that the net gains of such an analysis would be few: intellectual irony is lost on too many people. Nevertheless, it was tempting; not for Penck's sake, but for Ralf Winkler's.

Nancy Johnson (1983)

Published as "Nancy Johnson," *Parachute* 32 (September–October–November 1983). The exhibition under review was presented at A Space, Toronto, June 18 to July 9, 1983.

"Somehow it seems to fill my head with ideas—only I don't exactly know what they are," says Alice in *Through the Looking-Glass*. This half-forgotten complaint nudged my mind as I stood looking at Nancy Johnson's drawings. It wasn't that it was difficult to interpret them. Indeed many of them seem quite polemical in a gentle and somewhat negligent way. But in ascribing to each a clear meaning, I had an uneasy feeling that I was subverting the principal relationship which held me to the work. It is this feeling that seemed strongest, rather than any agreement or disagreement I might have with their more accessible "plain talk."

In a couple of recent reviews, I suggested that there were severe limitations in the use of symbolic form. I argued that a straightforward attention to ordinary experience communicated in as directly accessible a manner as possible is capable of producing a more effective understanding of our essential conditions of existence.

Yet, as Lewis Carroll's Alice reflected, and various contemporary areas of structural study—let alone psychoanalysis—have confirmed, the question left begging is what constitutes meaning in recognizable communication. If, as I implied, it is possible to distinguish between "plain speech" and symbolic expression, what distinguishes them, and how do they relate to our desire for "recognizable communication"—in other words, for some balance of accessible truths?

In the work dealt with through the two preceding reviews, it remains clear to me that the hermetic use of a simplistic symbolism in the one case— possibly a degeneration resulting out of the artist's escape from conditions which initially created its need—and the clarity and freshness of analytical understanding in the second case, were legitimate foundations for my suspicion that the use of symbol as a modus operandi is to a degree tautological; that it runs the danger of misapplying succeeding and ever-distancing layers of symbolism when the fact remains that individual human intelligence, already inescapably constituted by symbolic structure, can formulate its own symbols ad hoc more appropriately.

I am not sure, however, that tautology is the only problem. I want in this review to consider a bit more what appears to be the dialectic between plain speech and metaphor. I must emphasize that this is a dialectic, not a set of posed alternatives, and it is because I find this condition at work in Nancy Johnson's drawings that I want to examine it through her show at A Space.

The exhibition consisted of twenty-two ink drawings on paper, all identical in size at about eighteen by twenty-four inches, matted and mounted under Plexiglas directly on the walls, and organized in an implied linear progression around the entire gallery, like words or sentences in a text. These drawings comprise a series which, in contradiction to its arrangement, is not conceived as a narrative structure, but as a set of disparate and semi-coincidental interconnections which require us to read them backwards as well as forwards and select local relationships rather than an overriding general logic.

This disparate quality is set forth in the drawings themselves. Each is constructed of loose cartoon-like sketches and a fairly compact vocabulary of free-form solid shapes whose combined purposes are to imply human situations in certain states or containing certain actions. Each includes, as well, a text in the form of words or phrases in snatches of what can best be

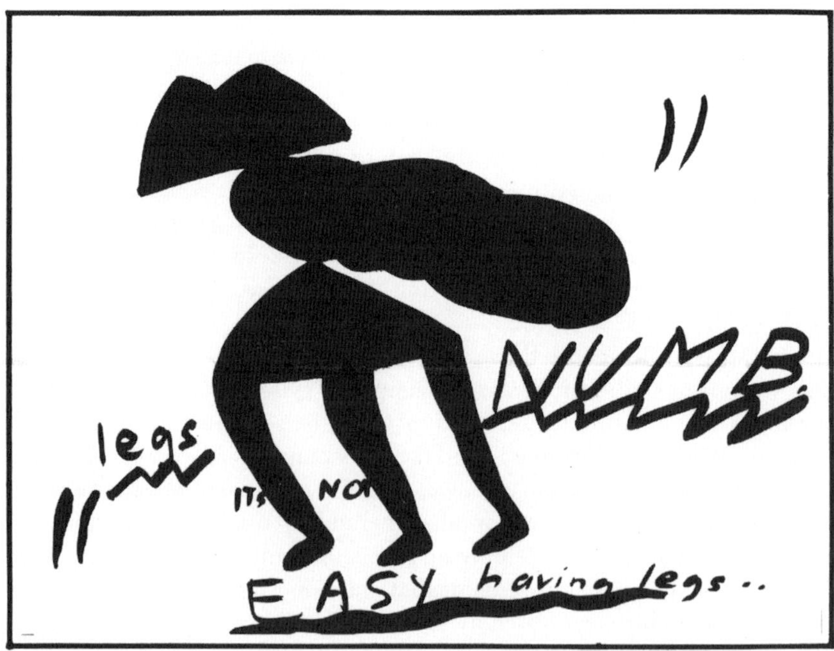

2.4   Nancy Johnson, *legs numb its not easy having legs*, 1983. Gouache on paper, 43.2 × 57.6 cm. Courtesy the artist.

considered thoughts not yet articulated into coherent language, rather in the way that we make our thoughts in language before we speak or write them. The status of these texts as still amorphous "thought-feelings" is confirmed by fragmenting their placement and size within the drawing so that they themselves take on an expressive function as an integral part of the drawing they help construct. For example, the drawing used on the mailer, and one of my favourites, includes the text "legs NUMB...it's not EASY having legs" against a harassed-looking "figure" composed of three different shapes—which we easily recognize as deriving from Johnson's established vocabulary of elemental symbols—surmounting three legs in profile. What seems to emerge on being with these drawings for a time, however different the situations they depict, is that they all share one particular state: sexuality. And interestingly enough, this does not seem on reflection too strange.

I said that I wanted to focus on the dialectic between plain speech and metaphor in Johnson's work. In each drawing the basic conditions for it are set by the juxtaposition of articulated experience, represented by the text (or more correctly by our instant understanding of the text), and unarticulated Being, represented by the picture symbols with their far more oblique accessibility. As a result, the text inevitably appears to us as explanation for the symbols; or rather, the transparency of the text—that is, its accessibility—becomes secondary to or founders on the opaqueness of the picture symbols. It is this process that caught me short in front of the drawings, and it seems to me that I found myself de-stabilized, as it were. And in order to re-stabilize myself, to reconnect myself to the world in some reasonable state, I found myself required to reverse my normal condition of creating symbols or metaphors as extrapolations out of perceived experience, and instead re-create perceived experience, normality, out of the symbolic representations which confronted me. This re-created normality, however, is not and cannot be ordinary or normal; it relies too much on memory and desire, as any public washroom will tell you. It is stripped of the complex specific quality of actual encounter. What is left is a residue of basic consciousness in varying degrees of imaginative fantasy, depending on the individual.

I am not going to pursue whatever reconstructions I attempted; I'm not sure I could. I do want to pursue the notion that what I as the viewer was forced into was what Johnson as the artist had already found herself forced into. In constructing a dialectic of this sort, she constructed for herself a state of primal consciousness; a state, that is, essentially erotic and sexual in nature. And this would be the case whatever subject matter she chose to select for these drawings. Now, I am not suggesting there is anything particularly new or startling in this. Quite the contrary; it seems to me a condition underlying all work which uses overtly oblique descriptive techniques, whether surreal, expressionist, or whatever else. Indeed, our ability to read in sexual meaning to even the most harmless passing remarks of normal conversation seems to indicate that we will interpret any open encounter in this manner. What I witnessed standing in front of these drawings, then, was not the apparent subject matter, but the inevitable one: the sexuality of their condition.

I mentioned just now that actual encounter of relations in the real world have a complex specific quality denied to us in symbolic encounter. The mailer for Nancy Johnson's show reminded the viewer—or programmed the viewer, if you prefer—with the knowledge that this was the fourth and last exhibition in a series curated by Tim Guest for A Space titled *Sex and Representation*. Of the four artists involved—Von Gloeden, Clemente, Steir, and Johnson—the comparison of Johnson's drawings with Von Gloeden's turn-of-the-century photographs of nude Sicilian fisher-boys dressed up in classical disguises seems the most seductive. Despite, and perhaps partly because of the absurd classical pretensions, Von Gloeden's healthy young nudes confront us with a reality we know and feel instantly a part of, voyeuristically at any rate. The boys are real people, with particular physical identities that naturally remind us of our own individuality, and that of our friends. We wonder how they felt being dressed up as young Greeks for an ageing German Count or whatever to photograph. We wonder about them as people. Faced on the other hand with Nancy Johnson, the viewer's response is far more intellectual and more primitive. We are forced to imagine and reconstitute a physical identity, a recognizable and meaningful reality, for her figures with very little more than our own inchoate fears and desires to work with. Because this reconstruction exists only in our own reality, it has no proper definition and no delimitation, and consequently no barrier to the shifting fantasies of our inner confusions and passions. Removed from a common reality, we are imprisoned in our own, just as Johnson herself becomes a prisoner of her own symbols. Nancy Johnson's representation of sex, in the context of this series, is the representation of sexuality as a constant internal state. Von Gloeden represents the diversity of "the other," and the physical state of longing which surely finds its crowning parallel in Thomas Mann's *Death in Venice*.

In attempting to distinguish plain speech from metaphoric speech, then, we seem to find two different orders of the same experience. Plain speech, which is as we all know full of metaphors, is in fact itself a form of metaphor. It seeks to place our thoughts in the open by admitting certain things and not admitting others, and in so doing to create a world of cause and effect and the implication that change can occur, one way or another; that states of being can be identified as good or bad, or at least discernable combinations of both. It is a very successful metaphor, and indispensable to Western thought. Symbolic expression, on the other hand, reflects a world which does not change perceptibly and is much narrower in its admission of possible action. It is, it seems, a world dominated by sexuality and aggression. It is our other knowledge underlying all strange encounter, and it is the terms of the dialectic we construct between these two different orders which gives us a coherent understanding and a moral perspective on experience.

Given their ability to pose this set of questions without being pretentious or vapid, Johnson's drawings are strong and honest statements that contribute an attractive sensitivity to an important discussion. I found certain conundrums, however. The most obviously damaging, perhaps, is that they seem somehow easy to dismiss, partly because they look familiar (as in "there's a lot of that around, isn't there"), and partly because they are familiar, as I have tried to show. The second conundrum is the challenge implied by the trap set in forcing us into ourselves: the difficulty of knowing what it is like, for a man, to be a woman; and of course the reverse. If Nancy Johnson's work has a major disappointment for me, it lies in my inability to detect in the drawings what the difference between these states might be. Johnson seeks to represent certain physical aspects of her sexuality which are more or less discernable, and more or less obvious. As a man, I inevitably bring certain dispositions to these drawings, and if the work has a particular value it would surely lie in the way in which her dispositions confronted my own. Like Alice, my head is filled with uncertain ideas, but I would like more; I want to know about the nature of those dispositions. I think this should be as true for a woman viewing these works as for a man. Johnson states that her work "concerns itself with the tangible difficulties of recognition and action, both private and public," and "describes aspects of the physical self, alone and in relation to others, its chains and privileges." If those difficulties and aspects were described more analytically for me, I would be better equipped to find a measure for myself. But they aren't, and I am left wondering if that is all there is. Perhaps Johnson is close to the truth in suggesting that her disposition is essentially elusive; it is a point I am more than willing to yield. But there are, I am certain, many aspects which are, as she says, tangible, and perhaps it is the dialectic she constructs between accessible and oblique information which is the cause of my discomfort. Perhaps if I—at any rate—had just a bit more plain speech, I would have a better understanding.

Winging It: Noel Harding (1984)

Published as "Winging It: Noel Harding," *Vanguard* 13, no. 3 (April 1984).

> I give a context for original experience, you have to develop the meaning.
> —Noel Harding, quoted by Chris Hume, *Toronto Star*, October 3, 1982

> A fantasia on the historic themes of light and hope, and
> on the contemporary theme of winging it.
> —John Bentley Mays, review of *1st, 2nd & 3rd Attempts to
> Achieve Heaven*, *Globe & Mail*, December 22, 1983

Solipsism: the theory or belief that the self knows and can know nothing but its own modifications and states. Mays may be on to something. This is a short article, and I want to clarify right now that it has limited objectives. I will spend some time considering five installation works by Noel Harding ranging from 1978 through 1983, works which I have actually seen. And in considering them, I will focus my attention on what I see as an intentional disjunction between work and audience. I will end with a short critical summary.

Since naming helps to solidify both a sense of purpose and a notion of criticism, let me begin by listing the five works which form the basis of my examination. They are, in chronological order:

Once Upon the Idea of Two (1978)
Enclosure for Conventional Habit (1980)
Scenic Events on a Path of Upheaval (1981)
Monument to Decision-Making (1982)
1st, 2nd & 3rd Attempts to Achieve Heaven (1983)

The action of *Once Upon the Idea of Two* is the process of constructing, filming, and presenting a "portrait of Barbara." In its essentials, the installation consisted of a large paper screen in front of which was placed a chair. Onto this screen was projected as a continuous film loop the activities—both required and incidental—surrounding the construction of the set of conditions for filming Barbara posing in Harding's studio in that same chair which now formed part of the installation. Since the chair in the film was superimposed on the chair in the installation, that chair became the focus for the representation of a past event whose purpose was its own re-presentation. With a difference, however: placed out of sight, but not out of hearing, behind the screen was a video monitor which carried a tape loop of Harding standing in front of his work describing the process of making the film and urging the audience to sit in the empty chair. Within the space of the installation, this tape became an unsynchronized voice-over for the film as well as a directive to the audience. And placed beside the film loop projector, a video camera hooked to a monitor facing the chair replayed the audience's performance—if any—of Harding's instruction. This performance became a separate portrait, this time of the viewer alternating and overlapping with the image of Barbara herself. "Once upon the idea of two" became the idea of unifying past and present, of engaging reflexive representation with chance encounter, of Barbara and a stranger—ourselves placed in an alarming contiguity of real and unreal.

To reduce *Once Upon the Idea of Two* to its central elements is, however, to misrepresent the work. Harding does not present it so tightly. In practice, it is a work which confronts its audience with a confusing range of material distractions arising not only from such elements as multiple layering of the film image on cheese-cloth curtains, and the constantly fluctuating unsynchronized relationships between film image, video voice-over and audience connection, but also from the casual and unstructured nature of the film. And at least as problematic, the action the audience was required to perform seemed inevitably impositional and simplistic, and therefore avoidable. Consequently, the installation had built into it distractions which modified and all but nullified—its central hypothesis. The question is why did Harding impose on it those conditions?

In *Enclosure for Conventional Habit*, two years later, Harding presented three elements to his audience: a tree, some chickens, and a central life support system. Centrally important was the fact that tree and chickens were kept in an almost constant state of motion: the tree slowly travelled a track back and forth from one end of the gallery to the other, moved, lit, fed and sprayed by a linking connection of tubes and wires to the support system, while a small speaker on its platform played a stately cello accompaniment; the chickens lived on a moving conveyor belt, against whose constant direction they had to run to obtain their food, which was housed in a feeder located at the leading end of the belt, where another small speaker played out a punk drum beat in an obvious mimicry of the characteristic movement of chickens. The life support system to maintain the tree and the chickens in this state was suitably immense, and by virtue of its complexity, mysterious. Perhaps that is why Harding chose to reveal it to the audience only as a darkly visible mass of components looming behind a semi-transparent

1   See the exhibition text for *Noel Harding: Enclosure for Conventional Habit* (Banff: Walter Philips Gallery, 1980).

2   Quoted by John Bentley Mays, *Globe & Mail*, May 5, 1980.

3   Ibid.

plastic sheeting, to the accompaniment of a saxophone playing through four evenly distributed speakers set above the sheeting.

The title clearly suggested that *Enclosure for Conventional Habit* was an enclosure for the conventional "habits," or attributes, of trees and chickens. But because such a purpose is unsatisfactorily banal, two others came to mind. Since enforced movement is not explained by the first explanation, enclosure can be read as "suspension," and the work then became a witness to the suspension of conventional expectations in our intercourse with trees and chickens. As the tree moved ponderously by us and the chickens pursued an *Alice in Wonderland* destiny, running to stand still, the piece became an elaborately enforced fantasy out of Harding's somewhat perverse sense of humour.

And thirdly, there is Vera Frenkel's suggestion[1] that the "conventional habit" referred to is our own set of expectations and anxieties about life and dignity, and the work can be read as a wry investigation of our own banality hearing cellos when seeing trees, or drums when seeing chickens, and expressing concern—as almost all who saw the piece were bound to do—over the well-being of half a dozen chickens in a public gallery, but not a thousand chickens in a chicken farm.

What is striking in reviewing the discussion of this work is the lack of a central focus for the discussion. Harding's explanation that it is a "comprehension of time and movement"[2] hardly suffices. More revealing is his comment that the work is "the result of a lot of work on a vision."[3] As in *Once Upon the Idea of Two*, *Enclosure for Conventional Habit* is less interested in the construction of a central hypothesis than it is in the profusion and diversion of its material elements—a view supported by the photographic and written documentation included in the Banff catalogue for the work—a diversion which in effect cloaks the work in a magician's mantle of obscurity and ambiguity. Why? Simply because it is a vision, Noel Harding's vision, and what is important is not a focused intent which would connect with its audience, but an idealized and isolated intuition by an artist who sees his audience solely as an aspect of his own vision.

The intentional separation of audience from artist evident in these two works can be tested in a curiously inverted manner in *Scenic Events on a Path of Upheaval*, shown at the Ydessa Gallery in 1981. Inverted, because in this work there is no necessity for such a separation, and—perhaps realizing that—Harding throws one in from the side, off-camera as it were, in an apparent contradiction of his statement I quote at the head of this article.

Scenic Events on a Path of Upheaval retains basically the same elements as *Enclosure for Conventional Habit*: the chickens on their treadmill become goldfish swimming in a tubular aquarium of plastic sheeting stapled around the perimeter walls of the space. Back and forth across the gallery travels, not a large tree, but a small lettuce patch on a tiny cart which passes through the plastic sheet separating a simple control system from the audience before returning once again on the endless journey set for it, while overhead a small speaker accompanies it, tinnily playing the sound of video games.

Now the title of *Scenic Events on a Path of Upheaval* has a descriptive pomposity about it that connects, whether accidentally or not, with the smallness of goldfish and lettuce patches to construct an interior gentle humour and a sense of pathos which allows an audience to share in that construction. The goldfish become substitute tourist, the lettuce patch on its track becomes a rural landscape obsessively busy with its own pre-ordained path of existence, and the audience finds itself invested with the infectious aura of robot-like video sounds. There is no profusion of irrelevant material or activity, no disconnections to distract the audience from a grasp of the work as a comprehensible statement about which they can form ideas with some confidence that they connect significantly with the work. The problem of Harding's isolated intuition, while implied by the title, is suspended as a problem.

When Harding then tells us, however, that the work is his response to the Soviet involvement in Afghanistan, and the state of international relations, he undermines the integrity of the work itself, let alone the possibility of an "original experience." It is not that I disbelieve him, or that such a response may be inappropriate, but that the work itself does not contain—or require—such a statement. The result is that it now becomes a series of scenic events for Noel Harding in an engagement to which the audience was not invited. If we let Harding have his way, it becomes, once again, a vision from and for the artist which excludes the audience from a meaningful engagement with the work. I will come back to this word "meaningful" a bit later.

At first glance, Harding's two works from 1982 and 1983—*Monument to Decision-Making* and *1st, 2nd & 3rd Attempts to Achieve Heaven*—seem radically different in their reduction, even from *Scenic Events on a Path of Upheaval*. The difference, however, is largely formal, and involves the substitution of materially stable elements for the performance-related elements, like film or video—let alone chickens in the earlier works I have discussed. Harding's views on the relationships between artist, work, and audience do not change, and the formal simplicity in fact dramatizes the nature of his position.

In *Monument to Decision-Making*, three tall, round, slightly tilted concrete columns dominated the otherwise empty gallery space which remained unlit except for a dim violet spotlight on the ceiling and a bare light bulb which, connected to a hidden mechanical device, continually swung and clattered against one of the columns. Unidentifiable taped sounds could vaguely be heard. The austerity this work introduced abolishes the material extravagance of the previous work, and the starkness of its monumentality seems to offer the audience a chance to make contact with its core. And there is no doubt that some contact is possible in a way that Harding previously disallowed.

But I said it seems to make contact, and I say that because on closer examination the work's elements add up to a highly personal set of conditions which elude social interpretation and elide together to form a private metaphor for "decision-making." While I can certainly enjoy the metaphor, as I enjoyed it in *Scenic Events on a Path of Upheaval*, I am also aware that the only factor which holds its disparate elements together is Harding's declaration that it is indeed about decision-making. I am left to speculate whether Harding means to deny the importance—or self-importance—of decision-making, or whether instead the work is an anguished response in the face of that importance. Ambivalence has a long history in art, and its relation to the concept, and attraction, of the riddle in mythology and literature is obvious. The crucial difference is that the components of a riddle are attached to the experience of the audience. The components of Harding's installation are not, and while the title therefore plays an indispensable role in whatever relationship the work can have with its audience, it plays that role in lonely splendour, and with desperate futility. And the reason has been clear all along: Harding has no interest in that relationship. The work, with its title, has meaning for him, and that solipsistic position cannot by definition include an audience.

1st, 2nd & 3rd Attempts to Achieve Heaven serves simply to confirm the consistency of Harding's position. A large shallow wall-like form, constructed out of unpainted heavy steel plate, became partly an embodiment and partly a frame of reference for a small pair of bird's wings, one attached to each side of the form, which flapped at a constant mechanical rate. Spotlights set inside the form cast a soft sequential rhythmic light onto the ceiling above, improbably suggesting the wings' progress in moving the form forwards against all odds. A beam of red light from a small laser fastened high up on the nearby gallery wall pierced the mass of the form at a steep angle like a bullet from the gods, signalling its presence with a small red spot like a blood spoor on the gallery floor.

The reference to desire and denial is obvious both from the title and from the relationships between the wings, the steel structure with its rhythmic lights, and the laser beam. The piece appears to resolve the problematic relationships between title and material functions evident in *Monument to Decision-Making*. Ironically, however, the very simplicity of the work's metaphor forces the fancifulness of the title to betray Harding's persistent isolation. And the comparison with *Scenic Events on a Path of*

Upheaval is important here. In the earlier work we could suspend our disbelief in Harding's attitude because the title constructed a condition which the audience could complete. In this one, the title's obscurity undermines the modest one-liner of the work's visual metaphor, and reminds us that Harding's vision sees things we won't. What *1st, 2nd & 3rd Attempts to Achieve Heaven* constructs is another private metaphor out of Harding's sketchbook. As audience we can only look at it and attempt "to develop the meaning." It does not help that we can develop roughly the same meaning one assumes the title encloses, because that meaning refers only to the wilful obscurity— and for the audience the distraction—of Harding's own understanding of the title.

I am aware that my insistence in this article on the nature of the relationship between Harding's work and his audience inevitably distorts a fuller evaluation of his work. I am not evaluating his work. I am insistent on what I see as Harding's intentional segregation of art and audience, not because it is unique to Harding, but because the solipsistic idealism it reflects accounts in large part for the continuing problems facing contemporary artists in connecting with an audience, and in pursuing a purposeful engagement with being in the world.

John Mays used the term "winging it" in a review of Harding's last piece at the Ydessa Gallery with an obvious journalistic flamboyance. But in fact, "winging it" is exactly what Harding has been doing all along, to the extent that he has made it his basic art practice. The quick sketch, the immediacy of the artist's intuitional vision, becomes an original experience out of which we are to develop the meaning. Perhaps we must ask what Harding understands by "meaning." What I understand by meaning is an elaboration of a signified purpose, accessible, at least in the context of artmaking and the dialectics of social existence. Harding comes to art after philosophy studies at Guelph, and while I do not doubt his sincerity, I am disillusioned by his apparent lack of sophistication, and his grasp of what artmaking involves. The disappointment is that his essentially romantic transcendentalism simply ends up by isolating its adherents in the emptiness and banality of the oldest convention of all: the lonely individual as misunderstood prophet amongst the philistines. Such a position is meaningful neither for Harding, nor for me.

How We See/What We Say (1986)

Published in *How We See/What We Say*, exh. cat. (Toronto: The Art Gallery at Harbourfront, 1986). The exhibition was curated by Carr-Harris and ran from April 4 to May 18, 1986. Author's note: The printed catalogue was accompanied by an audio cassette in which the curator read the entire text while including short interviews with the individual artists in the sections relevant to their work.

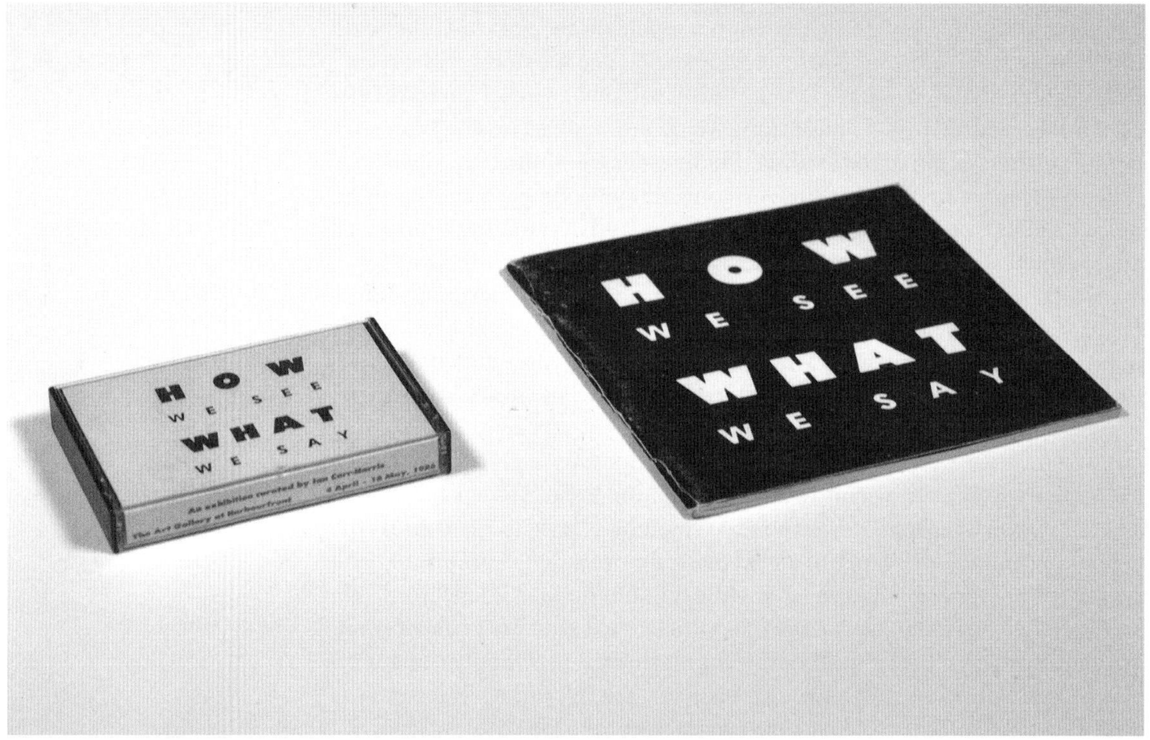

2.5   *How We See/What We Say* (Toronto: The Art Gallery at Harbourfront, 1986), exhibition catalogues (print and audio versions). Print catalogue: David Buchan, designer, b&w illus., 15 × 15 cm; audio catalogue: Ihor Holubizky, coordinator, reading by Ian Carr-Harris including interviews with the artists, 86 mins.

This is an exhibition of eight works by eight artists with quite different points of view. Their installation in the space of the Gallery has been concerned with underlining those differences by enabling you to consider them separately, while acknowledging that, taken together, they construct a context of shared concerns.

It must also be pointed out that this printed text is really a transcript to accompany the audio catalogue. My emphasis is important. The spoken word is richer in nuance and direction than the written, and therefore closer to my purpose, which is to demonstrate that artworks are conversational, and that ideas are passionate.

What you will not find in this transcript is something which only makes sense as audio documentation—views on their own work expressed by the artists, or by curators who have a special interest in the work. You will, I am sure, find them persuasive.

Let me begin by explaining what led me to organize this exhibition and what I mean by its title. As a working artist with exhibition experience, both as contributor and as viewer, I have been disappointed by the conditions under which the works of contemporary artists have generally been encountered. Consequently, I am not surprised by their failure to connect with those who come in contact with them. My disappointment concerning this double failure arises from a conviction that artworks—as artworks—exist solely within the public domain. It follows that if the work of contemporary artists fails to connect at this level, then that failure is profoundly serious. It is because I believe this situation is not pre-determined by, for instance, public inertia, and that changes can be instituted in this encounter, that I wish to contribute through this exhibition some ideas towards what is, of course, the very complex process of constructing directed meaning.

I want to indicate first what it is I am trying to avoid. Central to the public's alienation from contemporary artworks, it seems to me, is the status applied to the work itself. I believe there has developed a fracturing practice of staging contemporary artists as artists at the expense of the work they produce. This staging may proceed across a number of levels—focusing perhaps on an individual artist's intentions and personality, or perhaps on broadly shared connections of intention or thematic concern between artists, or often perhaps simply not focused at all, embracing a pluralism disguised as a commonality of medium or region. While all these levels of investigation reflect varying degrees of validity, they do not in themselves constitute a specific attachment to the works. The consequence is that contemporary artworks have come to be understood as simply, or merely, evidence. By evidence, I mean that the meaning of the work is understood not in productive terms—that is to say, in terms of its argumentation or logic—but in circumstantial terms: its existence as a circumstance, or artifact. As artifact, the work assumes a passive density, inevitably deferring to whatever forces are seen to have acted upon it. Those forces have been, typically, the artist as hero (rarely as heroine) and the curator as impresario. I want now, therefore, to examine very briefly how these two determinants have arisen, and how they act to override the work.

The artist as hero has had a number of complexions. The most common is secured in the romantic myth of the starving artist. It operates as well, however, with somewhat greater subtlety, in the more modern portraits of the artist as expressive genius; or the artist as lifestyle designer; or even the artist as people's cultural worker. This is hardly to deny the commitment that artists bring to their work. Rather, it is to warn against the dissolution of purpose within the frame of the work, and the consequent marginalization of the artist as just another "personality," a dissolution which seriously threatens this commitment. It is therefore important to understand that this distracting cult of personality is no simple misunderstanding, but a process deeply embedded in our history, and especially within the dominant and immensely powerful network of concepts known as modernism. I do not have the time to consider those concepts here, except to identify at their core an essential denial of historical dimension in favour of a transcendental Present. In eliminating the contingencies and debts implicit in history, modernism privileges the reductive absolute, and the individual's isolation. The work of art, consequently, is not seen so much as a construction of critical awareness—though it might in fact be precisely that—but as a residue of inspired struggle, a way station, in a spiritual search for an essential form. If this notion seems charming, it is nevertheless dangerous—for two reasons: on the one hand, we cannot evade history, and to attempt it is to render the artist irrelevant; on the other hand, the artwork—if it is merely evidence—hardly matters anyway.

The curator as impresario is in many respects a natural effect arising from the isolation of the artist. Stars need to be staged in particular ways, and at the very least it is considered unbecoming for heroes to stage themselves. What might at first be seen as essentially a service function can be seen as quickly assuming instead a controlling interest, controlling who is to be selected as hero and who is not. The function of impresario is therefore innately irresponsible, however much panache it may construct around the artwork. It is clear that it has nothing to do with the work itself, and that in fact it renders the work as evidence only of the curator's taste, or intellectual skill in delineating thematic motifs for which the artwork may conveniently serve as more or less appropriate illustrative support. Of course, depending upon who is acting as impresario, such a role can have diverting results. But this does not alter the fact that it ignores the specific meaning that the artworks must be seen to hold if they are to escape being merely evidence.

It is time, therefore, to consider first the meaning of "specific," and relate it then to the museum—the preeminent site of meaning and evaluation for artworks; secondly to the curator—whose purpose is to manage this site of encounter; and finally to the artist—who is at least responsible for making the work.

By specific we mean the actual conditions encountered. That, in turn, implies the question: what is different about this encounter? What sets it apart? Being specific means to construct difference, and difference involves the play of taking exception, of contesting understanding. It has been suggested that this contest is instituted, or inscribed, at a basic level within culture through language, within the dominant position that words hold with respect to ideas. Whether true or not, it has been normal experience across a variety of cultures, including our own, to define things by a process of establishing difference. This definitional procedure or location of specific meaning has been variously assigned to intentionality, to structural presence, to receptive disposition, or to historically "objective" criteria attendant on the means of production. While resolving those conflicting claims is problematic, perhaps even futile, it is clear that the process of describing differentiated meaning must proceed on the basis of holding a *specific position*.

Within the structure of the museum, it is the transcendentalist tendencies inherent within modernism which would seem to have caused museums to favour a false neutrality in presenting contemporary art. This neutrality is of course a doomed enterprise. This is so not simply because the physicality of architectural space can at best only construct an *emptied* space, implying by what it excludes the presence of those exclusions: it is also because we—as viewers—cannot be neutral. In straining our credulity by pretending otherwise, the museum's misplaced insistence on seeing the legitimacy of its empty spaces as illegitimately neutral displaces the viewer before the work and confuses the issue of how we are to experience the work's meaning. If the difference between neutral and empty appears to be subtle, it is, in fact, not. A neutral space assumes a positive and even aggressive state for itself; for that reason, changes to it for the purpose of accommodating artworks constitute a threat to its status. Needless to say, spaces conceived in this manner find it both impossible and inadmissible to adapt to the development of meaning; ultimately, neutral spaces betray their disguised ideological stance. A space conceived of as empty, on the other hand, is both demonstrative of its own conditions, and adaptable to the specific needs required of it. In this exhibition, the space of the gallery is conceived as empty, and its adaptation to the work has proceeded on the understanding that the specific conditions of each work must be endorsed by the gallery's space as a whole. If walls are needed, they will be walls, not partitions, and their existence will be contingent upon their specific purpose. It is in this contingent relation that the "empty museum" opposes itself to the "neutral museum" and recovers both an honest attachment to the space, and a reattachment to history and politics.

History and politics are, of course, determined by people, and in the museum those people are curators. I indicated earlier the dangerous inadequacy of the curator as impresario. But more fundamentally, this role for the curator fails because it is impossible. In the viewer's attempt to attach meaning to the exhibition of work, the curator's choices will be subjected to a search for significance. This significance is double-edged. If the curatorial role is to be significant, it will be so only to the degree that the work chosen supports the curatorial claims. For that to take place, the specific constructions advanced by the work must be clearly attached to those claims. The curatorial role cannot afford to be merely that of an impresario if it is to claim significance. On the other hand, if the artwork—centrally important to the curator—is to be seen as significant, that is, relevant, it can only be so to the degree that the curator is able to articulate specific claims of relevance related to propositions within the world. The work cannot afford a curatorial direction which fails to construct a text in which the viewer can operate confidently. This confidence will be secured to the degree that the context includes the presence of the curator. For both curator and artwork then, curatorial failure to ground the construction of significance in specific examination will inevitably erode or destroy that significance. The curator's role requires the same commitment to analytical reception demanded of the museum itself. As curator for this exhibition, then, I have chosen specific, existing works which I have found personally compelling, for reasons specific to the works, and for reasons specific to my understanding of their relevance.

If the construction of significance is double-edged, intersecting the curator and the artwork, what—for artists—is involved in holding specific positions, and speaking clearly, in the making of that work? To hold a position is to have stated it. Perhaps you have heard the story of the little girl who, when asked what she thought, replied: "But how can I know what I think until I see what I say?" If it is true that what we think is a function of what we say, it is also true that it is a function of *how we see* what we say. That is, there is reflexiveness—a reflection—within this chain, and the connection between saying, seeing, and thinking is neither casual nor linear, but collaborative—we could say "dialectical," constantly constructing what we are coming to be, often in surprising or confusing ways. Artworks are acts of "saying," or stating, and any attempt to understand them as dependent on "seeing" independently of "saying" is to misunderstand not only artworks but thought itself. Artworks say things, they "mean" to say things, and if there are ambiguities—as of course there always are in languages—they are the result of a dialectical process in which their meaning is a function of their applicability to specific conditions of experience. To speak clearly is to delineate how those conditions are experienced.

How we see, then, is intimately involved with what we say. And just what do we say? Of course we say many things, simultaneously. But one thing we always say—though rarely consciously—is what we think constitutes nature. The relations between art and nature are well known, if only in their simplest reduction as an opposition of values. But that relationship is the conventionalization of a much deeper relationship between the *fact* of nature and the *idea* of nature; and for the *idea of nature* we can read the *idea of culture*. Artworks, as perhaps the most advanced tool of culture, are the expressive vehicles through which we state our "reconstitution," as it were, of nature's *fact* as *idea*, because at the level of thought, of thinking about things, nature is, like everything else, an idea. It is out of ideas that we construct our actions. The fact that women bear children, for instance, or that we die if we freeze, are certainly facts, but their value as fact is no more independent of the ideas which can make child-bearing a joy or a calamity, or dying a blessing or a tragedy, than the little girl's thoughts were independent of her materialization of them. I have chosen, therefore, to consider the statements each of the eight artists in this exhibition advance within their work about the idea of nature. It is in, or around, our ideas about the delimitations of the natural that we define culture, and through it construct our notions of value and respect, of freedom and survival.

I have attempted to show the importance of specific attachment, and of speaking clearly to the attachment we adopt. It is only by revealing our identity that others may understand theirs, and enable us to reconstruct our own. It is precisely this process of understanding how we see, and what we say, that we look for and should expect from the museum through the space, from the curator through the exhibition, and from the artist through the work.

I want to start now With Paterson Ewen's painting of 1971 because in Canada, though it is true elsewhere as well, nature in its relatively uncomplicated guise as a subject with clear symbolic or transferable meaning has had a dominating history within the popular imagination. Landscapes—streams, mountains, lakes, jack pines—all have been used to express assumptions and desires. The enormous public influence of the Group of Seven painters is not the result simply of an ability to handle paint, or of having a good eye for pretty views, or of having clever collectors and dealers. It is the result far more of their understanding and attachment to certain commonly held beliefs and longings, and any useful criticism of their work must be a criticism of those beliefs. Ewen's *Rocks Moving in the*

Current of a Stream (1971) is precisely that: it sets itself in direct opposition to the Seven's conventional middle-class comprehension of the world we move in as an external reality that offers us—privileged voyeurs that we are presumed to be—desirable impressions or suggestive motifs for our appropriation. Nature—in this comprehension—is separate from us, and for those who aspire to greatness, it represents an opportunity for conquest. Or at least an occasion for safari. The jack pine's only interest is that it mirrors ourselves.

Ewen proposes instead an internalized or "apprehended" nature anticipated by our inquiry into the causality of its effects. Ewen's moving rocks are intentionally neither perceived—nor even perceivable as such—but are, rather, theoretical reconstructions comprehended by a knowing self-critical subject conditioned by and armed with language. Ewen's "safari" is undoubtedly better prepared than Jackson's for survival in the wilderness of nature whose effects have a cause.

Ewen's engagingly simple introduction both of the scientific revolution and, through his referencing to diagrammatic representation, of language into the Canadian landscape tradition may seem long overdue. That tradition has a history larger than the grip of the Seven would suggest, of course. Nevertheless, the strength of that grip is an issue. *Rocks Moving in the Current of a Stream* differs radically from Thomson's *Jack Pine* of 1918 in presupposing an active, investigative interaction with perceived experience. *Jack Pine* had no such supposition. The extraordinary elegance and seduction of Thomson's work is the seduction of the dreaming subject for whom nature is essentially unknowable, a vast panoply of tangled complexities—like the bush country itself; a reality which man may view, may indeed legally own and use or abuse, but which will always endure because it belongs finally to God, to a nature that is immutable and infinite. It is easy enough to see how the ambivalence of traditional notions about our place in the universe can service on the one hand a deep respect for the integrity of the world, while on the other hand permitting without demur the rape and destruction of its material manifestations. And material manifestation includes not only trees and lakes; it includes men and women as well. When God is in control, who are we but his servants, and his children?

In Ewen's painting, this equation is clearly shown to be insufficient. Not only does he recognize that, children or not, we know something about mechanics, and we can express more than simple awe at how things work: we recognize, standing before the painting, that if we discern pattern, if we construct knowledge, we construct also the power to intervene. In reconstructing nature as a force having its own laws and powers—as more, that is, than simply a majestic opportunity for contemplation or pillage—*Rocks*

Moving in the Current of a Stream clears the deck for a discussion about how
our relations to those forces may be seen.

If Pat Ewen's work represents a process of intelligent inquiry directed
towards a natural world whose forces can be anticipated, Murray Favro's
Still Life (The Table) (1970) represents a projection of that process toward
a level of abstraction which Ewen is careful to avoid. The reason is not
difficult to understand. Despite, and perhaps because of his awareness of
the inherence of force in the world, Ewen wishes to experience that world
as a palpable phenomenon—as an equivalent Being, one might say—whose
coherence can be experienced as one experiences or attempts to experience
one's own body. Favro is not concerned, however, with coherence—at least
not of the palpable sort. The forces that Ewen diagrammatically reconstructs as nature are for Favro quite separate from any such illusion and
exist on their own—perhaps rather like Michelangelo's figure caught within
the uncut stone—not as perceivable diagrams of figurations, but as principles of mathematics and engineering. *Still Life* is aptly named: it is, in fact, a
sophisticated contemporary affirmation of an ancient Western ambition—
the death of nature. For Favro, nature as such does not exist; what exists is
what we invent. Inventions are insertions of artifice into the fabric of the
Real—that is, Experience—and are hardly natural; their very existence is
highly contingent on perceptions of specific need and desire. Inventions
are manipulations, our manipulations. It is our insistent invention and
reinvention of the world through our fabrication of conceptual models that
constructs and reconstructs what we see as our imaginary coherence. For
Favro, what we see as nature is simply a set of models acting according to
principles established in tension with certain prevailing conditions.

Still Life (The Table) then, reconstructs rather than anticipates nature,
but it understands that reconstruction as a dimension in time, not—like
Michelangelo—of space. It understands, that is, that no absolute "eternal" construct exists to be reconstructed. Our experience of the world is
consequently not of an orderly equivalence, but of a "disorderly" array
of conceptual possibilities, of ideas about experience, in an undoubtedly
infinite progression of inventive experiments. What we experience is not
coherent equivalence, but divergent contingencies, and for Favro those contingencies are limited only by our imagination and our ability to materialize
them. If the *Flea* can fly, so much the better.

It is evident from *Still Life (The Table)* that Murray Favro locates these
contingencies pre-eminently within the theoretical arena of physics, or
physical perception. But the notion of contingency has implications for
other locations as well. To maintain that nature as a perceived entity is only
a projection or sentimental coherence—one that can be manipulated as a

replication according to formula—can be to maintain as well that nature as a term with ethical demands is also a projection of only sentimental interest. It is a question that lies at the heart of culture. Favro, understandably, chooses to ignore it, and in doing so joins Paterson Ewen in a tacit respect for process. In any case, Favro does retain a notion of the Real as cohesive principle, however circumstantial. General Idea, in *Snobird: A Public Sculpture for the 1984 Miss General Idea Pavilion* (1985) is not burdened by any notion of principles, mathematical or otherwise, as a definition of nature. *Snobird* not only accepts that nature does not "exist" as an entity, but—and this is critical—that nature is in fact only a memory of a myth within culture. So what if the *Flea* can fly? Reconstructing the Real is therefore out of the question; any reconstructing that is going to be done will be reconstruction of fictions, and what is "real" is simply cultural reference. If *Snobird* appears to be an artificially sophisticated one-liner referring, depending on the viewer's own sophistication, to certain specified events and evaluations—for instance a knowledge of Michael Snow's birds in the Eaton Centre—it is in fact exactly what it appears to be; because that, for General Idea, is all there is once certain assumptions have been made—assumptions such as those implicit in Favro's work and, for that matter, implicit even in the strained credulity of the dichotomy present in traditional middle-class views we discussed in connection with the Group of Seven. By extending those assumptions, the world becomes commentary and cliché, a network of one-liners in a closed critical text. *Snobird* is not about particular cultural clichés; it is, for instance, certainly not just a comment or attack on Snow's geese or on folk art appropriations. It is about culture as cliché, about culture as banality.

It is easy, and perhaps wryly appropriate, to dismiss *Snobird* and General Idea—as more or less humorous and more or less irrelevant to a serious consideration of general experience. In fact, however, for all its hilarious cartoon qualities, *Snobird* is deadly serious. Like Daffy Duck, it offers a critique of reality that examines culture's displacement of meaning from natural givens, or reference points, and considers the consequences of its power—or, rather, its actuality—as the sole producer and consumer of its own meaning. What is striking, therefore, is the extent to which *Snobird* implies a dissatisfaction with these consequences. It is an implication that cannot be found within the deadpan humour of the piece itself, but within the relations begged of the viewer. Those relations are clearly the classic ground on which all political cartoons base their ethical position and their power to influence: the *reductio ad absurdum*. If *Snobird* indeed faithfully represents our experience of the world, our experience is considerably more complicated and less extensive than we had imagined. Claustrophobic, in fact.

What do we have here, then? *Snobird*, carefully bracketed by its defined status as, after all, only a "public sculpture" for an elusive artwork always beyond whatever site it actually inhabits, is a committed act of ironic mimesis. What General Idea shrewdly realizes is that the power we profess in constructing culture depends for its existence on the continued presence of a nature that may submit to—or challenge—that power. Left to itself, culture—as an idea with the promise of unrestricted power—becomes a rather pointless narcissistic fantasy, caught—as *Snobird*'s subtitle reveals—in the decadent formalist maze of the fictional 1984 Miss General Idea Pavilion, with its self-reflexive entrapment of History, which is culture, in the future-past of a mirrored prison.

Snobird condenses a particular logic that stretches from the Group of Seven through Paterson Ewen to Murray Favro and reduces it to a desperate farce. But farce or not, the problem of value raised by that logic remains. How to attach ourselves to value, while accepting the idea of nature as mutable, is what Janis Hoogstraten considers in *Brook Trout*. *Brook Trout* seeks to cut the Gordian Knot that General Idea presents to us. Hoogstraten looks at Ewen's respect for an integrated equivalent nature and at Favro's engaging recognition of nature as invention and proposes a line of inquiry which secures the Fact of nature as inherent within the idea of culture, assumed by it, rather than one that is threatened with displacement by it.

This is a seductive integration, all the more so for General Idea's critique of the apparent alternative. *Brook Trout* switches the emphasis implicit in Ewen's paintings and places nature not so much as a set of external forces—or givens—to be witnessed and examined, however respectfully, but as a primary internalized instigator of culture in the first place. Nor is *Brook Trout* overly concerned with the representing or re-inventing of nature as a cultural achievement, as *Still Life (The Table)* is. While Hoogstraten recognizes the act of representation as a tool for examining and developing culture, whether used diagrammatically as in Ewen's work, or imagistically as in Favro's, *Brook Trout*'s central concern is with the functional relations those representations retain with their external reference—nature. It is important to realize then that by "external" Hoogstraten does not mean independent or "unknowable," but that which is apprehended as attachable to our purposes—to the purpose of culture. To modify Brecht's ironic pragmatism in the *Threepenny Opera*, we could say that Hoogstraten agrees that "First comes food, then comes culture." Indeed, *Brook Trout* is precisely about surviving: it is a lesson in how to identify and catch a good eating fish. This may seem like an innocent enough concern. But within the context of relations in the world, it is important to understand just what is being said. *Brook Trout* is a manual that instructs certain skills; that is, it recognizes that our ability to exist in reality, in the world, depends on our knowledge of those skills, which is to say on our construction of them as appropriate to their reference. And this, the painting is saying, is exactly what culture is. Culture is our skill, our ability to exist, and this necessary connection between the externally real—the Fact of nature—and the internally inventive—the Idea of culture—constructs an experience, our experience, that is one of continuous engagement.

In taking this position, *Brook Trout* occupies sensitive territory. *Snobird* aligns itself with a strongly held suspicion of so-called natural forces. A view of culture as itself positing nature has significantly positive implications for the reconstruction of power relations, most notably those—such as between men and women, or between rich and poor—which are often claimed to derive from natural order. It simplifies the argument to dismiss nature as an aspect of culture, and as we have seen, *Brook Trout* does see nature as an aspect of culture. But just how that aspect is grounded in necessity is at issue. *Snobird* exposed cultural narcissism as a farcical brand of hedonistic idealism, dangerously disconnected from both real material need and from ethical necessity. Hoogstraten, in attempting to ground value in primary purpose, re-opens the risk of encouraging those who would maintain the political status quo. The important question suggested by *Brook Trout*, then, is just what constitutes nature's legitimate references. How does the idea of nature work with respect to cultural necessity, and therefore with respect to power and morality? Hunger seems relatively straightforward; but is it, and what about other situations which are certainly not simple?

It is exactly this problem that is engaged in Susan Schelle's *A Home Movie*. As the title suggests, the subject is the family structure, and the arbitration through sexual division of moral necessity and the assignation of power. Schelle accepts *Brook Trout*'s premise that a solution must be articulated for the construction of value; that we cannot afford to treat the question as merely a cousin to perception, or as a farcical absence, but as the pre-eminent reference to be accounted for through culture. For Schelle, however, it is unfortunately not only a reference, but—as her text explicitly remarks—"a problem of control." And nowhere is the problem of control so acutely felt as in sexual relations and their impact within the family. Families are almost universally acknowledged as the kinship units which organize civilization itself. They are—traditionally at least—the arena where skills are transmitted, where boys learn to catch fish and girls learn to make dinner; the arena, that is, where our reconstruction of nature receives the kind of definition that affects personal identity. *A Home Movie* focuses on the controlling taboos and fears that characterize this process of reconstruction. It picks out, like a flashlight in a dark garden, the specific impact of this immensely complicated edifice on the friendship of a boy and a girl. Young people as a whole are arguably less skilled, or at least less socialized, than older adults; they therefore represent an area of greater tension between what is natural—what we conceive as natural—and what is cultured. The organized controls are consequently more pointed and less disguised. The boy and the girl are not free agents—they are accountable to the culture's perceived needs for its own survival. The boy is banished because he is male—a fact of nature, but only because he thereby implicitly threatens disturbance of cultural order. And Schelle's point is all the more telling for being staged in a gentle suburban garden, in a society that declares itself free.

If *A Home Movie* accepts *Brook Trout*'s basic premise, it nevertheless does so with a recognition that it is at those very points where culture must account for the "facts of life" that culture presses its power most firmly. That, in other words, the formalization of culture—its rigidity and its idealization—is magnified precisely as nature's reference points are sensed. If half the world, as we know, can be refused survival as a direct result of culture's regulation of its own process of survival, the outlook for changes in sexual regulation, for changes in power regulations, for social justice, seems slim. In *A Home Movie*, *Snobird*'s bitter evasiveness seems as logical a result of *Brook Trout* as it does of *Still Life (The Table)*.

But logic has many levels, and destiny is both interpretive and extensive. Destiny functions in history, and it is this view that is represented in Renée Van Halm's *Anticipating the Eventual Emergence of Form, Part 1 and 2* (1983). The work bears special relevance to the arguments put forward by Hoogstraten and Schelle. It is, in fact, a restatement of their positions for the express purpose of including history as a specific experience rather than simply a general corollary of culture. Indeed, it is neatly a double restatement; it takes as its basic text a painting from the fifteenth century by Piero della Francesca which depicts the Madonna revealing herself as "with child." What Van Halm does is to secularize the earlier work—to expand its theological statement of salvation—and reformulate that meaning as the process of lived history, the story of human generation. The single static, or ahistorical, snapshot structure of the medieval painting—with its appeal to a divine nature miraculously, or "immaculately" divorced from and triumphant over human understanding or action—becomes in Van Halm's work an album of intimately human experiences in the world. Not simply human, either, but specifically female, and specifically acted out within the contingencies of a freedom that is implied in the potential represented by the room within the piece; within, that is, the firm embrace of cultural construction and its history. This alliance of specific attachments—realized history, specific gender—aligns Van Halm politically and even strategically with Susan Schelle. But what is vitally important about Van Halm's position is her recognition that in the levels and modalities of history there lies a possible response to the question posed by Hoogstraten's *Brook Trout* and left unresolved, if more sharply defined, by *A Home Movie*. You will recall that the question concerned the problem of just what constituted nature's "legitimate" references. If existence is a function of skill, if culture is a function of nature, then it can be argued that changes to the cultural status quo that are not directly related to survival skills pose a potential threat to existence. In fact, Hoogstraten does use this argument because she sees the threat to existence as one posed in ethical relativism and its concomitant—the unfettered pursuit of power. But if culture is the site of value, as Hoogstraten certainly insists, the question becomes to what extent, if any, the Fact of nature as implicit in culture can allow for ethical challenges and redistributions of power. In *A Home Movie*, Schelle was dubious.

Van Halm confronts this question directly with the concept of history. History is a diachronic, or time-extensive, rather than a synchronic, or time-suspended, view of culture. That is, it introduces the idea of evolution, and with it of resolution, as inherent functions of time. For Van Halm, then, it is the seamless narrative of this evolutionary process of resolution, an immensely public narrative inclusive of—yet unanswerable to—specifically held and defended ethical or power positions, a narrative responsive only to its own implacably personal process of generation, that resolves the immobility within the synchronic understanding of nature and culture's relations, and demonstrates the opportunities at least latent in the evolutionary dynamics that constitute the idea of history. And Van Halm has cast history in sexual terms. For her, history—like sexuality and childbearing—is not about life and death as matters for resignation and fatalistic patience, of a natural stasis, but about life and death as an active arena within time, an arena of attachments and denials, and of cultural demands. It is the specific experience of power and morality as contingencies, as anticipations and eventualities, as triumph and loss, as struggle and achievement.

There is, of course, an irony in the notion of history rescuing us from natural stasis only to open the Pandora's box of infinite contingencies. To many, Van Halm's solution to *Brook Trout*'s question might seem merely a pyrrhic victory. But it is an irony that is anticipated in a paradoxical dimension of History's narrative always to be found implicit in our experience of the Present: the temptingly public yet fiercely private nature of our own identity. In a stark work titled *Three Dreams of Blood* (1981/82), Louise Noguchi constructs a container for this paradox. Like Schelle, Noguchi is acutely aware of the degree to which the constitution of the self is bound up with the intimate physical condition of the body. Unlike *A Home Movie*, however, *Three Dreams of Blood* does not directly concern itself with the question of power relations as they surface in cultural units. Instead, it looks at the specific experience we each have of ourselves—at our existential

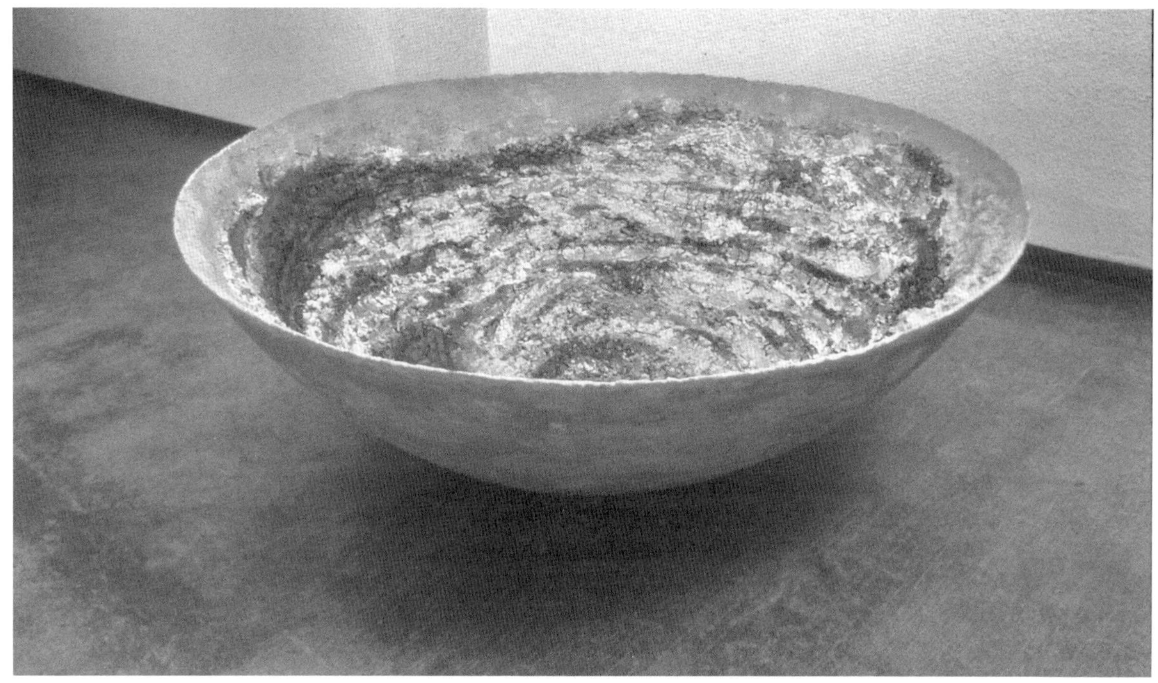

2.6   Louise Noguchi, *Three Dreams of Blood*, 1981– 82. Fiberglass, urethane foam, plaster, clay, bondfast glue, animal blood and linseed oil, 100 × 21 × 214 cm. Courtesy the artist.

experience of being-in-the-world. Now, it is important that this experience not be read—as it so often is—as by necessity excluding history and social responsibility. The connections between our experience of ourselves and our experience of others may be complex, but they are fundamental. In fact, Noguchi's stance represents another attempt to resolve the problem of nature's legitimacy in order to secure a position for ethics that neither founders on entrenched cultural practice nor threatens to disappear into the sands of time.

I said that *Three Dreams of Blood* seeks to contain the paradox of public presence and intimate privacy in their simultaneous constitution of our individual validity. And Noguchi accepts Van Halm's identification of history and sexuality. What Noguchi further clarifies, however, is that the sexuality we must address is not the specific factors of gender difference, or historical tales of sexual experience, but rather sexuality's pivotal place, or "site," as at one and the same time the connecting corridor between our outer and inner selves, and the link that binds us to the past and to the future. The bowl that is *Three Dreams of Blood* is a container that we construct in our self-identification as intelligent subjects; and the dimensions within the paradox of this validity include necessarily the paradox of being at once physical and reflective.

What does this mean? You will remember that Janis Hoogstraten talked about skill. Skill, she pointed out, is necessarily related to survival. But skill is also self-referential—it relates to quality, and through quality to ethics: that is, to questions of value and ultimately our own validity. We define our own validity to a significant degree by our acquisition of skill. It is this reflexive process, this validation of ourselves through knowledge and, inherent in knowledge, the acceptance of our personal physical and historical construction, that—like a skill—itself acts to justify us. Noguchi therefore reverses the equation established by *Brook Trout*: for Noguchi, it is not only that nature is presumed in culture, but that culture must be apprehended in nature. The ethic that *Three Dreams of Blood* secures, therefore, is one which maintains that for culture to make sense, that is, for it to have meaning and for it to be in fact distinguishable from nature, we are required to exercise a self-critical acceptance that we can call simply "having Grace." And for those who are willing to agree to the inevitability of debate and the shifting fortunes of human will, it is this quality of acceptance which secures the purpose of Van Halm's historically informed anticipation.

It is of course also true that "having Grace" is not by any means a prescription for social justice or for cultural change, and Noguchi has simply set that ambition aside in order to concentrate on what she felt was appropriate and possible for her to discuss. However, it remains all too noticeable that quality and existential compassion have little or nothing to do, as they say, with the price of beans, and it is therefore not surprising that Michael Snow's *Waiting Room* (1979) has nothing to say about either existential compassion or about social justice. It has nothing to say, that is, about meaning as a distinction between nature and culture. In *Waiting Room*, Michael Snow pays General Idea a return compliment, and not only agrees with *Snobird*'s critique of culture as "meaningless," but proceeds further to see "meaning" itself as meaningless. In *Waiting Room*, meaning—if it is to be located anywhere—is located in the formal structures which describe nature and culture. For Snow, reality does not exist except as a projected construct of shifting structures whose only connection, and whose only interest, is—well, structural. *Waiting Room* has no securely referenced existence; it is merely a photograph, a surrogate image of a model, a surrogate structure, imagined as a projection from a tiny cardboard mock-up, itself not only a surrogate but, in its absurdly sketchy disdain for simulation, an open mockery of the concept of defined reality. Significantly, the waiting room we see has no figures, has no apparent active function. In *Waiting Room* reality is only an imploded structure, as though a camera has been set for an infinite exposure which renders all contingencies—that is all history, all ethics, all

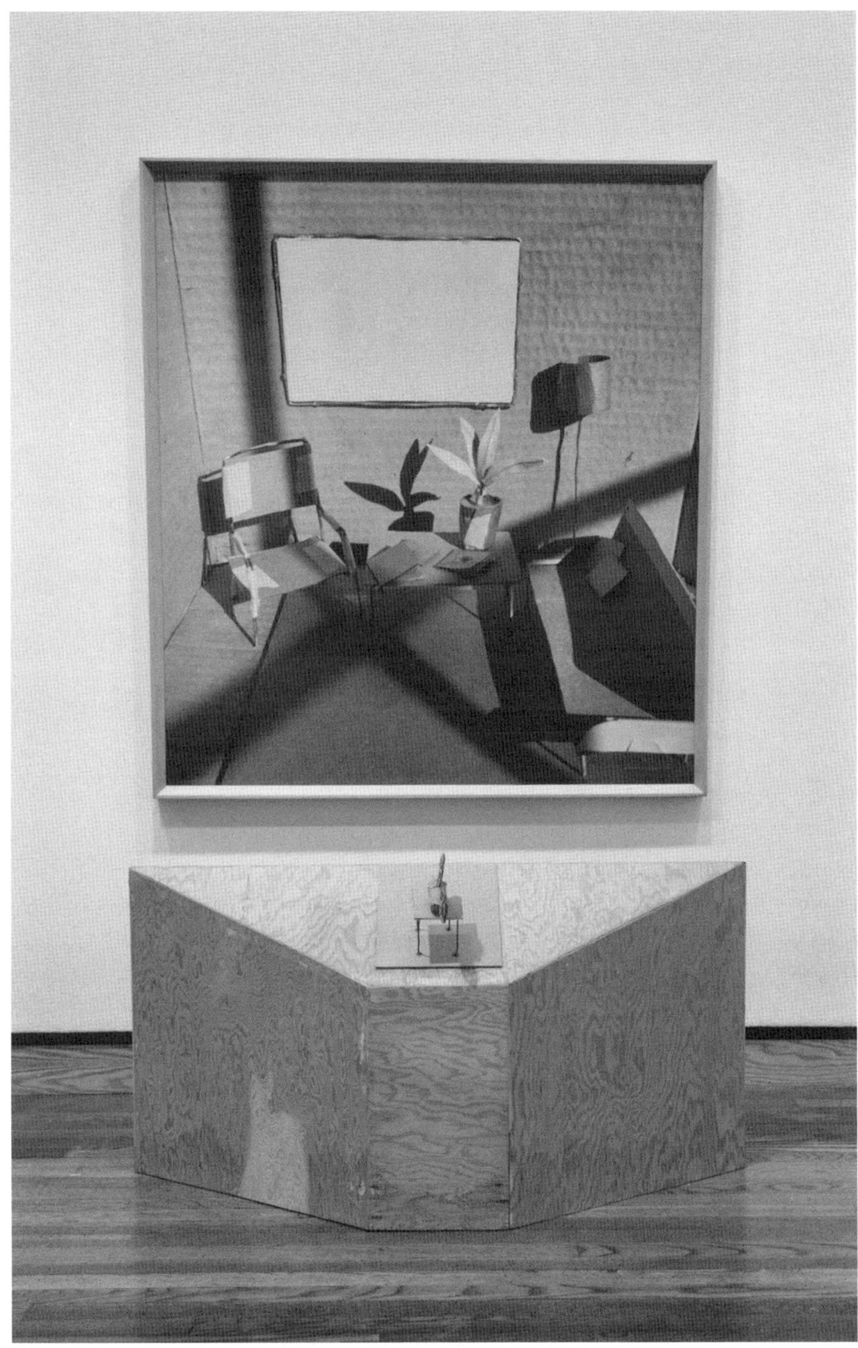

2.7   Michael Snow, *Waiting Room*, 1979. Framed colour photograph, plywood base, photo, 137.2 × 124.5 cm; sculpture, 121.9 × 60.3 × 36.8 cm. Collection Museum London, London, Ontario. Photo: Museum London.

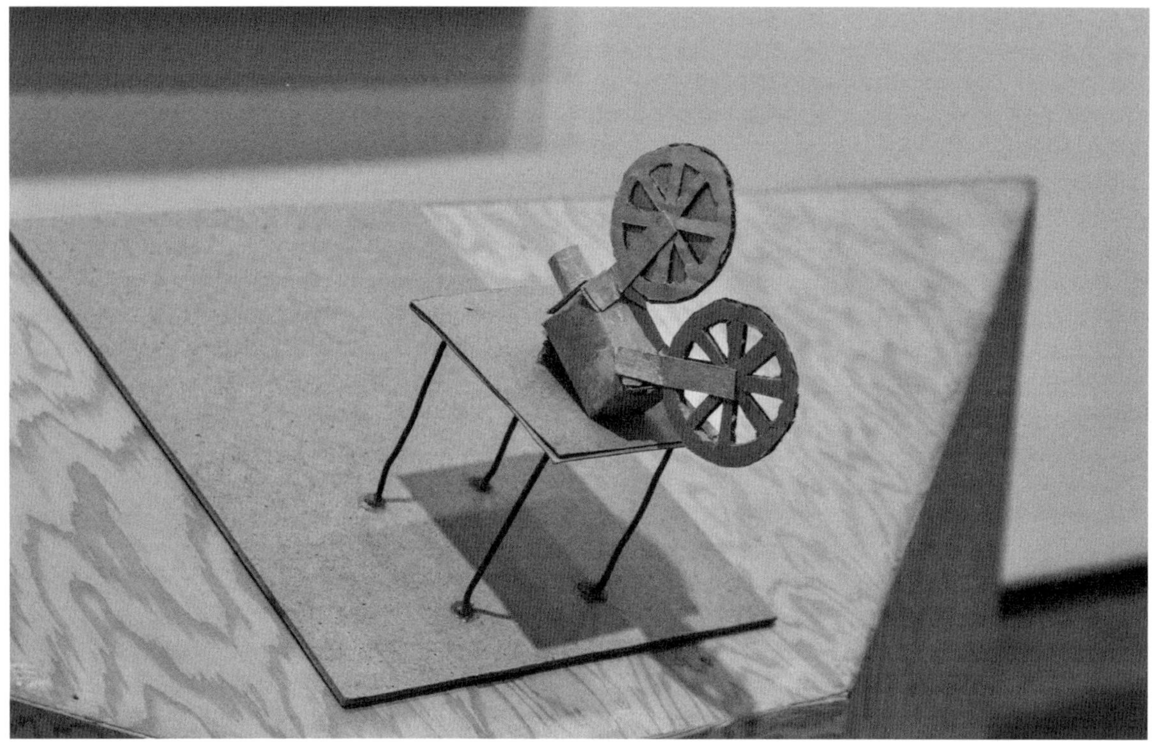

2.8   Michael Snow, *Waiting Room* (detail), 1979. Framed colour photograph, plywood base, photo, 137.2 × 124.5 cm; sculpture, 121.9 × 60.3 × 36.8 cm. Collection Museum London, London, Ontario. Photo: Museum London.

power—irrelevant and imperceptible. This *Waiting Room*, it is clear, exists at the end of history, beyond anticipation, beyond form itself.

In seeking to occupy a stance which makes no distinction between nature and culture, a stance of ever-interested, ever-disinterested observer, Snow in effect stalls any discussion about the nature of Nature. He is left with almost nothing to discuss. As he stated so eloquently in his 1969 film <---> *[Back and Forth]*, nature is only phenomena in flux, and culture is simply what we see on the screen. What Snow therefore sees in *Waiting Room* is what "one thing after another" looks like when it approaches the speed of light: a kaleidoscope of the Real which finally, like all kaleidoscopes, takes on a predictable sameness, an eternal difference which formulates its own essentially unified character. Beside Snow, Piero della Francesca's theology seems quaintly human.

While Snow superficially shares Favro's commitment to the notion of unencumbered invention, it is obvious that Favro's notion of constructive principles has no place in Snow's reductive position. *Waiting Room* has a specialized beauty, a peculiarly distant Purity that sets Snow apart from Murray Favro, and apart from the other works we have been discussing. For this reason, *Waiting Room* marks a polarity which allows us to consider and evaluate for ourselves the intellectual climate of our time, and the issues we must address. In its simplest expression, those polarities could be called on the one hand Grace, and on the other hand Purity. Perhaps we can say that it is in the subtle divergence of those appeals that we can witness the immense divisions we act out within the reconstructions of our "essential" nature.

Postscript

It might be useful to organize the statements represented within these eight works as a general concept of contemporary culture. But that is not my intention here. My choice of these works was determined not by an attempt to abbreviate cultural history, but by the clarity of purpose each work held. My text has been an elaboration of that clarity.

I do want to close, however, with two points. The first is that my choice spans three generations of artists, and our realization that each one contributes to a common debate that constructs a sense of historical meaning and continuity essential to a strong society. The second point is that this exhibition is founded on contingencies of space, opportunity, and purpose which render it paradigmatic, and not at all exclusive. There are many articulate artworks. Here are eight I respect.

Author's Note: Since only two works discussed in the essay are illustrated here, it seems important to include information on all of them. What follows is the original descriptive information for each of the eight works:

Ewen, Paterson. *Rocks Moving in the Current of a Stream*, 1971. Metal, engraved linoleum, plywood, 153.3 × 245.3 cm.

Favro, Murray. *Still Life (The Table)*, 1970. 35 mm slide, projector, projector stand, canvas-covered wood objects, wood table. 74.9 × 51.3 × 91.4 cm.

General Idea. *Snobird: A Public Sculpture for the Miss General Idea Pavilion 1984*, 1985. Cut-outs from 27 3.81 plastic bottles, suspended from the ceiling, 915 × 366 × 615 cm.

Hoogstraten, Janis. *Brook Trout*, 1985. Mixed media on canvas and paper on plywood, 244 × 244 cm.

Schelle, Susan. *A Home Movie*, 1984. Linoleum, wood, steel, carpet, projector, projected text and image, 9-slide sequence, 244 × 210 × 454 cm.

Van Halm, Renée. *Anticipating the Eventual Emergence of Form, Part 1 and 2*, 1983. Acrylic on plywood, plaster, and cloth, 244 × 305 × 61 cm.

Noguchi, Louise. *Three Dreams of Blood*, 1981/82. Fiberglass, urethane foam, plaster, clay, bondfast glue, animal blood, and linseed oil, 100 × 214 × 214 cm.

Snow, Michael. *Waiting Room*, 1979. Framed colour photograph, cardboard, plywood base, photo 137 × 124.5, sculpture 121.9 × 60.3 × 36.8 cm.

Women's Work (1987)

Published as "Women's Work," *Vanguard* (December 1987/January 1988). The exhibition under review was presented at Gallery 76, Toronto, September 15 to October 3, 1987.

Gallery 76 is housed in a pair of decrepit Victorian houses, 74 and 76 McCaul Street, built in a style typical of nineteenth-century Toronto's lower middle class. The last of its era on the street, it stands awkwardly counting the days. Some years ago it was semi-converted, almost accidentally, by the Ontario College of Art, into an ambiguous set of small spaces which make the artist-run centres down on Queen Street look, by comparison, like privileged modernist palaces. These conditions construct a sense of gritty intimacy that sometimes works to give artworks an urgency missing in more imperial environments. It works especially for this exhibition, *Women's Work* (co-sponsored by the Women's Art Resource Centre, Gallery 76, and YYZ) and for these six artworks by four artists whose concerns, as women, are focused on those very forces that construct the home—this former home—as the pre-eminent site appropriate to woman's place in the natural order. It seems, in other words, only fitting that this "appropriate site" be appropriated to investigate that ages-old assumption.

Now, the setting of this stage is not merely my speculation; it is established for us immediately on entering the house. The entrance hall is repainted a soft earth yellow with a rust-coloured stencil design found on the walls of the old basement. The intention is clear: we are in a house, a house with a history, a history of women, real women. It is also clear that we are not to bring to this exhibition our normal viewing of things as simply visual and discrete; indeed, the structure of this gallery as a house makes such viewing an effort. Much more readily, we find ourselves "visiting." These works fill their various rooms like friends gathered "of an evening" to talk and enter into those exchanges that go beyond talk itself. And what are these different exchanges, these discussions? Let's start with Carol Laing, the eldest.

In Extreme Circumstances takes the south parlour as its entire ground, introducing onto the white walls the original stencil design we found in the hallway. Against this reminder of women's traditional working space and the limits of their ability to represent, Laing has placed spoors of a very different world, the world "out there," the world of "great art." On the left wall, reproductions of small drawings by de Chirico—a foot here, a hand there, and index finger—construct the "hand of the Master." The wall carries, as well, its own admonition in a meticulously stenciled text: "He said, 'At all times you must be the master and do what pleases you.'" On the right wall, a colour photograph of a painting with several female nudes by the same artist is pinned to the wall; beside it is an enlargement from a book illustrating some classical statues of Woman as idealized form. Over the surface of the photographed painting is handwritten: "She said, 'I was a mere glove crumpled in the fist of a great artist.'" This wall carries also its own text: "She said, "My labor made it possible, but I am not its recipient.'" The two stenciled texts gaze at each other in sullen opposition. This parlour discussion gone wrong, this open war between two worlds gapes at us—intruders on a family quarrel at that sudden point when the disguises, the assumptions, the desperate attempts to "get along" give way to reveal, numbing in their clarity, the chasms and the hard resolves that characterize the reality we fear.

We have been standing with our back to Vera Lemecha. She catches us at another moment, one perhaps "later" than Laing's, a moment when that feared reality has been once again internalized, set aside enough to continue with our lives. But it is a reality that cannot be forgotten; there is left a heightened nervous anticipation, a contained excitement, a latent *jouissance*. *J'ouis Sens* is set in the south dining room and kitchen. In the dining room, wrapped around us in this small, square space, hang eight teasingly ambiguous texts whose history catches us between hints of the Delphic Oracle's double entendres and Barbara Kruger's deconstructivist posters. Like their antecedents, these words speak to the great questions of desire and destiny which haunt the intertwined fates of men and women. And they speak with privilege—sometimes of woman's self-knowledge, sometimes as woman's chronicler: "I PERFORM your silence beyond warmth we tumble"; "she licked his PROMISES, dipping her tongue in the absence of faith." These texts are small, uniform, set *sans serif* behind glass over which a black nylon netting is stretched to subtly retire the statements from the arena of public discourse into a private world of pathos.

These are whispers, sighs, even laments, and they are the silent voice for a series of eight colour photographs placed in a line across the kitchen wall directly facing us as we enter from the dining room. These photographs are not readable in the normal sense—their imagery, while apparently of "real objects," is so detailed that nameable reality has been traded for "felt" reality, a reality of things touched and not seen. And periodically, if you linger in these rooms, against these ambiguities, against their pathos, a women's clear soprano voice suddenly fills the space with a nameless aria, a song of strength and haunting beauty, that "Beauty" which so profoundly has been woman's consolation, and her imprisonment.

Back across the entrance hallway with its narrow staircases to the upper floors, Susan Kealey can be found in the north dining room and kitchen. *Is There Any Queen at All in It?* takes up the dining room. Seven roughly framed texts—like pages torn from a legal casebook—document the divorce settlement of Rosa Becker, whose decade-long, and ultimately successful, fight to secure some fair return for contribution to her husband's business resulted in legal precedent, and personal tragedy. Finally unable to collect the full amount of her award, and forced to turn over the rest in payment to her lawyer, she committed suicide. Her note, with its final bitter words to her husband, forms a subtext, a desperate codicil, across the arguments of the seven legal texts that plead their rationalism from the walls of the dining room. And, in the centre of this room, in the place formerly occupied by the table, the dining room table—that symbol of the patriarchal family—stands a beehive, ironic reminder of female power and female burden. Kealey's hive is also an embodiment of an image central to three poems placed below the seven texts. It is consistent with this work, and with this exhibition, that these poems have no acknowledged author. For women who, like these artists, have been troubled by and curious about their own history, no acknowledgement is necessary; they know the name of Sylvia Plath, whose own suicide was both warning and rallying point for a generation. So the hive stands there, in this old dining room, at the junction of two suicides, suicides over a power that is written in such simple things as dining room tables.

Surveillance, Kealy's other work, turns the north kitchen into a dark Victorian cupboard, the secret hiding place where children learned to find a world beyond parental authority. In this room we are once again those children, scared but free. Around us we hear a curious sound, like wind finding the minute cracks in the wall; and facing us, against an oddly uneven wall, we read, projected, one of those phrases out of Lewis Carroll: "to be is to be perceived." As our eyes adjust, we see that the unevenness in the wall is in fact a door set against it, a screen for this projection. And as we stand there, we begin to make out the smudged form of a person (a woman?) on this door, illuminated by this text. We realize we are cast as unwitting voyeurs, validators, engaged—as the work's title suggests—in surveillance, acting out against this simulacrum our permission to exist.

Lisa Naftolin has taken the north parlour for the work *Untitled (R. Budd Dwyer)*. Her text is a line of etiquette from Emily Post that begins: "Try to do and say only that which will be agreeable to others." Across this classic admonition to dissemble, to "behave," six Plexiglas panels hinge out from the wall on which the text is written, each panel imprinted with a successively enlarged image of a man in a suit holding his hand up in an instinctive act of protection. R. Budd Dwyer was the official found guilty of fraud who called a news conference to proclaim his innocence, and blew his head off in front of the assembled press. The obvious levels of irony operating in the inscriptions of proper behaviour, their validations, and invalidities across the conflicting boundaries of male and female authority, are left like an understatement, an innuendo, a misbehaviour, to cloud the politeness of this parlour.

Naftolin's second work, *Untitled (Diderot)*, sits quietly in the hallway bedside the front doors, against the earthy yellow wall and its stencils. It's a small work, apparently pages removed from Diderot's pictorial encyclopedia and framed behind glass. Two occupations are depicted—glass blowing, a male job, and spinning, a female job. The panels sit on the wall, pleasantly undemanding in their quaint eighteenth-century enlightenment style, seemingly curiosities of history, particularly of the polite history of classification and indexing, the science of "a place for everything, everything in its place." They remind one of those nice middle-class homes with antique maps and colourized engravings. Only we notice that certain phrases of the descriptive texts have been snipped out, that odd repetitions and incoherences mar the descriptions. The confident index, the complacently scientific character of this guide to "how things work" is undermined, and reduced to the simple question: what is so male about glass-blowing? what is so female about spinning? why is this "how things work"?

It is impossible to approach an exhibition such as *Women's Work* without finding oneself within contradictions drawn by the very desires, suspicions, and expectations inherent within both the acceptance by curator Elizabeth MacKenzie of the assignment to "organize a group show to complement a conference on feminism," on the one hand, and the very existence of the conference that created the assignment on the other. Under such circumstances, I find it is usually best to be naïve. My naiveté produced a single thought, and I suppose a recent cover of the *Village Voice* most neatly summarize that thought in all its complexities in the single ironic question: "What do women artists want?" Perhaps where Freud thought he could deal with whole gender, we know now that we can deal only with expectations. What do *these* women artists want? As this exhibition makes clear, they want an end to masquerade, an end to grand illusions. What interested me about this work was that at 74/76 McCaul, four artists engaged in an *intimate* conversation about being women, about what stands behind the elaborate construction of Woman. All these works carry implicit in their various critiques a deep anger that women's historical role has been characterized by disguise, by enforced roles which have constructed them as speechless witnesses, as silent victims. In *Women's Work* we see four women revealing what lies behind those disguises and that masquerade. If those revelations seem familiar, if they seem vaguely disappointing in that familiarity, and if these artists make them not for a grand audience, but only for some other women, I—as a man—find them both powerful and touching for their unassuming insistences, for their awkwardnesses, for their angry honesty, for their contradictory unfairness; for all those things that constitute the presence of revelation and the privilege of conversation over the vast and splendid indifference of authorized assumption.

Al McWilliams (1987)

Published as "Al McWilliams, Cold City Gallery, Toronto," *C Magazine* 16 (Winter 1987/88).

Al McWilliams would prefer that his work claim its own "being-in-the-world," unconfined by words. But as McWilliams demonstrates here, words are hard to escape, and they can focus desire with exquisite economy. I want to employ some of that economy to clarify what it is that McWilliams seeks to represent in his work. I believe too that this can only be properly understood within a context that recognizes that McWilliams has received critical acclaim and national recognition for his work.

We need to note then, some recent remarks by Gary Dault, published in *Canadian Art*. Discussing the Power Plant's inaugural exhibition, Dault reveals the existence of a Canadian "mainstream avant-garde," a "nationally constructed A-list" of favoured artists, artists with "a certain look, a certain stance, a certain way of being an artist." Dault describes this look: a stalwart *sang-froid*, an introversion, a lack of edginess, a strange tentativeness of emotion—a look that is "hard, clean, ironic, metaphorical, slick with doubt about what is real and what isn't."

Dault's critique is refreshingly candid, if a tad gauche, in its identification of a contemporary national style. It would of course be almost too simple to challenge his oversimplifications and take issue with his disappointments. But Dault is not alone in fingering a set of conditions linking artists who, for no easily locatable reason, have become Canada's international representatives. The National Gallery's Diana Nemiroff, commenting as a reviewer in 1983 on the Stuttgart show, noted "a surprising communality of strategies—mirroring, doubling, projecting, the dislocation of normal appearances and their turning back into themselves," strategies that she suggested were attempts to reconstruct the subject. McWilliams was included in that exhibition, and in a review of his work for *Vanguard* in 1981, Russell Keziere talks in similar terms about "theatrical ambiguity" and "the artist's intention of making a work of art that is either straightforwardly equivocal or equivocally straightforward."

Dault, it would seem, has simply collated the main adjectives, and expressed an unease about a "dominant history." It is important for us all to examine that history and Al McWilliams provides a focus by which to represent it.

All four of the works included in this exhibition were candidates for Dault's checklist. I think it is sufficient to describe two of them and illustrate a third. *Portrait* consists of two large, unframed, vertical drawings placed slightly apart and capped at the top by a colour enlargement of an adolescent's legs taken from behind, standing and spread to form an inverted "V" equivalent to that constructed formally between the drawings and photographs themselves. Only the legs are shown, the crotch and feet cropped by the edge of the photograph. Formal in composition, and ambiguous in gender, these legs are referenced further by the subject of the drawings—a simplified rendering of a generic upright chair clearly derived from mechanical and architectural aesthetics. The scale and the simplified masses of this chair, and of this piece, echo precisely the child's clean form, and imply an ambivalent correspondence between the usefulness of the chair, and the usability of the figure's body. It is a highly intellectualized work, disguising—or is it revealing?—a highly eroticized intellect.

Untitled (with beeswax, copper, and gas-jet flame) constructs a large, rectangular, painterly frame of reference. The ground is divided to construct a square on the right hand side, which is entirely and evenly coated with coloured beeswax. The vertical strip on the left side of the rectangle, not included by the beeswax square, is covered with a sheet of burnished copper in which are set two small, flaming gas jets. Within the square, there is sketched in a darker wax the cartoon-like outline of a male head wearing a fedora and leering knowingly at the two small jets of flame that penetrate the copper surface. The leering face instantly and "unequivocally" establishes the focus for this work, its eyes sliding sideways to rest on the dancing flames against the copper skin. But if the focus is the flame, the subject established is the face itself, the face of the artist as voyeur, imprisoned, like an unwary insect, in the seduction of his own making. The odd markings on the surface of the steel plate [in *and the man…*] are language—Braille, the language of the blind. Its text reads: "and the man liked the woman." The Braille script is formed with small jade balls penetrating the plate. The image of the woman, photographed in colour, is by Piero di Cosimo, around 1500. Nameless, she is only the subject of a painting. The work is constructed of ironic misalliances between the "man" and this woman. The woman's identity and beliefs are lost in history, while the man remains merely a vague reference in a contemporary text; the text is in Braille, a modern language that this woman could never have known; the woman is an image, and Braille is for those who cannot image. The steel plate, with its "words," separates itself metaphorically from the paper of the photograph. Across this complex gap there lies a barely contained desire, an introverted pornography instituted in the unwitting invitation of the woman's naked breasts, and a man's fumbling fingers on the hard, round surfaces of words becomes physical. The "confined" passion of this contradictory equation is exacerbated in the curious monotone of the text itself. "And the man liked the woman" is so impersonally neutral in its statement, so infuriatingly unsatisfying, that we are forced to disbelieve its neutrality, to read it as a poor disguise, as—indeed—an intentionally transparent act of dissembling.

I believe it is exactly this "intentionally transparent dissembling" that aggravates Dault and constitutes the project behind what he and others have described as the "look," or perhaps we could even say "the gaze," character-istic to a generation of intelligent artists, male and female, in this country. What has been dissembled is not necessarily the specifically sexual passion evident in Al McWilliams non-verbal confinements; what I think is being thinly, ironically, disguised—because disguise has been seen by these artists as the principal means by which to "reveal"—is our physical condition in the world, our productions, our dissolutions, our structures—the means by which we have defined meaning. It has been said that the artists of the '70s, the artists of the artist-run spaces, of "sociological investigations," of "feminist critique," were uninterested in surface and form, uninterested in artworks as vehicles for passion. I believe this is a massive misreading, and I think the complications in Al McWilliams's work represent a gen-eration caught between "passion and reason," caught within an awkward, far-flung frontier culture unable to define itself, and defined consequently by crushing indifference and hostility. No wonder there's dissembling and tentativeness. If that condition became the touchstone of a disaffected generation, if it became a "mainstream avant-garde," if it appeared in certain respects problematic, surely that is only to bear witness to the contradictory and always problematic needs of an era, and the power of an idea. And what evidence is there that the needs expressed in Al McWilliams's work, our needs, have disappeared?

Ransom Notes in the Mirror: Mark Gomes and the Amazing Fish (1992)

Published as "Ransom Notes in the Mirror: Mark Gomes and the Amazing Fish," *C Magazine* 34 (Summer 1992).

1   The shorter statement is from a telephone conversation with the artist; the longer was written for the Canada Council Art Bank.

2   Paul Feyerabend, "Against Method: Outline of an Anarchistic Theory of Knowledge," quoted in John D. Caputo, *Radical Hermeneutics* (Indianapolis: Indianapolis University Press, 1987), 212.

3   Caputo, 212. Although Caputo uses *dilige* in the sense of "love" (as in love of learning or "diligence"), I believe "commitment" is as appropriate a term to employ; it is in this sense that I have translated *dilige* as "be serious."

The use of image and of humour is a way of understanding or being more comfortable with what we don't know, with what we need to know.
—Mark Gomes, April 1992

I am making work that draws from and appropriates images of "homely speech." To these I apply the strategies of reconstruction and representation normally associated with the symbolic and the monumental. In this process, I ask questions of the "normal" cultural mediations that determine ownership and empower an object and text with authority. With this mixed breed, a kind of re-inventing having taken place, metaphoric possibilities allow for a different contextual perspective.
—Mark Gomes, February 1992[1]

A Dadaist is convinced that a worthwhile life will arise only when we start taking things lightly and when we remove from our speech the profound but already putrid meanings it has accumulated over the centuries ("search for truth"; "defense of justice"; "passionate concern"; etc., etc.). A Dadaist is prepared to initiate joyful experiments even in those domains where change and experimentation seem to be out of the question (example: the basic functions of language).
—Paul Feyerabend[2]

Dilige, et quod vis fac.
—Saint Augustine

Saint Augustine's dictum could be rendered: "As long as you're serious, anything goes."[3] The trick, as Feyerabend reminds us, is to know how to judge if you are serious. This is not an idle question. Whether cast as an anxious moment (if not a crisis) in the culture of critical modernity or as the triumph of modernity's mirrored nemesis, *post*modernity, the question cannot be answered by an appeal either to categorical imperatives or to end-less playfulness. The ethics of engagement have been destabilized and, like a Lenin without a programme, we are left asking not "What is to be done?" but rather "How can I be serious?"

I want to consider here what a basis for being serious might be and in particular how a number of works by Mark Gomes over the last several years have posed that question. Gomes tells us he is concerned with the "incoherence" of normal experience. His interest lies in returning us, as those who possess and are possessed by homely speech, to an accommodation with the way this speech defines the borderlines between knowledge and un-knowledge, between authority and its lack. His determination is that the different perspective resulting from this accommodation will, in an important sense, resolve the dilemma of knowing the unknowable. At the end, we may enter into a kind of serenity, as Ihor Holubizky has suggested[4]—although perhaps a state of grace, in Graham Greene's sense of dialectical acceptance, would also be accurate. Within this state, we may then determine (as we will be determined by) "what is to be done." I am going to approach both the work and the statement somewhat obliquely through a story and an allegorical development of that story, employing certain contemporary theories concerning the nature of our experience in the world. By this I do not mean that the works addressed in this article can be subsumed under either theory or a story; on the contrary, they confirm our own disequilibrium through their ability to impose on us a rehearsal of how we are determined within our own engagements: it is their exemplary condition—their existence as models—that credits for us the theories of engagement with which they seem to be aligned. It is because I am talking of models—of tangibility—that I would like to start with Borges—and for this I am indebted to Julian Pefanis.[5]

Jorge Luis Borges: A Story

In those days the world of mirrors and the world of men were not, as they are now, cut off from each other. They were besides, quite different; neither beings nor colours nor shapes were the same. Both kingdoms, the specular and the human, lived in harmony; you could come and go through mirrors. One night the mirror people invaded the earth. Their power was great, but at the end of bloody warfare the magic arts of the Yellow Emperor prevailed. He repulsed the invaders, imprisoned them in their mirrors, and forced on them the task of repeating, as though in a kind of dream, all the actions of men. He stripped them of their power and their forms and reduced them to mere slavish reflections. Nonetheless, a day will come when the magic spell will be shaken off.

4   Ihor Holubizky, essay published in the pamphlet for the exhibition *Literati* in the Toronto Sculpture Garden (July 14 to September 30, 1988).

5   Jorge Luis Borges, "The Fauna of Mirrors," quoted by Julian Pefanis in "Revenge of the Mirror People," in *Heterology and the Postmodern: Bataille, Baudrillard, and Lyotard* (Durham, NC: Duke University Press, 1990), 103–19. I am indebted to this work for unlocking the perspective I bring to Mark Gomes in this article, however, I have used Pefanis's material only in a partial sense.

6   Borges, quoted in Pefanis,
103–104.

7   The ensuing paragraphs
in one way or another restate
Pefanis, 103–19.

8   Terry Eagleton, *Literary
Theory: An Introduction*
(London: Blackwell, 1983),
185–87. The German *fort/da* can
be translated as "lost/found";
the reference is to Freud's use
of his infant grandson's game of
throwing a toy tied to a string
out of his pram, crying "fort,"
and pulling it back with a
gleeful murmur "da." With this
incident, Freud illustrated his
principle of psychic loss and
recovery.

> The first to awaken will be the fish. Deep in the mirror we will perceive a very
> faint line and the colour of this line will be like no other colour. Later on, other
> shapes will begin to stir. Little by little they will not imitate us. They will break
> through the barrier of glass or metal and this time they will not be defeated…
> In Yunnan they do not speak of the Fish but of the Tiger of the Mirror.
> Others believe that in advance of the invasion we will hear from
> the depths of mirrors the clatter of weapons.
> —excerpts from "The Fauna of Mirrors"[6]

On Mirrors: An Allegorical Argument

There are two striking events in reading the Borges account of the relations between the world of mirrors and the world of men. The first is to be informed calmly and without warning that, despite their history of easy passage from one world to the other, "One night the mirror people invaded the earth." Why? The other event is to realize, almost as an afterthought a few lines down, that we, as readers, have assimilated this with equanimity as natural, as how things are done. The Emperor is within his rights, we might say, whatever we may feel about, indeed despite what we may feel about those rights. Why?

The question of the allegorical invasion seems contained in our reaction and may go something like this: the time before the invasion is that time of original harmony before identity becomes an issue of difference.[7] The sudden inexplicable decision of the mirror people to invade "the world of men" marks the point at which identity in unity is already in collapse: the point at which the Yellow Emperor has perfected his magic arts sufficiently to ultimately frustrate and defeat the attempted invasion—an invasion surely undertaken, though too late, to prevent the deployment of those arts. The cause of the mirror peoples' anxiety about that magic is confirmed by the fate to which they are consigned: to become "mere slavish reflections." The true aggressor is the Yellow Emperor, not the mirror people and we, accepting automatically the triumph of the Emperor as right and proper, are guilty of complicity with irresistible power.

Again, why? When we comply, we yield to power. Compliance is therefore a form of defeat, however covert or considered or, indeed, indispensable. As such, it is the second agent in the defined opposition Victory/ Defeat (or in Freud's famous example, the *fort/da* game),[8] which exists by virtue of its recognition of indeterminacy or instability: if one of the agents in this opposition were always in defeat, always *absent* and the other always in authority, always *present*, there would be no opposition, indeed no significant relations of any kind; there would simply be two mutually exclusive realms—two arenas of mutual un-knowledge. Authority, then, is inherently indeterminate: like compliance, it is a fleeting condition arising from an inevitable, perpetual and inherent combat inscribed into the fabric of relations. In the mirror, we can anticipate revenge. Let's look at mirrors.

There are three distinct stages in the development of our ability to know ourselves and to construct meaning.[9] In the initial stage, we experience only amorphous fragmentation, a flux of unrelated sense impressions. This dream is suddenly and dramatically focused into relatedness, into coherence, when we see ourselves in the mirror—whether literally or through connecting the image of our own body with that of someone else's. What is established in this Mirror Phase is a powerful identification between ourselves and others: the self is imagined as identical to all other identities but most particularly the identity of the Mother. In this, the stage of the Imaginary, there is a bliss of unity: you could say we experience each other; you could say we are able to pass through the mirror.

The final stage, however, sees destruction of this harmony. The mediator this time is not the mirror but the social order in the figure of the Father and we enter now into the Symbolic Order. We are confronted with and confounded by both social and sexual difference and our alienation, our instinctive attempt to eliminate this threat of difference causes us, like the mirror people in the allegory, to invade the Law, to attack the Yellow Emperor.

But we know the story now: the Symbolic Order constituted in the Law of Difference employs the magic art of language, including homely speech, to mark the forbidden line between us. We become in consciousness "that which we are not," according to Lacan.[10] Held in the mirror and forced into mere reflections of the Law's image, we become split between what we are and what we are not and our desire to become again what we no longer are— the mirror people before defeat and inscription into the Law—is repressed and remains suspended in a state of unconsciousness, constant and unrealizable, waiting for the Emperor's magic arts to falter, waiting for the revenge that will forever shatter the conformity—the slavish reflection—imposed on us by the universal controlling law of the Symbolic Order.

Consequently, while in our conscious condition we reflect the Law, obey the dictates and "slavishly" support the Yellow Emperor, we wait behind the mirror for the destruction of that which we have become.

We wait for our own death.

On Language

In the thrall of the Yellow Emperor, we are in the thrall of language, and language, Lacan has suggested, is "what hollows out being into desire." It is the agency through which we are forced to give up all claim to the imaginary

9   I am restating Eagleton, 164–70, but see also Toril Moi, *Sexual/Textual Politics: Feminist Literary Theory* (London: Methuen, 1985), 99–101, which I have also used in attempting to clarify these processes.

10   Moi, 99.

11 See Eagleton, 128–30. I have, of course, greatly simplified Eagleton's restatement of Derrida's ideas.

12 Eagleton, 128.

realm of undifferentiated identity. We are split forever and from this point on we are bound to a chimera—the chimera of the Emperor's magic arts—as we lust for a forgotten bond in which identity is not bound but coincident.

What is the nature of this chimera? In a word, erasure.[11] Language reconstructs meaning as difference: terms (signifiers such as mother, father, good, bad, etc.) define each other through their difference from one another. But they must do so within a funhouse of alternative differences and any definition arising from their interrelationships must be transitory, always in the process of being overwritten by another. In the end, there is no fixed meaning just as there is no fixed end to meaning: there is only a "constant flickering of presence and absence together,"[12] as terms erase one another in a continual deferral of absolute meaning. No term is ever fully present in itself, never stable: in language we are always already absent. In the Emperor's thrall, we can only mimic.

"A kind of re-inventing having taken place, metaphoric possibilities allow for a different contextual perspective." It is surely one of the marks of language that its politeness betrays the hand of the Emperor. The perspective Mark Gomes would show us is not so polite: it is the dilemma of our enforced enslavement, of our rage that *what we need to know* is trapped within the mirror. How can we act when we dare not speak: when speech itself is at the very heart of the apparatus that imprisons us, makes us mere reflections acting out a comic-book existence?

> *A Dadaist is prepared to initiate joyful experiments even in those domains where change and experimentation seem to be out of the question (example: the basic functions of language).*

In Borges's story, "The first to awaken will be the fish." I'll begin with a particular fish.

Common of Piscary (1984/85)

An elegant space is opened up for us, defined by a table standing on a dais constructed of the same parquet design as the floor of the gallery on which it sits, integral to it. On this table lies a heavy roll of carpet, its red pile rolled in, its black canvas underside exposed. Most remarkably, balanced on this roll, an expansive trajectory constructed of steel tubing is described in space like that of a falling star. Facing this unlikely interior, resting on a second table—this one black and somewhat squat—rests a huge headless "fish," its body of the same rolled carpet as on the dais but in a curved and sinuous spiral tapering to a very fishy tail. Finally, between these two encounters, like a semi-colon, is placed a sensual squiggle of black carved wood,

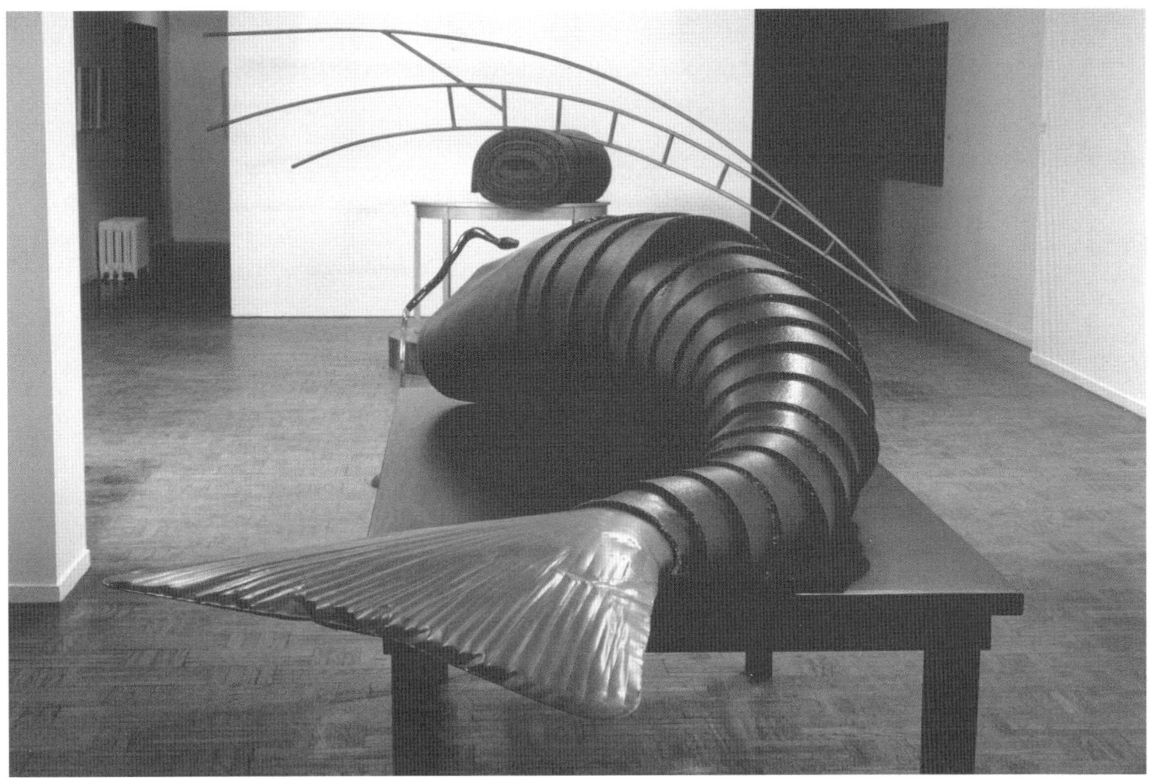

2.9   Mark Gomes, *Common of Piscary*, 1984–85. Mixed media, 1.8 × 4.8 × 10.5 m. Courtesy the artist. Photo: Michael Mitchell.

a sort of cross between a standing microphone and a snake: the figure of
the "trickster?"

> *The moment is one of precognition: an interior that mocks its designated space, a*
> *falling star, a fish that is no fish, a squiggle of a line that marks a line like no other:*
> *"Later on, other shapes will begin to stir. Little by little they will not imitate us."*

The Cynic and the Saint (1986/87)

Against a plain, arched panelling of red mahogany stands a rectangular red
mahogany table, puritanical in its simplicity, chameleon-like in its assumption of the panelling's colour and grain. Suspended over the table, floating
in front of the panelled wall, looms a bloated, white, balloon-like shape: part
trophy, part portrait, part animal—part human in its atavism. To one side,

on the right, we read on the wall an inscription, in effect a memorial: "The Cynic and the Saint—few could stand the strain of relaxing with them."

> *Like the Cynic and like the Saint, we wait for our own death; a death-watch in which our recognition of the absurd repetitions imposed on us by conformity with the Law is empowered by a sense of the shape that is like no other shape, by the stillness of a room that masks the mirror. "They will break through the barrier... and this time they will not be defeated."*

Perfect World (1989/90)

A great container made of grey-black coils stands half in, half on the wall in front of us. Below, a coloured silhouette of hands linked in a chain of interlocking closure like a child's paper cut-out forms an image across the wall that is half sentence-like, half like the surface of a sea. Anchoring these, rendered in low-relief and forming with the bowl and the sea an equation of great symmetrical beauty, hang the two words: *perfect world*, split apart so that they are not so much a coherent phrase as single word-signs floating above and below in harmonic balance with the images they now resemble. Enclosing this equation and also in relief, white brackets register a removal, a suspension of this state.

> *"Both kingdoms, the specular and the human, lived in harmony; you could come and go through mirrors." There is a familiarity about this equation, a connectedness that seems oddly mesmerizing; perhaps a glimpse from the corners of our eyes into that time before "the mirror people invaded the earth" and lost to the Yellow Emperor. A flashback into the realm of the Imaginary when the world could be depicted resting on the back of a giant turtle swimming in an infinite sea. A time in which there was no time, when all was centred, contained, linked together; a time now set aside, bracketed by language, by time itself, by difference.*

In/Out (1992)

A large dun-brown envelope, the padded kind used for sending documents or books, hangs suspended over a wire basket, the kind used for in/out trays on desks. But here, both basket and envelope are vastly out of scale. Monumental in size, the basket rests not on a desk but just slightly off the floor; equally huge, the envelope hovers above, neither in nor out, frozen in time. Eerily, we ourselves seem diminished, suddenly infantile, re-inscribed into a time when the world was a foreign country, a place in which our fears and fantasies held no value, a time when we found ourselves locked in deadly embrace with forces that, little by little, imposed on us who they determined we should be—forced on us "the task of repeating, as though in a kind of dream, all the actions of men."

"In those days the world of mirrors and the world of men were not, as they are now, cut off from each other." As we stand transported in front of, but also deliciously within this ironic interplay of the world of adult business with the world of children, we play again that fort/da game played by Freud's infant grandson: the envelope, neither in nor out of its basket, rehearses our terror of union betrayed and our joy at union regained; rehearses a history that took us from a time when "you could come and go through mirrors," through the long night of the magic spell, the Valley of Death, to that anticipated moment "when the magic spell will be shaken off" and the Yellow Emperor "will hear from the depths of mirrors the clatter of weapons." In our consciousness, Desire trembles in its insatiable determination.

Ransom Notes (1992)

In a corner of the room, ten or so cast-aluminum potatoes form a little pile against the wall; inconspicuous, almost unnoticeable. On closer inspection they are seen to be stamps, the sort that children make to stamp designs on paper. These, however, carry not designs but letters, the elements of language. We can read the letters but their message remains mysterious, undecidable.[13]

We try to make sense of them, but there is not enough: it is merely a fragment, premature or too late. It is impossible even to know from whom they come, to whom they are directed: we have forgotten so much, we have become what we have feared. "Others believe that in advance of the invasion we will hear from the depths of mirrors the clatter of weapons." Perhaps, instead, we will only find—from time to time, lurking in the corners of mirrors, mysterious and impenetrable—childlike ransom notes: a promise of reunion made mockery in language.

…et quod vis fac?

I am aware that in attempting to clarify the disinterments that Mark Gomes reveals—the fraught complicity that describes our forced engagement with the world—this too-brief article must paradoxically seem to fail

13   "Undecidable" in the sense that Derrida applies to language.

in its stated goal of re-establishing a use of Saint Augustine's permission to act. But the paradox, like all paradoxes, is only apparent: it is precisely in knowing that what we know is never precise and that what we can no longer be is also forever what we are that we can find a means of being serious that refuses to take itself seriously—as we examine at every step the implications and consequences of loss and re-establish in every moment the Grace by which to agree that "anything goes." Perhaps there lies immense wisdom in indecipherable ransom notes made by children.

A History of Manners: Susan Schelle's *taste* (1993)

Published in *Frame of Mind: Viewpoints on Photography in Contemporary Canadian Art*, ed. Daina Augaitis (Banff: Walter Phillips Gallery, 1993).

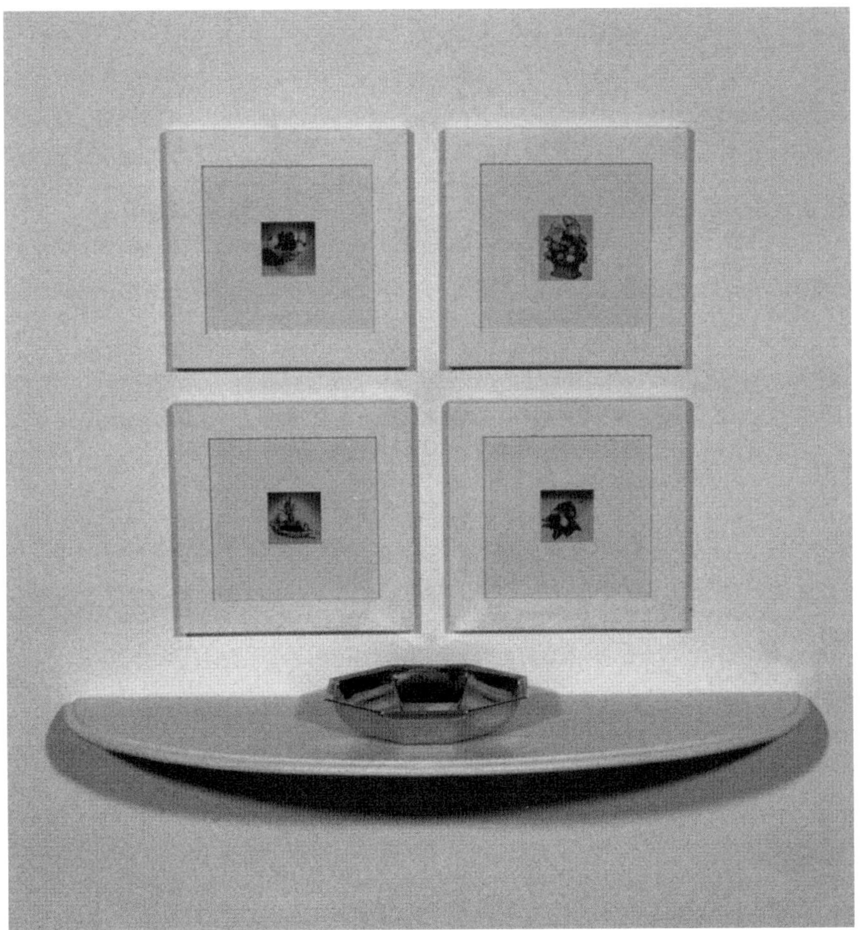

2.10   Susan Schelle, *taste*, 1988. 4 b&w silver prints, sterling silver bowl, painted shelf; prints, 36 × 36 cm each; shelf, 2.5 × 38 cm. Collection The Banff Centre, courtesy Walter Phillips Gallery, Banff. Photo: Monte Greenshields.

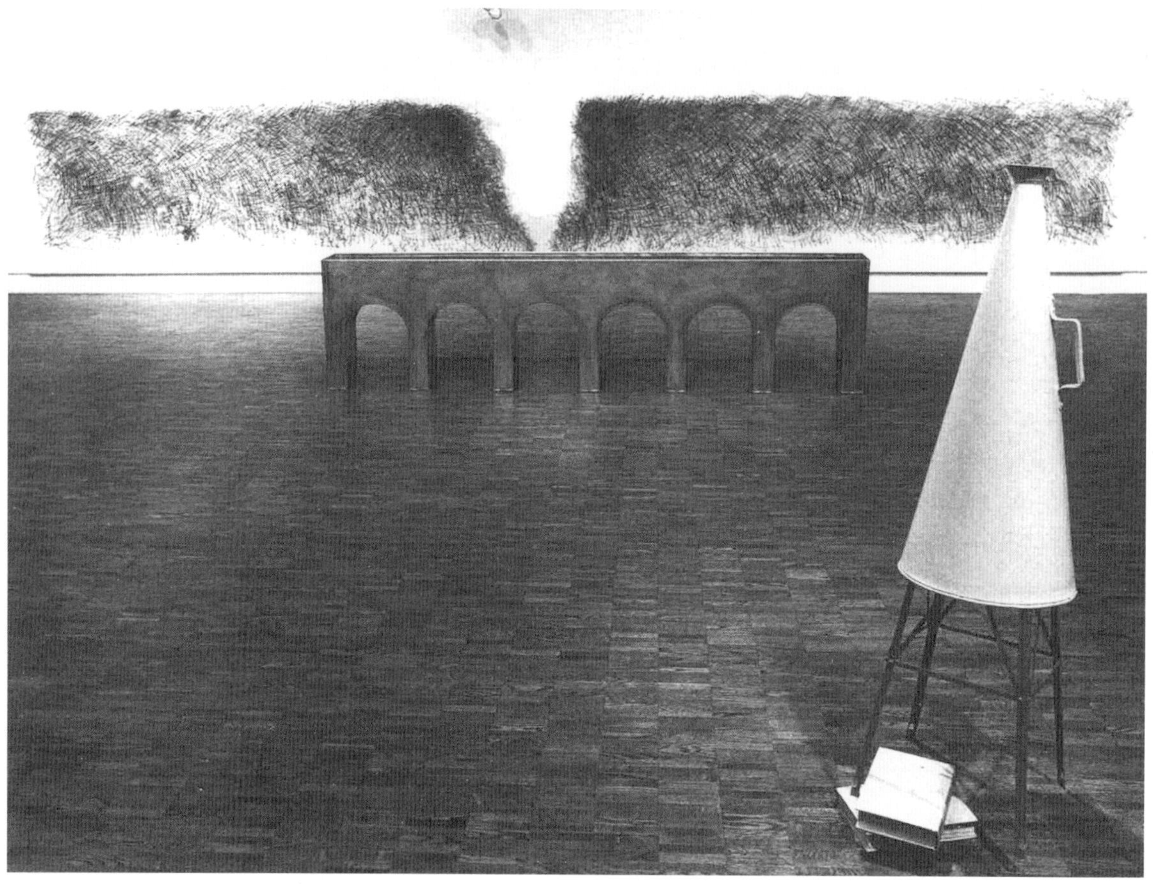

2.11   Susan Schelle, *Talking and Listening to the Man in the Moon*, 1983. Clay, plywood, graphite, paint, sheet metal, steel books, 7.32 × 3 m. Courtesy the artist.

> In patriarchal societies we cannot escape the implications of
> femininity. Everything we do signifies compliance or resistance
> to dominant norms of what it is to be a woman.
> —Chris Weedon[1]

> The effect is to highlight, or "highlight," and to subvert, or "subvert," and the
> mode is therefore a "knowing" and an ironic or even "ironic"—one.
> Postmodernism's distinctive character lies in this kind of wholesale
> "nudging" commitment to doubleness, or duplicity.
> —Linda Hutcheon[2]

> I am interested in the manipulation of the common. This often
> involves the use of imagery that deals with the phenomena of the
> physical world and the customs of a particular time or people.
> —Susan Schelle[3]

In 1983, Susan Schelle exhibited a work she titled *Talking and Listening to the Man in the Moon.* In reviewing that work, I criticized her for taking an isolationist position which I felt evaded the necessity to take issue. I now think that we were both right: it is necessary to take issue; and Susan Schelle *did.* What I failed to understand then was that in our culture "talking and listening to the Man in the Moon" is not a retreat so much as an apt description of the experience of women within male culture. How can one characterize the consequences of this condition if not as living in some kind of "midsummer night's dream," the source of Schelle's title? Very simply, her work described that condition.

It is useful to bear this digression in mind as an approach to Schelle's 1988 work, *taste.* The work is straightforward: four small photographs, square-framed in white with broad mats, are organized to form a larger square directly above an elegant semicircular white shelf with moulded edges. On this shelf is placed an octagonal silver bowl, shallow enough to be ambiguous in function, on whose interior surface is engraved the single word "taste." The photographs are clearly of illustrations from a magazine dating, perhaps, from the 1940s or 1950s; together they demonstrate fruit arrangement in four traditional and quite unambiguous styles of bowl—a cornucopia, a basket, a compote, and a boat. Everything is precise, attractive—polite, one might say. Even the rather unusual word inscribed on the silver bowl is easily explained as an amusing double entendre linking fruit and bowl. There appears to be no overt problem—no threat of unpleasantness. And yet...why is the word "taste" inscribed so meticulously on that bowl? *Why* are the photographs so small within their gigantic white mats? *Why* this inscrutable politeness?

1   Chris Weedon, *Feminist Practice and Poststructuralist Theory* (Oxford: Blackwell, 1988), 86–87.

2   Linda Hutcheon, *The Politics of Postmodernism* (London: Routledge, 1989), 1.

3   Susan Schelle, *Sans Demarcation* (Toronto: Visual Arts Ontario, 1987), 28.

It is this very sense of unease, of latent "duplicity," that Hutcheon
and others have located as a central agent in contemporary thought, and in
postmodern critiques of the subject. For both men and women—though for
polarized reasons—unease has a long history. As Weedon says, everything
a woman does, or has ever done, within patriarchal culture will inevitably
signify compliance or resistance, and at the root of male hostility towards
women and female culture there surely lies a nudging suspicion that compliance—or even complicity—remains circumstantial. I want to explore briefly
how Schelle's work describes a condition of duplicity centrally fatal to patriarchy itself, how it in fact *exacerbates* this condition in a way that perhaps the
earlier work did not, in order to demonstrate a critical disengagement; and
it seems useful to pivot this exploration on the title's own play of meaning,

Any "manipulation of the common" de-cloaks the investments of
authority—the common sense assumptions negotiated by generations
before us on our behalf. As such, it is a means of unravelling history. In *taste*,
Schelle addresses the history of manners and expectations which, while
binding on both men and women, have traditionally bound women most
fatally. This is a history of agreements whose fragility and self-
contradictions have been, for women, tantamount to a profound disguise.
It is worth noting this because the obvious double entendre in the title is a
mocking form of such disguise: we are not likely to be fooled by the reference to fruit; we know that the work is about style, even if we do not quite
know why. But the why is not so hard for those who know its effects: it is
the *form of the obligation itself*—the imposition of disguise—which is at issue.
In *taste*, the various containers—those in the photographs and, in a radically
different way, the silver bowl as well—carry a history of subjugation: the
subjugation of use to ornament, of women's work to "lady-like" behaviour
and of experience to language. It is important to examine just how the elements of the work function *against taste*.

The question of taste is pre-eminently a question of behaviour and
Schelle's choices explicitly link the question of behaviour to bourgeois culture. She is herself conscious of being a product of a certain privileged class
located in a certain privileged place: Ontario, white, Anglo-Saxon, middle
class. For this class, manners and obligations reflect the constrictions of a
patriarchal society in power; signs and codes do not slide too easily, and
ornaments, even inessential ones, are expected to keep their place. It is a
culture of extreme stability, of stasis; it is a culture in which uneasiness is
inescapable and one that Schelle can speak from with confidence.

But the linkage has more than personal significance: bourgeois
taste has legislated modern culture since the French Revolution. While
class-constructed, it is not class-bound: it operates for us as normative, as

common sense, and Schelle's work reads like a catalogue introduction to the culture of conformity as it confronts women. In one important respect, women do not fit within bourgeois values: for a system built on the ethic of work, on labour exchange (or labour exploitation), women's exclusion from work, their seclusion as ornament, places them outside the ethical system. Though women were excluded in important ways before the rise of middle-class culture, exclusion from work within a work ethic system amounts to exile. This marginalization finds historical expression in the greater importance given to art over craft such as embroidery and, within art, the long-standing privilege of history painting—the preserve of male artists—over so-called genre paintings of fruit, to which women artists were traditionally relegated and to which, despite shifts in theory, women in general are still. It is by no means incidental that Schelle has chosen fruit arrangements as emblems of exclusion, an exclusion further dramatized by the miniature scale of the photographs, their grainy, borrowed character, and by the vastness of their blank surrounding borders. Nor is it simply incidental that these arrangements are presented as impoverished versions of a distant original. Lacking aura, lacking the stamp of presence, they remain for us remote in time and place; they remain in an important sense *irrelevant*.

In stark contrast to this plane of dismissal, presence is inherent in the shelf and its ambiguous flat silver bowl. Sheer physical presence is significant enough, but in middle-class culture, with its dependency upon writing, on the whole apparatus of bureaucracy, there is, after all, something useful, even *natural,* about things on flat surfaces, just as there is something useless, even *unnatural,* about things that are hung. Positioned on the firm ground of a surface to which things cling, the bowl registers an authority which divides this work at the line between shelf and pictures, a line that signals a paradigm shift from the female exclusions on the wall to the confident assumptions of male power below. As I suggested earlier, the bowl's very ambiguity serves to position it in a radically different role from those in the photographs. Unlike the ornamental fruit bowls, with their specifically designed and gender-inflected function, the silver bowl lacks any single purpose: it is a designed *object*, independent of any natural purpose. It belongs, in fact, to an abstract order of representations whose sole metaphoric function is to signal control. In referencing, but not being, an ornamental use-object, in remaining both physically and formally independent, it acts like the linguistic sign engraved on its surface to mark both a distant association and a radical rupture with the world represented in the photographs. In substituting language—the word "taste"—for depiction, the bowl operates against the photographs of fruit as sign to its referent, though the photographs operate on their own as signs of exclusion. In displacing the photographs as signs, in effect emptying them of signification, the bowl unmistakably acts to privilege culture over nature, to flaunt male power and to signal female banishment.

taste would be an interesting work for its exacerbated portrait of simulated compliance alone. However, as I have mentioned, the title permits another reading of the shift line described above which allows a different, more active and transgressive view of the exclusions in operation. It is true, after all, that good taste bears a substantive relationship to "tastes good," even if it is a relationship denied by its cultural alter ego. Underlying the text, underlying its abstraction, its decorousness, there lurks its banished "other"—the *referent* that refuses to be merely an abstraction, which claims sensual gratification. There is, in fact, an ironic dimension to the sequestering of the word "taste" in its simple, geometrically correct silver bowl from the fruits in their complex, flowing containers locked away in "the world of women." It is an irony which, on the theoretical plane, has been described by Andreas Huyssen as a *complicity* tacitly acknowledged in bourgeois modernity's hierarchical privileging of high art over mass culture, a complicity complicated by a historical identification of mass culture with women, or more precisely the *threat of Woman as consuming Nature,* on the one hand, and of high culture with male rationality and *cultural control* on the other. In other words, despite its claims to exclusive authenticity, the male-inflected linguistic sign of *taste* acknowledges, as it fears, its banished life form, just as it acknowledges, and fears, the power it has consequently invested in women. With such a reading, this ironic *pas de deux* within the title becomes inevitably the central dialectic, or perhaps more aptly, the Derridean *erasure,* of Schelle's work.

In raising the problem of modernity's collusions with its own excluded partners, *taste* embraces a discussion central to contemporary art practices and theory. This discussion has notably been advanced through a realization that photographic practices in particular, including the history of film, are ideally located to offer the betrayals through which we can see what we have to say. The discussion consequently has a strong archaeological methodology and Schelle's work, with its precise and targeted investigation of pre-existing representations, offers us a perfect example of this determination that discovering meaning, like digging for gold, is less invention than close examination.

Angela Grauerholz: Fellow Traveller (1997)

Published as "Angela Grauerholz: Fellow Traveller," *Canadian Art* (Fall 1997).

> They are the images that we have from our memory
> of what the future used to look like.
> —Angela Grauerholz[1]

I'm standing, looking at a cluster of travellers boarding an airplane. The plane is not large, and there cannot be more than a dozen figures assembled on the wet tarmac. It's been raining, though it has stopped now, and despite the brightness in the sky's horizon, everything near is dark, smudged in the gloom of a rain-soaked pause. Within this ambiguity, a white line painted luminously on the surface of the runway intersects with me at the centre of my vision. My viewpoint seems picked out, as in a perspective study, and the scene before me, despite its indeterminacy, becomes an exercise in the appropriateness of things in the world.

I'm standing in the Olga Korper Gallery, looking at *Travellers* by Angela Grauerholz, and the indeterminate nature of the photograph is oddly replicated here. The sun at the moment is from the west, and its light passes through the clerestory onto the gallery walls and floor in ever-shifting intensities. A thin ray just touches one edge of the austere black frame, which gives this, and the other nine works in Grauerholz's exhibition, a sense of mourning reminiscent of the black borders on commemorative stamps[2] in my boyhood collection. I experience a sense of epiphany as I watch the sunlight's measurement of time deepen and intensify the image's own suspension of time. I think about Angela Grauerholz's remark about memory and future.

There is a point of view central to all these works, and *Travellers* is emblematic in this respect. Each occupies language in a double register. Let's call the first a declension, because it's about naming, or placing. As I occupy that view of the runway in the picture, it occurs to me I am privileged in several ways: by my apartness from the travellers, by the darkness which envelopes me, by the centrality mapped by the white line; by the black frame itself. There is a reiteration of separation; I had been *declined*. In precisely which grammatical case, however, remains obscure, and

1   Beth Seaton, "Angela Grauerholz: Mundane Re-membrance," *Parachute* 56 (October–November–December 1989), 23–25.

2   I think of those stamps issued in 1934 to mark the death of President Hindenburg, a moment that we now invest with the Faustian tragedy of a racial hubris set in motion. Like stamps, Grauerholz's photographs are unglazed. Their smooth matte surface offers itself to our desire to touch, to trace, and to feel. They seem more like treasured snapshots lifted from an album than the broad, open windows onto a vista that we would expect from their dimensions. And this point of viewing instantly returns to me: I am ten years old, looking through my parents' photo album, black and white on black, imagining myself in their place, in their time, a place and time which is to me, now, quite simply both appropriate and unforeseeable.

within that obscurity I am displaced, named a flâneur, a nomad, ironically a fellow traveller.

Let's call the second register a conjugation, because it's about acting, or timing. I have to think: what is it I'm doing on that runway? How is it that I'm there? And what does it signify that I am also *here*, in the gallery, watching the sunlight activate a photograph, watching it move gradually towards night? What tense do I occupy: past, present—future? Sometimes we need to listen to artists. When Angela Grauerholz speaks about her images as "what the future used to look like," I realize I can be in several tenses at once: I can be in the future anterior. And now I know my tense. I'm back in the future.

Moments in the Work of Margarita Andreu (2000)

Published in *Margarita Andreu*, exh. cat. (Girona: Fundacío Espais d'Art Contemporani en Girona, 2000).

What would I mean if I were to say that something happened a moment ago? Where would have been the event to which I refer?

What would it mean if I were to say I am free? Where could I be in my freedom?

I am sitting in her studio, speaking with Margarita Andreu. She has not posed these questions, but somehow they pose themselves as I listen, and find myself formulating a proposition that would embrace the body of Andreu's practice. That proposition could be simply expressed as taking the measure of the distance we experience, and the proximity we feel. And because, after all, Andreu is an artist, the field in which this proposition functions takes two quite tangible forms—the screen and the curtain. Tangible, but not necessarily evident, and I want to look at the evidence in order to explore the tangible.

Let us say I brush past you on the street. What does Andreu mean when she tells me that all her work could be contained in that simple moment of contact? And what does she mean when she says that to speak about space is illusory, that more precisely we can only speak within time, in stories rather than in space?

What I take her to mean is that I can only be in one place at one time—I can only be "here." I cannot get closer to spatial reality, since there is no concept of distance in space—space is defined by the contingency of shifting coordinates constructed in time. Curiously, I will always be apart from and not a part of space as it recedes into event, and consequently I can never be conscious within space itself. If I cannot "get closer," I can however tell different stories. Like Arthur Schnitzler's Lieutenant Gustl, you will tell a story about my brushing past you. The contact will remain a "time when," in which the space of that time is only a subject. Space will be subject to the stories you will tell, just as your stories will be subject to the rules of tense—the limits established by language.

I brush past you on the street, then. There are particular sensations attached to this act: feelings of transgression, the fluidity and resistance of bodies moving in space, the suspended quality of a momentary action neither anticipated nor subject to consequence. In short, it is an event whose significance rests on its construction of a reflexive moment. It is important to look at this question of reflexivity, and in particular its relationship to Andreu's tangible forms.

There is a central paradox concerning the nature of these forms that is deliciously apparent in the cinematic play acted out at the opening of every film screening. As the lush curtains slide away, signalling the origins of this experience in sexuality itself, the screen on which we are to watch the film is gradually and enticingly revealed to us as both a passive surface and a site of re-enactment. Indeed, because the film is projected even as the curtains part, we enjoy a thrill of passage as disguise gives way to, and colludes with, disclosure. The thrill is more than that of passage alone: what constitutes the separate identities of the curtain and the screen is thrown into doubt, and the conundrum involved in parting the certainties of identification from those of identity sets the stage for *our* collusion with the make-believe stories which, after all, we came to see. This same paradoxical position— curtain and screen as definitional collusions—occupies a similarly central role in Andreu's practice. Moreover, just as the sliding curtain is lightly touched by the intangibility of the projected film, Andreu's work depends as well on our recognition of two intangible elements implicit in both curtain and screen. These are the window and the mirror, and it is these subliminal elements which act to transport us, as in film, into the reflexive state Andreu calls "beyond reflection."

Curtains conceal. Yet in their concealing, they imply that which must be somehow concealed. In fact, in normal life we know exactly what they conceal: the window. And why? Because it is ourselves who need to be concealed—from the gaze of others, those beyond the window. So the curtain, in its logic, acts as mirror to our own image.

Screens may conceal, but they also reveal. Again, in normal life, we know the history of the screen as a decorative, even teasing division between subject and viewer, object of desire and unconsummated voyeur. The screen, too, acts like a mirror, returning us through our desire to our own "reflections." In contemporary life, of course, we know the screen as a site of projection, and here the screen becomes a window and ourselves, now, the consummated voyeur.

These, I believe, are some of the elements that constitute the ground— or perhaps it should rather be said, the narrative—that comprises Andreu's practice. A work from 1997 can serve as an example. In *Movement*, Andreu gives us the image of an office. The image is sensual, carrying that sense of intimacy associated with the stillness of shadows and filtered light. In the duration established through a series of four large-scale colour photographs, we notice in reading from left to right certain slight discrepancies: the light from the window changes, and the room becomes noticeably darker or lighter, more mysterious or less mysterious; spatial relations between objects in the room shift, suggesting our passage in time: a table's leg appears closer to a chair, a filing cabinet now hides the radiator. The entire framing of our view into the room itself is arranged differently too, as our positioning takes on an episodic fluidity. These shifts separate the experience of memory from the experience of space, prying apart our sense of engagement from our sense of order. Viscerally connected by virtue of their representation of a common place, each of the images establishes a different story, destabilizing the certainty of space through the instability of time.

Movement represents in photographic form Andreu's concern with passage and shift in her earlier site installations. In the 1996 work *Mirador* at Pamplona and Lleida, Andreu worked with these intangibles within the very tangible environment of large-scale architectural sculpture. In *Mirador,* a white curtain wall formed a proscenium entrance to the space, with three large windows—negative screens—piercing this curtain to provide visual and physical access to the space beyond. This other space faced a second curtain, now of glass, whose transparent screen prevented further access while offering a reflective surface—a mirror—to form an ambiguous barrier between "here" and the possibility of "there." In the catalogue, Annamaria Sandonà describes it this way:

> The white structure with three openings which obliges the visitor to cross it, passing through a darker area, is the obstacle, the dark initiatic path towards the light, within the work, towards a new obstacle, a magical one this time, the surface of the glass on which the reflection of your own image and the architecture can barely be seen. The alteration—caused by the work—of familiar and known space is a means by which a moment of sensorial hyperaesthesia is created, from emptiness into silence, from the confusion of life to the regressive and indistinct self, like the shadows of Plato's cave.[1]

I noted earlier that Andreu, in insisting on the primacy of narrative time over space, necessarily confronts us with the limits of language, and especially those imposed by tense. The questions I playfully suggested at the head of this text are cast in the subjunctive and conditional, and it is this acknowledgement of uncertainty with which Andreu works. Perhaps it is not even that these specific questions matter, but rather that it is their natural invitation to possibility that aligns them with Andreu's practice in my

1 Annamaria Sandona, "Margarita Andreu: Between Looking, Seeing, and Reflection," in *Margarita Andreu: Mirador* (Pamplona and Lleida: Ciudadela/El Roser, 1995), n.p.

mind. If language requires us to specify our place and time in the world, the conditional tense is our only permitted evasion.

Freedom, and our response to its terms, remains one of our oldest and most persistent stories, as Sandonà implies in her reference to Plato's cave. In *Lieutenant Gustl*, Schnitzler's parody of Viennese life, a young officer is consumed by agony and confusion as he debates within himself whether he must challenge the man who has brushed against him on the street, or alternatively to simply commit suicide. Andreu takes up that same event, not as parody, but as a kaleidoscope moment of situational improbabilities. For both, what happened a moment ago can only be a story we tell ourselves, and freedom is locatable only in doubt. In Andreu's words: "I thought I was free, when I was only being precise." In her work, Andreu's precision parts a curtain, revealing the hesitant stories which constitute the projections of our freedom—as we brush against one another for a moment in passing.

Staging Painting in the Work of Ulrike Nattermüller (2000)

Published in *Ulrike Nattermüller: Prospekt*, exh. cat. (Köln: Salon Verlag, 2000).

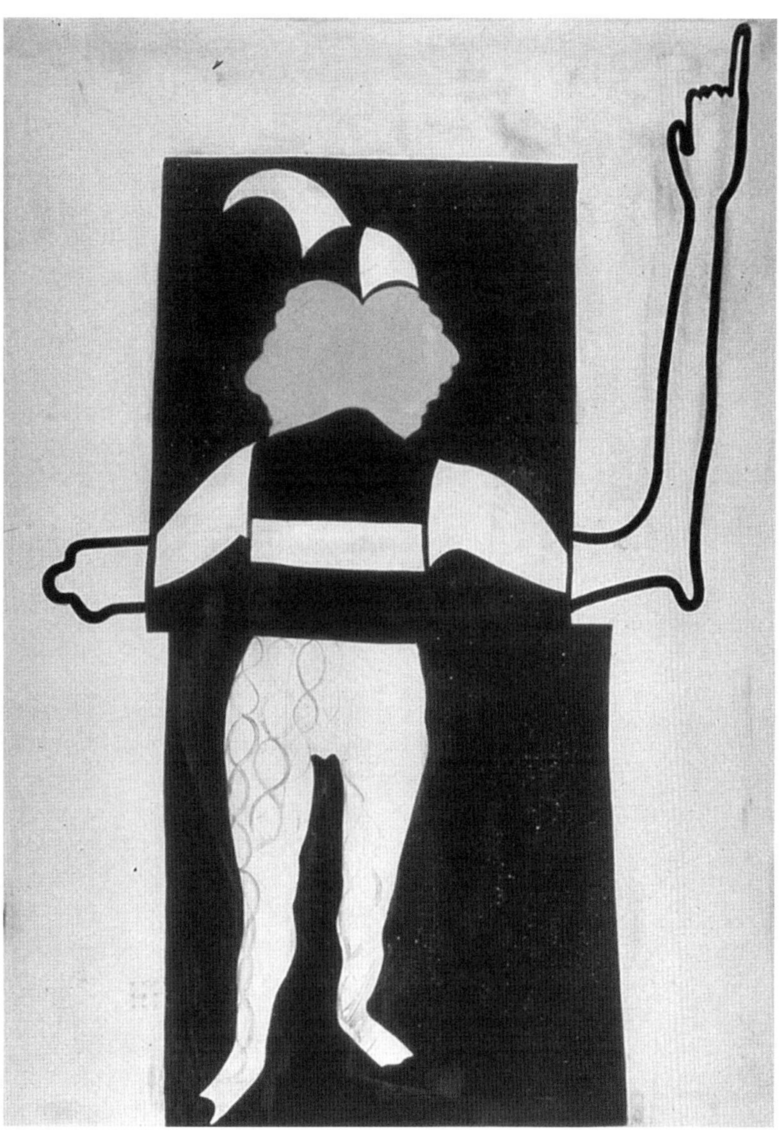

2.12   Ulrike Nattermüller, *Idole No. 2*, 1995. Acrylic on canvas, 170 × 200 cm. Courtesy the artist.

1)   The figure is deformed. A depiction not so much of natural deformity, but of those distortions of form arising from perception, from point of view. We see this figure—those figures—through collage, pieces patched together from different angles, fragments re-forming form to pose their ironic title: *Idols*. And just how are we to idolize? Where is that point of reference at which we could rest, from which we could admire? Where is the order of things? Perhaps in the painting itself, in its upright rectangularity, in its poster-like advertisement of demonstration. Yes, perhaps here, in the fact that—all depiction aside—it is possible to grasp the edge, to handle this object, to take it down, put it away.

2)   Yet I remain anxious, and my problem is to know why. What, after all, have I experienced? The surface of this painted canvas is, reassuringly, simply paint. When the light catches it from the side, I can see the action of paint on surface. Nonetheless, I am not reassured. It is not the frankness of disclosure that I feel, but the urge to conceal. What if this figure were, in its depiction, a natural deformity? I would be reassured. Bosch, for instance, whose figures—phantasms moulded from nature—serve only to confirm the coherence of our imagination. In Bosch, my fascination overwhelms any dismay as, secular though I may be, I take pleasure in the orderly assertion of Divine Judgement over Evil. Nattermüller's figures, however, provide no such coherence. Faced with her *Idols*, I feel their resistance, their quiet disruption of natural order. There is no position from which I can claim to find myself—their bodies provide no vantage for my own. It is this that disquiets me: I cannot assemble an image for attachment. I remain unattached, even from myself.

3)   The figure is out of place, as it is equally displaced: a doubled sign, both hermetic object and monumental proportion. These *Monuments* disturb and disorient, contradicting rather than affirming their dedication. They intrude and obscure. We are required to peer around and through them to detect what is concealed. But in fact they are obscurity itself, offering neither form nor context. It is as though in their lack of form they contaminate all around them, concealing not only by their mass but by their presence, so that what should remain untouched, inviolate, orderly, even natural—a landscape, a building—shifts and dissolves, becomes indeterminate. Obscured.

4)   Ulrike Nattermüller has mentioned the importance that Francis Bacon and Georg Grosz hold for her own practice. The possibility of comparison is useful. Central to both Bacon and Grosz is the question of corruption, of the flesh and of the spirit. The consequence is to effect in their work a

strong element of satire. What can we say about satire? That it proceeds out of despair, that it identifies its object of despair as an implacable enemy, that it is clear in its pursuit of that enemy's ultimate destruction—even if, as in the case certainly of Bacon—the enemy is the self. There is always horror present. This is not the case with Nattermüller, for whom, rather, the appropriate strategy is parody. Parody proceeds not out of horror but out of courtship, and its position is not confrontation, but correlation. Like paradox, it resembles—re-assembles—a parallel in order to parade, even exaggerate, its notation of respect for the other. Its object of otherness is conceived not as an enemy but as an ally, willing or otherwise, in an alliance—a dalliance—whose purpose is to define in respect to this or that quality a parallel authority. The *Idols* and the *Monuments* elicit desire, just as concealment, fragmentation, and displacement elicit loss. We want what we can only glimpse in Nattermüller's parade.

5)   The figure is displayed. More than this even, it is splayed, its interior manifested, its exterior moulded into a matrix whose sign-like flatness, familiar through Kitaj, Hamilton, or Warhol, advertises this reversal of form. Like a child's drawing or a doll's house, the surface no longer contains but simply frames events whose address is to masquerade. In these *Interiors*, edge and frame are separated, just as in a child's game rules are subject to shifts of logic, and the game of "dress-up" proceeds seriously without being taken seriously. The permeability of boundaries and the ambiguity of iden-tity collapse our normal processes of identification, something also made familiar through fashion, music videos, and magazine advertising. A kind of stage is set, and these works initiate a play of possibilities whose processes engage us through a theatre of exchange and encounter rather than through a theatre of transcendence. If Francis Bacon is one point of comparison, perhaps Allen Jones, whose paintings promote a collusion between static voyeurism and aggressive exhibitionism, provides another: when we dress up, when we display, we can do what we cannot otherwise permit.

6)   It is as though the *Interiors* rescue me from the disquiet of the *Idols* and the enveloping obscurity of the *Monuments*. Where I felt abandonment and loss, I feel here a disturbing intimacy, as though my initiation of a desire had been confirmed. Why this is so may be that abandonment has shifted to the self-abandonment of display, and loss—of identity, of identification—has been established as a condition of authority. Eviscerated and opened out, like a dissection, like the spread pages of a book, I feel "stripped bare by"— what, if not my own volition? I feel my volition as I feel my violation: not inviolate, nor indeterminate, I experience possession.

7)   These figures triangulate. Deformed, obscured, displayed, they form a familiar trinity whose model of the Real is the pornographic image. If pornographic, there is no hint of licence or judgement. This *body* of work is an address to the body, specifically the female body as the singularly shared representative—the mother's role—for our polarities of intimacy and autonomy. Central to pornography has always been abasement. If to the naive or unwary the result has been debasement, Nattermüller's work suggests the contrary: that in abasement lies the power to negotiate with value. The *Idols*, the *Monuments*, and the *Interiors* construct the terms—disguise, deferral, and display—for just such a negotiation. We have already named it, as Lacan has, *masquerade*.

8)   *Figure in a landscape*. A cursory review of the tradition of Western painting would show that the figure in a landscape has been our most compelling image of identity. Confronted with the forces of Nature, the figure may be recognizable, sharply delineated as a specific individual, or it may be vague, a cipher or sign for ourselves. In either case, the figure does not stand alone but is inscribed into a dialectical relationship with the external world, and in this inscription the figure becomes a sign for the struggle to survive. We read not an individual but an insistence. As we peer past the figure to the landscape itself, it is our own struggle with the otherness of Nature that compels us, and it is this with which we must negotiate. The figure's articulation acts for us only as an emblem—a possible resolution—for this struggle. A second order of triangulation consequently surfaces between the figure of our observing self: the figure for ourselves within the painting, and its landscape, the figure of Nature itself. In the English language, "figure" has a triple connotation embracing form, cipher, and reason: we are obliged to reckon with the figure. Which is why Lewis Carroll's Alice falls through the crack.

9)   There is a sense of falling—a subtle vertigo—in Nattermüller's Galerie Klein installation *Interieurs* of 1998. Here, Nattermüller constructed a doubled set. Playing off the gallery's given environment—a three-sided white exhibiting space penetrated by Erhardt Klein's domestic interior—Nattermüller hung six of her *Interiors* paintings, two per wall, to form an open envelope for the viewer. Within this envelope, and situated so that it faced Klein's domestic insertion into the gallery, the artist then inserted her own three-sided exhibiting space—a knee-high model environment whose "walls" were curtains hung from rectangular wooden frames and on which were hung miniature photographic copies of other works in the *Interiors* series. Dividing this space, two gold mesh square cut-outs were hung from a wire stretched between the opposing walls, leaving a centre square opening.

On alternate sides of these two transparent curtains stood two obscure figures. These figures were somewhat particular. Projections into three-dimensional space of an image from one of the small photo-paintings, they each occupied the position of viewer—an inversion of their role within the painting. Poignantly, they nonetheless cannot take a form other than that which they held in the painting, so that their independent status retains their representational dependence. In a sense, they have fallen out of the paintings.

There is one other pivotal element. The Swiftian reference of the modelled room—we become Gullivers in Lilliput—is further complicated by the disjunction between the falling motion and embracing folds of its curtains and the implacability of the gallery's hard plaster walls. As though to offer a fulcrum for our ambivalent position within this polarity, a wooden folding chair is placed just beyond the limit of the model so as to occupy an ambiguous relationship to both model and gallery. It is, perhaps, the equivalent of the mirror or the rabbit-hole in Alice's "adventures." Perhaps it is, ironically, a chair for Gulliver. Its folding action folds us from one state to the other, from standing body to body at rest. Which is to say, from being on guard to being guarded.

10) It may be that folding—the folding of our bodies—marks the shift between day and night, between struggle and rest, between work and play, between strong and weak: between "raw and cooked," exterior and interior. As I consider folding my own body into the chair set before me in *Interieurs*, I hesitate. I become, in this public space, aware of the significance of my action. On the one hand, I will be demonstrating the physical architecture, the mechanics of my self, revealing to others the specificity of my separate parts in motion, a display that raises ambivalent desires. Do I dare to enjoy the role of image? I look again at the two strangely monstrous de-formed viewers in Nattermüller's model. Do I dare, like them, display my own extraction—my own mortality? I am tempted to return to my role as standing observer, viewing the model and the *Interiors* as though their invitation to the Masque could be noted, and ignored.

I know already it is too late.

11) There is a connection to be made with Matisse in *Interieurs*. In 1923 at the Galerie Berheim-Jeune in Paris, Matisse hung his exhibition of paintings on curtains around the walls. Of all the Moderns, Matisse is perhaps the most strikingly feminine—in our contemporary sense. His depiction of women escapes the dual traps of sentimentality and hostility common to male artists and demonstrates a lived appreciation of their awkward grace and their human power. Nattermüller's quotation of Matisse—even

to titling the installation in French—confirms and extends Matisse's
insight, folding it into a genealogy of beauty. Matisse's famous remark
that he made paintings to be admired from an armchair resonates within
Nattermüller's work.

12) Beauty is in the trace. The trace of a hand across a face, the trace of sunlight on a floor. And to trace is to re-visit, to make a tracing, to copy out—as
we used to copy out a text, before technology disguised the event.
    But as I think about it, perhaps beauty is that intimacy we constitute out
of paradox and the vertigo we express in discounting our material experience. What fascinates us are the definitions and deferrals, the contradictions
and transgressions that endlessly collude as texts to defy our perception of
the obdurate nature of that experience. To re-trace, to re-write, to re-touch
those texts is to employ the dimensions of space and light required to
negotiate with these linguistic relations, to negotiate with beauty itself.
In *Interieurs*, the curtains re-trace Matisse, but the Text re-traced is more
extensive still: it can be found in the *Winged Victory*, as it can be found in a
Cranach or Vermeer. In the simple fold of cloth lurks the trace of our desire.

13) Dividing this space, two gold mesh square cut-outs were hung from a
wire stretched between the opposing walls, leaving a centre square opening. On alternate sides of these two transparent curtains stood two obscure
figures (see section 9 above).
    Like the chair, these two simple quasi-curtains offer a puzzle to be
reasoned out, to be—again, in English—"*figured* out." And like the chair,
they are pivotal: they are reflections of, or references to the small square
"painting" from which those two figures are derived, and which now are
situated as viewers before these two curtains. Curtains that are in fact
screens, and as they veil each figure in turn, they offer their surfaces as the
junction between here and there. They extend and focus the nature of both
the surrounding curtains and the folding chair, balancing us in an oscillation
between our lived experience and the reflective experience of painting.

14) Too late to retreat into objectivity. *Vanity Fair* called Nabokov's *Lolita*
"the only convincing love story of our century." Like Humbert Humbert,
I confront in the chair and through those two screen-curtains with their
parodic figures the ecstasy that every little girl knows—the intoxication of
playing with dolls, of dressing and undressing, indeed of the whole giddy
anticipation of unfolding potential itself.

15) Nattermüller is no stranger to "dressing up." Her interest in fashion is
grounded in her own experience with designing clothes. Perhaps, instead,

we could call them her "costumes to be worn," and since costume's mode is
an application to the body, the idea of the Odalisque is central to her work.
What is the Odalisque but the female body stretched out, folded out even,
the quintessential "luxury object," that *something of value* for which empires
have fallen. Referencing Goya's famous example, the *La Maya* double portrait playing, one might say, between shift and shiftless, Nattermüller brings
to the Odalisque the realization that through the operation of the fetish,
the whole can be traced in the detail, through the shift, in what the psychoanalyst D.W. Winnicott calls the transitional object. Just as the costumed
Maya transfers us to the naked Maya, and just as the surface of the painting
operates as a transitional screen, the curtains and chair in *Interieurs* operate
for us as moments of transition in our passage from observer to lover.

16)   In an eerie way, Nattermüller's work is reminiscent of a central motif
in Liliana Calvani's *The Night Porter*: the convergence of a dress and an
address. In the film, it is Charlotte Rampling's school-girl dress and the
couple's imprisonment in the address of the apartment that carry the peculiar sexual charge and poignancy Calvani enlists in her portrait of that same
"obsessive, devouring, and doomed passion" that Humbert Humbert felt
for Lolita. In the doubled space of Nattermüller's *Interieurs*, the dress and
the address are collapsed from narration into emblem, retaining *their* sexual
charge and poignancy as a network of ambiguities with which to catch and
hold our own—yes—intoxicating ambivalence.

The Art of Travel: Forever Engaged in the "There" beyond the "Here" (2001)

Published as "The Art of Travel: Janet Cardiff's Here and Robin Collyer's There," *Canadian Art* (Fall 2001).

1   See Lewis Carroll, *Through the Looking-Glass, and What Alice Found There* (New York: Random House, 1965), 32. First published in 1871.

> "Well, in *our* country," said Alice, still panting a little, "you'd generally get to somewhere else—if you ran very fast for a long time as we've been doing."
> "A slow sort of country!" said the Queen. "Now, *here*, you see, it takes all the running *you* can do, to keep in the same place. If you want to get somewhere else, you must run at least twice as fast as that!"
> —Lewis Carroll, *Through the Looking-Glass, and What Alice Found There*[1]

I like the weight of trains and the feel of that weight lifted into speed against the resistance of the rails. I like train stations the way I like public squares, as natural meeting places melting effortlessly into the streets of cities at the far reaches of my imagining. That is why I like carrying my own bags along the platform and up into the carriage. I like the fact that my friends can stand outside and remain with me to wave goodbye as I settle into my seat. And as the doors close and I feel track and train merge into motion, I can watch as buildings, then fields, roads, forests pass like living stage sets on either side. For anyone curious about such things, and trains seem to provoke such curiosity, the relationship between travel and other experiences becomes a matter of interest. Since my major preoccupation tends to be how art functions and for whom, it is the connection between art and travel that comes to mind as my train pulls out from Amsterdam Centraal this June morning on its way to Paris. This article, if that is not too grand a term for what amounts to some personal travel notes, is the measure of that journey.

I was quietly laughing my way through Nicholson Baker's *The Size of Thoughts* when a relatively large one snuck up on me. Reflecting on certain possibilities in the cliché "I don't know much about art, but I know what I like," it occurred to me that stepping onto this train was to step into a particularly positioned moment. I'm talking History. Because trains do not fly. They run. On steel, on the ground. Trains are the last great public marker of our inevitable mortality. Unlike cars, whose ethos is illusory control pushed to a disembodied panic speed, the train's implacable schedule releases us to the materiality of time and place. Unlike planes, and very much like Alice, however fast the train runs, it does not leave my "here." When I step out onto the platform at Paris Nord, I will be in a "here" whose connectedness over the last several hours and hundreds of kilometres remains tactile and unbroken. As in a child's game, I can connect the dots, and this makes me neither a tourist nor a pilgrim, but a traveller. And, I want to insist, it makes for a significant way of looking at art. Now, I don't know much about art either. But I do know what I like as I rummage about discovering, retrospectively, reasons to think about it, connecting the dots that accrue, as it were. It's like picking flowers and finding a bouquet—or like travelling on a train and finding myself here.

Around this largish thought, then, I want to suggest a few contributing thoughtlets on how I see art functioning. In this regard, two works in particular are of interest: Janet Cardiff's *A Large Slow River* at Oakville Galleries' Gairloch Gardens, and Robin Collyer's *Yonge Street, Willowdale* from his series of four retouched colour photographs.

If you are not familiar with the general nature of Cardiff's work, this beguiling quote from the Oakville Galleries' spring newsletter may help: "Janet Cardiff will produce an audio walking tour that will guide visitors through Gairloch Gardens...Cardiff's reproduction and sequencing of life-like sounds plays with the visitor's senses, suggesting movements that do not occur, and people and things that are not there."

In *A Large Slow River*, Janet Cardiff intercepts our assumption that artworks are to be unravelled, read, or otherwise decoded and produced by us in a sort of eager quest for meaning. We are escorted, politely but firmly and somewhat brusquely, along a path that has already been travelled by Cardiff herself, and which we are now directed in following at her pace, in our time. As we struggle with this duality, we find ourselves drawn into a complex of memories from that time-before-us, now re-enacted not as a singular narrative—a story for our time—but as a series of fragments, or found experiences, whose contingent immediacy finds equivalence in the variance between Cardiff's path and ours.

In other words, her directions and memories open up a gap between her "here" and ours. We realize that, while of *this* here, they are not of this time, and that her narrative, so elliptically inscribed as to disassociate us from narrative itself, is from another place. Vital to Cardiff's project is our recognition that while her directions and stories are disassociated from our experience, the work has enrolled us as intimate companions and participants in what constitutes a parallel experience that is also a palimpsest, a superimposition, linking her with us. We *are* on that same path; we *are* following her directions as we skirt the landmarks she describes, both those

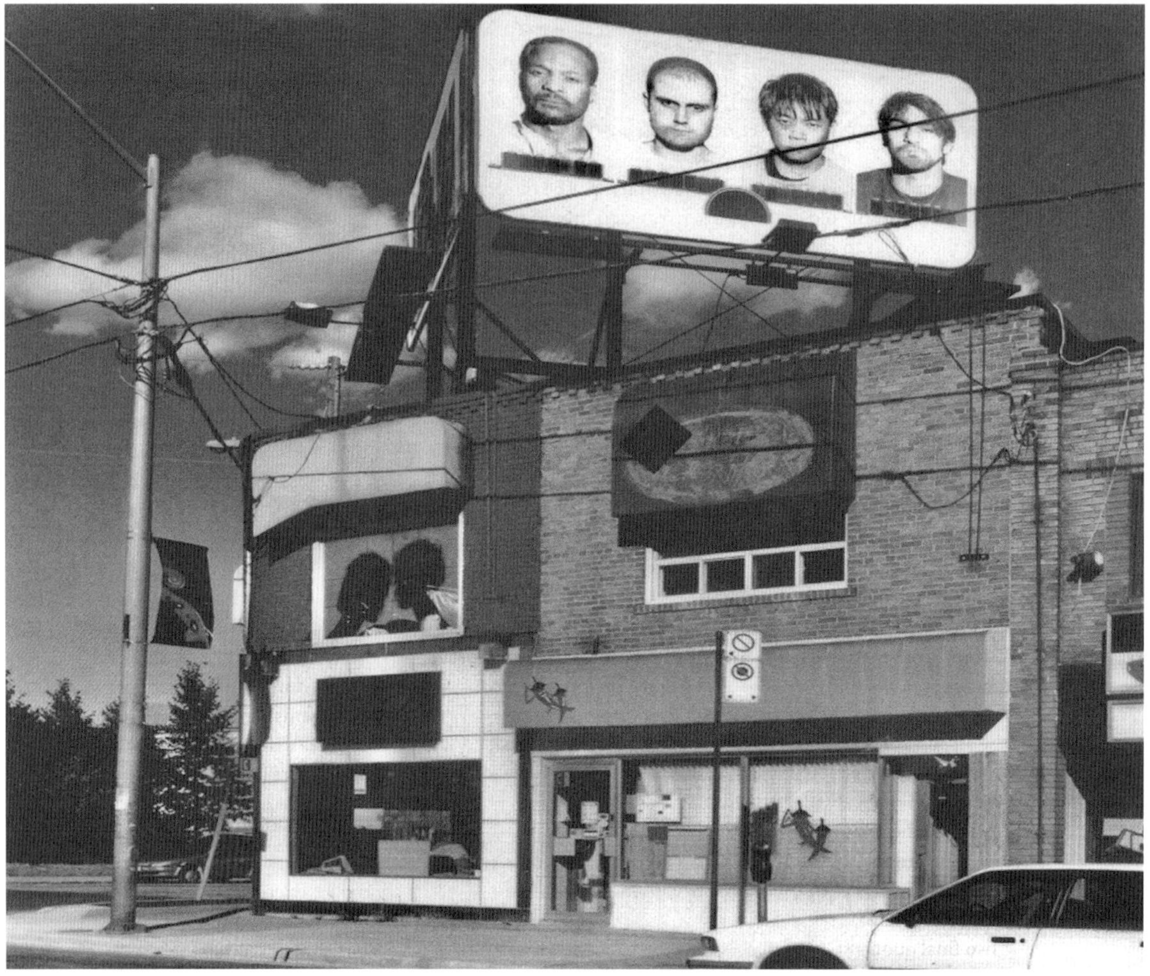

2.13   Robin Collyer, *Yonge St. Willowdale #3*, 1994. Retouched colour photograph, 50.8 × 61 cm. Courtesy the artist.

that exist for *our* here and those that existed only in *her* here. And central to these links between her and us is that we inevitably stumble, get left behind, go astray and have to catch up to…what? To our here through hers, on a path which has always been plainly in sight, and whose destination was always already connected to where we began.

Walking through the garden with Cardiff's voice in my head, I'm unsure whether I'm tracing her path over mine or mine over hers. But standing in another here, at the Art Gallery of York University a year before, I'm quite sure that I'm where Robin Collyer has placed me: face to face with *Yonge Street, Willowdale*. The photograph is there, I am here.

But like the artist, I too live here—in Toronto, and this is my town. So this "there" is also pretty well here, brought here, as a sign for what I know exists across town as something I can travel to, by streetcar and bus. And whether I live here or not, I know from the title that this image is of Yonge Street, Willowdale. A "there" that could be a "here" if I were to go *there.*

Fair enough, you might say, but after all this is what photographs can do. What Collyer has in effect done, however, takes a moment to register— like watching a photograph emerge in a developing tray. In the space between recognizing the photograph's reference to a locatable here and recognizing that he has dislocated image from language—or, I am about to say, relocated image across language—my experience of *his* there becomes an experience of *my* here. Because, you see, there is no text, no language, no index in the billboards and signposts that continue, quite normally, to populate Collyer's *Yonge Street, Willowdale.* There is only the *form* of the signs, the street and the objects, and language has been displaced to a connecting link between myself and the image. The language *within* signs has been converted to the language *of* signs, and once again—as with Cardiff— we find ourselves on an oscillating plane, in a shift between the terrains of the viewer and the viewed. If Collyer's use of language seems at a polar opposite to Cardiff's, they come together here, at the point where Alice discovers that getting from here to there is—like travelling—a matter for the far reaches of an imagination firmly anchored in the "here."

Meanwhile, remember that I'm on a train, and reflecting on how that experience represented a positioned moment. I believe I said I was talking History. I was going to say that while trains verify real space—in which time is a function of experience, and the realm of the traveller—air travel occupies a fictive transcendental space, where time is divorced from experience and we enter the realm of the tourist.

For the tourist, space and time are collapsed into a projected and even Platonic desire: sensation reduced to a checklist, an anticipation to be annulled, or crossed off. Increasingly, we have become inured to tourist time. Indeed, we have become tourists to ourselves. Perhaps this should come as no surprise, since modern life has always been premised on transcendental notions of revelation and progress. In any case, this minor historical illumination led me to the matter of art. These thoughts seemed to make sense on the TGV as I jotted them down, comfortably accompanied by panoramic fields, stretched buildings, and snapshot figures, because what had caught my eye was a preview text in the special issue of *Beaux Arts* magazine devoted to an exhibition I was thinking of seeing in Avignon. Specifically, and I quote: "Taken from the love stories of the late Middle Ages, such as the *Songe de Poliphilie* or those by Petrarch, 'Beauty in Fabula' is designed like a fable. It is structured like a long quest with many trials along the way: the visitor vacillates from inner turmoil and doubt to the pleasures of carnal delight and spiritual ecstasy." Don't get me wrong. I'm as ready as anyone to enjoy carnal delights and spiritual ecstasy. But to me, a journey, a pilgrimage, a progress such as the one described has the closed quality of an entrapment. We're talking the difference between a miracle play and Shakespeare.

So, the first of my two thoughtlets related to art therefore has to do with the fact that it is not my experience that carnal delight and spiritual ecstasy—both of which I strongly endorse as central to art—can be choreographed as a narrative. Watching the Dutch and then the Belgian and French countryside pass by, I felt the gratification of surprise—delight and ecstasy, you might say—as minor and completely circumstantial epiphanies were stitched together by the implacable weave of the train's uneventful passage. There was a narrative, but one constructed by my own recognitions as the train—and I—together traced the here of what was already there. Just as my walk in the gardens with Janet Cardiff, or my apprehension of the Real while standing before Robin Collyer's photograph, provided a similar set of recognitions. As Gary Larson, the *Far Side* cartoonist, might have said, first the story, then the tale.

My second thought, a corollary, really, has to do with proximity—the need to touch and be touched. Janet Cardiff's voice reaches us viscerally, even to the point of forcing us to suppress an urge to turn in her direction, to face her physical presence. And just as *A Large Slow River* uses language to connect her path through a landscape with ours, Robin Collyer employs the language-title *Yonge Street, Willowdale* as a linking index, returning a landscape stripped of language to a palpable form. In other words, we are led into both these works through felt experience. Like Saint Thomas, first the touch, then the embrace. No air kisses.

But in Venice, during a biennale, air kisses abound. I'm tempted to reflect on the rightness of this. Venice defines itself at the crossroads of historical decadence and modern tourism. Everyone else has long since picked up on the exquisite perfection of the site as a set wherein to situate the tragic comedy of desire. And, since Venice is the city of Casanova and Marco Polo, let alone of Thomas Mann, air kisses seem to suggest acknowledged limits and a healthy option.

It is, of course, the city of this year's *Platea dell'umanita*; part two, one might say, of Harald Szeemann's grand linkage between the *then* of the twentieth century and the *now* of the new millennium. I'm here—in another June—to pursue those two thoughtlets of a year ago a little bit further through Janet Cardiff and George Bures Miller's work *The Paradise Institute*, shown here under the curatorial direction of Wayne Baerwaldt. Taking my cue from Venice itself, I'm interested in pursuing the linkage of time with that of place: in returning to Venice, I am in a place that connects Cardiff and Collyer across time—eight years, 1993 and 2001—through place, the same site—Canada's ambassador pavilion to the biennale. I want to reconsider Collyer's sculpture *Kiosk,* shown along with four similar works from the early 1990s in the Canadian pavilion that year by curator Philip Monk. In the process, we add *then* and *now* to here and there.

My notes tell me that the biennale of 1993 was directed by Achille Benito Oliva, the Italian art critic known for his invention of the term *Transavanguardia*. Benito Oliva's biennale carried the title "Cardinal Points of Art." Its theme, he explained, "is indicative of an overview of how contemporary art is the result of cultural nomadism." Writing in the introduction to the catalogue of the current biennale, Harald Szeemann states, "We do not find ourselves facing new art revolutions…but in a climate of increasing interest in human behaviour, in human existence…Art today… searches for the dissolution of borders, which is the characteristic of the

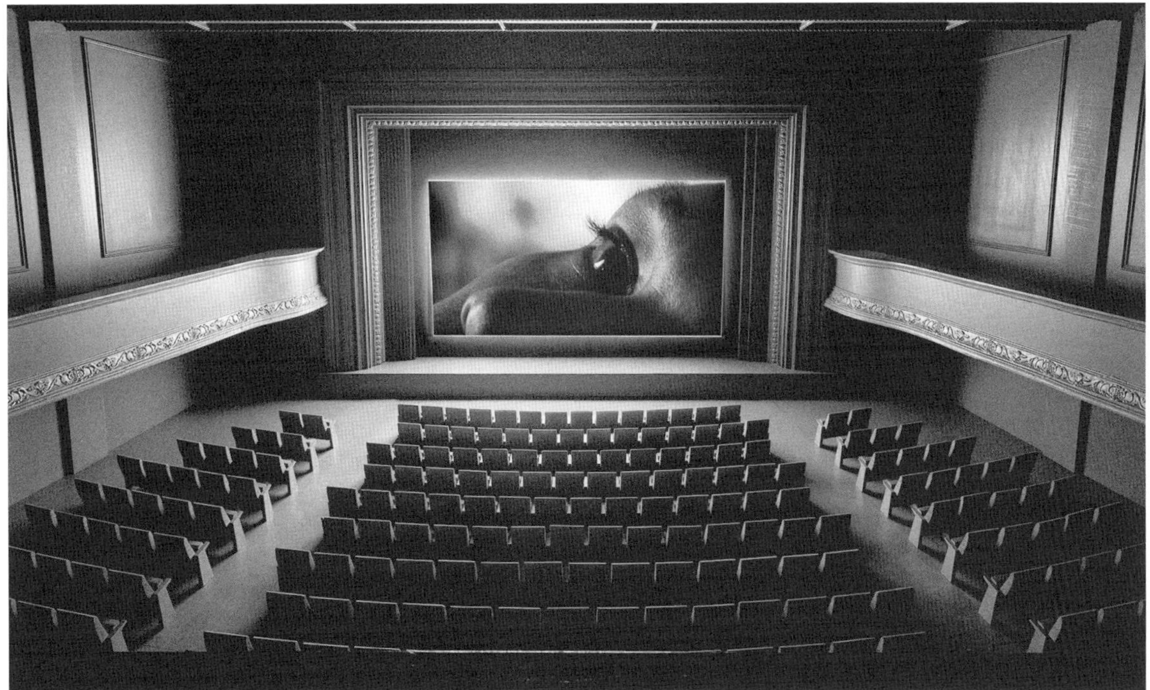

2.14   Janet Cardiff and George Bures Miller, *The Paradise Institute*, 2001. Wood, theater seats, video projection, headphones and mixed media, 5.1 × 11 × 3 m. Detail of the theatre and video projection, 13 mins. Courtesy the artists and Luhring Augustine, New York. Photo: Markus Tretter.

'trend towards global artwork'…. This however remains a utopia. Every art has its own laws, conditions, its own way of making use of space reception."

My point, if it doesn't seem too naked, is that the contest between Benito Oliva and Szeemann's differing positions reflects precisely the struggle with proximity that informed my train journey from Amsterdam to Paris. A theory of nomadism or the dissolution of boundaries is, as I've noted, a variant of transcendental dissatisfaction with the limits of proximate experience. It is forever engaged in the "there" beyond "here," an anticipated future "then" against an exhausted "now," utopian in Szeemann's phrase.

These positions are worth quoting here, because they make clear that this is no small matter, but one viscerally inscribed as a debate into our demands on what we view as significant art. It is not my concern to examine the biennale as such, but Szeemann's leitmotif, flickering through the entire exhibition, could be framed as a recognition of the urgent need for human contact, even for an extraordinary intimacy, that seems coexistent with a fundamental conflict concerning the implications of that need for individual freedom; perhaps, we could say, for individual desire. The need itself seems poised against the desire.

The Paradise Institute is all about being poised between need and desire. It starts with a line-up. At the biennale, this is not extraordinary, but this is no ordinary line-up. The model here is cinema in the old-fashioned sense, when lining up around the corner to see a show was part of the experience. Except that the level of control exerted is heightened by the small numbers able to enter and by the need to "prepare" viewers to cooperate in the tasks assigned to them by the nature of the work. As Wayne Baerwaldt describes it, "*The Paradise Institute* is a repository for memories elicited by our shared knowledge of the artifice of cinema. The most visible portion is its form, a seventeen-seat self-contained screening room, set within the spiral shape of the Canadian Pavilion."

A screening room with a difference, however, since it is also a set in which the viewer feels convincingly transported to the upper balconies of a classic movie theatre, complete with rows of seats drifting off towards the central screen far below. To be inscribed into this artifice, the viewers must be ordered into rows, ushered in, seated and instructed on the use of the headphones before the doors are closed and the work engaged. Like a movie, but with a level of control more reminiscent of the airports and flight arrangements by which I came to sit now in this darkened faux movie theatre, this set in which I am expected dutifully to conform as a passive, entirely isolated recipient of the "show." The show itself is described as a "10-minute original video…like a hybrid genre derived from spy novels, murder mystery thrillers and *film noir*…structured like a cubist collage."

Two final quotes are useful. The first is again from Baerwaldt: "It is a murky environment where viewers make up stories in their minds about immersion and reconcile themselves to the juxtaposed voices of authority…a seamless bridging of the artifice of cinematic experience with the personalized realities, and the fleeting revelations of Truth." The second is from Janet Cardiff: "We try to fool people about which reality they are actually in by screwing up the information reaching their senses."

My first point concerning artworks and their effectiveness was that carnal delight and spiritual ecstasy cannot be choreographed. I have deployed Janet Cardiff's *A Large Slow River* as a touchstone for what I mean. But Cardiff and Miller's *The Paradise Institute* is a very different work. It demonstrates those tendencies that I have defined as less a process of recognition than one of entrapment. The work builds on the internal narrative sequences, or collages, that have always marked Cardiff's productions, including *A Large Slow River*, to the extent that those narratives now redefine this work as cinematic rather than expeditionary.

More than that, even, the work is cinematic in a very specific sense: it pushes cinema into the virtual, where the *here* of the viewer's space is negated by the *there* of the director's purpose. No longer allowed to intervene as a participant in the choreographed event; unable, that is, to display or even indulge a shuffle or a whisper, my disembodiment is employed to presume effects that in fact only I can legitimately produce. I am reminded of Walter Benjamin's remark that the greatest illumination film can achieve is a condition of distraction. Benjamin was talking about going to the cinema as a public act of free will: together, in a crowded room, whispering to our friends, joking, laughing, coming and going. There is no coming and going allowed in *The Paradise Institute* other than that imposed by the ushers, and the representation of whispering is no substitute for the fact. Need, with all its uncontrollable urgency, cannot be successfully subsumed under the imposition of assumed desire.

If my second point about artworks involves the need to experience physical connection, *The Paradise Institute*'s expansion of cinematic narrative to substitute itself for my own can result, at best, only in a reception of ironic withdrawal from delight and ecstasy, a withdrawal that, moreover, seems central even to its conception. The presence of memory as delivered through the collage of film noir and John le Carré has the whiff of Poe about it. The "then" that imposes itself so strongly in Cardiff and Miller's piece is a "then" rife with paranoia and dread, a nightmare projection from the past, intangible, fragmentary, haunted—a work for a time of troubles, a time where the dissolution of boundaries can be a very dangerous enterprise.

As with *Yonge Street, Willowdale*, Robin Collyer's *Kiosk* in the pavilion in 1993 was clear about its boundaries. The pavilion itself was conceived around the discrete nature of the visual artwork, its historic definitional status as an implicit commentary on, rather than elision with, affairs in the world. To enter the Canadian pavilion that year was to enter into an assembly of five iconic three-dimensional images, each of which, like *Kiosk*, acted with respect to one another as words in a sentence. I want to insist on this comparison, because I made the point earlier that, with Collyer, the language within signs has been converted to the language of signs—in this case the palpable form of the sign: *Kiosk*. Language in this mode as both title and object becomes itself palpable, very much *here*, and assumes an equivalent dimension to the icon to which it refers, to the "there" of the object-image. It is this contiguous relationship of here to there that connects *Yonge Street, Willowdale* and *Kiosk* to the viewer within the oscillation I have described as a form of travel.

Alice ran hard to find herself in the place she never left, about to embark upon a game whose moves were clearly established while their possibilities remained entirely undetermined. Collyer's pavilion in 1993 presented the viewer with a set play of five "moves," like those sketched out for Alice by the Red Queen. Striking about all of them, *Kiosk* included, was their quotation of suburban culture and the fabrication of interlocking specific objects whose anonymity produces the realm of possibilities out of which are generated the recognitions that provide the viewer the "carnal delight and spiritual ecstasy" experienced when confronted with Collyer's work. The viewer of *Kiosk* is free to move from their "here" to Collyer's "there" unimpeded. If *The Paradise Institute* is overdetermined, in both the technical and popular senses of the term, Collyer's *Kiosk* is underdetermined, indeterminate and open to moves in a game whose evolution is to be determined by the viewer. Delight and ecstasy thrive in an environment of ambiguity where possibility can be both recognized and invented, where the terms at issue are driven neither by deception nor by imposition. With *Kiosk*, I know where I am, even in a strange land.

There is another aspect that is important to stress: *Kiosk* carries the sign of the toy or model, and consequently the proximity that I suggested in my second thoughtlet. The power of models is that they collapse the distance between that which can be touched and that which can't, and erotically assert permissions that can be fulfilled only in the imagination. The choreography lies in the modelling. *Kiosk* appeared at the 1993 biennale within a context of cultural nomadism which, as Szeemann noted, carried an expectation that the ordinary constrictions of definition could be dissolved. The suburban anonymity that Collyer cites might seem to connect his work to themes of dissolution, but it is this very anonymity presented as a stable object, specifically a toy or model, which connects the work instead to a "here-thereness" that defines a space for recognition between viewer and object.

It might seem that I'm making too much of all this. I don't think so. To get technical about it, I'm talking about the way in which we encounter meaning, and the difference between thinking of something as dictated by intention or a search for value and thinking about value through something encountered along the way. It's my experience that you never find what you search for, but that there's infinite delight and ecstasy in recognizing where you are when you're already there—like looking through the window on a train from Amsterdam Centraal to Paris Nord.

Torie Begg: The Art of the Apparent (2002)

Published as "Torie Begg: the Art of the Apparent," *Contemporary* (Summer 2002).

Note that *Contemporary* was founded as *The Green Book* by Keith Spencer and renamed *Contemporary Art* in 1993 under the ownership of Gordon and Breach Publishing (G+B). In 1996 it was renamed again, as *Contemporary Visual Art* (later abbreviated to CVA) before being acquired by Art21 and reappearing as *Contemporary* in January 2002. It ceased publication in 2008.

She was English. I had first met her years ago in a French city at the elegant apartment-gallery of a friend, a collector and dealer, in connection with an exhibition of her paintings. She came for breakfast on her way to the airport. But I remember she was late, and breakfast became a flurry of half-drunk coffee and heartfelt exchanges as the taxi waited below to take her to some other place where, I imagined, someone else would meet her in some other apartment, in some other country, over a breakfast much like this one.

She is English, and she is Torie Begg. We have met many times in the years since. But first impressions last, and I find myself returning to that morning and the reflections that crossed between artist and work. Impossible to catch then, intriguing to consider now. Central to the intrigue is a word: apparently. It is the modifier Torie Begg has attached to various colours in titling her "painted objects," and, on reflection, it has come to mark the ground that held my fascination.

Is it admission or critique? Regret or dismissal? Conviction or acceptance? Where would I begin?

I can begin here: like Jane Austen, Torie Begg presents a façade of conventional desire behind which she represents a central condition of that desire: the impossibility of its self-admission. Puzzled by my own reactions to the work, puzzled, that is, by the sense of flirtation that I experience from a project that seems so determined, both in its evidence and in Begg's discussions on it, I catch myself attempting to lift the veil, to see that which has been forbidden for me to touch. That attempt requires alibis, and I want to test a few against the possibility of that touch.

The Determined Project

I deal with paint as matter, as something with body, making a three-dimensional "thing" using paint not as a pictorial element but as a building material.
—Torie Begg, *Contemporary Art* (Winter 1995)

It is through the cracks that you see things.
—Torie Begg[1]

1   In-person conversation with the author, London, UK, April 28, 2002.

Before the alibi comes the event, and the event here is one characterized by the artist as a form of architecture, a construction or "building up," an edifice whose final corporality has been elaborated unsentimentally through strategies designed to remove the architect from the architecture, the painter from the painting, or, more broadly and with Yeats's famous question in mind, "the dancer from the dance." Interestingly, this architecture is independent of material support. While Begg has employed the "natural" painting support of canvas, stretched and then re-stretched to define the surface as a field inclusive of its edge, she has enrolled, as well, such unconventional supports as shoes, bricks, mattress springs, and so on. The point is made: it is not the support that is of value, it is the event, the architecture, not the building. And the point is extended to that other natural support, the space within which the painting exists, when Begg arranges her "things" into spatial installations that insist on their eventfulness in contradistinction from the space in which they are housed.

If, in other words, there is at play here a dematerialization, it is one that directs itself to that abidingly eroticised anticipation of the figure that lies behind the veil, beneath or beyond the surface, at the core: the bride stripped bare, even, one might have said. If, therefore, there is to be any lifting of the veil, anything to be touched, there will have to be an account of that other event, present as an exclusion, implied in Begg's sly insertion of "apparent" within a tradition of painting that would elevate truth over appearance. It is this disturbance that provokes the counter-event which, as Near-Eastern cultures have always known, exists simply in anticipation, in implication, or rather in "being implicated," in absence as presence. Begg's determined project, then, is to assemble a cover story whose disrobing can only call into question the act of disrobing as anticipation itself. How to tell the dancer from oneself? Dangerous territory for the incautious, and the first alibi must involve some assertions on the nature of reality.

The First Alibi: The Real as Residue

Conventional notions of adequation, often called truth, such as that if it looks black it is black, depend on what Lacan refers to as reality, the amalgamation of image and symbol, or, to be more precise, amalgamation of the self-identifying realms of the imaginary and the symbolic. But if such is the case, truth is inadequate. That is, there is a crucial difference between reality and "the Real," and this can be summarised in two ways. Firstly, it is widely accepted that it is impossible to access in any direct manner the "real world," that which lies outside us, because our only means of doing so are limited to the senses and the symbolic structure of language. Nonetheless, as Freud noted with respect to the phallus, our apprehension of an object includes its absence: its "realness" exceeds its reality, or we could say that the real exceeds or is in excess of reality and its constituents, meaning, and signification. The Real is that which is excluded from our reality. Lacan calls this excess "residue." Torie Begg calls it "apparent."

Secondly, Lacan picks up on Freud's proposal that an obdurate "silent force" exists in the human psyche that finds expression in repetition and compulsion. Lacan refers to this force as *jouissance* which, while often understood to mean a state of pleasurable ecstasy, he casts as an intensity which lies outside the limits of reality and may be characterized as an emergence of the residual Real, of "excess." What is significant about this is that as an individual forms a social identity, *jouissance* is relegated to the permissible margins, primarily sexual excitement. The Real in its residue and Sexuality in its abandonment become linked. Torie Begg might call this the "crack" in the crust of the surface.

The Second Alibi: The Palimpsest as Cover Story

A central aspect of Torie Begg's work arises from and extends the ancient expectation that painting mimics its referent. Imitation is a complicated affair, and the mimetic tradition collapses that complication into realism, roughly the terrain of what is popularly referred to as reality. Its mischievous twin is mimicry, and it is this terrain that approximates Begg's project. Mimicry is a form of doubling in which imitation serves to both copy and critique. Virginia Woolf remarked that Jane Austin's mastery of character description "stimulates us to supply what is not there," and this ability to so refine a surface as to invite its penetration is a device that has been explored as a form of palimpsest. Sandra Gilbert and Susan Gubar are especially well known for having applied the term in reference to women's writings, for instance in Brontë's *Jane Eyre*, and it is they who have described the operation as a "cover story." In a palimpsest there are two levels of signification. One, the accessible surface convention, depicts or imitates what we see. The second involves the implications that we discover when we look through that surface to encounter a deeper, obscured meaning whose existence threatens to disrupt the very surface that provides our vantage point. It is in this respect that the palimpsest and the mimetic tradition converge as mimicry. And it is in this respect that Torie Begg's assumption and separation of painting's mechanics—on the one hand paint, layer upon layer of paint, and on the other any support, from canvas to bedsprings, that can hold the paint—converge as a cover story borrowed from the conventions of modern art for a body whose embodiment has been "flayed," unstretched from its frame, re-ordered for us into a parody like bones in the Paris catacombs.

The Third Alibi: The Supplement, Derrida's "Shameful Other"

It could be said, indeed it has been,[2] that Torie Begg's paintings are, in effect, cancellations. This cancellation, in opening up a void, inevitably constructs, in turn, the requirement of a compensation, and we could therefore say that Torie Begg offers us painting as compensation.

Any compensation is supplemental to its absent or suspended reference, and this is how Jacques Derrida addresses the necessity of writing with respect to speech. Derrida can be mischievous himself, and in a famous passage directed at Rousseau he discusses the parallel necessity of masturbation as a supplement to intercourse, thereby slyly connecting language with sexuality. And there is more to it than mere necessity. As Rousseau himself admits, masturbation's advantage over "natural relations," and writing's advantage over speech, lies in the possibility of greater articulation. The supplement is capable of a greater "presence" than its privileged partner, or, to press the point more exquisitely, any naturalized convention carries an innate inadequacy for which it inevitably seeks a compensatory presence in its "artificial" twin. Moreover, supplements are extensions. If historical commentary can also be seen as supplemental to historical events, it is clear that there is a privilege of elaboration at play. Torie Begg, in cancelling painting, offers us a compensation that theatricalizes and elaborates on painting's processes, and in that process supplements painting with its own, superior, absent presence.

The Fourth Alibi: The Surplus

Look closely at a Torie Begg painting and you will find a "flaw." This flaw will take the form of a stray hair, or a flake of paint from the ceiling of the studio, a corresponding accumulation of paint as Begg's patient layers succeed one another and invest the fault to move on. You may find this distracting, and you will be correct. Consider this a surplus.

Consider this also a Text, as Barthes uses the term when he writes: "The Text is not a co-existence of meanings but a passage, an overcrossing; thus it answers not to an interpretation, even a liberal one, but to an explosion, a dissemination." The Text as a dissemination—the erotic word dramatizes his point—is a weave of signifiers, meanings crossing over one

2   "The construction of the field by means of its own cancellation signifies an engagement with, and subsequent erasure of, what is left to painting after the nominal end of its history." Richard Dyer, "Reflexive/ Iterative, Object/Painting: Karate Tactics and Decoy Deconstruction in the Work of Torie Begg," in *Torie Begg— Apparently Grey or is it Jello?*, exh. cat. (Graz: Gallerie Eugen Lendl, 1998).

another to form an infinite and playful metonymic chain of engagement. The Text offers a surplus or plenitude that yields not an aesthetic field of concentration, but an erotic field of multiplicity.

An erotic field of multiplicity is, of course, the terrain of feminist renegotiations of gendered difference. Irigaray suggests that women's sexuality is distinguished by its capacity for multiple and heterogeneous pleasure. It is autoerotic and plural. And this extends to women's language, non-linear, "incoherent" to "male" language centred on the logic of "reason"; a language one must listen to differently to hear an "other meaning" constantly in the process of weaving itself. And Kristeva codifies this "other" language as a semiotic chora that represents a feminine, though not necessarily female, libidinal energy that supplements as it simultaneously subverts the masculine symbolic order.

If painting is a field in which language is materialized, it is clear that those surplus stray bits of "apparently distracting" detritus embedded within Torie Begg's layered surfaces take on a central significance, ensuring an intimacy of infinite deferrals that disrupts the confines of the established order.

An erotic disruption, quite apparently.

The Fifth Alibi: Marginalia

The fifth alibi would have taken as its text the concept of overdetermination. Coined by Freud to evoke the multiplicity of causes that determine any given dream, it has also been appropriated for Marxist analysis by Althusser to suggest that any historical moment, like a dream, can reveal many determinants, even if it is the economic that may in "the last instance" secure the fate of that moment. That alibi would have lifted a particular veil to reveal the inevitable admiration that must be felt in the presence of sheer virtuosity, the multi-faceted control over the means of production that is the hallmark of an artist who is both profoundly inventive and positioned to command the capital required to exercise that invention. We can call it allure. A Torie Begg has allure.

But there is no need for the fifth alibi. Indeed, there was never a need for any alibis at all. I could never have been present, just as Torie Begg, the work, is absent too, lingering in the supplement, a residue between the lines drawn by gender and the Symbolic Order. Nor, therefore, need there be any excuse for a text that is, after all, itself a supplement, marginalia on a document for others to erase. Merely anticipations at the dance.

Johanna Householder: Ambiguous Redemptions (2004)

Published in Johanna Householder and Tanya Mars, eds., *Caught in the Act: An Anthology of Performance Art by Canadian Women* (Toronto: YYZ Books, 2004).

> I believe in the oblique, the almighty ambiguity, the forgiveness of earnestness, the resurrection of the body politic and the low-tech life everlasting.
> —Johanna Householder[1]

Cheeky. Not quite blasphemous, really, as manifestos go. Cheeky. A cause which usually appears as its effect: "Don't be cheeky!" This is important. It sets up immediately an opposition that is fundamental to Householder's work—that between "good" behaviour and "bad" behaviour. What is also important though, is that when uttered, the stricture is more often than not ambivalent. Posing as a rebuke, it indulges the possibility of encouragement, or at the very least, it restricts itself to a formal notification that a limit has been breached. To be cheeky is to calculate the inevitability of this effect. As in, for instance, reaction to Andy Warhol's *Brillo Boxes* in 1964 at the Stabler Gallery. Mixed, to say the least. As in, for instance: "'What cheek!' giggled/gasped Mrs. Parsons."

And what, fresh from her 1964 visit to the Stabler Gallery, might Mrs. Parsons be watching a few evenings later? It could have been, in 1979, *The Secret Life of Sgt. Preston*:

Scene: a bare stage, barely lit, with LP sound of dogs barking; enter furtively two women (Johanna Householder and Janice Hladki) dressed in large red overcoats. They proceed to neatly arrange the contents of their purses on the floor, then stand around looking vaguely guilty, suspect. Suddenly they are in an office drawn from an Edward Hopper painting— typewriter, filing cabinet—putting on lipstick; they place Mountie hats on their heads and proceed to work, scanning giant file folders, typing rapidly with the aid of a pair of high-heeled shoes. Behind them on the wall, a film plays a close-up image of a woman's bare belly against a table re-playing the task of emptying out her purse. Slowly the two women slide out of their chairs—slither, really—onto the floor, lie supine, file folders covering their faces. Now they struggle carefully to rise without dislodging the

1 Johanna Householder, "For the Re-materialization of Objectional Art," in *Performance au/in Canada, 1970–1990*, ed. Alain-Martin Richard and Clive Robertson (Quebec: Les Éditions Intervention; Toronto: Coach House Press, 1991), 191.

files. Putting on lipstick again, this time with increasingly exaggerated relish, they begin to suck, then eat their lipsticks. One of them pulls a toy remote-controlled car from the filing cabinet and....

The thing about being cheeky is that no one—including you, me, or Mrs. Parsons—is sure just what to do with it. Outright parody plants you smack in the middle of "those who know." Satire plants you way out among the "holier than thou." And as for blasphemy—well, you get strung up high.

To get this straight then: are we talking some kind of cloaked subversion? The "Hey, wait a minute. What was that all about?" sort of thing? Yes, but not quite. Because Householder is nothing if not straightforward. She's from West Virginia, for gosh sakes! Baton twirling!

So how about an innocent in the world. "Being unsure" about being unsure is at the core of this approach to the idea of work, and to Householder's convictions concerning what we might call the daydreams of life as we live it day by day. Let's watch another piece, a recent video work co-produced with b.h. Yael: *December 31, 2000*:

Scene: reddish lighting, extreme close-up on a speaker, sound reminiscent of a spaceship's interior; cut to close-up on Johanna's face inside a space suit, moving purposefully, heavy sound of breathing. Suddenly the connection is made: the soft, alluringly passive voice of Hal, the computer-gone-wrong from *2001: A Space Odyssey* breaks the tension: "Just what do you think you are doing, Dave." Johanna, as Dave, ignores the voice, continues to move forward through what becomes quite obviously the basement of her house, up the stairs to her kitchen. The cinematography recalls the jarring, angled shots in *2001*. "Dave, I really think I'm entitled to an answer to that question." Johanna emerges from the refrigerator into her kitchen, pulls a corkscrew from a drawer, moves towards the stove. The sound of breathing continues implacably. "I know everything hasn't been quite right with me," continues Hal's voice. "But I can assure you now, very confidently, that it's going to be all right again." Johanna/Dave inserts the corkscrew into a knob on her stove, turns it. Bends down, inserts it again, turns it. Close-up of Sama espresso machine. Opens oven door, climbs in. Noticeable on her suit's shoulder is the Canadian flag. "I feel much better now. I really do. Look, Dave. I can see you're really upset about this. I honestly think you should sit down calmly, take a stress pill, and think things over." Johanna/Dave emerges from the washing machine....

In *December 31, 2000*, Johanna speaks not a word. She simply acts, as Dave, to kill Hal. But listening to her talk about the piece, there's a flatness in the voice very different from Hal's smoothly seductive coaxing. It's a flatness one imagines to be bred of controlled patience—not the patience of the naturally patient, but the patience that comes of contesting conventional habit, of finding out that what seems only logical or obviously true carries

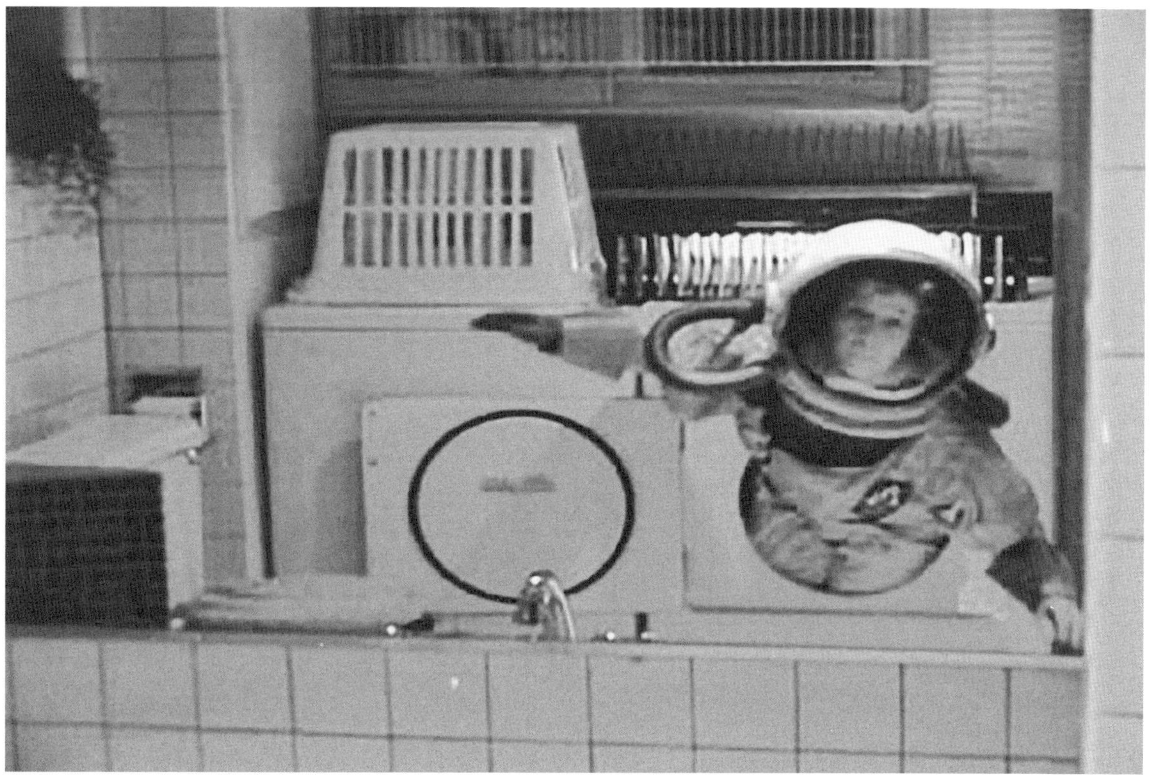

2.15   b.h. Yael and Johanna Householder, *december 31, 2000*, 2001 (video still). Video, colour, 7:22 mins. Courtesy the artists.

little weight in the world; that being earnest about oneself can be seen as absurd. There are consequences, and the most available is to recognize—and act out—the absurdities in the ruling convention.

With this thought in mind, I want to return to the daydreams of life, and being innocent in the world—day by day. Householder's West Virginian innocence was given a grammatical boost in 1968 through finding herself at a performance of the Grand Union, a group that included Yvonne Rainer and Steve Paxton. This propelled her into dance studies in England and subsequently by the mid-1970s to York University and collaborations with George Manupelli. But also, more tellingly, it propelled her into the conviction that collaboration was the means by which the artist could undercut the inherent trap of narcissism at the heart of modern art's ambition "to astonish."[2] From this vantage point, Householder proceeded to work within the practice that has come to be called performance, and in association with a diverse range of artists that included John Oswald, Francis

2   This is not to say, however, that there was no intention to astonish. As Householder writes in her manifesto: "We were not anti-spectacle, we wanted to reclaim the authorship of spectacle. And to own ourselves as performers."

3   Michael Fried, "Art and Objecthood," as reprinted in *Minimal Art: A Critical Anthology*, ed. Gregory Battcock (New York: E.P. Dutton, 1968), 134–35.

4   Clive Robertson, "Performance Art in Canada, 1970–80: Tracing Some Origins of Need," in *Performance au/in Canada, 1970–1990*, 11.

Leeming, Janice Hladki, and Brenda Nielson. And then, of course, there came The Clichettes.

The 1967 summer issue of *Artforum* carried Michael Fried's attack on the minimalist, or literalist artists: Judd, Morris, Smith, and so on. Fried's complaint was that the work of these artists represented a subversion of the idea of art, one that essentially supplanted art with a form of theatre that shifted the centre of the work of art from the work as an object to the audience as a subject. In addressing Tony Smith's experience of a night-time drive along an uncompleted turnpike, Fried makes the following statement concerning this shift:

> What replaces the object—what does the same job of distancing or isolating the beholder, of making him a subject, that the object did in a closed room—is above all the endlessness, or objectlessness, of the approach or on-rush or perspective. It is the explicitness, that is to say, the sheer persistence, with which the experience presents itself as directed at him from outside (on the turnpike from outside the car) that simultaneously makes him a subject—makes him subject and establishes the experience as something like that of an object, or rather, of objecthood.[3]

As Fried's account makes clear, there's something cheeky going on. Specifically, and this is where innocence and the day-by-daydreams of life come in, persistence trumps gesture, and the subject challenges the object on stage, where art becomes some kind of performance.

And what on earth is "performance art" anyway? A recent cartoon in the *Globe & Mail*'s comics section has one convict huffily reprimanding another with the line: "Convict! I'm not a convict. I'm a performance artist objecting to the injustices of the legal system." Clive Robertson, in his lead essay for *Performance au/in Canada, 1970–1990*, tracks the recent history of performance as an art practice—recent in the sense that the Bauhaus avant-gardist experiments lie outside his reference—and notes the often-vague distinctions between Happenings, Events, Body Art, and so on. But what seems common to these various categorizations remains the intent to perform, or *re-perform*, a task rather than to simply appear as a performer in, for instance, a play. As Robertson writes about the emergence of performance: "The notion of task was central to Happenings and Fluxus (the usage of everyday or non-art skills)."[4] If we apply this to the cartoon, our convict is making a distinction between on the one hand passively performing the socially scripted role of a bitter convict "caught" (in the play *The System of Justice*) and on the other hand actively "performing" the task of being caught in the System. If we apply it to Householder's work, we can append to Robertson's task-related description of performance the comment that central to this is the concept of the *anti-task*, a concept notable in the work of Fluxus. The distinction requires a re-reading of context in order to wrest authority from those agencies that have by custom exercised it. At the core of performance lies precisely this determination to offer a re-reading.

Or, one might say more appropriately in Householder's case, a *reiteration*. To reiterate means, of course, to say something again, and repeating something, as any child knows, can be employed ironically. Once launched into public space, the original "something" is now fair game for critical examination and the play of manipulation. This quotational gambit runs deep in our contemporary and allegedly postmodern culture, and aside from the obvious and by no means solely postmodern craft of parody, it surfaces in what Roland Barthes has attempted to characterize as the third or "obtuse" meaning—the first and second being literal and symbolic meaning. For Barthes, this obtuse level of signification marks the presence of the work of art, though his description of it is elusive. "Nevertheless," as Craig Owens remarks in his influential essay, "The Allegorical Impulse," "the third meaning…has 'something to do' with disguise; [Barthes] identifies it with isolated details of make-up and costume (which properly belong to the literal level) which, through excess, proclaim their own artifice."[5] At the risk of injecting here a somewhat technical language, I think it is useful to note that Owens goes on to quote Barthes on what this is supposed to accomplish: "It is no longer the myths which need to be unmasked… it is the sign itself which must be shaken; the problem is not to reveal the (latent) meaning of an utterance, of a trait, of a narrative, but to fissure the very representation of meaning; not to change or purify the symbols, but to challenge the symbolic itself."[6] The symbolic, after all, represents who we thought we were. Aren't we supposed to be the symbolic animal? Isn't art supposed to symbolize something for us? Isn't art supposed to *mean* something!

And Householder's meaning is, actually, quite clear. It is to reiterate the behaviours we take for granted, those behaviours that symbolize our conformity with the social values that in turn stand as symbols describing our "dignity" or humanness, and "misplace" them; to, in effect, *mis*behave. This strategy recalls a comment quoted by Clive Robertson and made by a curator in referring to Gathie Falk's performances as "childish things."[7] Whether made pejoratively or not, the comment is useful for assembling a key constituent of Householder's practice. It is no secret that women find themselves infantilized in the male-authored cultural frameworks that dominate the planet.[8] One response—and this is the case here—is to adopt the stigma wholeheartedly and use it. This could be said to be the arena in which the women's movement and good old-fashioned broads meet to

5   Craig Owens, *Beyond Recognition: Representation, Power, and Culture* (Berkeley: University of California Press, 1992), 82.

6   Owens, 85.

7   Robertson, 12.

8   I'm tempted here, by the way, to invoke Michel Foucault's interesting observation that the "author function" is a particular institutional tactic of assigning or claiming responsibility that is not to be confused with who was "actually" responsible for whatever was produced.

9   They have done five:
Orchid, SAW Gallery, Ottawa,
1993; *amygdala*, in.attendant,
Toronto, 1997; *Last Year at
Marienbad: the missing scenes*,
DeLeon White Gallery,
Toronto, 1998; *Rehearsal*,
a-level, 2000; *Rememberance
Day*, Dovercourt House,
Toronto, 2000.

10   Owens, 54.

11   Owens, 54.

agree, though with clearly differing expectations and operating proced-ures. As a woman, to act "childishly" is to work both within and against the system of behaviour. To define that point of excess in the disguise, as Barthes calls it, at which behaviour is not simply misplaced, but *displaced*, is to call behaviour itself into question. And where does that leave you, Mrs. Parsons? And what about Mr. Parsons?

Running off to therapy, perhaps. But may I suggest instead one of Householder's performances, the ones she does with her daughter Carmen.[9] You could have tried, in 1998, *Last Year at Marienbad: The Missing Scenes*. The description goes:

> Set against the backdrop of the 1961 film by Alain Resnais—a film which shaped certain ideas about the possibility of art for me when I saw it as a little girl. In which we [Johanna and her daughter Carmen] enter the image and retrieve the phallus in the form of a trombone.

> Scene: a typical Toronto industrial loft interior, with two large win-dows across which is rear-projected the original film. Johanna and Carmen (ten years old) are sitting at a table, dressed in loose-fitting white gowns, rather reminiscent of a Lewis Carroll photograph. Mother and daughter play a game with matchsticks. Johanna blindfolds Carmen, moves to one of the windows and watches the film. Suddenly Johanna breaks the window and hauls out a large white cloth as though retrieving the film itself. Carmen produces a trombone. Johanna and Carmen arrange the cloth over their heads, with Johanna high up and Carmen below, who now starts to play "Wild Thing" on the trombone....

Within the trope of the child-woman—with its rehearsals, reiterations, misplacings of behaviour—Householder's collaborative use of herself and her daughter stages a kind of laboratory for actions that offer up, in Craig Owens's terminology, an allegorical, and therefore *supplemental* meaning.[10] As in "Well then, how about this?" The catalyst for this is dissatisfaction. You can practically hear The Stones being played in your head! However, one thing that can be said for paternalism is that it issues its own form of license. The Canon is a secured territory around which may flourish—because irrelevant—all sorts of weird and wonderful things. This can, of course, also be immensely frustrating, maddening for those—historically women in particular—who have been consigned, as it were, to the dustbin of history. But one must remain philosophical, and it helps that the dustbin is history, that it is *precisely* the place, the laboratory, where other possi-bilities can be framed. To push Craig Owens's point, history, as a form of commentary and critique, is itself allegorical "insofar as these are involved in rewriting a primary text in terms of its figural meaning."[11] With *Last Year at Marienbad: the missing scenes*, Johanna-Carmen workshop the (canonized) film, launching a doubled allegorical figure—woman-child, mother-daughter, spectator-plunderer—against the film's interiorized formality, providing an extended and messy otherness to its staged reductivism.

In this short profile I have left it for others to discuss Householder's work with The Clichettes, a central part of her history, and one that is complex enough that it has been treated separately in this book. It is equally important to note that Householder is, you might say, a household name in the business of instigating and promoting performance in Canada, DanceWorks, 7a*11d, and the Women's Cultural Building in Toronto among them. Her commitment to the local scene follows on her commitment to the concept of the lab, and Householder employs opportunities when and as they arise to inject her sassy—did I say cheeky?—guerrilla tactics into the local celebrity scene. Finally, I have also not treated her important contributions as a teacher at the Ontario College of Art and Design.

Rather than detail these involvements, I would like to fade to white with one of her recent performances, *Diversionary Targets*, an action for twelve performers that began and ended in Toronto's Grange Park on Saturday, September 27, 2003. Here is Householder on *Diversionary Targets*, a collaboration with the *4 Cardinales* web project coordinated by Leonardo Gonzales and Alexander Del Re from Chile:

> Inspired by the global nature of the project, and the image of the compass as a target, *Diversionary Targets* is a response to the increase in global warfare and the targeting of civilians in military actions. In this participatory event the performers were given target hats to wear throughout the day of the action. At 9:00 p.m. we reassembled to recount our experiences and convert from being targets back to being points on a compass.[12]

12   Unpublished notes by the artist.

Michael Snow/Nothing to Declare: Notes on Two Exhibitions at the Power Plant Art Gallery (2010)

Delivered as a Sunday Scene lecture at the Power Plant, Toronto, January 24, 2010; unpublished.

Why are we here—in this exhibition—in this public gallery?

We are here because we share with Michael Snow and the artists in *Nothing to Declare* an interest in the difference between similarity and resemblance, or between images and the indexical methods, like language, that we employ to refer to images. An interest in what it is to represent something.

Let's call it the network in which life and art are enmeshed.

Let's call it the problem of language. But what is its problem? Or perhaps we can ask: what is its game? Because, and here we are indebted to Wittgenstein, to represent something, to use language, is to enter into a game. Games use rules or conventions. This is as true for life as it is for art, but art can draw our attention to the rules in play.

It is his rigorous adherence to this simple dictum that has, I believe, characterized Michael Snow's practice and career, and the reason we are here now—enjoying *Solar Breath (Northern Caryatids)* (2002). I think that enjoyment is rooted in a recognition of Michael's sense of play, the play of the game.

Note that he loves to play with his own name, which conveniently references the white stuff, winter, weather, figures of speech (snowed under, "snowed," as in "manipulated through flattery," and so on). Word play has always been a feature of Snow's practice.

Note also that he can play with his titles, allowing for alternate versions, some of which recall the Marx Brothers.

But let's for a moment take Snow seriously—serious if not blinding Snow. I want to draw our attention to a few reference points that may throw a light on this Snow.

I've mentioned Wittgenstein's concept of language as a game. But Wittgenstein also famously remarked that what we cannot speak about we must pass over in silence. I think this silence is a salient aspect of Snow's work—the silence of what lies beneath or within language itself. How does meaning surface in Snow's work then?

In 1986, I curated for the Power Plant's precursor, the Art Gallery at Harbourfront, an exhibition in which I included Snow's 1979 work *Waiting Room* (note the omission of the definite article, which shifts the title from a noun to an ambiguous state, a room that is waiting). In the catalogue essay, I suggested that Michael sees "meaning" itself as meaningless, that for Snow, "reality does not exist" (as meaningful) "except as a projected construct of shifting structures whose only connection and whose only interest is, well, structural."

I would now amend this, however, to link Snow's position to Lacan's concept of the Real—analogous to Freud's unconscious—the realm that we must pass over in silence because language cannot penetrate it. The Real is real enough, but it can only be inferred, not defined—it is the actuality, the confrontation of being in the world that underwrites language, is in fact caused by language. For Snow, language—structure—is the catalyst for apprehending the silence of that of which we cannot speak, where meaning must remain "meaningless."

What does "Solar Breath" mean? We cannot say. We can only listen to the slap of an image on a gallery wall—the sound of one image slapping.

I will come back to the Real in a brief look at *Nothing to Declare*, but I'd like next to consider Snow's *Serve, Deserve* (2009). Here there is another reference I feel is worth declaring, and it is Roland Barthes's proposal that meaning can be construed on three levels: the informational, the symbolic, and something he calls the obtuse, which he claims is the level—in combination with the first two—that compels us to think in a manner that propels us into the arena we generally mark out as "art," including, of course, entertainment.

We can approach *Serve, Deserve* certain in the information presented that we have before us a table on which appears in narrative succession a full dinner that is offered and then retrieved, ad infinitum. Note the word play in the title, and the subtle suggestion that "we deserve what we get," which here would appear to be a form of contempt for middle-class or "proper" manners. Not only is the meal thrown at us to land all over the table (rather like those caricatures of the messy abstract artist throwing paint at a canvas—another trope that Snow is clearly having fun with, perhaps with a reference to many of his old Ab Ex comrades at the Isaacs Gallery), but having been tossed at us, it is then sucked back, rather like taking a vacuum to the mess, only to be thrown once more. Symbolically speaking, we have been insulted, critiqued for our pretensions. But is this it? Is that all? If so, all we have is a social critique, and we "get it," move on, and quickly file it, ultimately amused but unmoved by its eccentricity. After all, if that is art, it's easy.

But that is not all. Because Snow has allowed in his title for a more carnivalesque approach to his work than merely a critique of social aspiration. In writing into *Serve, Deserve* a clear invention, lodging against a real word "serve" a constructed word, "de-serve," Snow snaps our attention back into the game—language—that all along has been *his* game. Any disruption such as this within the rules of the game is received as comedic, which is to say that we are enjoined to enter into the game, to engage in a food fight, you might say. Barthes calls this the level of the obtuse because it is here that we can be free to invent, to imagine without prescribed limits, to see where this might take us. We can cease to be serious. If Snow is serious, it is because he can afford not to be.

The third work of Snow's I'd like us to consider is his *Condensation (A Cove Story)* (2008–2009). Again of course, Snow is playing through the title with a "doubled meaning"—possible only in language—that links the natural processes of weather (rain or fog is condensed vapour) with the structural properties of cinematic film, here fronted by time-lapse photography and editing processes. This is all clear enough, and Snow is helpful in bringing all this to our attention. (Note that snow/Snow itself is a form of condensation!) But the work offers another layer for thought, and the reference I want to employ here is one that is associated with the German philosopher Kant and his elaboration of what is called the Sublime. This is tricky terrain, and to keep things simple, let's just say that what is at issue is the gap, or incommensurability, between our ability to conceive of something and our ability to describe or represent it—particularly if it is something big, like the weather in a cove in the Maritimes. What seems to me to be relevant here is that from this perspective, language will always fail us when we most want to express how we feel, to describe what has meaning for us. If I earlier suggested that for Snow "meaning" is meaningless, it is because we cannot encase meaning in language, where it will always be "less." There is a technical way of referring to this, what poststructuralists would call the play of the open signifier, which is another way of saying the openness to play of the rules that govern meaning in language. In *Condensation*, Snow (himself condensed) provokes us with the "inadequacy" of his title, of his structure, in the face of the vastness the image content of his work imposes upon us. The dissonance or incommensurability between the playful artifice of his title and the majesty of his image can only overwhelm us with a sort of melancholia, a sigh that somehow meaning has escaped the grasp of the structure that seeks to contain it. I hear Lara's theme from *Dr. Zhivago* playing in my head. Is the work therefore somehow a missed opportunity? Has Snow pushed this one a step too far?

Not if you agree with the French philosopher Jean-Francois Lyotard, for whom this incommensurability, this failure to bridge conception and representation is the very condition that ensures our alertness to the power of critical reflection, to the recognition of our responsibility to remain awake, to be in fact conscious.

Nothing to Declare

I think we can make a connection between Snow's exhibition and the companion exhibition, *Nothing to Declare*, that suggests certain continuities in art practices as they are situated today. I might even risk suggesting that there exists today an accent on the melancholic to which I've alluded.

But I don't feel equipped right now to consider *Nothing to Declare* as an exhibition. I want only to suggest a couple of things with respect to three particular works that are included, and how I think they relate to the title, and to Michael Snow's work.

To begin with, I want to pick up again on the concept of the Real that I mentioned before. If there is *Nothing to Declare* in the exhibition, I would take this to mean that a declaration must appear only in language (I declare that there is something here). But this "here" is within the conscious realm. In the realm of the Real, or the unconscious, declarations are not possible because the Real stands outside language. No declaration can take place. There is nothing to declare. This nothing is therefore all that can be "said," it is the realm of the boogeyman, the spectre, nameless horror, and such, but also of free association. It is the realm, as Freud suggested, of substitutions and transferences, which once articulated in dreams, converted into language, offer up in-sights into what we must otherwise "pass over in silence." If there is one thing that in this culture invites silence, it is death, or rather the dread of death, and its companion stricture, memento mori. This is therefore the realm of melancholia, where the open signifier of foreboding dare not close on the signified of oblivion. Or as Woody Allen said, "I'm not afraid of death. I just don't want to be there when it happens."

The three works I want to note here in one way or another seem to me to touch on this, and perhaps the other works in *Nothing to Declare* offer various routes to the same end.

I'll start with James Carl's piece from his *jalousie* series, and I'll treat it as an instance of the grammatical term "metonymy," which is to say that its structure reflects a series of transferences rather than a metaphor or symbolic unity of substitution. From the position of the viewer at the midpoint

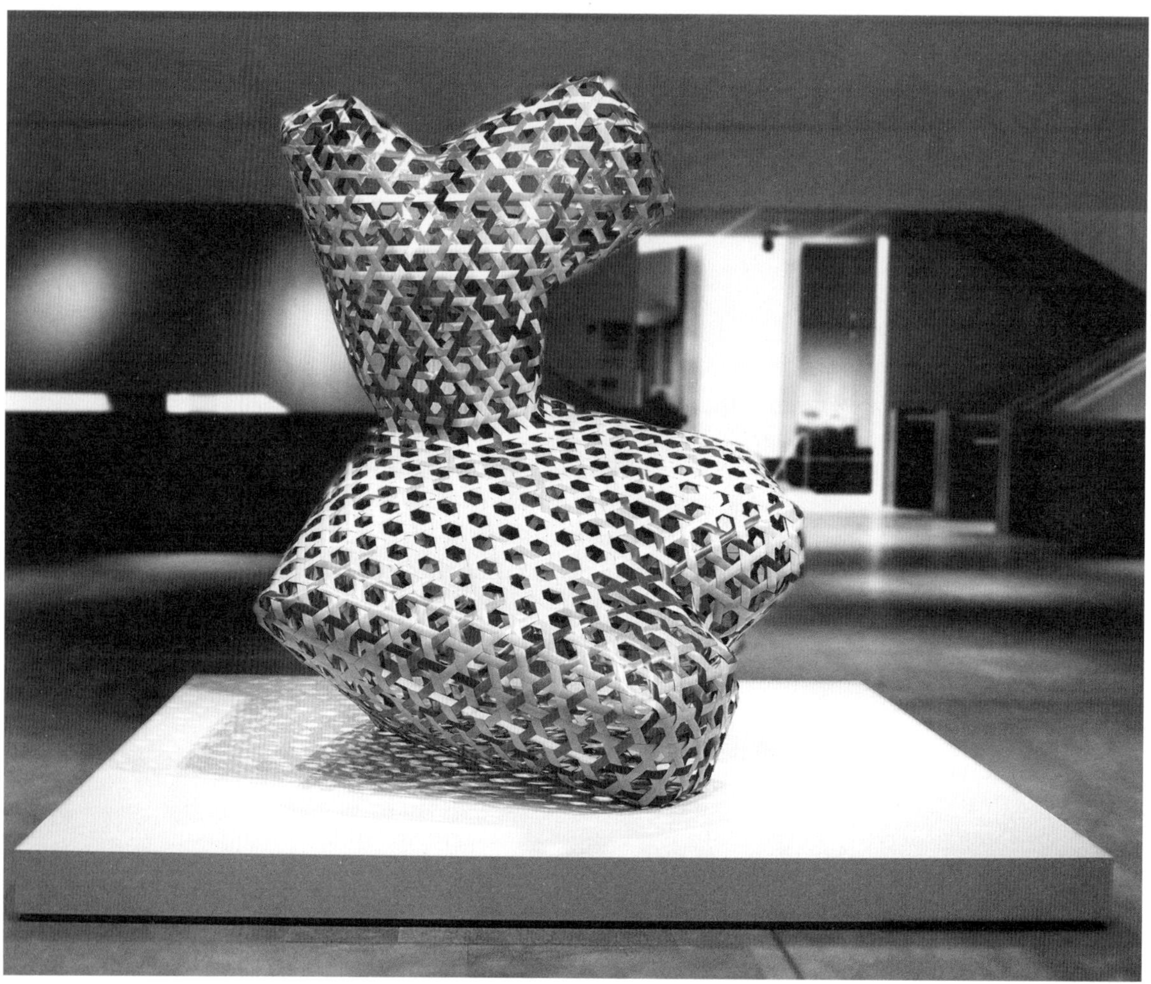

2.16   James Carl, *jalousie (pink)*, 2009. Venetian blinds, 2 × 1.3 × 1.7 m. Courtesy the artist.

of a line linking Middleton's piece and Magor's to Carl's across the gallery, *jalousie* takes on the image of a classic modernist figurine, the kind of precious object that employs the nude torso in a compact essay on form in space, suitable for display on the clean lines of a mid-twentieth-century modern side table. And where could such a table be situated, but in proximity to a large glass window, perhaps even in Philip Johnson's famous 1949 Glass House. And given this exposure to the light, would not this figurine's form be crossed over by the slatted light thrown through a Venetian blind, or in French a *jalousie*? But *jalousie* in French can also mean jealous, especially in a sexual sense, so Carl's nude becomes enmeshed in both the sensual play of filtered sunlight and lurking sexual possession. Possession comes with fear, fear of loss, whose greatest expression is death. This "nude," which is not just a nude, cannot escape the silence of its episodic death, or what we might call its own undecidability.

At the other end of this arc that cuts obliquely through the exhibition is Tricia Middleton's monster, *Portrait of a Mountain Sadsack* (2009), a kind of Bermuda Triangle of bits and pieces forged out of the flotsam and jetsam of childhood fears, all the mundane objects that in the night transform into the monstrous, the thing under the bed. Middleton's conglomeration reflects the Real in its inarticulate repository of that which language cannot form, an apparent antithesis of Carl's series of transferences, yet like Carl's figurine, a figure of silence and what Barthes or Lyotard would call the impossibility of representing the unrepresentable.

Within this arc lies Liz Magor's contribution to the exhibition. Magor's work has for some time investigated the tableau, the frozen moment that oscillates between the living and the dead, between real and artifice, where both reality and representation collapse into an interrogation worthy of Magritte's "Ceci n'est pas une pipe". Magor has perfected the realistic modelling of natural forms and cultural artifacts with the effect of extending the embrace of finality, the passage of time, the search for security, the need for protection, the solace to be found in form itself. But another word for solace is consolation, we think of Boethius's sixth-century *Consolation of Philosophy*, and therefore inevitably, once again, the memento mori, the recognition that in the midst of life you will recognize your death. Peculiar to Magor's recent vocabulary of artifacts has been the deployment of casts of real albeit dead animals from stags to mice as part of the mise-en-scène. Typically these "nature mortes" retain the colour of the natural plaster-like material that forms the cast, and this doubly artificial intrusion disturbs the easy acceptance of the general artifice Magor presents, reminding the viewer of the "impossibility" of such artifices, returning us to the incommensurability of concept and representation that Lyotard considers the mark of the Sublime in its melancholic mode, and what Lacan might call the elusive quality of the Real.

Parentheses in the Work of Yvonne Lammerich (2010)

Contribution to a brochure for the two-person exhibition *Yvonne Lammerich & Joan Key: Incidentally*, The Nunnery, London, UK, April 9 to May 9, 2010.

1   Bertrand Russell, "The Study of Mathematics," *Mysticism and Logic and Other Essays* (London: Longmans, Green, and Co., 1918), 60.

2   Artist's statement for *Island*, "Nature in the Garage: Exploding Wonder" (10 artists), Toronto, June 29 to August 6, 2006. Curated by Janet Bellotto.

3   Excerpt from a poster for a studio gallery exhibition, "TMCA (Toronto Museum of Contemporary Art) – a proposal," Toronto, 2009.

Mathematics, rightly viewed, possesses not only truth but supreme beauty.
—Bertrand Russell[1]

I came to art through painting, initially as a formal inquiry into visual language within a bounded picture plane. Increasingly, however, my interest centred on the nature of the viewer's reception of this inquiry, and my conviction that while the form was visual, the sensory experience was more complex. This led me to understand the plane of the picture as a form of tympanum, a resonating membrane possessing both a projective and a receptive dimension, like a cone capable of both hailing and hearing: not so much a "page" as a doubled projection. This opened up the flatness of the picture, unfolded it as an active rehearsal of the body's spatial experiences from touch through hearing.
—Yvonne Lammerich, 2005[2]

Yvonne Lammerich's work is a sustained investigation of the trajectory linking the mobile space of the viewer to the suspended space of representation. For Lammerich, it is the act of viewing that precipitates a transmission or projection, an arc, which catches the viewer in an infinite series of collapsing moments that constitute the pleasure of the image.
—Ian Carr-Harris, 2009[3]

The pleasure of the parenthesis is its invitation to a digression. Perhaps we can even say that pleasure itself constitutes a digression—that it lies only within, or dependent upon, that obtuse level of self-interrogative meaning that Roland Barthes suggests is the realm of art, but which might also be the evocative realm of plenitude, amplitude, beatitude, solitude, similitude—the 'tude words (see Google's list!) for states that suggest something beyond the reach of closure.

At any rate, the parenthesis qualifies, interpolates, intervenes in the structure of linear meaning, it enlarges our relationship to something by

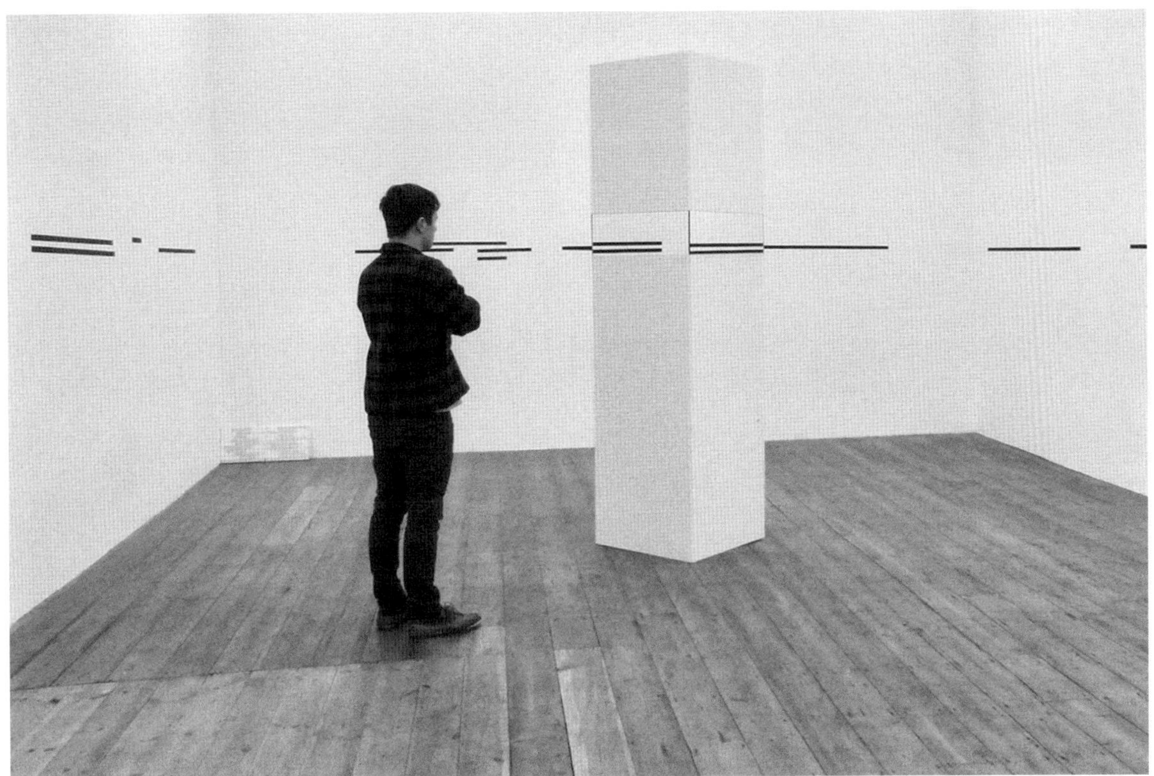

2.17 Yvonne Lammerich, *Sight/Lines (reflections and connections)*, 2010. A square column 2.5 m high and 60 cm on each side includes a 20 x 60 cm mirror set at eye level on each of the four sides. This column is positioned obliquely at the centre of three adjoining walls. Painted lines spaced around the perimeter walls of the gallery appear to connect or flow into one another when viewed in the mirrors from sites marked around the base of the column. Installation at The Nunnery, London, UK. Courtesy the artist.

interrupting our concentration from within. It destabilizes one truth by the simultaneous delivery of another. It is this simultaneity of the incidental, this interpolation, that operates centrally in Lammerich's work, and which is specifically located in the title of this exhibition at the Nunnery.

The interpolation that has woven itself most contentiously through our negotiation with the idea of art has been the position of the viewer, in both the sense of proximity and response. In her doctoral dissertation on the nature of belief structures, Lammerich noted that in the long span of Western history, from Pompeii through Giotto to Monet, there can be seen at once a recognition of location as a space of mobility, and an attempt to find a strategy by which to arrest the gaze. Baudelaire went on record in 1846 that sculpture was boring simply because the viewer's gaze could find no secured resting point that would determine the precision of its image. Michael Fried lamented in "Art and Objecthood" that Judd, Morris, and others had so privileged the viewer's sheer presence that the autonomous "presentness" of the work of art was translated into a "merely interesting" object.

For Lammerich, these struggles with the image, as Canadian critic Philip Monk has put it, are part of the game. It is a game written into the grammar and syntax of language, in fact into the dialectical relations existing between the mind that reflects and the body that engages. *Sight/Site Line*, for instance. A tall square column with mirrors at eye level on each side occupies the centre point of a square gallery. Intermittently painted black lines precisely spaced around the gallery's perimeter walls connect as a single line in the four mirrors when perceived from set positions in the space. In effect the painted lines and their reflected images combine to fold the envelope of the space into a coherence constructed for the viewer from the collapse of physical and virtual experience, creating a moment of uneasy simultaneity. Within that moment we are, incidentally, neither the one nor the other.

Figure: On the Artist Gordon Lebredt (2011)

Published in *Gordon Lebredt: Nonworks 1975–2008,* ed. Lin Gibson (Winnipeg: The Centre for Contemporary Canadian Art and Plug In Editions, 2011).

> The artist and the writer, then, are working without rules in order to formulate the rules of what will have been done. Hence the fact that work and text have the characters of an event; hence also, they always come too late for their author, or, what amounts to the same thing, their being put into work, their realization (*mise en oeuvre*) always begins too soon.
> —Jean-François Lyotard, *The Postmodern Condition: A Report on Knowledge*[1]

> You think I have been wandering from the point? Avoiding your question? I admit I am not answering it directly. And people may think: he's just wasting time, ours as well as his. Or he's playing for time, putting off his answer. And that would not be entirely false.
> —Jacques Derrida, *Deconstruction: A Reader*[2]

> At first sight—nothing.
> Perhaps we've come at a bad time, timed our arrival all wrong. Or, then again, as chance would have it, it could be that we're just in time: in time or in step with what, at any moment, is about to make its appearance. As luck would have it, we've arrived before time, in time, it turns out, to see it come about or come around.
> —Gordon Lebredt, "Visitations: Image, Figure, and the Other Side of the Phenomenon"[3]

Perhaps we've come at a bad time, timed our arrival all wrong. There's an appeal in Lebredt's use of the plural "we" in recording his visit to an exhibition. Is that "we" a subtle avoidance of the more restrictive—and misconstrued—"I", a plea for a necessary commonality of experience? Or, an easy explanation, he came with a friend? Perhaps, though, given Lebredt's nuanced alertness, this "we" could be read as an elision, a recognition of identity as multivalent. And this might suggest something even more likely, that this "we" is an

1   Jean-François Lyotard, "Answering the Question: What is Postmodernism?," in *The Postmodern Condition: A Report on Knowledge*, trans. Geoff Bennington and Brian Massumi (Minneapolis: University of Minnesota Press, 1989), 81.

2   Jacques Derrida, "The Deconstruction of Actuality: An Interview with Jacques Derrida," in *Deconstruction: A Reader*, ed. Martin McQuillan (New York: Routledge, 2000), 531. Originally published in Derrida, *Passages* (Paris: Gallilée, 1993).

3   Gordon Lebredt, "Visitations: Image, Figure, and the Other Side of the Phenomenon," an unpublished article originally submitted to *C Magazine* in 1995.

oblique reference to another order, the order of language itself: Derrida's
différance—where difference is always deferred, where—lacking a present
tense—no "I" can properly exist.

If I too have timed my arrival all wrong—in coming to a consideration of Lebredt's work—I can find no better entry than a text that Gordon
wrote on his "visitation" to a project of my own in 1995 for the space at
137 Tecumseth Street, the Susan Hobbs Gallery in Toronto, and from
which the quote above is drawn. As I re-read his writing—the tense here
is neither present nor past, and Lebredt's work is all about *writability*—
I find another inflection to his use of the personal plural: that I as reader,
as the artist whose work is being discussed, as his post facto collaborator,

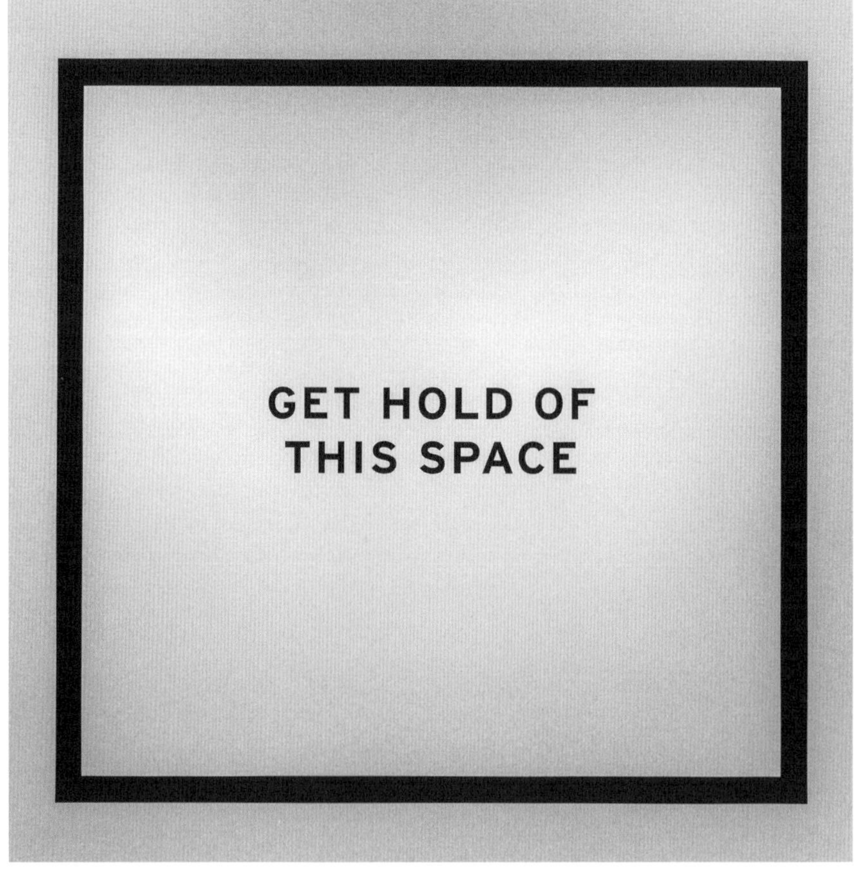

2.18   Gordon Lebredt, *Get Hold of This Space*, 1974/2010. Latex paint and vinyl lettering,
dimensions variable. Courtesy the Art Museum, University of Toronto.

am drawn into that discussion as a participant to the point where intention gives way to reception, invention to re-invention. Simply put, I *arrive again* at this work, *137 Tecumseth*, not once but *again* and *again* as "we," Gordon and I, consider and discuss the time of arrival. And this arrival becomes the rolling out of time as words exploring other words, as words implying images encompassing and transforming yet other images, where the actual and the hypothetical become indistinguishable, become both elusive and concrete, where the appropriate tense to describe this engagement initiates an unrolling of the future anterior condition: *that which will have been written—will always already have been written.*

What, then, are we to make of *137 Tecumseth* in that time before its arrival in the space, before Lebredt's arrival in the gallery? Looking back—to 1994—the project that came to be known as *137 Tecumseth* had a history, which is to say a text, and that history amounted to another—that of a child watching late afternoon sunlight in a semi-darkened Victorian drawing room pass slowly across the wall opposite to the large window whose shape determines the image of that light. The child would look forward to that extended moment, and over time note the changes in location and angle of the projected light. Over time, the child would reflect on the passage of that light into a history, where—over time—that passage of light would be re-enacted time and time again, and every time mark a moment whose extinguishing could only lead to its inevitable return.

So in 1994 the project was to re-enact a history for others to share, to secure that deferred moment of pleasure in a time, the time of the re-enactment—approximately twenty-five minutes. A simple project, really, a piece of theatre, requiring only the construction of a device—a projection system projecting only light—capable of endless replay. Time redux. Start.

But where, actually, to start? Is there a beginning, a middle and an end—a narrative? "*At first sight—nothing.*" In my notes, it is clear that a narrative was assumed, one that "began" with the first sign of light and "ended" with its disappearance into a hiatus of—well, "nothing"—a "marking time," a separation of one reiteration from another.

If this was originally the extent of the choreography, Lebredt's text anticipates a crucial inversion, where the narrative of appearance and disappearance—arrival and departure—is collapsed into a potential inscribed into that hiatus:

> Now if I haven't got my times mixed up, if I'm on the mark insofar as I'm in step with Ian's device, the mechanism by which he can make some "thing" not simply appear and disappear but, at the same time, disappear in its very appearing, I will venture to say that what he "produces" here is not theatre. Or, if we must retain such a designation (and

I believe we must), it will be in order to take notice of this "is not," this nothing which exceeds its own staging.

Everything—the entire operation to come—will hinge on this interval, this time in-between time(s) of what, having already come to pass, has not yet come.

I have borrowed on Lebredt's unpublished article for two specific reasons: the first and most playful perhaps is that it was indeed unpublished—a match for a catalogue of his "unrealized" Nonworks from 1975–2008. The second is to have been able to demonstrate a key component of Lebredt's thought and the subtlety of his insistence—informed doubtless by his philosophical attachments—on the interval or "no-thing" which is also a "some-thing" that *persists in the absence* that is provoked by the projected appearance of the "thing." This catalogue, or rather ~~catalogue~~ is itself a "nothing," a collection of "non-works," yet it is also something—a trajectory of images over time that persist, have persisted, will have persisted—whether "published" or not—in the greater trajectory of the "we" that is constituted in the figure "Lebredt."

Nature Morte: Any Sharp Knife Will Do (2011)

Published as "Nature Morte: Any Sharp Knife Will Do," in *Any Sharp Knife Will Do*, exh. cat. (Regina and St. Johns: Dunlop Art Gallery and The Rooms Provincial Art Gallery, 2011). The exhibition, a collaborative installation by Seema Goel and Lee Henderson, was curated by Jeff Nye and Bruce Johnson, and was presented at Dunlop Art Gallery, June 3 to August 4, 2011, and at The Rooms Provincial Art Gallery, September 21 to December 2, 2012.

> Bring Me the Head of Alfredo Garcia!
> —Director Sam Peckinpah, released 1974

> Garcia's head is worth a million bucks because Garcia, it turns out, has impregnated the daughter of a rich Mexican industrialist. The millionaire is almost a caricature of macho compulsiveness; he simultaneously puts a price on the head of the culprit, and looks forward with pride to the birth of a grandson.
> —Roger Ebert[1]

Any sharp knife may indeed do—whether to bring home Garcia's head, or as is more deeply clear in Peckinpah's film, cut into the gossamer layers of discretion that shield us from our unwilling admissions of lust, terror, greed, and control that are the subjects of Seema Goel and Lee Henderson's at once disturbingly queasy and delicately framed project.

I saw a head once some years ago—in a medical specimen museum. I found it easy at the time to remove myself, to see it as a curious object. It was only subsequently that I realized my mind lingered on it, as though that head refused to let me go, as though my mind was forced into some other realm of the imagination where that head as an identity, a sentient being, refused to be consigned to mere object.

In 1998 the Lacanian psychoanalyst and cultural critic, Julia Kristeva, curated an exhibition at the Louvre—*Visions capitales*—on decapitation. Kristeva's subject is the necessary intersection between the body and language, and she views the image as our link to the sacred: In the beginning was the Word, and the Word was God. That link is rife "with the terror that provokes death and sacrifice, with the serenity that follows from the pact of identification between sacrificed and sacrificing, and with the joy of representation indissociable from sacrifice, the only possible crossing."[2] Which brings us back to Peckinpah's film, and Garcia's head as trophy—now

---

1   Roger Ebert, review of *Bring Me the Head of Alfredo Garcia!*, August 1, 1974. See https://www.rogerebert.com/reviews/bring-me-the-head-of-alfredo-garcia-1974.

2   Julia Kristeva, *Visions capitales* (Paris: Réunion des Musées Nationaux, 1998), 11. English translation from the French quoted in *Psychoanalysis, Aesthetics, and Politics in the Work of Julia Kristeva*, ed. Kelly Oliver and S.K. Keltner (New York: State University of New York, 2009), 6.

wrapped in a dirty fly-trap canvas bag and befriended by its captor in that bizarre pact of identification Kristeva raises. Ebert again:

> Somewhere along the way Oates, as Bennie, makes a compact with the prize he begins to call "Al." They both loved the same woman, they are both being destroyed by the same member of an upper class, they're both poor bastards who never asked for their grief in life. And slowly, out of the haze of the booze and the depths of his suffering, Bennie allies himself with Al and against the slob with the money.

The complex of associations I am drawing here involves the link between representation—whether Peckinpah's film or Goel and Henderson's installation—and our fascination with terror. Strikingly, *Any Sharp Knife Will Do* deploys our relationship to the staged animal figure through a conjoinment of the museological devices of taxidermy and the diorama with the semantic relations between photography and the trophy in its investigation of the sacred and the profane. It is an accepted trope that the animal represents aspects of ourselves, and when Kristeva suggests that the particular body we inevitably hold in awe is that of the mother, she who knew us before we knew ourselves, it seems clear that in their specific connotations these familiar animals—mice and dogs—represent our conflicted attachments to the origin of our very existence, a conflation of awe and abject rendered visible in the feminine gender ascribed to Mme. La Guillotine.

It is of course common experience that the body of the other invites a vertiginous impulse in our own. This is the very meaning of the sacred, and the alienation of the profane. Sensing the draw of the abyss, we draw back. In *Any Sharp Knife Will Do*, Goel and Henderson play with this in dividing the installation into two parts, a smaller reception space through which one passes before turning a corner to encounter the final mise-en-scène. The play involves the dialectic of text to image: In the anteroom, text rules the image. A series of various writings—stories, instructions on taxidermy, musings on decapitation—entirely cover the black walls, providing commentaries loosely keyed to five small inset vitrines, three of which contain trophy-mounted mice heads, the other two a vintage photograph of a young man and a close-up shot of a dog's nose. Inevitably one is seduced by the written word, whose presence dominates the space. The effect is to slow down, draw out one's thoughts. Here one is in the preservational presence of the archive, in the presence of death's suspension of purpose.

As a consequence, entering the large room beyond, the shift to the immanence of action is profound. No longer in the archive of the Dead, we stand riveted before the scene confronting us. Three dogs of various breeds have assumed the attack position, the intensity of their gaze directed towards a group of three large framed photographic images of animal trophy heads, images whose content is itself inscribed with the absent gaze of the camera viewfinder. Despite ourselves, this nature morte resonates with anticipated explosive purpose as we in turn look intently at the dogs, coiled, waiting for the pounce that we also know will never occur. We look, again despite ourselves, for the smallest twitch, the tremor in the fur that precedes the rush. We are in the presence of the image, in the realm where the image rules the text, in the realm—to close the loop—of the sacred. We are where Benny finds himself driving across Mexico talking to Al's head, oblivious to the separation of life and death because we, the audience in Peckinpah's film, cannot ourselves sustain that separation, cannot sustain the separation of the living body from the suspended moment of the image.

And why is that? Perhaps because just as we cannot separate life from death—we cannot imagine the void that is death itself—we cannot separate what we have come to call the sacred from its complement, profanity. This is edgy territory, the domain of what Lacan calls the Thing at the heart of the Real—that terrain that marks the fundamental disconnect between what we say and what we feel.[3] And the Thing? It is that place beyond words, beyond image, beyond signification itself where awe and wonder are crossed with fear and trembling—in a word, with terror. Where words fail. Where we babble to a stinking head, or with Goel and Henderson return to the image and the word in quiet desperation to simply stay alive.

3   For an interesting discussion of Lacan's ideas see Philip Shaw, *The Sublime* (New York and London: Routledge, 2006), 131–47.

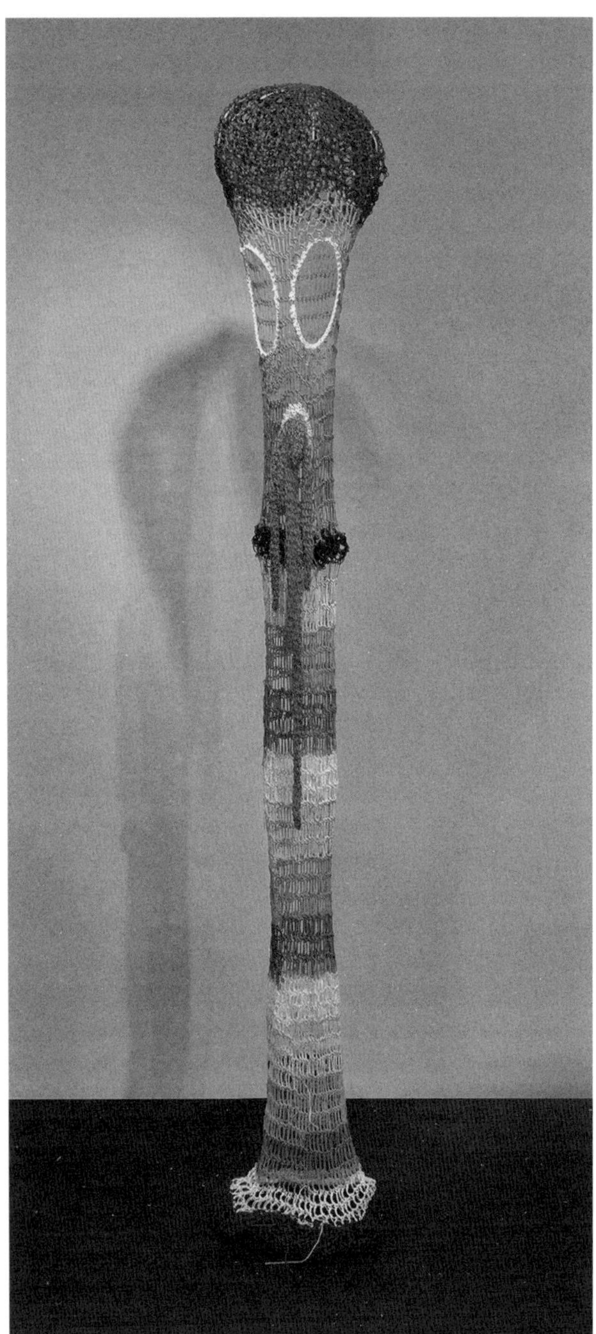

2.19   Omar Badrin, *Sickly*, 2016. Nylon industrial fishing and Mason line, 290 × 50 × 50 cm. Courtesy the artist and The New Gallery, Calgary.

Omar Badrin's Masks

Published as an exhibition essay for the New Gallery, Calgary, February 19 to March 25, 2016.

> Nothing of him that doth fade,
> But doth suffer a sea-change
> Into something rich and strange.
> —William Shakespeare, *The Tempest*

It is intriguing that we seem drawn to masks. From the Lone Ranger to Darth Vader, from Venice's Masquerade Ball to the masked terrorists of ISIS, the mask beckons to us, flirts with us, challenges us to recognize the paradox of our own identity. Paradoxes can be fun; identity, however, rarely is. Identity is a prison; identity is death.

Which brings us to Omar Badrin's masks. Developed from a particular type—those used by skiers and terrorists—these masks appear to speak the sound of silence. Like flayed corpses with gaping mouths, they hang before us like a dread reminder of life's tragically brief encounter.

But hold on! Are they not crocheted in pleasant pinks and yellows, purples and pastel greens? And come to think of it, *Deflated* seems more like a sad clown than an existential nightmare. *I Dies at He* seems a candidate for *The Simpsons*. What are we to make of such a paradox?

The question of an artist's own experience, their biography, is always a touchy subject. We are torn as to whether we should read the work through their history, or our own; to read the work as propositions we can apply, or as a narrative to enjoy. Omar Badrin's history is as entertaining as it is illuminating, and since he quotes it, we are obligated to consider it. Born in Malaysia to Malaysian parents, he was shortly after adopted by a Newfoundland couple who brought him back to be raised in the fishing-dominated community of the island. There, Badrin found himself within both a loving, female-centred home and an estranging white culture. Referring to his work, he says: "one might say that I am rejecting a culture that I have always felt rejected me. It can also be interpreted as abandonment, which results in a subconscious void." Yet on the other hand, Badrin is also quick to point out the depth of his debt to that very culture—to its hands-on relationship to making and mending, the significance of repetitive action in the craft-based business of fishing and working with the sea, to the titles borrowed from Newfoundland speech. These conflicting factors are clearly evident in his masks—the crocheting that he learnt from his mother, the net-like materiality of the work, the warm pinks and purples of their hues. All wrapped up in masks that suggest the trace of death.

So what do we make of Death? Shakespeare's "something rich and strange," or—as Badrin hints—Lacan's terrifying void of the Sublime experience bereft of articulation? What proposition can we apply ourselves in our confrontation with Badrin's work? Perhaps one finds it in the first line of Shakespeare's quote: "Nothing of him that doth fade." For a moment these paradoxical masks suspend us wordlessly between horror and reassurance, between the mark of the void and the marks of the hand: between death and life.

Liz Magor's *Chee-to* (2016)

Published in *Liz Magor*, exh. cat., ed. Lesley Johnstone (Montreal, Zurich, and Hamburg: Musée d'art contemporain de Montréal, Migros Museum für Gegenwartskunst de Zurich, Kunstverein in Hamburg, 2016). This catalogue was published in conjunction with the exhibition *Liz Magor: Habitude* at the Musée d'art contemporain de Montréal, June 22 to September 5, 2016; the Migros Museum für Gegenwartskunst, Zurich, February 18 to May 7, 2017; and the Kunstverein in Hamburg, June 30 to September 10, 2017.

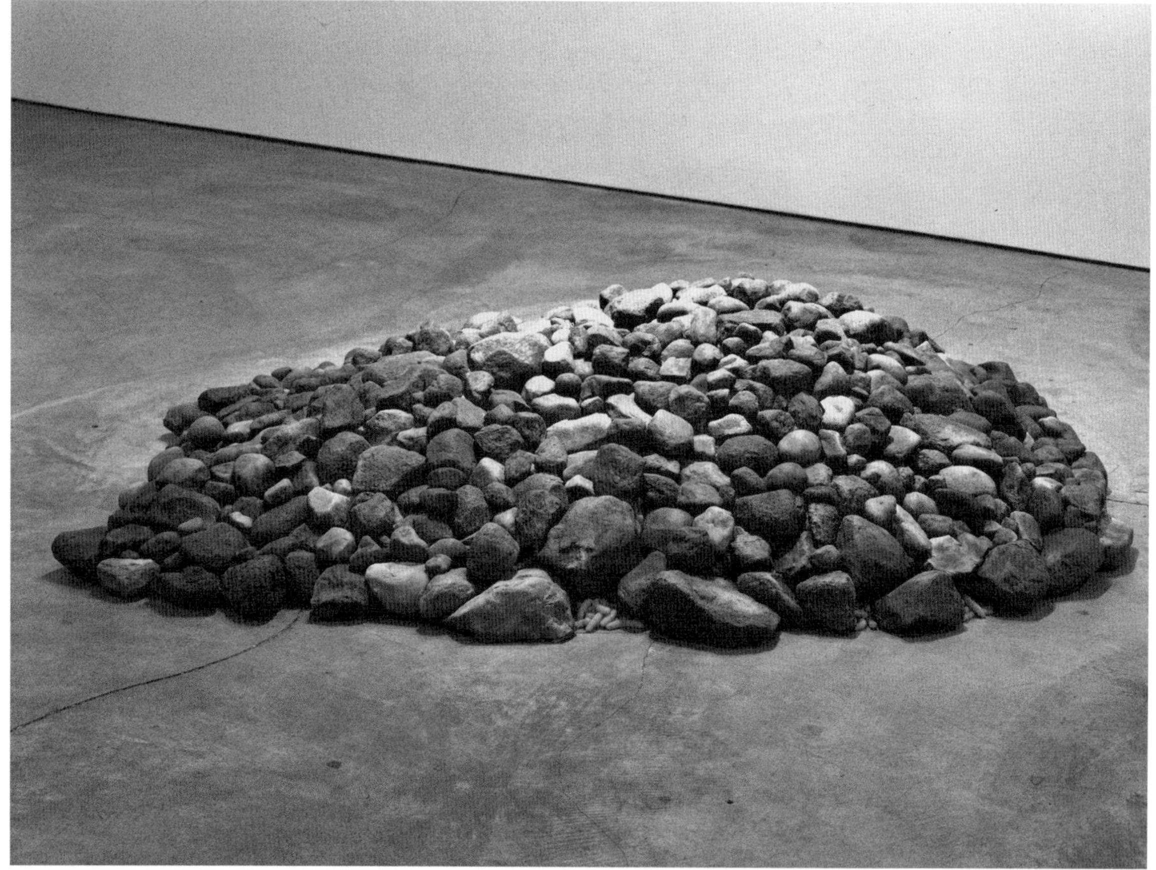

2.20   Liz Magor, *Chee-to*, 2000. Polymerized gypsum, Cheezies, 42 × 167.5 × 200 cm. Courtesy Catriona Jeffries, Vancouver.

Certain images pass for (and perhaps preclude)
the authentic in spite of their obvious fakery.
—Liz Magor[1]

Pierre Menard did not want to compose another Quixote—which surely
is easy enough—he wanted to compose *the* Quixote. Nor, surely, need
one be obliged to note that his goal was never a mechanical transcription
of the original; he had no intention of copying it. His admirable
ambition was to produce a number of pages which coincided—word
for word and line for line—with those of Miguel de Cervantes.
—Jorge Luis Borges, "Pierre Menard, Author of *Don Quixote*"

A Little Song, a Little Dance, a Little Seltzer Down Your Pants.
—Chuckles the Clown (George Bowerchuk), from the "Chuckles Bites
the Dust" episode of the *Mary Tyler Moore Show*, October 5, 1975,
screenplay by David Lloyd

The main thing is honesty. If you can fake that, you've got it made.
—various attributions, including Ed Nelson and George Burns

Nabokov is famous for his remark that if satire is a lesson, parody is a game.
Liz Magor is known for her exploration of that which we think of as real
or authentic, and that which we know to be fake or inauthentic, and the
confliction that we experience in the face of their confrontation. *Chee-to*
is a classic instance of her fascination with this tension, and I want to
explore this myself through the quotations I have placed at the head of this
short essay.

Let's first review just what *Chee-to* is. The back story here is Magor's
deployment of survival narratives within the framework of Nature and
History. As a sculptural object, we are presented with a polymerized
gypsum casting of a pile of brown-grey stones about six-feet-by-five-feet-
by-sixteen-inches in height. Spilling out from under the pile can be seen
what seems to be a second, barely hidden, pile of Cheetos (the real thing—
cheese-flavoured, puffed, cornmeal snacks courtesy of Frito-Lay/PepsiCo).

Magor writes that "certain images pass for (and perhaps preclude) the
authentic in spite of their obvious fakery." That images may, despite or
even because of their fakery, *override* the authentic, or apprehended, reality
is not new; here's Picasso in 1923: "Through art we express our conception
of what nature is not."[2] But Magor goes a step further in suggesting that art
can preclude that which we see as authentic. In *Chee-to*, the (fake) stones and
the (real) Cheetos work together to assemble an image experience that is

1   Email to Diana Nemiroff,
October 11, 2000. Quoted
in Diana Nemiroff, *Elusive
Paradise: The Millenium Prize*
(Ottawa: National Gallery of
Canada, 2000), 82.

2   Picasso approved this
statement, made in Spanish to
critic Marius de Zayas, before
it was translated and published
as "Picasso Speaks" in *The Arts*,
May 1923.

3   Reid Shier, "Crack in the
Rock," in *Liz Magor*, exh. cat.
(Toronto: Art Gallery of York
University, 2000), 84.

neither fake nor real, but an elision that remains *undecidable*, a conundrum of two idea structures we apprehend as one.

In "Pierre Menard, Author of *Don Quixote*," Borges teases us with a similar conundrum. Pierre Menard manages to produce, after a lifetime of dedication to his task, only a fragment of an authentic *Quixote* that is to all appearances word-for-word identical to the original. Menard's *Quixote* is far richer than Cervantes's for the fact that it functions as a palimpsest, a text through which we re-read the original, a re-reading that inevitably constructs a game that Nabokov alludes to as a parody, and the state of empathetic sadness or loss that parody embodies. In his story, Borges opens up a game in which the original text is not the authentic text; it is, rather, Menard's fragmentary re-visitation—word for word—that can claim authenticity within the limits of the game.

But, one might say, what has this to do with Magor's *Chee-to*? Simply that it is not sufficient to speak of Magor's work without recognizing her deeply parodic sense of humour. It is, for instance, hard not to connect *Chee-to* to Felix Gonzalez-Torres's elegiac *Untitled (Portrait of Ross in L.A.)* (1991). Magor the parodic clown lurks within Magor the equally passionate examiner of functioning reality. On an anecdotal level, anyone who has spent time with Magor has enjoyed her playful and often biting appreciation of logic and argument, and the space of extrapolation that is opened up in everyday conversation. In *Chee-to*, Magor shows her hand to a degree less evident in other works, or as Reid Shier puts it: "*Chee-to* is an eloquent exercise in complete overkill," a "hoax that doesn't know when to quit."[3] It is for this refusal to quit—this willingness to push to the limit—that I believe places *Chee-to* among the most persuasively personal of Magor's works. A little neon-orange seltzer down the pants is bound to wake us up.

Magor's practice is often cited for her ability to pull off the fakery of her objects in order to establish the honesty, or truth, of her enterprise. Yet Magor's admittedly accomplished ability to construct her casts, to "cast them" as viable portrayals of reality, seems no greater than that of many artists who deploy such methods. So I think there's another element to her work, and again *Chee-to* is emblematic of this. To successfully fake truth, or honesty, as George Burns implies, is to enter into the very heart of truth itself, the heart of its darkness, one might say. And it is here that *Chee-to* reveals its erotic pull—the object of desire (and what are Cheetos anyway if not a void of desire?) all but buried under the weight of guilt. Lacan, in his take on *Antigone*, pursues the concept of a void at the core of our identity, a void resulting from the chasm between our socially constructed self and the pre-social implosive entity that formed our original un-nameable "self." Antigone, in defying her uncle in order to bury the brother she desperately loves, enters into that space that has no boundaries, the space of absolute attachment, of absolute truth—a space that cannot be known—an infinite regress that brooks no articulation, no place. Insofar as they remain suspended within the conundrum of the Other, Magor's casts fake the truth that cannot be borne.

Dance With Me: Notes on the Work of Ginette Legaré (2017)

Written for the exhibition *Ginette Legaré: For the Time Being*, presented at Birch Contemporary, Toronto, March 23 to April 29, 2017.

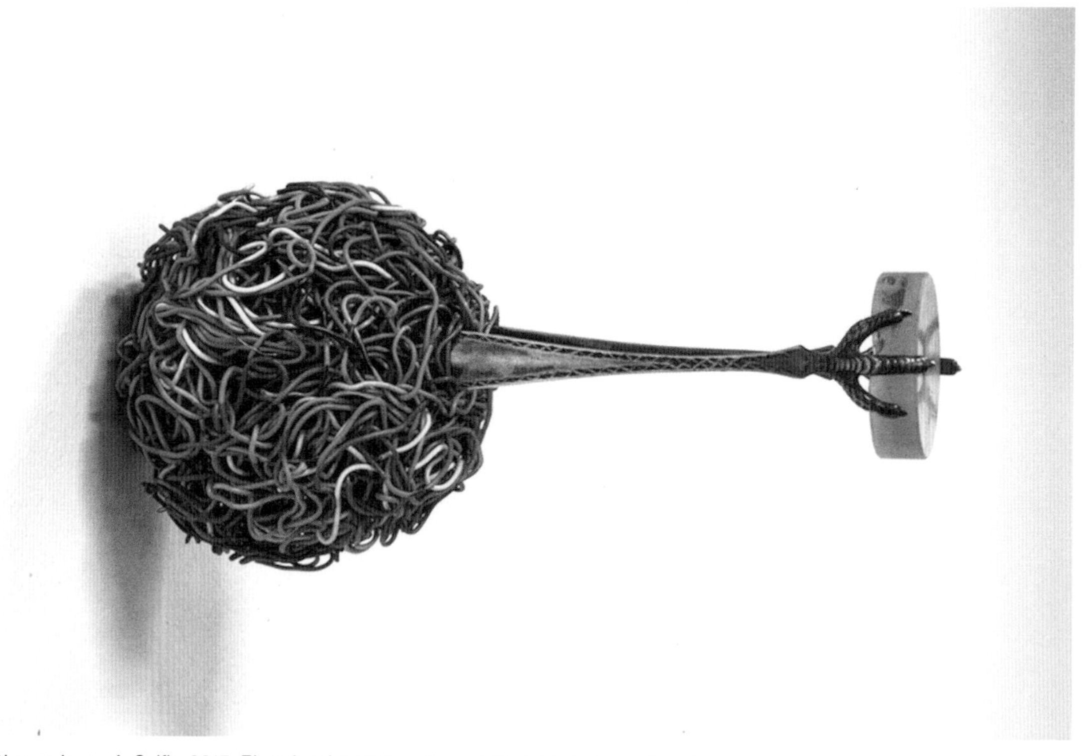

2.21   Ginette Legaré, *Selfie*, 2015. Electric wire, tongs, glass lens, 8 × 8 × 16 cm. Courtesy the artist and Birch Contemporary, Toronto. Photo: Toni Hafkensheid.

Though much has been said about objects,
they remain disarmingly intriguing.
—Ginette Legaré[1]

Much *has* been said about objects. To the point, perhaps, that we are no longer quite sure what an object is. The object—that *other* to ourselves—has become a site of intrigue, of mystery, the epicentre of our search for meaning and the resolution of suspense surrounding who we are. We seem, somehow, to be in an Agatha Christie play—one that includes a butler.

There is a butler—Judith Butler, American philosopher and gender theorist. Butler has been a central player in the concept of the body as material more than merely physical, a site of materiality or embodiment that can be characterized as performative. Inherent in this position there is an insistence on the discontinuity of fixed paradigms, a sense of the in-between-ness of things, of the linkages between ourselves and the material world within which we are embedded. This material world is not simply stuff, it is the matrix within which ideas about ourselves are constructed, similar to the way an artist constructs a work of art through the intersection of ideas and material—the materialization of an idea.

Ginette Legaré is well-versed in the discourses that circulate around the body and the identity of things. For Legaré, materiality has been central to her work from the beginning, and while childhood experiences at home played a part, so did her university studies in the early '80s—undergraduate at Laval in Quebec City and then the graduate program at York University in Toronto. To remark on this is not simply to establish a personal history, but more importantly to introduce the intellectual ground for Legaré's work. Two events—one public and the other personal—offer a useful context. On the public side, the social politics of the era cannot be ignored. The 1961 Quiet Revolution in Quebec saw the collapse of the Catholic Church's hegemony in Legaré's native province, a period coincident with her childhood. At the same time, the genial humanism of Steichen's 1955 *Family of Man* was coming under increasing attack from critical thought, largely under the umbrella of French poststructuralist theory. Finally, another parallel revolution in sexual politics, dating to Simone de Beauvoir's 1949 *Le Deuxième Sexe* but politicized in 1970s America, was disrupting the patriarchal structures of society. Taken together, the world that Legaré entered was radically different from that of her parents' generation.

On the personal side, Legaré remarks in a recent interview that as a francophone student in Quebec, her training at Laval was marked by an engaged familiarity with poststructuralist theory and politics—in French of course. Entering graduate studies in Toronto with only French, she found

1   From a brief text intended to announce Legaré's exhibition *For the Time Being*, in an email sent March 11, 2017 by the artist to Rebecca Travis, then gallery assistant at Birch Contemporary.

as she struggled to master the English language that she experienced a miscuing or misreading between her prior knowledge of the French texts and the English translations she was reading. She describes a folding of one culture over another such that the texts took on a *différance*—or conceptual differentiation and deferral of meaning. The cultural differences structured into translation became for her a performance in the malleability of language, and consequently of perception. In the one there is the other.

But language has a reference, and the "other" that was already Legaré's concern lay in the material world of objects, or more specifically "the overlooked and elusive relations among objects." Not just any objects however, since for her the materiality of things is best examined within the quotidian environment of everyday life—the home, the office, the workshop. We linger in these spaces, and it is here that perception, or the perceiving eye, finds the time to challenge assumption and open the door to the possibility of art.

What are the possibilities for art in these familiar things? To return to the body as being material rather than simply physical matter, materiality is—as noted—in essence performative, gestural, playful and comical, absurd, and even dangerous. For Roland Barthes, a central figure in French post-structuralism, this is in fact the terrain of art once it is liberated from its instrumentality as an agent of political change or as a signifying marker. We may dismiss office politics or family relations as apparently inconsequential daily struggles, but consider Samuel Beckett's 1955 play *Waiting for Godot*, and banality has its darker, insistent side, a side that as Barthes suggests opens up to art.

So it is precisely here, in the world of familiar objects that attend on these struggles, that art finds special purchase. In turning our attention to these objects, Legaré invites us to allow ourselves a moment to enable them to break open their silence and speak to us of—well, ships and shoes and sealing wax. And in breaking open that silence can sealing wax, or ships and shoes, ever be the same afterwards? After Heidegger has had his way with a broken hammer, can a hammer ever be just a hammer again?

I've just taken the liberty to connect Legaré with Beckett, Lewis Carroll, and Martin Heidegger. And my justification is that Legaré's familiar is no return to a genial sense of reassuring familiarity. The objects that she brings to our attention occupy a realm of estrangement not unlike the territories explored in Saul Steinberg's *The Inspector*—a territory in the guise of comedy yet rife with a sense of the after-image that follows on the conversion of image to reflection, to dis-illusion, and even to the terror of mortality. The mystery of the object I alluded to earlier is encoded in the silence of the object—and the urgency for us is to break apart that silence to reveal or un-conceal a truth about things. To acknowledge their mystery and to find authenticity in their apparent transience or disposability—their unseen gestures or moments "not fully decanted"—represents a glimpse into the dimensions of truth.

With Lewis Carroll in mind, let's return to the malleability of language mentioned previously in connection with Legaré's experience of stitching one language over another. A characteristic of language is its openness to wordplay. If objects are silent, language is noisy, messy, more massage than message. Language is an invitation to a dance in which one partner has little forewarning of the steps, where missteps in fact are the rule. If in her titles, Legaré announces the dance, it is for us to interpret or invent for ourselves the moves. This leads to a speculation that borders on invention, but building on her familiarity with the work of such writers as Irigaray and Kristeva, the broken silence of Legaré's objects can be seen to speak in the voice of the feminine register, a voice renegotiated as "other" to ourselves rather than a lack, devoid of speech. If her transformational objects no longer lack voice, it is because they dare to confront us with their otherness to the simple objects from which they were born—the tools and devices we take for granted. "Look at me," they seem to say—"No, *look* at me!"

Perhaps the most iconic image of the last few years is the ubiquitous selfie, whether posted on the internet or observable as a work in progress in practically every bar or roadside attraction, including, of course, the galleries and museums. *Selfie*, a recent work from 2015 breaks open, or to use Heidegger's term, un-conceals the selfie as the subject encoded in the object. The object here is about sixteen centimetres long and consists of a seven-centimetre-diameter ball of rolled multi-coloured electrical wire into which are embedded a pair of Victorian sugar tongs holding out towards us a small double concave lens clasped in its silver claws. Peering into the lens, or of course looking out from the lens as the object/subject, we find ourselves diminished, near impossible to make out. The self as tantalizingly remote.

Selfie is a complicated work. The ball of electrical wire speaks to the world we've built, one dependent on electricity to power the electronic age of digital communications—and selfie cameras. Reaching out towards us, however, are those silver sugar tongs with their antique bird-like claws, like a crone offering us a twisted mirror into which we look to our own despair. The object's silence, once broken, offers not the self that we think we know, but a self we must rediscover as we feel ourselves, like Alice, falling into the abyss.

There is at least one more point I'd like to raise with Legaré's work, and the sugar tongs direct us towards it. The character of her objects is often reminiscent of devices and tools we associate with the framework of a period set slightly back in time from the current culture of throw-away plastics. This character lends her work a sense of the classic novel, or novella, or perhaps an image from an old movie. The authority of time, its aura—to bring Walter Benjamin into play—gives us the rhythm of the dance, cheek to cheek, late at night as the guests leave and the last couple slow-dances to the mysteries of love and its illuminations.

Projects, 1975-2020

An Approach to Criticism (1975)

Published in *Parachute* 1 (October 1975).

I have been asked to publish here photographs of my work. I have chosen three that have been exhibited at the Carmen Lamanna Gallery in Toronto in the last two years, and to make them intelligible they require some discussion.

Throughout all my activities there is an interest in analyzing ordinary structures into basic elements, and in my work especially, an interest in the implications of this within the context of art. Or more simply, an interest in details and the assumptions underlying concepts; details which allow us to see things not intended or not "significant." Insignificant things offer room for manoeuvre and definition beyond the limits of their original context, and it is within the analytical and expressive power of art to objectify these elements into persuasive conceptual and sensual language, using in the process simply the ordinary elements of normal reality.

I am the Queen of England focuses this interest in a simple, direct way. Itself restricted in size to a small, two-dimensional plane, it is composed of two simple elements or details: a fragment of a sixteenth-century popular rhyme and a photograph of a splendid detail from a queen's portrait. These elements are placed together in a visually discrete relationship in such a way that the work manages to exist without unnecessary complications, openly balancing official elegance and popular irony. As such, it is a pleasing object.

Implicit in the piece, however, is the element of time and context: within the more familiar modern context of washroom graffiti, the piece assumes an ironic irrelevance to any important reality, becomes insignificant as a social or political gesture, and crosses the line into the parallel reality of art.

As an art object, the work performs as an analytical vehicle fusing layers of perception within defined boundaries. By affording a content derived from normal reality, and by placing certain unavoidable changes on this reality, the work acts as a ground from which to operate on a variety of levels within the viewer's consciousness, with as little intervention on the part of the artist as possible.

Indeed, this position is crucial for the aesthetic implications and significance of the piece, and of all three pieces illustrated here. The artist is in

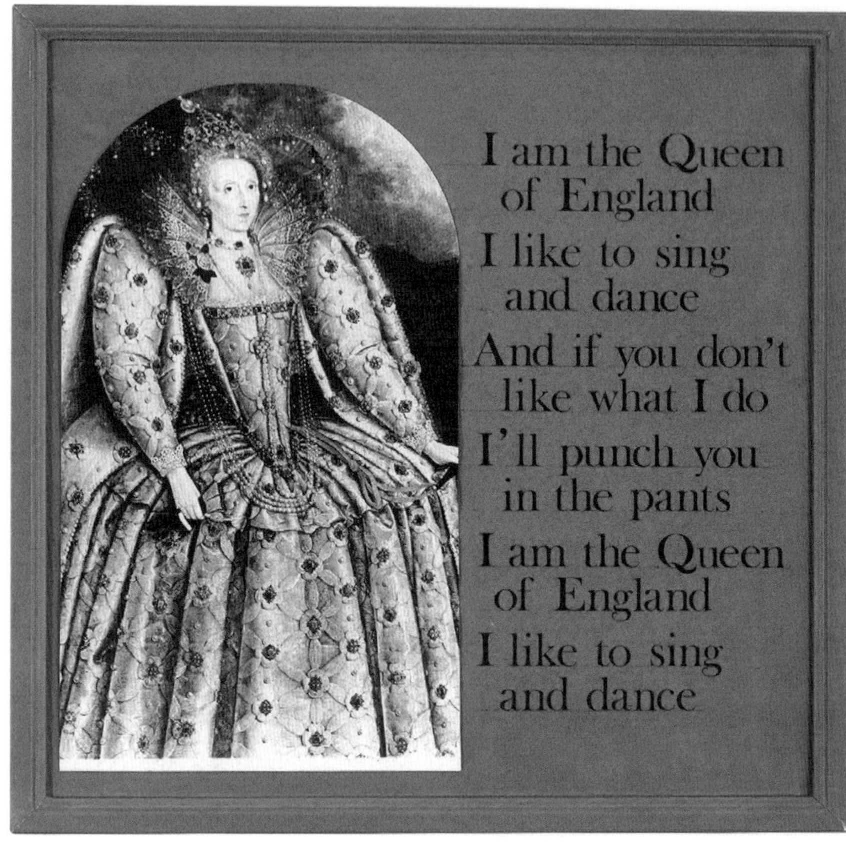

3.1   Ian Carr-Harris, *I Am the Queen of England*, 1973. Photograph on painted Masonite with frame, 61 × 61 cm. Photo: Henk Visser for Carmen Lamanna Gallery.

effect assuming the part of impresario, coordinating and scheduling events and situations in order to activate responses of a highly reflective and sensual nature in those who come in contact with the work. The work becomes, in fact, static theatre, occupying a position between art object and public performance in order to see more closely what seeing is.

I am the Queen of England focuses this interest in a simple direct way, while providing for implications which concerned me further in later work, particularly the other two pieces illustrated here—*The Violin Lesson by Balthus* and *A Thing of Beauty*.

Restricted in size to a small, two-dimensional plane, it is composed of two simple elements: a fragment of a sixteenth-century popular rhyme, and a photograph of a splendid detail from a queen's portrait. The work is simple enough that it manages to exist without visual complications. However, while appearing simple, even banal, its presence provokes questions, in particular the question: what does it say about art?

It is significant that the work is based on elements borrowed by the artist from normal reality; and the change of context in time and place from sixteenth-century politics to twentieth-century irrelevance operates as the crucial detail in removing the work from that reality and placing it into the parallel reality of art.

The work goes further than this, however. With the hint of infinite repetition in the rhyme, with the use of photographic documentation, and with the use of a title which is simply the first line of the work itself, the piece occupies a position somewhere outside the two-dimensional physical restrictions it possesses and approaches sculpture, and beyond sculpture, on theatre, and beyond theatre, on normal reality, perceived now from a position of detached involvement. It is this concentration on the relationships of structures that is essential to the artist's intention of defining an aesthetic occupying a fluid position from which to analyze and objectify the structure of relationships.

Author's note: The intent of this contribution to the magazine was to suggest that a critical essay could be written in different ways, that any piece of writing involves a fluid set of inventions that may be prised apart, that there may be a near-infinite series of essays implicit in the one that is selected for publication. This essay suggests two possibilities.

Look (1978/2000)

Originally exhibited at the Carmen Lamanna Gallery, 1979; with technical improvements, 2000.

Installation with an original text and screenplay.
Voices in order of appearance: Ross Young, John Massey, and Ian Carr-Harris.
Actors: Janis Hoogstraten, John Massey.

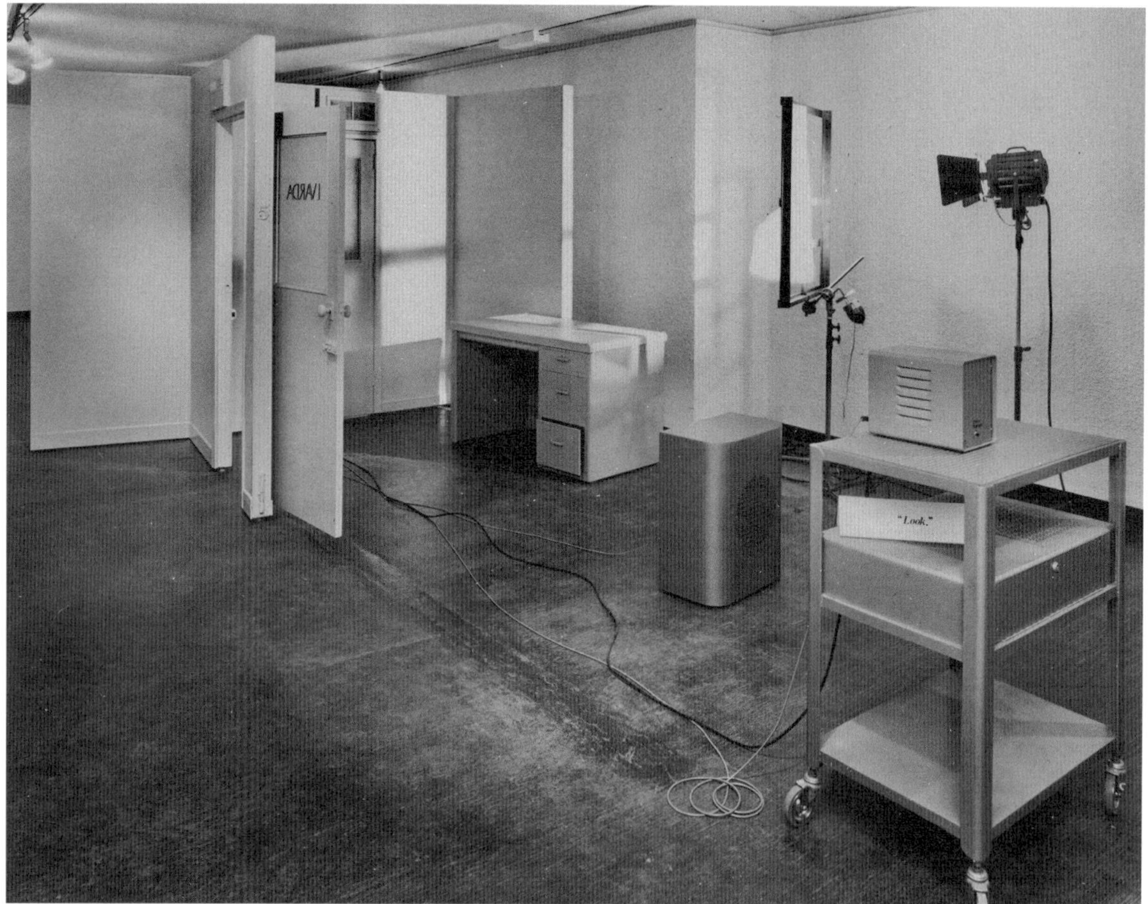

3.2a   Ian Carr-Harris, *Look*, 1978–79/2000. Painted wood constructions, synchronized 16 mm sound film, projector & audio deck with floor speaker, glass window with rear-screen material, spotlight on metal stand, fan, curtain material, push-button operated electronic control unit on a/v cart, viewer-controlled, automatic re-setting cycle of five-minute film & separate audio. Dimensions approx. 9.14 × 4.6 × 5.5 m. Original installation, Carmen Lamanna Gallery, Toronto, 1979. Subsequent installation, 2000, at Ydessa Hendeles Foundation, with 16 mm film converted to video projection. Photo: Henk Visser for Carmen Lamanna Gallery.

Its purpose was to frame a reference—to detect not evidence, but identity: the identity not of a witness, nor of a victim, but of an experience.

"And what experience?" you might ask.

"But what experience?" she asked. "What is there to be said about that figure falling against the glass?"

****

The room sits, a stage within the larger space. It confronts you with its own condition. Across its walls—mere sketches of another place, perhaps another time—the light of late afternoon plays softly shifting patterns of artificial light and shadow. In front, a large speaker sits mutely on the floor.

You pause because its presence interrupts your distance, disrupts the protection of your power to pass on by, untouched. Besides, it is obvious—you already know—that you have the power to play the work. The switch sits squarely, discretely, on its ventilated box. Your presence, and the room's, collide. The voice is a young man's voice, not unsophisticated, nor yet unmoved.

PRESS SWITCH TO INITIATE THE CYCLE (4:09 minutes)
(transcription of audio)

Look. It doesn't matter what it was. It's what it is. That's all that matters. I was standing around the afternoon it happened; at this place, one of those really dumb places. The kind that attract dumb business. It was getting late in the day; must have been about 4 o'clock or so. I remember the sun was pretty high still, but sort of moving real fast. Anyway, the shadows were getting longer. The elevator wasn't working, as usual, so I got to climb the stairs.

It's funny, sort of. I always hated that building. I wasn't too crazy about the reason I went there. Nothing bad, you understand. Just kind of...well, kind of grungy. I could never think of enough reasons for the reason I was there.

This particular afternoon I was really blown. The walls sort of shimmered or something. They kept disappearing, and there I'd be in a travel poster someplace. Anyplace.

So anyway I was real nervous. I had to wait for an invoice, so I started wandering the corridors. Anything to keep moving. It was real nice, because everybody'd closed down for the day and there was no-one around. The emptiness was like a real relief, you know? It made me feel really good. Kind of absent. The next thing I knew I was facing a blank wall at the end of the corridor, but there was this empty office beside me, and the sunlight coming in the window was really nice, like liquid gold that time of day. I've always liked late afternoon. I guess everybody does.

Well, there was nowhere else to go, so I went on in. There was some guy's name on the door—Vardas or something, it doesn't matter. A desk too, looking kind of lonely. Just sitting there, like someone's dog or something, just left behind. So I walked over to it and touched it and got to thinking about it. What it had been used for, what was going to happen to it—stuff like that. I was beginning to feel really close to that desk. I was even thinking how I could take it home with me. I was feeling pretty sentimental, I guess.

Then I began to hear these noises. They seemed to be voices, coming from behind a door beside me. Someone turned on a light, and I could see shadows against the frosted glass of the door. I felt kind of like a kid—you know, watching something you're not supposed to. So I kept real quiet. The voices were low, but it sounded like some kind of argument. The shadows seemed more and more like something was going on, you know what I mean? One of them sounded real nervous. I was getting pretty nervous too. I mean, here I was, uninvited in a place where it didn't look like there was supposed to be anybody. Especially me. And there was this thing happening.

The voices got lower and I couldn't hear much for a while. Then this guy's voice says: "OK kid," and I hear this shot and there was this face against the glass and hands sliding down and I could hear the sound of the body falling on the floor behind the door. It happened so sudden. I just couldn't believe it. It was like the movies, but not even as real. Disappointing, really, now that I think about it. But it did something to me, you know? I can't explain it, but it freaked me right out. And then I heard the kid's body being pulled away from the door, and I thought: Christ, this is no place for me. So I edged over to the door real quick and got out of there faster than you'd believe.

It's funny, you know. I've never told anyone about this, till now that is. I sure as hell didn't want to get involved. Being a witness for that kind of stuff can be a pretty heavy scene. But I keep thinking how nice that room was with the sun and the shadows and the quiet. And all that other stuff happening in the room right beside me - just ten feet away. It makes me light-headed just thinking about it. Kind of makes everything seem, you know, too relative or something.

Anyway, the walls sure don't shimmer at me anymore, I can tell you. And disappointing or not, I've never felt the same since.

And what is there to be said about that figure falling against the glass?

I'm listening to a story. I'm in that story, a late afternoon in a vacant office, somewhere. I am there, as I am also here in this other space, a gallery. Suddenly a body falls against the office window, its hands reaching out to touch me—and together we collide as flesh and blood.

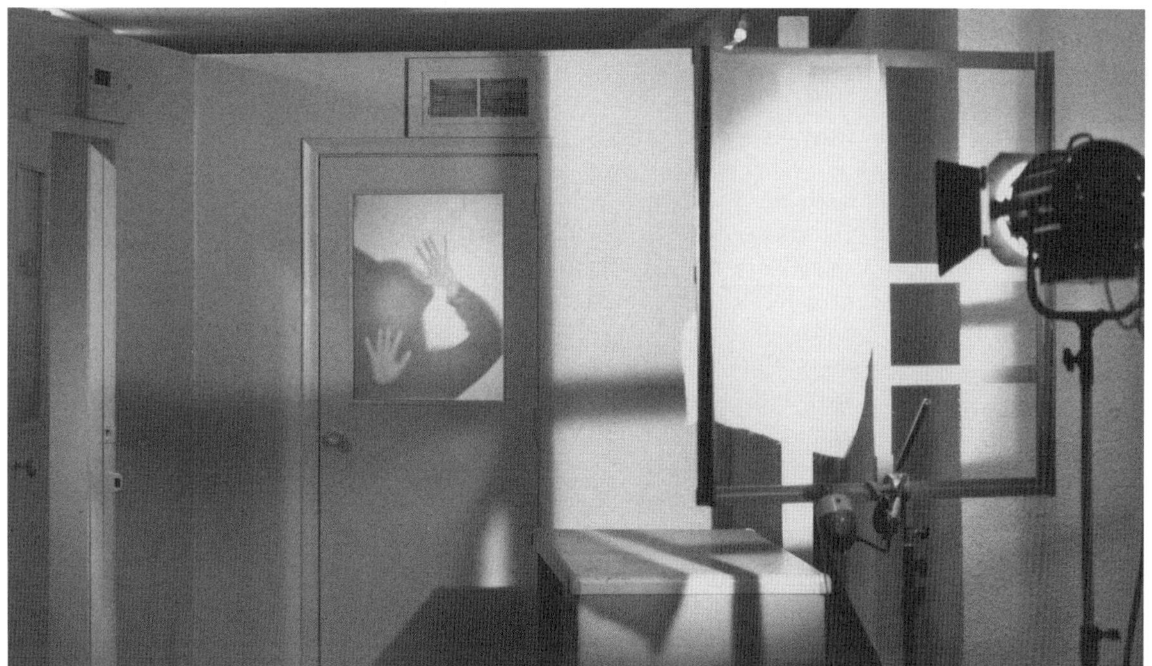

3.2b   Ian Carr-Harris, *Look*, 1978–79/2000. Painted wood constructions, synchronized 16 mm sound film, projector & audio deck with floor speaker, glass window with rear-screen material, spotlight on metal stand, fan, curtain material, push-button operated electronic control unit on a/v cart, viewer-controlled, automatic re-setting cycle of five-minute film & separate audio. Dimensions approx. 9.14 × 4.6 × 5.5 m. Original installation, Carmen Lamanna Gallery, Toronto, 1979. Subsequent installation, 2000, at Ydessa Hendeles Foundation, with 16 mm film converted to video projection. Photo: Henk Visser for Carmen Lamanna Gallery.

Personal Image for Social Space (1980)

Written for *personal image for social space/L'image personelle dans l'espace collectif: seven artists' concepts that rethink the nature of glass in Canadian architecture. A mailed exhibition*, 1980. This was a mailed art exhibition contained in an envelope and folded paper holder with a single poster/text by each artist. It included an introduction by Stuart Reid, plus Jurors' Statements. Participating artists: Ian Carr-Harris, Stephanie White & Warren Hamil, Frederic Urban, Robert Jekyll, Gerald Ferguson, J.F. Granzow. Jury: Greg Curnoe, France Morin, John C. Parkin.

There is, as everyone knows, a tension existing between the roles of the artist and the architect or designer, a tension arising logically out of the difference between free conceptualization and task conceptualization.

For this reason, I have selected a site which no longer performs an active function. I am proposing that the abandoned service garage in the attached photograph (a BA garage in the fifties modernist style) be "re-activated" using as the sole functioning element the glass pane on the front door of the office.

What interests me in this situation is the dual nature of the windowpane. Buildings—architectural structures—operate on us not only as objects having mass, but also as containers having space. Indeed, it is this ambivalent nature of architectural structures that gives them their power over our imagination. In stark terms, external mass provides us with the potential of visual judgement, while contained space provides us with the potential inherent in the relations between people. Buildings as objects are simply design problems; buildings as internal space are complexities of human history.

Specifically, I am proposing therefore to re-activate the old service garage as a containing space by presenting a glimpse of its internal dynamics to the external viewer—a glimpse of the life which originally filled the space—through the recreation of the image of its original occupant.

The process is straight-forward: the window is backed with rear-projection material, and an automatic film-loop projection system—timed for intermittent operation—projects a segment of film onto the window. The content of the film is intended solely to present to the external viewer the figure of a man as he would have been seen from outside the door.

Out of the darkness of the interior he emerges to lean his elbows on the internal sill of the window frame. He is an older man in his indeterminate fifties with a rough-lined face marked with stubble and grease, dressed in grey garage overalls. A red rag is stuffed into his breast pocket, and he wipes his forehead with it before reaching for a crumpled pack of cigarettes. He lights up, takes a long drag, looks out the window with that distant expression produced by years of fatigue and meaningless struggle. Suddenly he turns his head back towards the interior of the shop and yells in reply to someone: "Ok, Joe. Coming." He looks out at us with one last drag, stubs out his cigarette on the sill, and shuffles back into the gloom.

This "appearance" would probably last about three minutes or less, and would involve a simple one-hundred-foot 16mm looped film automatically controlled to replay at any interval desired, but no more than once every fifteen minutes. The technology is simple and inexpensive.

It will be readily apparent that in this proposal the window plane is being considered not as transparent window on the external world, nor as a source of light for the interior space, nor as a decorative element, but purely for its power as a focus of our memory, our imagination, and our expectations.

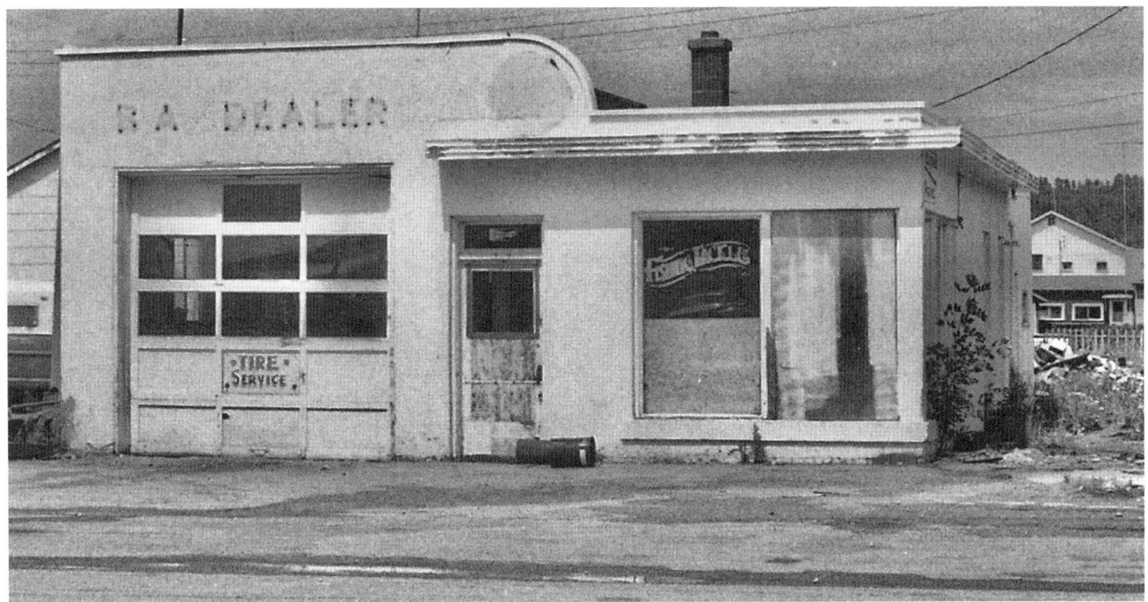

3.3   Ian Carr-Harris, untitled project for Stuart Reid, *personal image for social space: a mailed exhibition: 7 artists' concepts that rethink the nature of glass in Canadian architecture*, 1980. Envelope with individual folders, introduction by Stuart Reid. Courtesy the artist.

Let Me Explain (1982)

A project for *Impressions* 30 (1982). *Impressions* was a Toronto-based photography magazine that ran from 1970 to 1983. The original editors were John Prendergast and John F. Philips, co-founder of the Baldwin Street Gallery of Photography, Toronto. Subsequent co-editors would include Shin Sugino and Isaac Applebaum.

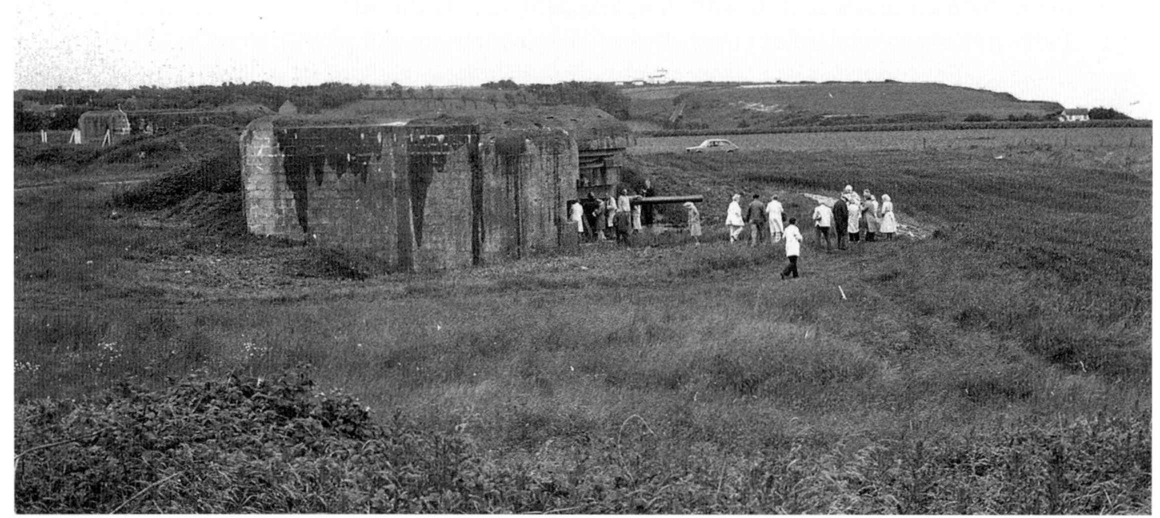

3.4   Ian Carr-Harris, *Let Me Explain*, a project for *Impressions* 30 (1982). Text piece with image, facing pages. Courtesy the artist.

Let me explain.

My friend and I had gotten up early to go and visit the old German gun emplacements that still stand along this part of the Normandy coast. The photograph looks a bit flat because it was raining in a casual sort of way; just enough to make our skin feel cold and strange.

For quite a while we were alone, tramping more or less in silence through wet grass and peering into the foetid remains of art deco at war. We climbed a small hill to look around; or perhaps to be more precise, to have one last look in that futile attempt we all make to turn certain experiences into more than just a memory. It never works; but in a curious way we came close.

A bus appeared. One of those incredibly modern continental buses, the kind which make our Greyhounds seem quaintly old-fashioned. We watched as it picked its way elegantly through the mud to stop to the left of the picture. A Mercedes, with West German plates.

As we walked slowly towards our car, we could hear the tourists calling to each other across the sodden field, helping each other on with their coats; excited by yet another point of interest. Nebraska voices, flatly rooted in common sense America; middle-aged female voices introduced by Reiseverkehr into a French field to exclaim mid-western banalities over German art deco guns pointing in memoriam through another rain at Omaha Beach.

That's when I decided to take this photograph.

George (1984)

Presented as part of the group exhibition *Vestiges of Empire* at Camden Arts Centre, London, UK, November 16 to December 23, 1984.

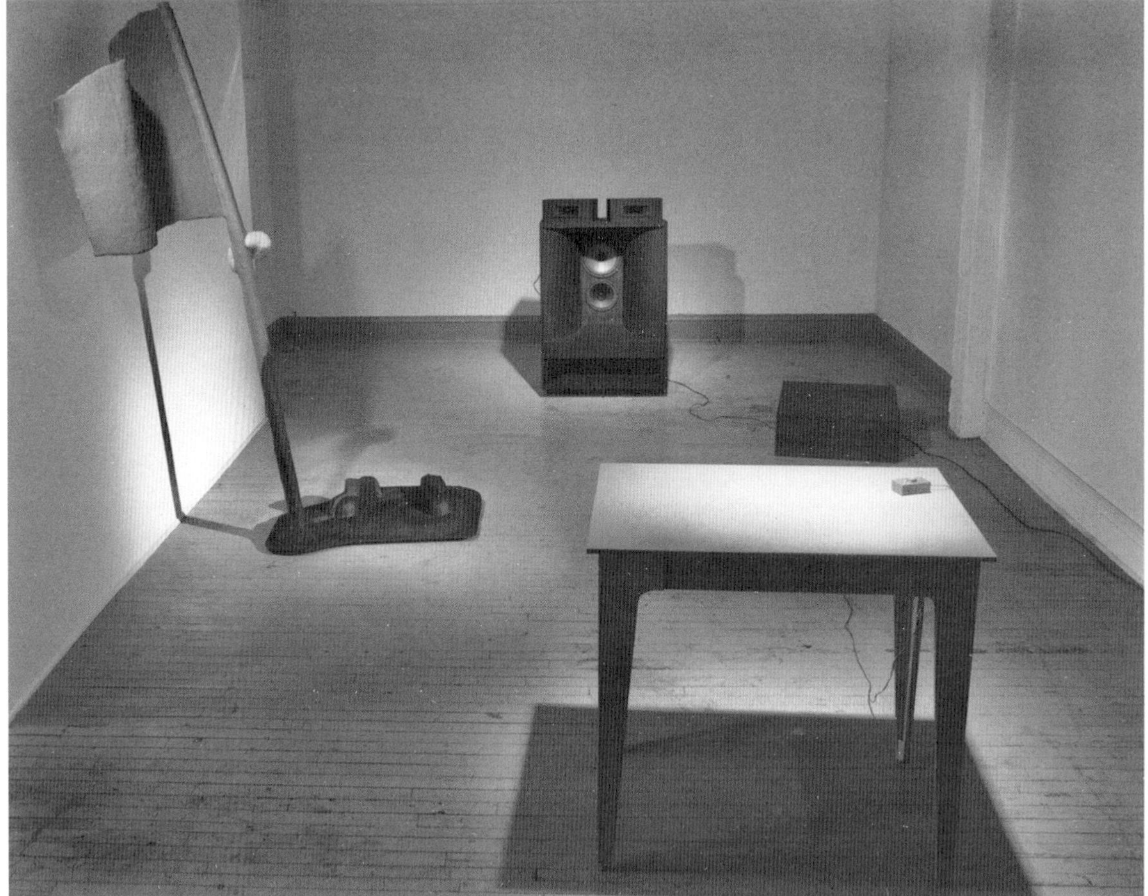

3.5   Ian Carr-Harris, *George*, 1984. Painted wood floor speaker, painted fiberglass "toy soldier with flag" construction, painted wood table with push-button, viewer-activated audio on cycle of four minutes, amplifier with audio deck, installation variable. Studio installation. Courtesy the artist.

This work is conceived as direct theatre, with its action initiated by the
viewer. Each action is a self-completing cycle of four minutes on audiotape
loop and includes the following text for female voice with two interviews.
The work is about beginnings.

(transcription of audio)
Where should I begin?

After all: (duet)   beginnings can be bright!
                    beginnings must be right!
                    beginnings should be...

I won't go on.

I'll get back to beginnings later.

So let's just say that George, over here on the left, is a good beginning.

Once upon a time:
        sitting with the others that I barely knew
        feeling very strange and cold on the vast hardwood floor below the
                distant mesh-screened December windows
        the question (the possibly innocent question) hung on the brittle air...
        no. Forget the air: dropped like a giant fat spider onto my thin
                child's chest
        "And where were *you* born?"

Years later, I decided to do a bit of research:

(male voice)
        "I can remember...I can remember going to Montreal when I was a kid,
        because I had, uh, I had an aunt there, and thinking that this was what...
        this was what Europe was like, that this was really exciting. In a way,
        going to Montreal or going to Quebec was like going to Detroit, that
        it, uh, it just seemed...it just seemed so, uh, so much more exciting, and
        it *looked* good. Everywhere I looked it looked, it looked interesting.
        People carried themselves well, and...And these were all things of, sort
        of culture and style, but I was really impressed by them; and just, just
        the kind of, liberal attitude towards things, and a casualness about the
        way they were and the way they presented themselves—and it was just,
        it was just like a different country altogether. And that's—and I didn't
        think about it, about any problems with it belonging in Canada, or any,

uh, any real differences, except that it seemed very special in the context of Canada as I understood it at the time."

And since I'd learned to check for balance, I did some more:

(female voice)
"My picture of John A. Macdonald is so cynical. Um, I always think of him as sort of this…this sort of overblown…(laughter)…this overgrown Tory with a, uh, who had a severe drinking problem, and a retarded daughter, and nothing but problems all his life—and his big pie in the sky was the railroad. And that's just how we treat our heroes, you know. Anything that's had an influence on Canadian history, we always, uh… Maybe it's, (laughter) maybe Canadians love gossip, and the seedy side of people's lives, but that's how you see it, you know.…And also when I think of John A. Macdonald, I think how he exploited the Chinese…and how many lives were lost in that…in his sheer determination—to build that railroad."

And listening to the quickness in their voices;
And listening to the frankness of their stories;

And listening to the clearness in their hearts:
    (well, relatively anyway)

I remembered George:

Poor, imported George;

When-we-were-just-beginning, George;

And maybe…

And maybe we're still just beginnings…George and I.

5 Explanations (1985)

Published as "Ian Carr-Harris: *5 Explanations*; notes," *Descant* 16, no. 3 (Fall 1985): 31–36.

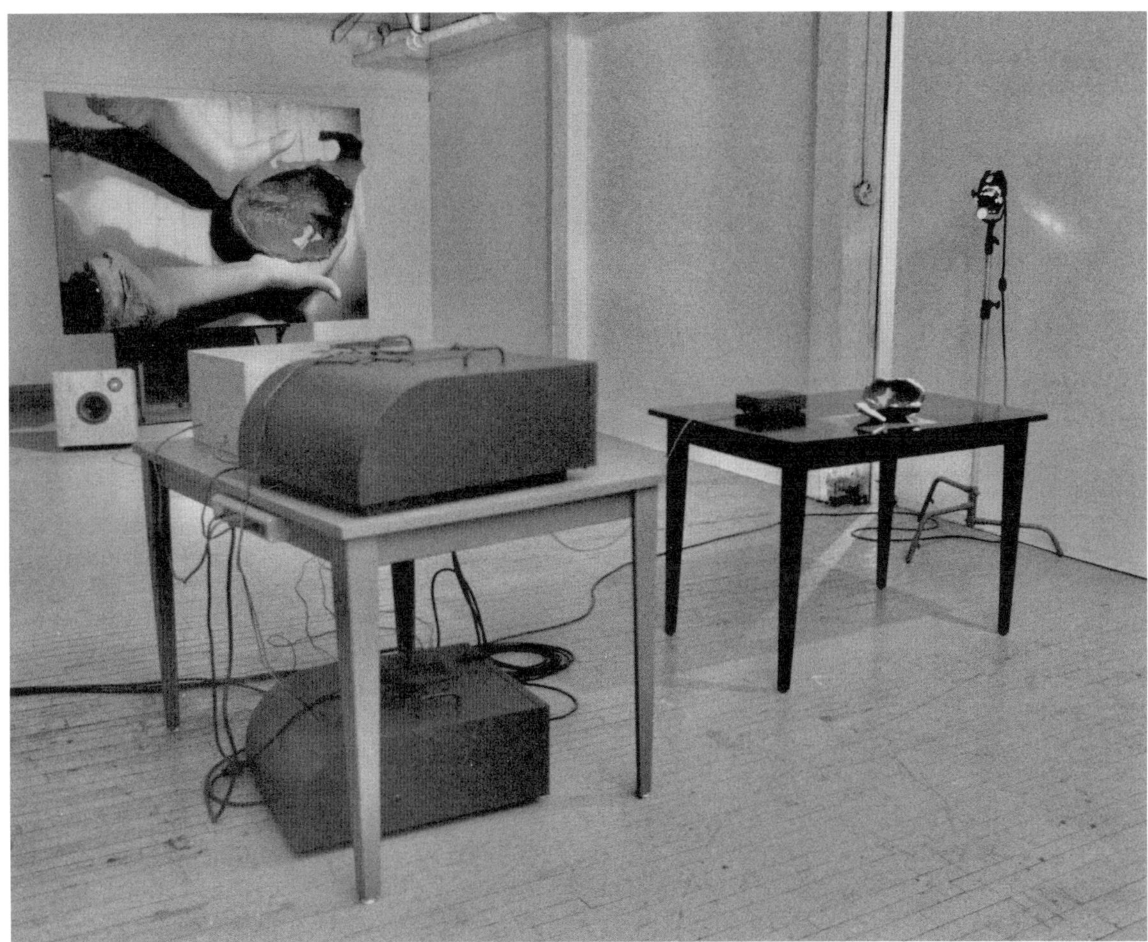

3.6   Ian Carr-Harris, *5 Explanations* (detail), 1983. Painted wood and fiberglass-resin construction with metal support structures, spotlight on metal stand, audio deck and three floor speakers, audio tape of voice-over (originally with viewer-controlled push-button, later changed to continuous play); voice-over consists of five different texts each suggesting an "explanation" for the image, each separated by thirty seconds pause; total running time of all five explanations approx. 20 mins. (Viewers not expected to remain the full duration.) Dimensions approx. 4.25 × 7.6 × 2.4 m. Artist's studio installation, 1983. Courtesy the artist.

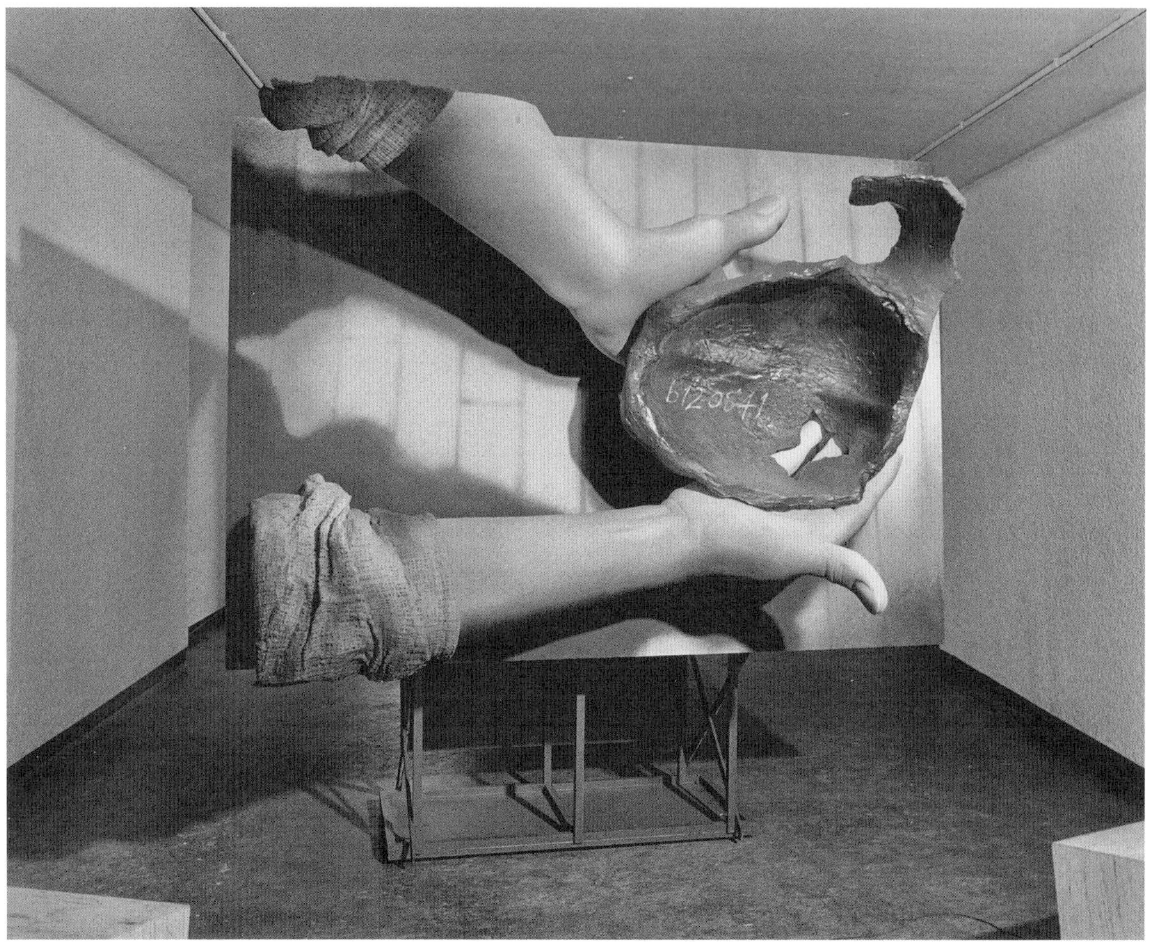

3.7/3.8 (*this page and opposite*)   Ian Carr-Harris, *5 Explanations* (details), 1983. Painted wood and fiberglass-resin construction with metal support structures, spotlight on metal stand, audio deck and three floor speakers, audio tape of voice-over (originally with viewer-controlled push-button, later changed to continuous play); voice-over consists of five different texts each suggesting an "explanation" for the image, each separated by thirty seconds pause; total running time of all five explanations approx. 20 mins. (Viewers not expected to remain the full duration.) Dimensions approx. 4.25 × 7.6 × 2.4 m. Artist's studio installation, 1983. Courtesy the artist.

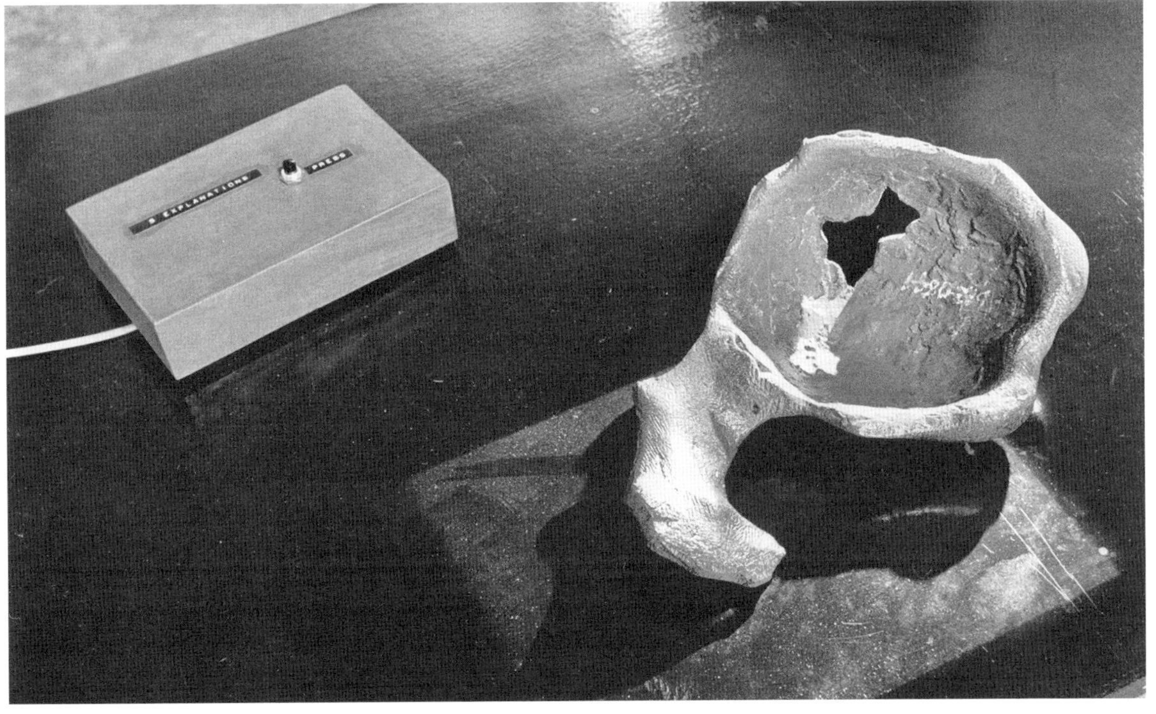
5 EXPLANATIONS PRESS

It always took me a long time to read the weekend comics. Not because I didn't understand them, but because understanding them was less important than *looking at* them, or—shall we say—experiencing them. And what is true of comics is even more true of certain loaded images.

The work *5 Explanations*, which I did in 1983, takes a particular image—a photographic format of a pair of hands holding an ambiguous object—and seeks to address our experience before that image. Two considerations were of principal importance: the image is reconstructed as a physical, material presence, while retaining an enlarged and even filmic photographic reference; and any singular understanding of its content becomes the subject of a critique developed through a voice-over commentary which both supplies the title and represents the central focus of the piece.

The work is installed so that it both fills the room in which it is housed, and directs our gaze: first at the image, from a point in which its components form an illustrational rectangle; and secondly towards the elegant black enamel table set immediately in front of the viewer. On this table is placed a life-size, or scaled-down, copy of the object held by the hands in the "picture," as well as a control switch mounted on a small box and connected to the mechanical housings which completely fill the second, utility, table. It is clear, given the three speakers facing us in the space between ourselves and the constructed image, and given the switch on the table, that the work is not simply visual, or formal in its disposition, but is in fact organized as a demonstration or explanation, and that this explanation is accessible only at our invitation.

There are five explanations. But they are assembled so that each is complete in its relation to the image, and each is disassociated from the other. Technically, they are recorded on an audio loop whose cycle is divided into five separate and independent sections, each section a finite cycle in itself. As a result, a given viewer may experience one or perhaps two or three of these explanations, but not likely all of them.

The formal structure of this work derives not from the installation alone, but also from photographic and by extension media imagery, and from theatre; it is in many ways a kind of private performance, and its lighting is vitally important for choreographing our sense of relationship to what is in effect a staged event. When activated by the viewer, the normally diffuse lighting of the gallery is extinguished and substituted by a harder spotlight fixed to the ceiling and focused frontally against the image. This flattens and simultaneously floats the picture as a kind of illusion in the room, while another smaller light near the viewer projects a rectangle of light across the object on the table, constructing an intimate, possessable echo of the larger abstracted object to which it refers. The viewer becomes not only an observer, but also a possessor.

Only two of the five explanations are reprinted here. It was never the intention of the work to reveal its entire sequence as an object to be understood, but rather as an occasion to frame the ambivalent desires of our look.

Audio 1

I must have spent a lot of time, when I was growing up, looking at old copies of *National Geographic*. There wasn't any television in Ottawa then and in Quebec—across the river—we weren't allowed to go to the movies. Not that I felt particularly deprived: a photograph stuck right in front of your nose, on a rainy afternoon when you're a kid, is not really much different from VistaVision, or whatever else the Americans were bringing us at the time.

There is one difference, though. If you look at something long enough or see it often enough—after all, there's a limited number of even *National Geographics* in the world—it becomes a part of you; and what may have seemed at first arbitrary, or frightening, or simply inconsequential, becomes bit by bit familiar, expected, even coveted. It becomes, that is, quite material, and the relationship between its status as a reproducible image and its status as a real thing, or a real event, becomes a dialectical reality—and a transparent distinction.

The image you see here became for me a symbol, or condition, of precisely this conceived desire, and exists now not merely in my memory, but in my soul. And I want to say why, and what I think that means.

This reconstruction is of course a composite from the past, and therefore has no factual existence. It's a fiction, but it's important to consider its active elements, which are three: a woman's hands, cradling a Paleolithic fragment for us to examine. It is, in fact, an act of demonstration: and the reader, or viewer—who is usually eavesdropper or voyeur—becomes instead a privileged and even welcome visitor.

What absorbed me when I was a child was how this simple inversion seemed centrally important to my existence. Like Alice in the looking-glass, if I gazed at the image long enough, its surface would dissolve, and I'd be there, in that place, bending down to look at that mysterious thing whose presence and history transformed the woman's hands into a vortex of imagined temptations. The frozen dullness of the photograph would vanish in the immense subtleties of real space, and real time, and the silence of its text would explode into the sound of her voice gently explaining the significance of that something from long ago, while the soft, almost inaudible, brush of her skin on the skull she held would speak to me even more gently of the still greater importance of something confusingly, passionately close.

And this, it seems to me now, is what that image was about. It was about desire and constraint: about wanting to know something you will never know; about wanting to touch someone you will never touch; about privilege, and its mockery.

Audio 4

(The fourth section starts with a short "chant" read by a female voice which fades out as the male voice begins. The chant comes through the plywood speakers near the image, the male voice through a larger speaker near the viewer.)

> With visible breath I am walking.
> A voice I am sending as I walk.
> In a sacred manner I am walking.
> With visible tracks I am walking.
> In a sacred manner I walk.

There is a story told by Black Elk, warrior and medicine man of the Oglala Sioux, of the way the sacred pipe first came to his people. And I want to read it to you, because it has something to do with what you see in front of you now.

A very long time ago, they say, two scouts were out looking for bison, and when they came to the top of a high hill and looked north, they saw something coming a long way off; and when it came closer, they cried out, "It is a woman!"; and it was.

Then one of the scouts, being foolish, had bad thoughts and spoke them; but the other said: "That is a sacred woman; throw all bad thoughts away." When she came still closer, they saw that she wore a fine white buckskin dress, that her hair was very long, and that she was young and beautiful. And she knew their thoughts and said in a voice that was like singing: "You do not know me, but if you want to do as you think, you may come." And the foolish one went; but just as he stood before her, there was a white cloud that came and covered them. And the beautiful young woman came out of the cloud, and when it blew away the foolish man was a skeleton covered with worms.

Now, I am not telling you this story because it is well told, or because it is interesting as myth, or even because it can be read as a moral.

Instead, examine yourself closely. Consider the image I've constructed in front of you as roughly analogous to a photograph. It is a photograph, then, of a woman holding something—it doesn't matter now just what it is—for you to see. It could just as well be a man walking down the street for that matter, but this particular image is, I think, appropriate. Now imagine that that woman is real, and that she is showing you something. As she talks, you are aware of many things that have little or nothing to do with what she is saying: the tone of her voice; the smell of her sweat; the muscles moving in her arms; the warmth from her body. You can see the blood in her veins. You fight against her physicality—against her womanness—as you attempt to register what she says. Above all, you fight to maintain that illusion you must both uphold that your entire response to her is contained in the logic of her information.

You will notice, however, an odd aspect to this physicality. If you think carefully, you will realize that it has as much to do with yours as it does with hers. There is, you might say, a photographic quality to it, as though while acknowledging her independent status you nevertheless simultaneously impose on her the condition of a projected and incestuous desire, and like a photograph she ceases to be independent and becomes instead a reflection of your own body and will.

You will recall that the wise scout in Black Elk's story resisted the seduction of that reflection in the knowledge that to violate the sacred woman—to violate the photograph—would be to destroy himself.

And that—not pious stories or moral rhetoric—is how things are.

On TV (1986)

This work was produced for *Luminous Sites*, an exhibition of Canadian video installations curated by Daina Augaitis of the Western Front and Karen Henry of Video Inn, Vancouver, February 25 to March 13, 1986. Works by ten artists were installed at galleries and public sites throughout the city.

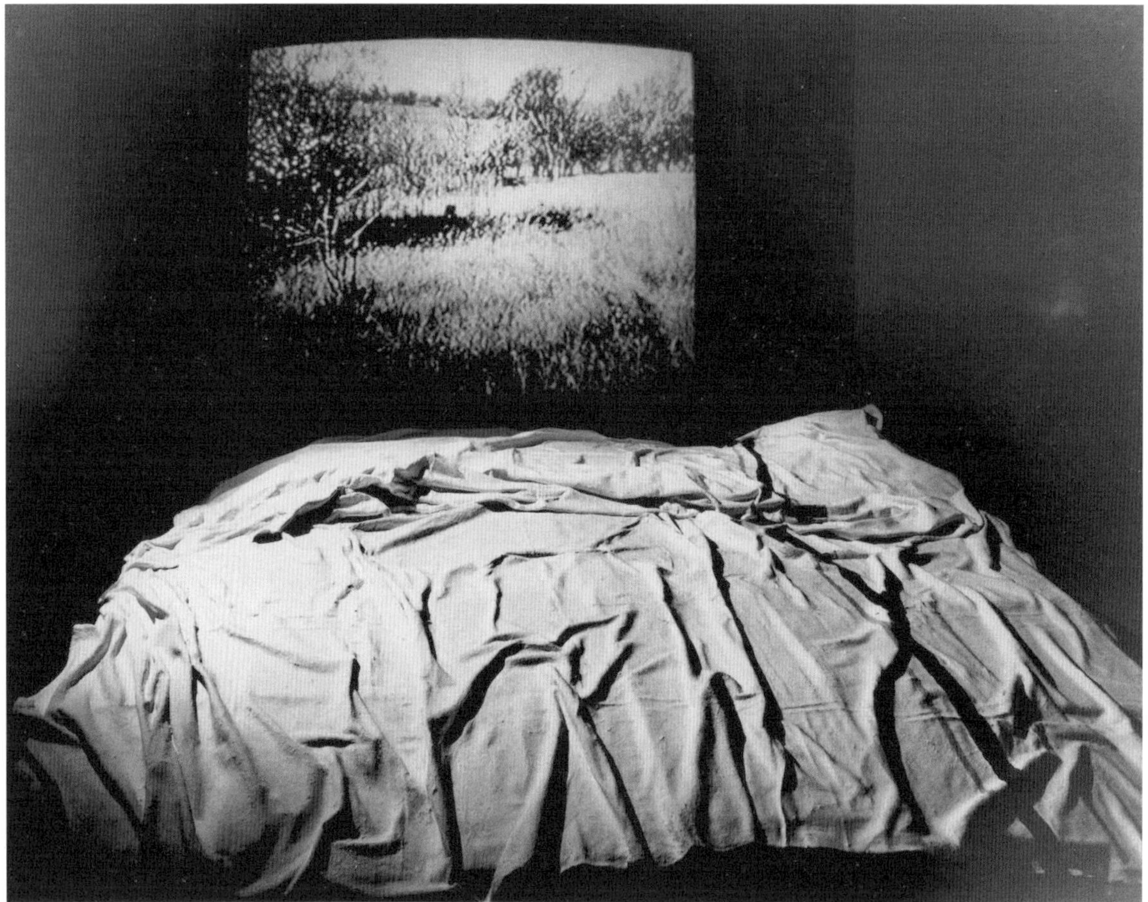

3.9   Ian Carr-Harris, *On TV*, 1986, installation Carmen Lamanna Gallery, 1986. Painted plywood screen, painted fiberglass-resin-impregnated sheet, painted plywood base, floor speaker, 35 mm colour slide, slide projection through rotating fan, audio cassette on continuous repeat, stereo amplifier in housing, spotlight, spoken text about ten minutes between short intervals of "TV noise." Photo: Chick Rice, Western Front Gallery, Vancouver.

I have a number of concerns about what artworks can accomplish, and
they fall roughly into two intersecting categories. These have to do on the
one hand with their suggestiveness and the meanings they can construct
dialectically in the imagination of the viewer by virtue of their permissive-
ness; and on the other hand with the intentions of the artist—who holds
at least responsibility for the existence of the work—in directing meaning
and presenting to the social consciousness of the viewer particular codes
of value. When taken together, and all artworks exhibit both these categories, they act to define and to counter our own individual productions
of meaning. They both produce and deny these productions—this is what
they accomplish.

For artworks to produce meaning they must be specific. That is, we
must have a point of departure, from which, as the viewer, we can move. For
artworks to deny meaning, the references denied must not only be specific,
but their identity must be clarified, whether through representations of
language or through mimetic construct.

On TV constructs through its imagery an implied location of the viewer,
an attachment. That location carries ambiguities which the work's audio
text proceeds to ground in a set of clear intentions, intentions that become
at once a demonstration and a reminder of the work's status, and the viewer's position. The text is a lecture on two paintings by Manet, and through it
an investigation of the act of seeing.

As with all my work, *On TV* derives from my conviction that we understand things for ourselves out of specific encounters that embody their own
particular penetration of social value.

(transcription of audio loop: lecture alternates with fifteen seconds of
TV "snow" or static)

I am going to assume that if artistic practice cannot change the world, it can
at least be useful in demonstrating something about what would be involved
if changes are to be made. I therefore want to talk about two paintings by
Edouard Manet, and to consider in particular his *Luncheon on the Grass*, or
Déjeuner sur l'herbe.

From its execution in 1863, that painting has been most remarkable—to
the majority of its audience—for a conjunction of two deceptively simple
statements. Most obviously, unlike the two men beside her on the grass,
the woman is naked. Moreover, also unlike her companions, she looks out
directly at the viewer. Despite her nakedness, she in fact clearly, and calmly,
acknowledges our presence. Above all, these statements are remarkable
because the painting makes no appeal to symbolic truth to justify them.

For most, this has meant that *Luncheon on the Grass* can be seen either as a tasteless and unredeeming narrative of questionable intention about prostitutes and students; or, alternatively, as a critical intervention disrupting the polite conventions both of art and society as they existed in the golden age of the European middle class. And both views have their merits.

I am interested in another reading, however, one which is less ambitious as an ethical model, but which nonetheless retains a solid critical value for the work. I said that the woman's gaze, directed at the viewer, remains notably calm. In fact, her look is entirely normal, expressive of the same vague interest she would hold for any casual passerby were she completely clothed. In her own look, she is as dressed as we are. Now let us also assume, since Manet was male, that the constructed viewer is male as well. Is this, then, simply the familiar privilege of a voyeur? Partly, and I believe intentionally so. But Manet's naked woman is not so easily an object of erotic acquisition. Her body is not laid out for male desire, nor is she placed in an unaware or compromised position. Her stance is functional, and Manet has lit her with the unsentimental directness of passport photos or cheap TV talk shows. More especially, her gaze is that of an intelligent subject, and we are addressed neither as authority, nor allowed to assume anonymity. We are, in fact, addressed by her as present, equal, and inconsequential. And this establishes a fundamental change in the privileged relationship, one which was not lost on its original audience, whose central complaint was precisely the discomfort that this naked woman provoked in her—male—viewers.

What are we to make of this changed relationship? What I believe Manet constructed around the woman is an inescapable realization of accountability, and the critical power that this subjective realization exerts over the seduction of objectification. As we stand before the painting, we become physically aware that in spite of our attempts to define experience as discrete and irrational—as standing safely outside ourselves—we are actually in reality immensely vulnerable to dislocation. *Luncheon on the Grass* defines a set of relations that exists primarily not within the painting, but between the painting and the viewer. Through the woman's gaze, we are rendered conscious of our own look, rendered aware that our own extended gaze—seeing her naked—is an act of our, not her, volition. *But*, and this is crucial, it is an act we did not invite. We have, as it were, been ourselves compromised into an encounter we might otherwise have invited; and it is we who are as a result surprised and confused, not the woman. In distressing us, and making us accept responsibility for this distress, Manet constructs a position of disturbance for the viewer which can, and finally must, be addressed self-critically.

It is clear, then, that the important subject of this painting is not nudity or even nakedness, not decadence or issues of painting as such, though it certainly includes discussion on these. The real subject is the nature of our relations in the world, and these Manet defines as both subjective and operational in the site of the viewer rather representational within the frame of the painting. The real subject of *Luncheon on the Grass* lies not *on* the grass, but we could almost say *in* it—it lies in our encounter and within our reconstruction of it.

Luncheon on the Grass was completed by Manet's second painting of that year, his *Olympia*. The naked woman rests now not on the grass but on the rumpled sheets of a bed. The ironic equivalence constructed in *Luncheon on the Grass*, first between ourselves and the woman, and then expanded within the painting as an equivalence between the woman and her oddly ineffective "natural" landscape—a landscape that looks suspiciously like a badly painted theatrical back-drop—is repeated even more ironically in *Olympia* with the suggestion of a sardonic equivalence between the woman and the cut flowers the maid ostensibly presents to her, but more obviously to us. And on the sheets at the woman's feet a small black cat, its back arched, and painted expressly to mock the viewer's own hidden alarm, echoes the direction of the woman's gaze and stares out at our intrusion, confronting us again with our presence by this bed, within this surrogate landscape. In *Olympia*, Manet more blatantly and more suavely reveals his proposition: not only that the landscape we innocently came to view must surely, if unexpectedly, include ourselves; but moreover, and inevitably, that this encountered landscape is a trap of projected and self-conscious ironies. Exactly fifty years later, Duchamp signed this proposition into the twentieth century.

What does all this mean, then? In both paintings, Manet has signalled that the discussion of our accountability, our subjectivity, is necessarily an ironic discussion of equivalent relations. I noted before that the paintings can be considered to construct their viewer as male, and it is vitally important that we see this as neither an imposition nor a social assumption—though it is of course both—but as an intentional and necessary corollary, an additional irony, if you like, to Manet's responsibility for the work. Vital, because this responsibility assigns the logic of the interlocked gaze Manet has set between the viewer and the woman. In constructing us as male, both *Luncheon on the Grass* and *Olympia* confront us disconcertingly with our own sense of difference. And precisely because we are placed self-critically before that recognition of difference—because the woman recognizes no authority and remains our equal—we may distinguish but we cannot separate the categories of difference and similarity. The woman constructs an ironic equivalence between herself and the viewer, and the additional ironies Manet has built into the paintings are projected now as a recognition by the viewer that we are caught within a dialectic of observed and anticipated experience. And it is within this dialectic that we can distinguish the ground and conception of moral value and responsibility.

I remarked at the beginning that the reading I have given here differs from most in being less morally ambitious. The standard critiques, while differing sharply in ideological attachments, share a belief in the effectiveness of a moral imperative. Not surprisingly, this ultimately involves the deployment of power pursued as an argument of closure. The critique I have favoured here, the critique of ironic equivalence, while it recognizes the importance of power, recognizes as well that that power must be understood self-critically and dialectically if it is to have moral significance and political credence.

I have talked about Manet because he has entered history, and we look to history to stand outside ourselves, to—in effect—more easily experience our own critical position. Most of us, however, are not likely to be concerned with the *Luncheon on the Grass*, or the *Olympia*, and rightly or wrongly look to what we know in the present. If what I have discussed seems merely elitist in its assumptions, look carefully then, and consider what you find yourself actually doing—as both engineer and client of your own look—when you catch yourself next time watching something on TV.

Art and Document (2020)

Written for *Voices: artists on art*, an artists' project conceived by Yvonne Lammerich and Ian Carr-Harris and held at Harbourfront Centre, Toronto, September 23 to December 24, 2017. The project was collected in a book self-published by the authors in 2020. The project is also archived online at https://voicesartistsonart.ca.

It started in a pub. When Yvonne proposed *Voices*, the conversation had turned to our memory of an exhibition no one remembered. So this project began with the sense that memory is a fragile entity, and that to try to communicate to others the impact that art can have tests our ability to reimagine another's experience, and our ability to transcend the present moment. This led to a question: *how* to reimagine another's experience, *how* to transcend the present moment?

Eventually we cobbled together twenty-three questions we felt we ourselves would like to be asked about the experience of being an artist, and which we thought other artists would find equally interesting. One of those questions involved a concern over the durability of art in our current culture. Certainly a characteristic of contemporary art has become its increasingly performative nature. An issue that has arisen in performance is whether it speaks to impact and memory rather than to research and reflection, whether its documentation is useful or even legitimate.

The issue extends to how art and history is experienced, and in this respect one interesting strategy within contemporary art is the emergence of re-performance, which in an important sense touches on a debate around spoken and written language, a debate that reaches back to Socrates and Plato and the very nature of what we take to be authentic. Socrates, as we know, insisted that Plato's written language could not possibly be as authentic as the performative power of the spoken word, and that writing or recording would be the death of memory and the free extrapolations of storytelling and invention.

But Plato persists. We live in history and abide by the text, and if memory and storytelling is lost, we at least have the document, and the document enables its re-performance. More than that, however, it also enables its extrapolation, what one might call its reinvention. *The Republic* is nothing less.

We live in history, but we no longer need live without the spoken word. The new technologies stretching back to the invention of the audio recording and now to the ubiquitous smartphone video have revolutionized the status of the spoken word, the role of the performer, and the framing of the artist. It is as though the artist, as in those trompe l'oeil paintings where the figure steps out of the picture frame, can give voice to their thoughts—like Socrates holding forth in the marketplace, as Plato writes.

Curiously, the *Voices* project itself began as a discussion in a marketplace—the ByWard Market in Ottawa, and specifically the Aulde Dubliner pub on the corner of William Street. And curiously, as well, the subject of our discussion had been a memory—Dorothy Cameron's important National Gallery of Canada exhibition from 1967—the one that we had both independently seen. The memories soon turned to storytelling and the realization that despite its groundbreaking status few if anyone had ever mentioned it in the fifty years since. One could say it had been erased, were it not for the fact that a few precious copies of its catalogue remained. Along with our memories.

What I took away from *Sculpture '67* was that somehow Canada was on the map—it was the centennial year, and I hadn't yet been to *Expo '67*—though I wasn't sure what the map was about. Canada seemed an interesting place to call home, if only because it didn't suffer from over exposure—an in-between sort of place where something could happen (whether or not it might). And I was in-between, about to go, somewhat late in the game, to art school. Perhaps that exhibition was in many respects my first semester at the Ontario College of Art.

In any case, from storytelling we moved to documentation. It occurred to us that our discussion was about the document, and how it could be understood as the work itself. We knew that logistically, *Sculpture '67*, as an exhibition, could never be re-performed. But we reasoned that the exhibition's document—its catalogue—could be. Luckily, we found a copy of the catalogue on eBay. Moreover, Cameron had constructed it as simply a series of artists' statements with images on facing pages, so in effect it was a true exhibition catalogue, a catalogue of the exhibition's fifty-one artists and their work. For the *Voices* project, the catalogue entries therefore became the re-performed exhibition, and in the spirit of performance, Iain Baxter& (a.k.a. N.E. Thing Co, with Ingrid Baxter), Michael Snow, and Françoise Sullivan to our delight agreed to read their original statements on camera as a parallel speaking document.

Another critical element surfaced somewhat indirectly, its source a remark made in an article by art critic Robert Fulford that appeared in the Summer 1967 issue of *artscanada* (Barry Lord's precursor to *Canadian Art* magazine) shortly after the exhibition's premature closing by the National Gallery in mid-July. Fulford closed his piece with this: "The National

Gallery's show has given us a chance to judge [Canadian sculpture's] direction, but it will be a long time before we understand their destination."

Fulford's statement, which we took as a challenge, nicely articulated the relationship between the National Gallery's project and the project that *Voices* has pursued in its interviews with artists working in the following decades. I'll return to this relationship a bit later on. For the moment, I want to follow up on the issue of the document as an artwork.

While it's one thing to re-perform an exhibition as a document, it's quite another to view the document as an artwork. Is *The Republic* a work of literature? There are those who view Plato as a clandestine artist. What is an artwork? What *makes* an artwork? What shifts the meaning of art? These questions have been crucial since Duchamp's 1917 *Fountain* in the definition of art, artists and the audience itself. Our conversation in the Irish pub had quickly turned to the question of contemporary artists and the familiar artist statement as well as the more recent emergence of the artist interview. Could the statement or interview now be seen as the work itself? Writing almost fifty years ago, Roland Barthes suggested that the work of art should more properly be called a "text," in the sense that the art as object is extended by the contexts of its existence, that it is not bounded by its apparent objecthood. The work of art, in effect, exists on a continuum of possibilities. What was good for Barthes seemed fertile ground for us, and we decided to video-interview fifty-one artists as an artwork. So, *Voices: artists on art* was born—in an Irish pub, which seems only fitting given James Joyce and the Irish love of storytelling. *Voices* pursues the work as text, one might say to the edges of definition, where art impacts on document, and document folds itself into art, where *what* artists say and *how* they say it becomes art itself.

Our project is therefore not simply an exhibition of work by artists, but an e*xhibition of artists speaking as itself a work.*

I'm aware that the matter of form is always contestable. It would be easy to say that as video the project has a ready-made form, one pre-set by the language of film and specifically documentary film, with ourselves as artist-filmmakers. But our intent is more than would be appropriate for that defence. Our claim, instead, is that *Voices* is an umbrella artwork, a *Gesamtkunstwerk*, comprising not simply the project as installation, but as one formed by each of the fifty-one encounters with individual artists, one in which the artists speaking to *being* artists represents Barthes's unwrapping of our conventional expectations for the artwork. In effect an artwork of multiple identities.

To test this further, there is Borges's "Pierre Menard, Author of *Don Quixote*," one of the stories in his compilation *Ficciones*. Borges's fictional novelist, now deceased, has spent a lifetime writing some small sections of *Don Quixote*, Cervantes's 1580 masterpiece. Astoundingly, Menard's "Quixote," though unfinished, is word-for-word identical to Cervantes's original passages. No matter. Menard's work is an original *Don Quixote*. Why? Because Menard has written it centuries later, and as a consequence, embedded in the words he has written are all the circumstances that have occurred since Cervantes wrote *his* "Quixote." Indeed, inherent in those circumstances, is the fact that Menard is not Cervantes, that his words are formed from his own experience rather than those that informed Cervantes. Cervantes's words may appear to be the same, but they are not: words embody what the author has experienced.

For *Voices* the implication is clear. The artists' works, like Menard's words, are embodiments of experience, that of the artist as well as that of each individual viewer in the presence of the work. As Julia Wood and Robert Cox put it in "Rethinking Critical Voice: Materiality and Situated Knowledge," we all "live embodied lives, constrained, informed and framed by material circumstances such as living and working environments, food, and medical care." To speak to that materiality is to reveal the work in its becoming, its essential, if contingent, Being. The artist's statements, the voiced responses to our questions in the project are in all respects an engagement with the intended meaning of a work of art, inescapably entangled with it, its other identities.

Voices: artists on art, Five Interviews (2016/17)

Art without conversation is decoration.

It began with a conversation about a National Gallery exhibition, *Sculpture '67*, that we had both seen in Toronto's Nathan Phillips Square the summer before we went to art school. It featured fifty-one artists from across Canada, including Françoise Sullivan from Quebec, Michael Snow from Ontario, and Iain and Ingrid Baxter's N.E. Thing Co. from Vancouver.[1] Groundbreaking in its support of the new idiom of minimalist and conceptualist tendencies revolutionizing the art of the twentieth century, it was a hit with both public and critics. No one remembers it.

So memory—or the loss of it—became an inspiration. Because with no memory there is no meaningful present, no conversation. What to do?

It was here that a thought was born. What if instead of a statement tacked to the wall, statements by artists became the artwork itself? What if voices would *be* the work—the voices of artists speaking to their interests, to the interests of their viewers—conducted by artists. By us. So *Voices: artists on art*—a work about how work *works* in the context of the world and the values artists and viewers share.

Artists make art to be heard. Making art is a process of gathering evidence—whether that evidence concerns the materiality of the world expressed in line and shape, or whether that materiality concerns the social constructs that dominate or infiltrate our experience in the world. Art can frame what moves us, or destabilize our assumptions, and the artists interviewed in the *Voices* project interweave these elements in their practices. Based on a belief in the agency of artists, this project is our contribution, our work as artists, to an ongoing conversation on what is art and what it can become.

About the Project

Limiting ourselves to the same number of artists as the fifty-one represented in the 1967 exhibition, the interviews that Yvonne Lammerich and Ian Carr-Harris conducted for the *Voices: artists on art* project were based

This preamble is an edited version of remarks introducing the project, organized by Ian Carr-Harris and Yvonne Lammerich, in the book *Voices: artists on art*, self-published in the spring of 2020 to accompany the original exhibition, which was presented at Artport Gallery, Harbourfront Centre, Toronto, 2017; Southern Alberta Art Gallery, Lethbridge, 2018; and Zayed University, Dubai and Abu Dhabi, 2019. The project is archived online at https://voicesartistsonart.ca.

The writer, curator, and artist Lauren Fournier closes her book *Autotheory as Feminist Practice in Art, Writing, and Criticism* (Cambridge, MA: MIT Press, 2022) with these lines: "While autotheory is predicated on the self, it is by no means solipsistic. The singular can be a gateway to the multiple. And in theorizing together we may, after all, hear ourselves." Listening to artists the better to have that conversation is the purpose of these interviews.

1   Iain Baxter legally changed his name to IAIN BAXTER& in 2005.

on a series of twenty-three questions formulated over several weeks in the summer of 2016. Organized under three sets—On Work, On Practice, and On Impact—the questions were designed to probe the artists we selected on such issues as how they came to be artists, their work processes, their views on the art system and the audience for art, the value of originality or authenticity, and the sheer persistence required to maintain a practice. To prepare for the interview, we sent these questions to each artist several weeks before the scheduled meetings which were conducted in studios across the country, including Toronto, Montreal, Winnipeg, Calgary, Vancouver, Victoria, and Moncton. With a long history of interest in making films, Yvonne Lammerich assumed the role of videographer, both lighting and camera, while Ian Carr-Harris acted as the interviewer.

The following transcriptions represent only a small selection of those fifty-one video interviews. They have been edited for length and to bridge the shift from spoken to printed word. While every effort has been made to remain true to the voice of the artist, clearly the hesitations and occasional repetitions that make the spoken word come alive require careful and selective editing to preserve the articulation of thought that is expected in the written word. These transcripts have therefore been constructed in such a way as to respect both the living voice of the artist and their intent in what they have to say.

Raphaëlle De Groot

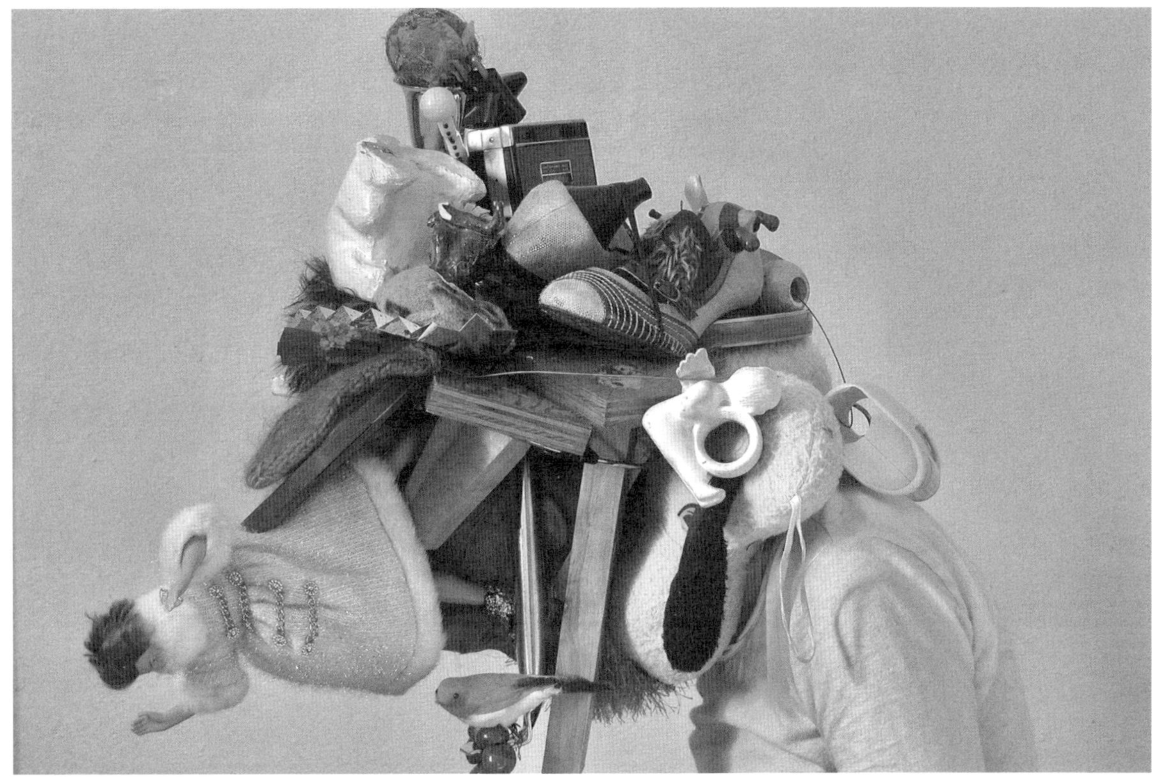

3.10   Raphaëlle de Groot, *Port de tête*, 2010. Digital print, 51 × 71 cm. Courtesy the artist. Photo: Mirko Sabatini.

This interview was recorded on December 7, 2016.

Born in Montreal, Raphaëlle de Groot's performances, videos and installations raise questions about the relationship of art to the body, identity, memory and material phenomena. De Groot has worked with artists and historians to consider the relationship between "dead" memory locked in documents to that of "living" memory anchored in the present.

(Editor's note: One especially engaging aspect of the interview with Raphaëlle is that while clearly at home in her use of English, she speaks with the subtle intonations of her native French language and the very expressive sense of presence more typical of Quebec than of English Canada. While in many significant ways it is Raphaëlle's gestural language throughout the interview that lends urgency to her concerns, hopefully the transcription carries this same intonation if it is to adequately reflect the lightness and infectious engagement she brought to the process.)

The gallery at Harbourfront Centre in Toronto is a large space with one wall consisting almost entirely of floor-to-ceiling windows facing onto the main traffic corridor of the Centre. A reception desk sits to one side of that wall, and this becomes the location for the interview. The space is flooded with daylight, it is mid morning, so lighting can be supplementary. Today the gallery is closed, and Yvonne is working to place the lighting to counter the daylight streaming through the windows. There is a certain amount of traffic noise from the corridor as well, and Yvonne finds it necessary to situate the cameras so as to reduce the effect on the recording. Raphaëlle decides to place herself by the reception desk. Ian remains standing several feet from Raphaëlle near the centre of the gallery. Yvonne signals that the cameras are ready and the interview begins.

CH: Why does one become an artist—it's a question for many who see it as romantic at best. Why did you decide that this was what you wanted to be?

RDG: Yes, well, I don't think I ever really did. In such a clear, "Oh, I want to be an artist." And somehow it's a choice or a commitment that is constantly renewed. Because it's not really easy (laughs). So, you know, like you constantly have to renew your desire and your will and conviction that this is what you want to do. So I would have a particularly interesting story in terms of how I came about how to be an artist, but certainly—my grandmother was a painter, so I grew up in my house with paintings, and her art was very much, for my father at least, represented a memory of their history of exile and immigration from Europe and then from South America and then eventually to Quebec. But then, you know, the art she did had nothing to do with—was not, let's say, contemporary art! She painted flowers, people, landscapes, in oil, watercolour. So I grew up with this around me, but I never thought that I would be an artist, in that sense.

  Then what happened is that I actually wanted to go into stage design and I didn't get into the schools I wanted to, but got into an arts BA program, and I thought, good! I'll get a good ground and then if I wanted, I could apply to go into stage design. And then I don't know what happened, but I was—probably because of the teachers I met and what happened there—was that I found myself so interested in what was happening there in my classes and, I don't know, I just stuck with it. And kind of got lucky.

Right away when I got out of school I did a year as an exchange student in New York and came back from that experience with a body of work that I proposed at an artist-run centre and they had—in their programing, they were lacking someone, and so right away I was able to show that work, which was quite exceptional, and then from there things started to kind of evolve.

And right through all of that I also was trying to figure out how the hell was I going to make a living, right?! (laughs) So this whole balancing act thing you try to put in place, and that's when you really figure out, should I continue doing this, should I do a Masters—but then somehow should I do one in anthropology or maybe I should go to a conservation school, like when you restore artworks, and trying to search for ways that—In artworks you actually have to work to find out a way to earn money, and parallel to that, time and space to do your work. So I was trying to figure out how to put that in place, and for some reason I always ended up thinking well, no, the space where I can do what I really want is to be an artist. If I go in anthropology or if I go to this other thing, there's a frame around these other things that's not like what I have—what art gives me as a platform, as an open space to, to—I wouldn't say challenge, because that's not the spirit that drives me, it's not challenge-based—but to search for boundaries of sorts and in the arts I felt that—especially in contemporary, actual practices, that's where I'm most alive, in that kind of intellectual questioning of things. And so that's how at one point I kind of resigned myself, saying, well no, it's not searching for another thing to do, this is where you need to be!

But still, you know, I feel that's very fragile and I think, and I really know, that I can be successful in terms of getting grants or recognition and all that, but still that's not enough to confirm that I can still be around. I wonder how—you know, for me you guys are a great example of that because you're still around, you're still doing it. And probably you went through the same thing I did, where you're like: how can I continue doing this? Also, when things are changing so rapidly around us, constantly— Yvonne is a video artist (laughs), and you're doing this project in films, and you know, your practices. And so that it's an evolution that you're doing this. So we constantly have to, well constantly—part of the nature of what we do is also a constant reinvesting, re-engaging, re-, re-, re-... (laughs) I don't know if that answered the question!

CH: I'd like to use your word "boundaries." If one has a boundary, then one has a sense of purpose, that somehow something has to be done. So did you have a sense from the beginning, or did you evolve a sense of what an artist can do or does in order to circulate around these boundaries?

RDG: Well, for sure, as I said, growing up with these paintings, with a very clear idea of what an artist is—you know, my grandmother she's a painter, she has her stuff, a place where she does that and it was kind of close to me direct from childhood—I could see that. And then there were, you know, the films, you see Camille Claudel, and you see Rodin in films, and you see—you have this image of Jackson Pollock, you know! The drippings, the energy! So I guess I internalized a kind of media-romantic—through a romanticized vision—representation of an artist. Picasso (she mimics Picasso's gestures and laughs). That, and from this other, my grandmother, this other—not contemporary at all, you could see these two sides—but somehow what I was doing in school, I went to just doing a lot of painting, these paintings I installed in relationship to the space of architecture and I always ended up putting myself—let's say in a student exhibition, you know everyone wants the best wall, to shine. Just give me the worst angle where you'd never think you'd put your work there—I'd go there! I did not want any part of that "give me the best wall." And so that's part of the impulse, not being where you'd look there. Probably I would have rather been the artist who wants the best, the best spot, you know, but that's not how I was working!

So I think I've lost myself in your question, because you were talking about what an artist can do. It's this kind of attitude, I guess, put myself outside of the frame in some ways—situating the, the—*la graine*, the seed of a project outside the frame that got me to suddenly discover that I was completely thinking of that romantic idea of the artist, but completely outside of the representation I had of the studio, you know, the space where you're this kind of white, blank page where you create from within your— (she makes a tumbling gesture that suggests something coming from the gut, and laughs)—from within, or you have this inspiration that comes from above and the artist has this, this *being* that materializes this inspiration or expression, you know! I needed to move away from that. But still this idea was there in the back, like a glove where you have the outside and then you flip it around and then there's the inside. The two sides of the same thing, dynamically engaging. And so I guess that's the thing that got me engaged with boundaries—finding myself to think of projects, to think of art but in places like a textile factory or a congregation—nuns—or a public library, doing things there, actions, that didn't use any conventional tools or mediums or anything that had to do with my art background, what I had learned in school. Traditional discourse. But still doing things that had to do with unveiling or a kind of looking at things in a different way, trying to, to bring to the surface things—which is pretty well I think what an artist in a way does. Differently, you know, but art's about that.

CH: As you were talking, I was thinking about a particular work, the *Summit Meetings*, and that work would seem core to your practice. Would you say so?

RDG: You think so? (laughs)

CH: Well, I'm asking! From what we're discussing, it seems like a quintessential piece.

RDG: (laughs) Yes, well, I'm happy that you're mentioning this work, which is kind of an ethic for me to put together. In *Summit Meetings* it's true that—how can I say—it brings together the things that go to the beginnings of my practice. So the *Summit Meetings* in itself is a gathering—even though it's a show, which you see at an exhibition, I see it as a gathering. So for me it's an event with physical objects in a room, a gathering of objects that come from this whole kind of project I started in 2009 that I call *The Burden of Objects* where I collected from people in many different contexts and scenes and countries. I collected from people things that they had at home, that they kind of put away in a cupboard, hidden somewhere. So, things that they were never able to throw away but nevertheless, you know, they don't live with these objects around them, constantly. They're kind of put aside.

And so I was offering people the possibility to free themselves, in a way, of these things they had—saying, well, you can pass on this burden to me and this burden of yours will become part of my drive for art. (laughs) And so I've received many, many things, and collected each time a kind of story or anecdote in relation to these objects and especially also why people were ready to let go of these things. So things could be, like, for example, a gift you received—you really liked the person but the thing they gave to you not, no, you can't. Or, for example, things that belonged to an ex-boyfriend. You don't feel authorized to throw away but you've lost touch with the person so you're stuck with the thing. Or things that have to do with a loss, or also things from your teenage years, you know, another period in your life, so many of these objects were at the kind of boundary with people trying to turn a page on something. When they gave the object to me, it became also for them not only to free themselves of the material accumulation, but also of the immaterial weight they attach to some things that they have and can't let go of that.

So I have this collection of things, the smallest being, let's say, a bead and the biggest, an armchair, and eventually these things, I travel with them—not all of them at once, but I travel with these things and I started really carrying the burden and trying to—not re-purpose it, but constantly *address* it, and the movement in the work—taking things from under the carpet, or under the bed and just taking them out, and so now I become the guardian of these things and so I—it doesn't make any sense if I take them back into a cupboard or put them in a box, I have to, you know: Hey, you exist, you exist, what do you mean? Hey, you Thing, what do you stand for here now in my hands? So I did this for about seven years (laughs), in many ways just to—of course, things are in suitcases but then taking them out of the suitcase and then maybe bringing them to somewhere so they can—so it's not just the objects I have with me, but the stories and the people who gave me these objects.

And so these objects would turn into my companions and I would then, let's say I would travel to Mexico and I would choose to bring with me a sample of my collection and so I made groupings and they're like friends and families that I would put in suitcases together and then I would think I'm going to Mexico and there's a particular relationship to Death, you know, and I'm very curious about that and I have objects that deal with that, so I bring them with me and then when I get to Mexico I bring some of these objects in my bag to go visit a cemetery and then once I'm there I see a grave, full of objects on it. It's a child that died at one years old and it's known that the tomb opens up once in a while and the ghost comes out and because the baby was afraid of the dark, so the people will keep giving him toys and leaving him toys and I had—one of my objects was a telephone, a bad news telephone, and the person who gave it to me told me that he received through the telephone notice of his mother's death and then his father's death and then of his last uncle and his last aunt and best friend and so on, and he said to me I don't want this phone anymore. So I had this phone and other objects that had to do with loss, and there I found myself in the cemetery with these things, and I just asked the clerk that was there and could you please put this phone on the grave—and just trying to really project myself into these objects and imagine that they can have conversations and could help each other in some way or—and so I had an example of that, a red telephone cord that this young woman, girl-woman, when you're right in that age there, in-between! And she gave me this cord saying, well when I was young my father went away during the weeks to work and so every night I waited for his telephone call to say good night and the only telephone we had was this red telephone and I would be sitting waiting for the telephone call and playing with that cord and so she said eventually the phone broke but I wanted to keep the cord—it doesn't have any value, it probably comes from Zellers or Walmart but I couldn't throw away the cord. And so, for me, that cord represented the relationship, the love-bond between her and her father. And so I just plugged that cord into that bad news telephone and wondered what would happen (laughs)—nothing happened, I didn't receive any call through that telephone, but I mean, for me, these moments were—and these were not public moments, they were very private in my life, in my travels, in my—but it really happened to me, I started to look at things in a different way, when we think of it, art does that, or it did to me, really transforming my way to relate to the world and see things.

And so eventually, with that new look on objects, I started thinking, well, wait a moment, my objects are full of relatives, you know, so maybe they have relationships with other objects that are in museums. And so from the very beginning of my work I did this immersion in various museums. That work of museology became very important, and from then on, I became also conscious of these spaces where things are kept with an idea of forever, right, where you have temperatures so things will last as long as possible, and there's a whole set of gestures and a way to place things and treat things. But still, all that behind closed doors. And sometimes the objects that are there get to go out and be shown and have their own sort of glory. But there are so many things that are kept like that and that we never see and never get any attention, really. And so I started thinking that maybe my objects from my collection could be meeting with relatives in museums that were also kind of left, put aside or fell in the cracks, or objects you'd never think maybe are in a museum collection. So through all this looking at value systems, what we value, what lies behind that—my objects, you could really see there is a lot of emotion attached to them. But then, you think a museum is an institution, you think maybe there's an objectivity to that, right, and certainly there's a way that museums are set up, this idea that they're scientific in their approach, it's not what they feel they should keep—it's a study. But I'm not that sure, really. I think also, as cultures, we have this value system intended to put aside things and marginalize things, or to cover things and not look at things, or not value things, and what does that mean, what we exclude—or include? So the *Summit Meetings* was about that—trying to bring altogether these objects in museums where then me, collaborators, museum staff—we would be at the service of the objects, and not the opposite, where objects are at our service—that we would have to deal with all this material accumulation and what it means, and what is our relationship to it?

CH: Great work!

RDG: I didn't have a lot of feedback on that work. When you're actually in the room with that work it's a huge quantity of information to absorb (laughs).

CH: We are of course familiar with the conceptual movements of the 1960s and '70s. Is there a mood like that today? What is contemporary today?

RDG: Well, when I started in the late '90s, and I was a young artist, not with these ambitions because that isn't me, but with these hopes—history, you know—as many young artists—also I find when I am teaching, something characteristic of young artists, where you feel maybe you have to invent something of your own, right? Anyway, in my case it was a bit like I was conscious of certain movements, but not just the '70s—much broader. I was more interested in history classes than art-history classes and I felt the need to have a perspective, like, from the Renaissance to now, but also a mentality—no, a history of ideas, ideas I guess, so, ok—you're asking me about today, and in the '90s I could feel this kind of tension between, well, either you do stuff outside the gallery space and you go and do these things, and you know what? Fuck the gallery space, you know!—and what's that, the white cube, you know—and you know it's like all this '60s and '70s, in a way, that's what they did too, you know, so it's like playing back that disc again. And then you say, well, if I do it outside, how will people see things, see the work, and how will I get recognized and all that thing, and it felt a bit like you're either the one or the other. But then I think we were a bunch of people who said instead of "it's one or the other," no, well, you can be there and there and you can also bridge things and open up. So actually, my movement outside the more conventional recognized art spaces and all that was not because I was against the—but it was really a search, maybe, trying to bridge and tunnel and connect things more than open a new—like maybe in the '60s, '70s.

And so today it's like a constellation—there's so many different ways to show your work, you know, and now you even see the DIY scene, and the young emerging artists are saying, we don't want to be an artist-run centre, and though the artist-run centres really come from the artist, the artists who did this to have a place to show other than institutions and private galleries, and now you have artists who are saying, we want to be doings things now and just organizing themselves and using their house, apartments, and it's not about being in the gallery space or being in a white cube or outside a white cube—it's just about being able to do things at the moment that's relevant and where they feel the necessity here, *now*, to do something.

So I don't know about a Zeitgeist (laughs) but for sure more, even more than when I started almost twenty years ago, much more diversity of—diverse possibilities, and also more independent initiatives from artists. Well, the *Summit Meetings* and *The Burden of Objects*, it's a project that came out of gradual, many years of bringing things and people together, and institutions. It's not a curated exhibition in the sense of a curator saying, "Hey, Raf, do you want to do something in our museum"—it's me, like, saying, "Hey Museum, you know, I'm doing this thing, I'd like to do a great 'Summit,' you know, a summit of objects, and I think it's a cool idea"—and then getting another museum, getting museums together and then getting them to collaborate together—a different way of just thinking, not thinking of organizing an exhibition like these people inside the institution—they're the ones thinking about what they should show in the institution, and, "we're going to get artists and show the work and that kind of movement—"

CH: Yes, the Zeitgeist, always a question! But that brings in the matter of theory since Zeitgeists always seem to beg a theory. Is theory of interest to you?

RDG: Well, how can I say? I think a lot! (laughs) Yeah, I think a lot. At the same time, I have a kind of *resistance*, a resistance, in—I resist theory because for me theory is interesting when it's a practice. Yes. So for me thinking is making—well, I don't do too much with my hands. So sad! In my case, doing is gathering things, sorting, putting together, assembling—that's my way of doing, I guess. And that's OK. And other people think writing, and theorize writing with words and projecting this kind of, projecting in this world concepts and notions. Which I think is awesome. But I want to do that through experience and through a direct relation to things in the world, and people—then it happens, and I can read—"Hey, man, would this do that? What this woman is saying in her book is—I get it! Because that's what I'm doing." How's that! You know. So that's for me my relationship to theory. So for me art *is* theory. As practice.

CH: Do you read much, in literature or—

RDG: I have periods where I have the necessity to read, and often it is related to the projects I dive into. For example, now I'm going to be reading a lot about Indigenous people, like accounts and stories, and their culture, and decolonizing methodologies. What I'm doing has to do with this. I'll be reading a lot of history, a particular place. It's a kind of what I read is always very focused on my field work, let's say. Yeah, so that's kind of disappointing, right? (laughs)

CH: I want to pick up on something that I feel is running through our discussion, Raphaélle, which is a deep-rooted sense of humour, or I guess almost a loving embrace of something that could be understood through comedy, or through a sense of play.

RDG: Oh, you mean in art? Well—

CH: In your own work.

RDG: Well, I'm a bit of a clown! It may not show. And also, it's very serious, what we've been talking about, it's very serious! And I mean, for me in art there is a deep sense of urgency, of survival—it's serious shit! (laughs) But at the same time maybe it's my way of being. Trying to bring back things, ground things, to just think who we are as humans, which is kind of funny, more funny creatures.

CH: We are funny creatures, and all the more so when it comes to responses people have to work. What kind of responses have you had to your own work, and what do you make of it?

RDG: Well, the most responses I've had has been to my performance work—the work where I wrap my head in things and do things without seeing, and just become this weird thing. And then people don't know what to do with this weird thing that seems nevertheless quite vulnerable. In that particular work I think what you experience when you see this kind of transformation is that you always have, you're always conscious of me the under the thing, me under the mask, and so you see me in that situation and people project themselves in that—and we fear, a lot, losing our sight—a lot of people claustrophobically close their eyes and play to be blind, right. So people see that and then people see the thing on top of me, like another being and then there's this—between the two things happen, and so you find yourself kind of thinking it's funny but at the same time kind of tragic, or at least you're kind of not tragic but you're like—"Oh, she's going to fall down I've got to—how can she even breathe," and (pants) engage physically in the performance.

Once I did—Oh my God, poor public. And I got reactions *there*! I was pregnant, I think like six months, and my husband wasn't there, thank God—he would never have let me do this. And so I did one of these performances, wrapping my head, but I did the performance ending up on a chair and I did it purposefully with a chair that was kind of rocky (laughs) and with one leg shorter than the others. So people were on the edge, they couldn't stand what was going on! My purpose wasn't really to put them in that situation—they told after that they were so happy I got down off the chair. And I didn't start on the chair right away—for a while I sat on it—it was gradual, I brought them (laughs) to that moment. And you know I had—I wanted to create this beautiful image where I would be standing on the chair, and I had put a fan so that I would have wind and then I would have these party—but black and white, you know—Yvonne, you would have loved it! (laughs)—black and white streamers. And so I would be throwing them and they would be flying in the wind, right, and the image I had in my mind would be this great—But I was all, like, bulky and pieces of these like legs and arms sticking out and kind of my things falling apart and of course these *guirlandes*—they looked like gone in the wind, they looked like *that*! But that's the work, the work is that.

So reactions sometimes are, well—often these reactions help me see what I'm doing because I'm inside, I'm just trying to do things without seeing or thinking—for example, I'm a foot, you know, thinking of reversing things. We often have this idea of the artists' gesture—you know, Picasso, Pollock—what if the artist was a foot (laughs), what if we had to be in the world instead of with our eyes, with our ears, instead of with our hands or our feet—what kind of world would we live in socially if we reverse these things? So these are the kinds of questions that go in my mind and bring me to do this type of performance weird work—if you would have told me that I would have been doing performance work I would have laughed so much. I would say impossible, because I hate it! I don't understand anything about it, I'm never going to be doing work like this! And then I did work like that! (laughs) And still in front of other performance work I can be very uncomfortable and *still* I don't understand why we do these weird things.

Yes—so, reactions. I was saying that people's reactions, in these particular cases, they help me see what it is I'm doing. I remember one guy saying to me—"well, you're like me when I'm in the morning, I have to be doing things, I have a list of things I have to do during my day," and he was talking about entanglement—how we are entangled in our lives and how there's this sequence of things, very precise, that we plan our life, we plan our day, or mornings, afternoons, we plan every minute of our time and we need to be efficient, we need to be efficient within that planning. And my performances, in a way, I'm thinking are completely opposite to this. But they're so planned, and what I mean by that is because I don't see and I've brought materials in my bags and I want to be adding these materials in a particular sequence, so there's—they're never rehearsed, I never rehearse, it's a situation that I put myself in. But I want to be getting somewhere with my actions, like I said, I want to be on this chair, I want to have this wind, I want to be doing this! I want to be *at the top of the world*! I want to be doing *this*! And so I need to have a plan because I don't see—So he just said to me, you're like me, stuck with my plan during my day, during my life. Because what I produce, like I said, I have this image of the *guirlande* going in the wind—but it doesn't really work, it doesn't fit, things fall—you know you try to do something but then it doesn't work, it doesn't go as planned. And doing these performances! That's not what I wanted to be doing, necessarily, it's all intuitive, but then people give you this feedback—that's what I'm doing—I'm showing a side of our human kind of nature—what am I doing? I don't know! But—so, reactions. Yes.

CH: What about critical reaction? Have you found that has fed into the work?

RDG: I find a lot of people studying my work—you know, Master's students, or PhD students, and I kind of discovered also at one point that teachers were showing my work to their students as an example of this or that, of course—whatever, and that really got me thinking—I remember I had done this project in Ottawa, in an old bank, it was called *Making Real*, a group exhibition, anyway, and I was meeting people coming and choosing ID cards I found in the bank and I invited people to guide me in making portraits of these clients and I had this mask on my face—a white piece of paper I would put on me and then the person choosing the colours just guiding me in how she would see that client's face and I would be doing that portrait on me, on my face on the paper. I did this project. And then—

Anyway, years later I had an email from this person saying "Hey, here's my thesis—it's about your work and it would be lovely to have a coffee with you some day." And so I started looking at that thesis, and it was one of the persons who participated in that particular project, and did a portrait with me. And it was for him this moment that was revelatory, anyway, and this experience was very strong. And somehow, he described that this experience was partly one of the things that motivated him to do a Masters in art history. And this thesis, I was reading it, and—Oh, I felt so weird, so weird, like I was being dissected, being like, being really opened up and looked inside. It was overwhelming, the sensation of—so I had to stop reading it. I found it was too much, not because of, you know, what this person was writing—not because of the quality of what he was saying, it was very high quality, what he was saying, very rigorous work and not the kind of quality where I have to close it because it's bullshit, right—that can happen too, it does, it does! (laughs) So the opposite maybe, because it was too close, and you have to preserve in some ways these areas of shadows in your practice because then you need yourself to—you know, what would you meet in that shadow corner?—it's very important for an artist—you need to go there yourself. And find a way to light it in a proper way, and not too much because then it loses any interest. So, you know—

So, critical. Critical. It has helped me a lot, but at the same time you have to know when—because I think there's a danger also as an artist, you shouldn't speak—your voice as an artist needs to be yours. It's easy, it could be easy just to take—"Well this person wrote this thing about my work, *and it's so right!*" But is it, really? Because it's not the same thing, you know. As an artist, what drives what you're doing, you have a voice, even if you can't write properly, maybe, or as nice as this person did, or clear maybe—but you have a voice and it's from within, from the making, doing aspect of it.

And it's only you that can have this voice, it's your own process—no one else can speak for you about this process (gestures to her gut). So that's a place that's important. And so—and it's not the same thing as someone from the outside, even though another artist, let's say, would comment on your work—it's awesome! It's nourishing!—But it's not the same. So you have to, gradually—well, part of growing up, not being a baby artist anymore, it's acknowledging that voice more and more and more and kind of trusting it, well, not trusting it, but being confident because—It can be easy in the art world, the authority on the work—in a way. You, *you*, the artist, has this—you're the Boss, Man! You're the one deciding is it black or white, red or blue, and you know why you do these things. So then why should it be more valuable, why should, you know, why should it be considered more valuable what someone else from outside says. So what someone else from outside says is awesome because the work has a life of its own. But if we talk about *practice*, of what does it mean *to do* work, and, you know, those decisions within the work, well then you have—it's your voice. Sometimes critical views, they're mixed, they overlap—you know—so you have to learn to differentiate where these voices come from.

CH: A few minutes ago, you opened up this question of the authentic for me by suggesting that it's rather like a mystery story, it's not something you pull out from the shelf, it's not something you pull out of your being and say there it is—it's authentic. From what you're saying the authentic is more a kind of becoming. Would you say that?

RDG: Becoming. Well, that's very interesting. Authenticity as a becoming. A kind of basic definition of what authenticity is—in art or anything else, whatever it is, is being true to yourself, right? And I think in the arts, or in art practice, being true to yourself in the practice always brings you somewhere else, somewhere you didn't expect, right? You start somewhere, but you don't know where it's going to bring you or how it's going to end. And so in that sense being true to yourself is having this capacity to listen to what your work is actually producing almost before it's outside of you. It's also, in French we would say a *sortie de soi*, where we get out of our self, where, instead of the attitude where you do something because you think that's where we want you to be, or a gallerist wants you to be, or a curator wants you to be, or the public wants you to be, or your lover wants you to be (laughs). It doesn't have to be from the art world, even. Sometimes we have these internalized expectations, so it's not about—this becoming is being true to what *is* coming,

Bonnie Devine

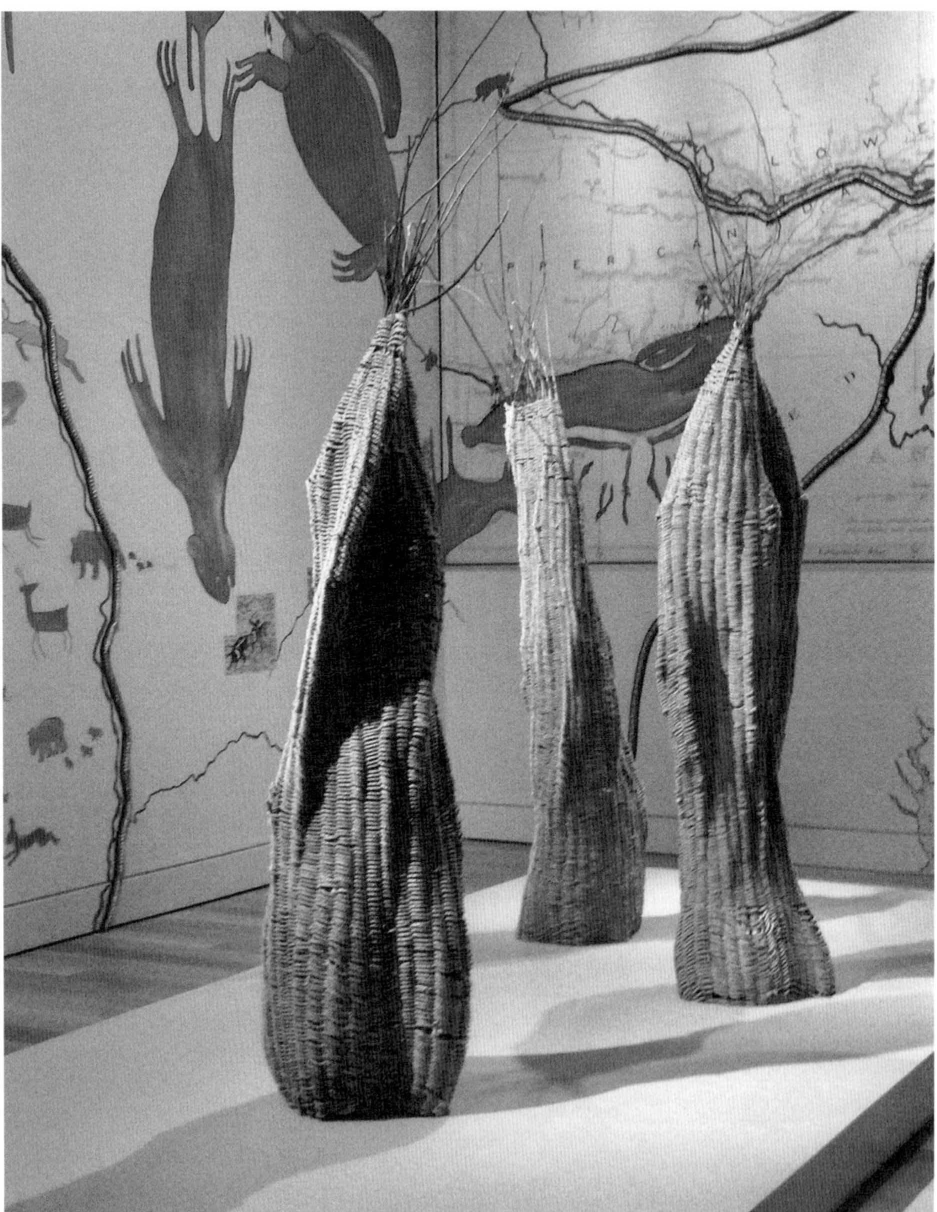

3.11   Bonnie Devine, *Battle for the Woodlands*, 2014–15. Acrylic and mixed-media mural/installation, 9.14 × 3.96 m; with Bonnie Devine, *Anishinaabitude*, 2015. Twigs gathered at the Don River, the Serpent River, and the St. Clair River, sea grass, kraft paper, 167.64 × 76.2 cm. Installation, Art Gallery of Ontario, Toronto. Courtesy the artist.

This interview was recorded on December 9, 2016.

Bonnie Devine is a member of Serpent River First Nation, Genaabaajing, an Anishinaabe Ojibwa territory on the north shore of Lake Huron. Her work emerges from the stories, histories, and image-making traditions that map contemporary Anishinaabe identity in the land called Canada. Her art explores issues of narrative, environment, treaty, history, and land.

(Editor's note: No transcription can fully convey the tone of an interview, and it is important to note that Bonnie's reflections on the issues this interview brings into play are conveyed with a quiet determination threaded through with a sense of humour that, for this interviewer, lent her appeal to our need to reconsider the idea of Canada all the more urgent).

Yvonne Lammerich and Ian Carr-Harris are set up in Bonnie's studio on an upper floor of an older office building on Duncan Street south of Queen in Toronto. The studio is a smallish rectangular room with typical large warehouse-style windows on two sides. The area is a downtown intersection in the core, and the noise of traffic from the street is a constant reminder of the intensity of inner-city life. Despite the sparseness of the room, it has a comfortable feeling. Bonnie is sitting on a recliner couch in the middle of the studio and on the floor in front of her is the large knitted work Medicine River. *It is late afternoon, and as the daylight gradually fades, the room is soon lit with overhead fluorescent lighting. Yvonne has positioned the two cameras, and she will be moving between them during the session. Ian sits opposite Bonnie several feet away. Yvonne signals that the cameras are ready, and the interview begins.*

CH: Bonnie, you've written a very nice piece about where you come from, where you grew up. Everyone has a different story of course, but we really enjoyed yours, and in some respects that could be a great opening to the question I want to ask, which is how you came to be an artist.

BD: Do you want me to tell that story?

CH: I'd love that!

BD: My people come from the Canadian Shield, the north shore of Lake Huron in central Ontario. My grandparents were trappers, and loved what would now be termed a traditional life. I feel very privileged that I witnessed that, and also to have witnessed the transition from that into what is now my life here as a professional artist in Toronto. So there is a trajectory in my life that I can trace, as well, to a cultural history, if that's not too grandiose a claim. Because for sure in essentially one generation we, my family, have moved from living very traditionally on the land—completely self-sufficient, sovereign lives—to what we have now, which is struggling to understand ourselves, and for me as a contemporary artist working within an academic situation with all of the European context that that implies... (pause) I don't know whether I've skirted that issue or not...

CH: I know that you studied art, at OCAD of course, so what brought you to those studies?

BD: I knew from very early on that I had a story to tell. I saw a transformation occurring in my homeland, in the lives of my parents and my grandparents, that no one had words for when I would ask, you know, "What is that over there"—because industrialization was beginning to happen in our part of the world. They discovered uranium when I was very small, thirty kilometres north of us, and the mining around the discovery of uranium was what transformed us from a small, self-sufficient trapping community into a site of incredible devastation as a result. So I was witness to that as a young child, and my parents and grandparents, probably out of a sense of protection for me, wouldn't talk to me about what was happening. So I grew up with a central mystery in my life, and I think it was the resolve to somehow understand that mystery that made me want to be an artist, that gave me the...I think an art practice is always rooted in a question, a problem-solving kind of mode of thinking and acting in the world, and for sure that was right in there—this deep question about, well, what is going on, you know! We had these deep piles of yellow powder that suddenly emerged in the middle of our community. They were beautiful, they were abstract images, they were big triangles, they were big domes, they were this brilliant yellow, and the ground all around them had been turned all black by the action of the sulphur.

I found out afterward that this black was sulphuric acid—and this was being used in refining the uranium. But they were leaving it raw on the road, in the middle of our community! No one could explain that to me, and I remember as a little girl lying in bed in my grandparents' house, thinking to myself: I'm going to find out what those are, and I'm going to tell people what that is.

CH: Well, that raises another question, and this would seem to introduce it. There are a lot of misconceptions around what an artist is, or what an artist does or can do. So for you, what does an artist bring to a culture? Perhaps, as you were saying, would it be to try to understand something, to reveal it as a true story or a metaphysical story? Is that what you think an artist can do?

BD: I think my understanding of what an artist is and can do continues to evolve. So when I began to think about how to be in the world, it wasn't to say, well, I'm going to be an artist. It was to say, "How can I find a job that will allow me to engage with this information, these phenomena, that is in a way active and satisfying to me?" Yes, so when I was first thinking about art, when I was first thinking about my life as something that I could actually do something with, this took me a long time. And I don't think that everybody regards themselves in that relationship with their life as artists do. I think that, as an artist, one assumes that one can respond to something, and in my family that notion of responding to political realities, or social realities, or even the materiality of life, is quite foreign. I come from a family that didn't have very much agency, and I think that it was difficult for me to really get hold of the idea that I could respond in an individual, meaningful way. And the way I learned to respond, to do that, is as an artist.

CH: Is that something you brought to your studies, or something you took away from your studies?

BD: That's interesting. I brought longing to my studies. When I entered university to begin studying artmaking, I was starving, lusting for an opportunity to engage with my reality in a responsive way, and OCAD gave me the tools to be able to respond. So those things developed, and actually, that's why I say that my view of what an artist is continues to evolve. Because I become ever more responsive as I learn more techniques for perceiving and then replying, I perceive more nuances in my artistic practice.

CH: I'd like to turn to the question of what coheres within a practice. How do you see a coherence within the strategies you have developed? Can you talk for instance about the *Tecumseh Papers*?

BD: So, a couple of things with respect to that particular body of work, which has to do with history, history as it is written, history as it is received by those who read what is written, and then narrative, as it is not written but experienced. To go back to this notion of receiving, with a more subtle nuanced ear, that which has almost disappeared, so as to develop a kind of antenna for the historical truth. That lies within the words that have been written. So the thing that coheres, I think, throughout most of the work that I have been doing in the last twenty years, is to trace out the between-the-lines story that is not written but is present. This is what I came here to do, and I realized this as I moved through my studies and began to be able to hear—almost as my instructors were speaking—to hear another voice behind them, one that wasn't necessarily a contradiction, but was correcting with some assurance, and this voice of assurance—who knows where that was coming from—certainly was not from my lived experience (pause). The fact that there was another story behind the written story was an insight that toppled everything that I had hung my life upon, and so I needed to build another structure. And I would say that the resulting work has been to develop a new structure that I can build my life upon, that I can trust, that I can move around—it has mobility, it's not fixed. And so this is freedom, and also truth in some way, a deeper kind of truth. So I would say that's what my practice is about on a really personal level.

CH: Would you care to talk further about the *Tecumseh Papers*?

BD: Yes, certainly. It was quite arbitrary. I was given the assignment by a curator at the Art Gallery of Windsor. She said to me: would you be interested in coming and looking at these two busts that we have? They have two terracotta sculptures of General Brock and Tecumseh, and this was ahead of the anniversary of the War of 1812. It was a very celebrated, iconic event and they wanted me to do some work around these two figures. So I looked at them and I began to read the histories about General Brock. There was not a great deal about Tecumseh. Although an iconic figure, he was not chronicled or accounted for at the depth or level that I was seeking, and I quickly—for that reason—was attracted to him because his absence was like a magnet to me. And Brock was so present, he was so illuminated that I lost interest in him and began to focus on Tecumseh. I began to look for Tecumseh. I ordered all the books I could, I searched for him. I walked where he had walked, I went to the places I thought he had been, I went to Michigan, I went down to Ohio. I really looked for him. And I didn't find him! And I was responsible to create this body of work about this figure and I had nothing. Some friends gave me an opportunity to travel to Italy. They had a house in the northern hills in Piedmont and they invited me to go and spend a month there and it was four months before the exhibition was to open. I had copious notes, I had notebooks, I accumulated a lot of knowledge, but I didn't really have anything to show. And on this crazy whim—almost irresponsibly—I decided to go to Italy. And it was there that Tecumseh came to me—and I found him. I think it had something to do with the isolation of the little house where I was staying and the remove from North America and all the expectations that were building here for the cele-brations around 1812, the 200th anniversary of this great battle. He walked into the kitchen in that little house! (pause)

I had begun a practice that…I had a large biographical novel about Tecumseh, and I had been reading it and circling various words in the text. Every time it said "war," I circled that, every time it said "gun," I drew a circle around it, every time it said "Indian," I drew a circle. So I had this 700-page book and every page had been written and covered in these arrows and circles. And one day it just sort of fell away and I saw the story behind and I began to draw that story. So, for me, the notion that history, as it is received in Canadian consciousness, and the history of this lived Shawnee man who found himself at the very edge of this tremendous struggle for our home-land—it needed a kind of letting-go for me to be able to receive that story. (laughs) Should I say more?

CH: Please!

BD: I just ended up cutting up the book, I ended up pulling apart the history books and making work out of those books. So I made a cloak, I made images for the wall, I made plaques, I drew on top of those books, because I felt that I wanted to challenge their story, but not only challenge it, but to enrich it, not completely erase it or burn it, or throw it away, but to say, look, there is this other part to this, you know, and if you just look a little this way maybe you'll see it too and how beautiful it is. So yes, Tecumseh for me is still a moment in my own life as an Anishinaabe woman where I actually touched against a spirit of something that is true.

CH: Just as an aside, one of my former students, Sona Safaei, mentioned that in her Iranian culture, one typically looked not at the line, but at what lay between the lines.

BD: Aha, yes. For sure. The negative space. As a sculptor, one is very aware of the negative space. This happens in text—it's very evident in text. In Western thinking, when one is transcribing or reviewing a text, one figuratively pierces and un-pierces and pierces and un-pierces this filament of paper that surely contains the truth within it. But, in my thinking, it needs to be pierced and pierced and pierced (Bonnie makes a circular gesture) because you need to look around and under it. And so, I made three large treaty belts that are documents, Western, English, and American, translated into treaty belts for the same reason—to look at the way that the textual representation of history is not sufficient.

CH: Of course, we have, present here in the studio, a large work that is impossible for us to ignore, (laughter) and I'm very curious about it. Would you talk about it?

BD: Well, I made this in 2007, so it's actually quite old. I was thinking about—this was at the very beginning of the awareness in Canadian consciousness of the difficulties in the very far north of Ontario. So there is a town called Kashechewan. Kashechewan First Nation is a Cree Territory on the Albany River, and news began to filter down into the CBC and onto the pages of the *Globe & Mail* about this town that had a boil-water advisory and had been living under one for decades. And this despite the fact that it was on a far northern river that Canadians like to think is pristine wilderness. So how did it happen that this community had contaminated water? Moreover, they had issues with substandard buildings, the children in that community had no school because the school had been condemned because it had been built on PCP tanks, and also had black mould, so they had been getting their primary education in unheated portables. And all this news began to come down to us here in the city of Toronto, and I thought that I wanted to make a river, I thought that through my hands and through the knitting of this object I could somehow in some way instigate a healing. Not that this would heal the water necessarily, although there is some metaphysical connection there, but that it would assist me in reconciling to this truth, to take action. So I took copper audio-wire, the kind of cable you would use to carry sound, and I began to knit this long river, and as I was doing that I composed a musical piece that could be played through this river. It was coincidental perhaps that in that same year a scientist in Europe managed to map the human genome. And so miraculous is our technological age that I was able to download the human genome in these lines of coded genes—eight pairs all in rows—and I set that to music. And that's what plays through the river. What I was trying to talk about was that they cannot eternally poison the river—they will try but they cannot eternally poison the river. So that's what this is—it's called *Medicine River*.

CH: I'm interested by this relationship between metaphor and historical events, the relations between history and artmaking. I'd like to raise the question of art history, our relationship as artists to other artists both in our own community and across generations, and I wonder how the practices of other artists is a factor in your own thinking.

BD: Oh, absolutely. I think this is one of the wonderful gifts of a formal education within a Western academy, for all of us, but especially I would say for Indigenous artists who are attempting in some way not to integrate our voices but add our voices to this discourse. It's enormously important that we understand the various strands in our history, where we transgress them, where we concur, where we walk side by side—that's the beautiful part, I think, of this profession—the fairness, the respect, the regard for this history. So I have been deeply influenced by my instructors and other practitioners from long ago, and I very much feel compelled and honoured—responsible—for passing this on to younger people as part of a chain of continuum. But Indigenous art practice hasn't necessarily been included within that larger conversation. And this is something I want to rectify.

CH: When we speak of a discourse or conversation, perhaps this leads to another question, whether there is a particularity to that discourse, a specificity that—though I hesitate to use the term—could be construed as a Zeitgeist or set of issues that speak to our condition, globally and here in Canada. Would you see such a set of issues in play currently?

BD: I think there is a notion of a Canadian approach to enlist that in practice—I believe there is a multivalent dialogue that is ongoing and profoundly engaged. Being close to the centre of the city, and especially to the Ontario College of Art and Design, close to the University of Toronto and Ryerson, and other academic centres here in Toronto is enormously nourishing to my practice and I would imagine to that of others. The conversations I have with my colleagues and my students, and my friends, help me to untangle some of the complications and obscurities that we are constantly facing and to, again, peel back some of the obfuscations that we are bombarded with to find that truth. And in the peeling back of that to create a space where something can be made in response. So while many things have changed in the city, I don't think that the particular condition of the artist has changed, the condition of conversation with others and the recognition of others' work. There are so many people in this city doing important work and to be in conversation with that is just wonderful.

CH: I want to read you something that I was quite struck by, something that you brought up in the panel discussion at the Art Gallery of Windsor. And it comes back to your *Tecumseh Papers* that we just talked about: "As viewers of the *Tecumseh Papers*, Devine asks us not to be mere spectators but to pay attention, to live for a moment in the complicated world such as that inhabited by Tecumseh, and by doing so to think compassionately about the present circumstances of First Nations people and ways to move as allies together into an uncertain future." In light of your panel statement, I wonder if you have any ideas about the relationship of your work to the general public, and indeed to a committed audience, as well.

BD: This is an interesting question, and it gets to the notion of the pedagogy that is embedded in a lot of my practice, actually—it has to do with this trying to rewrite, in some kind of material sense, the history that we live in, and the way that history has consistently compacted us into a certain kind of behaviour. So my hope is that by altering history, or knowledge of the history, we can perhaps behave differently. (pause) But this is very complicated for me, because I'm not sure that I like art to be pedagogical, and I don't like the idea that somehow, one way or another, I am representing to an unsuspecting—however compassionate—audience a unitary voice for Indigenous peoples. I have ambivalent feelings about that. So I find curators and commentators will attempt to say that that's the goal, and in fact it isn't, actually. I am simply trying to respond, I'm trying to enliven the object, the art object, as a participant animate creature within our cultural sphere, to animate that so it can speak. So there are some complications around this. I'm not sure that Canadian artists who are not of Indigenous ancestry face these dilemmas. I would be interested to hear if they do. Do they? Do you?

CH: Personally, I've never imagined speaking for anyone. I imagine myself speaking *about* something, even a community, but not speaking *for* that community. Perhaps that's because I don't have a committed attachment to a community, though of course I have an inherited identity. I wouldn't even speak for other artists. I can only speak from my own judgments.

BD: Yes, well I think that the problem is very common for all artists of colour. (pause) I shouldn't generalize here, and I do agree that it's very subjective, but I do find that others complain about this matter, about the idea of representation within their work as a burden that other artists perhaps don't have. So what I try to do is to shift the burden to the objects and to reawaken those objects in some way that gives them voice.

 CH: That does remind me, to your point, that some have said that the contemporary world that we work within, the world of the last couple of decades, growing perhaps out of postcolonial theory, has in many ways become a world of competing identities, and if one is searching for a dominant discourse, it is the discourse of identity. I'm not sure if that's true or not.

BD: Yes, I'm sure that there are areas within the art world where identity is absolutely at the forefront to be spoken about. I'm not sure that's where my work would locate itself. The written record, the written account, I'm interested in responding to that, thinking about that. I speak very clearly about these things from a different perspective, my own perspective, and I'm clear and direct about announcing that. For some, this may infect everything I say, but hopefully for others this may open up that space where one may speak. (pause) But I am not so much interested in speaking about identity as I am about a more common-wealth, or a commonly held narrative, and how do we all contribute to that.

CH: Bonnie, you teach, of course, and as I listen to you, I wonder to what extent theory has played a role in the development of your thought?

BD: Of course, and I would say one of the wonderful things that has happened in my career as an academic has been the emergence of an Indigenous scholarship, and Indigenous texts and theoretical discussions on aesthetic structures, and on narrative structures. And so those theoretical frameworks are really important in both my teaching and in the making that I do. For instance, the notion of postcoloniality is something that I contend with because I don't feel we are in a postcolonial world. I don't think we've emerged yet. I don't think we have a correct or full understanding of what colonial pressure is on us that we are burdened with. And so disentangling that has become a big part of what I would call Indigenous theory. And so, yes, I am very interested in that, and it is very influential in my teaching.

CH: I'm reminded of something that Zhou Enlai said in response to a question about the importance of the French Revolution. He said: it's too early to say.

BD: (laughs) Yes...

CH: But I'd like to ask, concerning critical attention, whether there has been a perspective brought to bear on your own work that has been interesting or useful to you?

BD: No, I would say, no. I think that critical attention to my work that is meaningful to me will have to come from someone who understands the issues that I'm dealing with, and unfortunately most of the critical world is still extremely European-centric, and comes at these questions of aesthetics or of practice or of structure from a set of frameworks that I don't fit into. I become still the exotic, the other. So I don't look to that particular area for understanding. There are a number of younger scholars who are beginning to write their doctoral papers and so I'm beginning to interact with those individuals from all around North America, actually, and those younger scholars are bringing a different kind of understanding to what I am doing.

CH: Well, of course, committed scholarship works and flourishes within an academic system, as you yourself have pointed out. Just as an artist's career happens within the art system. What's your experience of that?

BD: I've been very fortunate in that I've found curators who are interested in exploring with me what is of interest. I've been fortunate in being given space to do that work and time to do that work with some very generous and perceptive individuals, so this has actually allowed me to grow the perspectives that I have. In terms of the gallery system, within a comfortable kind of timeline of this activity here and that activity there, I've managed to craft a good working balance and I've managed to travel and expand the extent of my investigation in unimaginable ways. I'm very grateful for the way that the art world—in this particular limited way that it deals with me—has been good to me.

CH: A final thought. You talked about honesty earlier, what is real, or truthful, what we can hold in our hands, something we might call what is authentic as opposed to the demands and strategies of the art systems. How does that problem emerge for you in how people see your work?

BD: That's interesting. Of course, art and artifice are close, and we are, after all, in the business of constructing artifices in many ways. The notion of fantasy and the notion of the identity of the artist as a sort of iconic figure— we're always dancing around that. People will always assume certain things about you because of the work that you do —and then they meet you and everything collapses!

All of that aside, I have been led by something that Carl Beam said many years ago. He said, "I want to get my hands on meaningful things." This has stayed with me and reminds me of what I would call truth. Because who knows what is really true. But I do know what is meaningful. And I want to get my hands on meaningful things too, and that's where I find my ground zero.

Lee Henderson

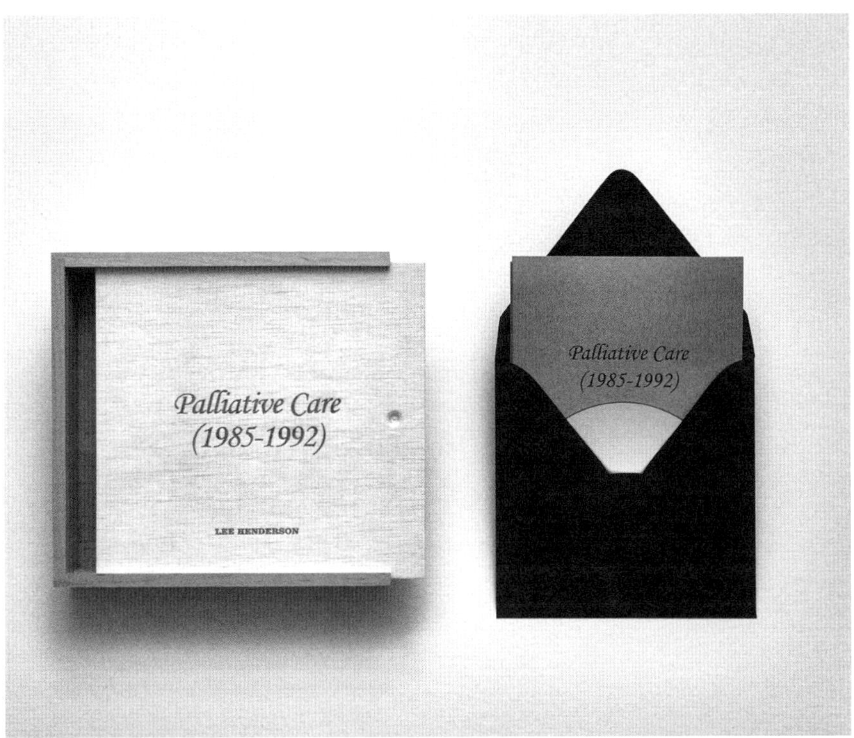

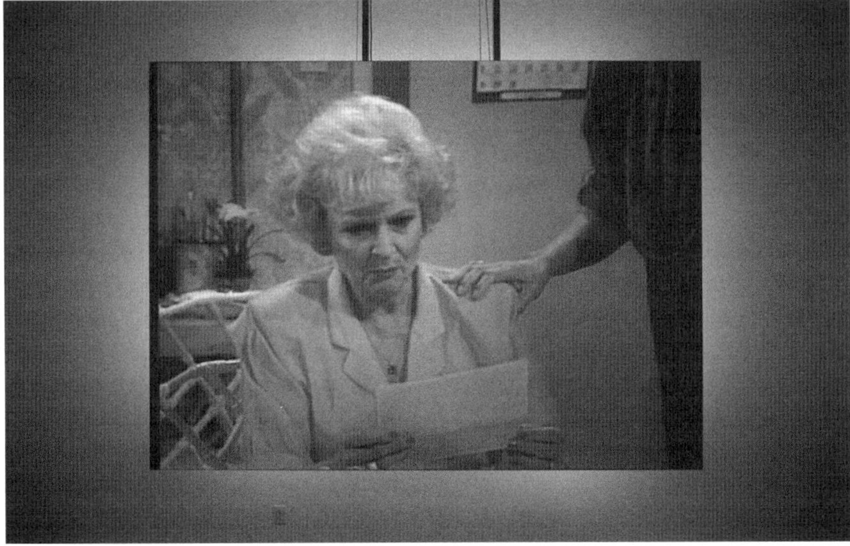

3.12   Lee Henderson, *Palliative Care, 1985–1992*, 2016. Artist multiple, edition of 20+AP; DVD, booklet, pine box, 22.8 × 22.8 × 6.4 cm; colour NTSC video, stereo sound, 25 mins. Courtesy the artist.

3.13   Lee Henderson, *Palliative Care, 1985–1992*, 2016 (detail). Installation view, Latitude 53, Edmonton, 2016. Video installation of custom projection screen, lighting, chaises longues, heating, dimensions variable; colour NTSC video, stereo sound, 25 mins. Courtesy the artist.

This interview was recorded on April 21, 2017.

Lee Henderson grew up in Saskatchewan and has studied art in Canada and Germany. His work moves in constant contemplation of death, somewhere between the persistence of collective histories and the brevity of individual lives.

(Editor's note: What stands out for this interviewer is Lee's ironic humour and pervasive sense of distance from the traditional art establishment and its conservative, one might even say timid approach to what can be uncovered if one really looks at art beyond the comfortable assumptions built into the art system).

Yvonne Lammerich and Ian Carr-Harris are set up in Lee's apartment-studio on an upper floor of an older office and retail building on Yonge Street in Toronto. The apartment is modestly spacious and filled with film equipment, a small kitchenette promises coffee. Morning daylight from windows on the west side mixes with the overhead lighting. Lee sits on a chair in a corner of the apartment that serves as a library/office. Yvonne positions the two cameras and frames them to place images of Lee's work in the background and a bookshelf to his left. She will adjust this from time to time during the interview. Ian positions himself on a chair several feet away to the right of the cameras. Yvonne gives the signal and the interview begins.

CH: Lee, you talk about false problems, in art or philosophy, and I wonder where revealing false problems might take you. What it might actually involve in making artworks.

LH: Well, I guess that depends on what false problem is being addressed.

CH: Name one?

LH: Death! Death is a false problem.

CH: I'm glad to hear it!

LH: (laughs) You're welcome. Or the apprehension that precedes it, let's say, and the grief that follows it. I suppose the nature of what it means to look at that as a false problem is to look at it also as sociology, political criticism, cultural criticism, explorations of visual culture or religious theory, all of these different ways, or a constellation of ways, by which we've tried to address it as a problem—and have failed to do so because it's not really a problem. I suppose in that respect, with respect to making art, it means bringing in lines of semiotic inquiry that pre-exist the creation of the artwork, and mine those existing vocabularies of how we talk about death or how we address death, how we frame death culturally or consciously. And using those or combining those as the raw mineral of what gets reconstituted as an artwork. (pause)

There's something in the role of the artist that allows things to be followed to their natural conclusion. So allowing a set of assumptions that we make to sort of play out in an intellectual free space, the playful atmosphere of the studio, let's say, and then subsequently the exhibition space. What happens, in effect, if we follow something to its natural conclusion, how wrong-headed can that thing get.

CH: A student I had many years ago, Leah Glushien, had a marvelous statement that was exactly one sentence long. Picking up on what you're saying, Lee, she wrote that "In an effort to improve my outlook on life I look for absurdities and work to emphasize their charms." Are you emphasizing the charms of false problems?

LH: Absurdity is curious. I don't spend a lot of time thinking about absurdities, but I do spend a lot of time thinking about comedy.

CH: Comedy? Well, I'm interested in the core ideas that filter through your work, and Death of course, or the Terminus, is one that you've raised.

LH: So, I did an ongoing project I'm calling the *Refinement Pavilion*, and it's a series of urns. Each of the urns houses the ashes of the first edition of the first printing of a book whose author wanted that book destroyed unread and unpublished at the time of their own death. Vladimir Nabokov for instance, his book *The Original of Laura—Dying is Fun* is the subtitle Nabokov gave his unfinished novel—he wanted that work destroyed because it was unfinished at the time of his death. Destroy, burn it, never let it see the light of day. And for decades afterwards his son wondered whether he should publish this work, but whenever he brought up the idea he was met with consternation and controversy. He did eventually publish it in 2009, I believe, and the Nabokov scholars at the time were appalled that he would dare go against the great author's wishes, but they were also really happy because they had this new work to study, right? And a lot of them were saying it would have been his best work had he been able to finish it. So I'm interested in that kind of ambivalence around heeding the wishes of the dead, the ambivalence around what constitutes its authorship and what the author gets to say about their work or not say about it or what kind of agency they're given over their work after they've gone. I think we talk about artworks as outliving people, as a form of immortality, which is ridiculous because they become their own entity that then gets fussed with and gets transmuted, for instance with Nabokov, into a book when it was originally just note cards—or alternatively into ashes. So I got interested in where does that end point actually sit in the decision-making process.

CH: There's another work, *The Known Effects of Lightning on the Body*. Would you care to talk about that as well?

LH: *The Known Effects of Lightning on the Body* occupies a low-lit room with the walls all painted a deep sort of blood red—actually the name of the colour is "smouldering" in the paint catalogue!—and there's one half-chromed light bulb hanging from the ceiling. There's low-benched seating in the room positioned around a campfire-like small projection onto a piece of copper sheet about two feet square facing the viewer. The projection shows an unlit wooden match held vertically, and this match is then lit by another match that enters from off-camera. We hear that other match being struck, so the trace of it having been struck exists as sound before we see it on fire when it enters the projection. So now the second match ignites the first, which bows as it burns down the shaft, surrenders, gives in. When the match extinguishes, it fades off the screen and is replaced by another match, and so on. So each of those burnings starts with a kind of flash point and it becomes this process of extinguishing—the flames give off this final gasp of smoke when the flame is finally extinguished.

For me, the point of thinking about the terminus in that work is not dir-ectly but in a near-allegorical way of asking, how can a space provide room for you to reflect on your own mortality or on processes of grief or loss? It's like the game of peek-a-boo that Freud describes, where as an infant you have to see your parent vanishing and re-appearing so that you become comfortable with the idea, so as not to be disturbed by that as a loss.

CH: I believe you're interested in Eastern philosophy and the near-allegorical seems somehow to invite that. A quotation of yours that I quite like is "I stumble, I grope, until something reveals the mortal banality of its associations." A simple match. Could you speak to the processes within your work?

LH: I think in the case of the work I just described that it grew from an observation I had made when I was holding a match that was burning, that the match head became even more visible as a real head as its body curled towards its spine. I guess it goes back to what I was saying before, taking something to its conclusion and then exploding it out. As something worth spending attention on.

CH: Looking closely, then.

LH: Precisely.

CH: You've said that making an artwork is every bit as absurd, direct, and fruitful as rearranging furniture just to see the pattern on the floor. So this leads me to ask how you see the interplay between idea and material. I imagine it can be theorized or personalized. Any comments?

LH: I think it comes from the desire to allow someone to come to their own realizations, but of course a set of manipulated realizations. So an outlining of a path that a person ends up following, ideally not even when they're in front of the work itself. I like the idea that an artwork can, by means of deception or aesthetics, material seduction, lull you into thinking about it one way while you're standing in front of it, only to reveal itself in a different or subversive way further down the road.

CH: The question frequently comes up as to whether there's a current discourse, a mode of inquiry that an artist's work adheres to, or of course doesn't. Any thoughts with respect to your own practice?

LH: I have lots of thoughts about it, but no conclusions. It depends upon what one means by the time—this year or this epoch—or even what geographical location are we addressing. Is it in terms of the global online community, is it emerging/mid-career or senior groupings—and so on. I was talking to Michelle Jacques about Toronto art and Canadian art and what is the thing that can or should be celebrated about it, and we were positing that it is intellectualism, that it is a kind of familiarity with and proximity to academic or critical theory, and a kind of…The specific theory we were talking about is McLuhan, and the affinity people have had with his theory, in pop culture but also with those who work with his theory themselves. So I don't know, but it sort of starts to nudge us towards a sort of geographic or national sense of a discourse here. But I don't know whether anyone can know this, really, when you're in the middle of it. Sort of "what is water to a fish?"

CH: Sort of what is a trend to an artist! Trends or not, in your own practice, how do you see that practice in the context of what you see around you?

LH: I guess it's consistent in that I borrow from pop culture, not that it's omnipresent but that it's consistent. I'm reluctant to rely on a single medium, or discipline, I guess it's pretty rare that I think painting or photography is "enough," enough, that is, to answer to the issue of complexity and that mix of significations that become an embodiment.

CH: If we were to quote Žižek, and I'm not sure if Žižek is merely a trend or not, but he has important things to say about art and culture. Would you have an empathy for positions he takes?

LH: An empathy for some positions he takes, though I'd have to say I have greater or more consistent compatibility with comics than I do with professional thinkers, but…

CH: I'm sure Wittgenstein would appreciate that!

LH: I like Wittgenstein too—he was pretty funny. He had an interest in jokes, at any rate. Žižek is funny too.

CH: You mentioned comedy before, and do you want to talk a bit about how you see that operating in your own work?

LH: Sure, I've described it before as the work being all about death, but funny like King Lear is funny. And I'm not being cheeky, I really think King Lear is hilarious.

CH: You'll have to follow that along!

LH: Sure. I mean, because it is absurd—so there, I am interested in absurdity!—to think you can fully, completely plan for your own death, that you can set in motion all these plans of authorship or control or authority that will persist and that will unfold the way you had intended in your perfectly tactical brain. Because when you throw other people into the mix, you throw expectation—or birthright in the case of King Lear—or admiration or grief into that mix as well and it unravels. So King Lear is about this guy trying to plan for his own non-being, and failing utterly to do so in any effective or useful way. And I just think that's really funny.

CH: And that idea of failure in thinking about death as outside of circumstance, and the comedy that ensues, runs through your work?

LH: Yeah, I think so, in some ways as a kind of alternative in suggesting well, what if you don't spend the time worrying about it and the consternation and anxiety around it? And let's say also there is a kind of destabilizing of death and humour as oppositional, or death and life as oppositional. I'm thinking about a project I did last year called *Palliative Care 1985 to 1992* which is a video compilation of all the voiced references to death in the Golden Girls series on TV. It's twenty-five minutes long, and it's pretty solid in the ways in which death of one kind or another is referred to, with occasionally the laugh tracks left in—and actually the most unsettling moments are the laugh tracks. It's most unsettling when you have this juxtaposition of an artificial insistence on forced laughter.

CH: Lee, you are very well regarded as a teacher at the university, and since you enjoy the process, do you want to talk about that?

LH: Sure, you had mentioned Eastern philosophy before, and I suppose that has a fascination for me because it's the way I approach teaching art as well. I don't know how this really is from experience, but I understand that if you approach a Zen Master and say, "I want to study with you in your temple," they'll say no, they'll reject you. And you're expected then to sit on the steps of the temple night and day until they eventually let you in. It's a bit cartoonish in a way, but there's something in there about, well, unless you have a great doubt, or unless you have a profound curiosity that you can't manage to resolve on your own, then there's really nothing I can do for you. So I tell my students that if you're not curious, if there's not something that really drives you to think about or to know about, then I can't do anything for you.

CH: You should make them stand outside the door night and day!

LH: I should, you know! But I don't think you're allowed to do that.

CH: You have a gallery, you are about to embark on a residency in Scotland, and you write. So it would appear that you've developed a number of approaches to the art system, and I wonder, how does that work for you?

LH: Ahh, fine (laughs). It works fine.

CH: Ask a question, get an answer!

LH: Yeah, well, I guess it's having a nomadic disciplinary practice. We were talking a while ago about the present, and one's difficulty or inability to define the present in any definitive way, and I'm thinking again about Marshall McLuhan and his idea that the artist is the one that sees the present and finds ways to make the present intelligible to other people.

We could undermine that argument if we claim that if the artist can't define
their own present, how can they define it for anyone else. But I think that
sense of piecing together your own constellation of modes of working and
of contexts and communities to which you want to belong, or interface
with, that is the present. The idea that you have a single institutional path
that's fixed or that's exclusive, that is systematized and has clear instructions
or clear expectations—I don't know that this has ever existed, but I don't
think it exists now. So I think that's the present moment—it is this cobbling
together. We see that in labour as well, where everyone has to become a
freelancer—the gig economy is our moment. I suppose artists are more
accustomed to that.

CH: You've sketched out a multivalent practice, but is there a multivalent
audience? What do you imagine as your audience?

LH: I don't really spend any time thinking about audience, I think about a
viewer. I think there's something crucially different about the two. If one is
thinking about an audience, one is thinking about groups of people, about
people with already a defining set of characteristics, and I think it's a term
we probably borrowed from, yes, theatre, but more likely from advertising and branding—the target market sort of thing. I'm more interested in
what kind of experience the individual viewer can have. I'm fully aware of
reader-response theory, that people come in with their own stuff, and the
stuff they come in with depends on who they are and what their experiences
are, their allegiances or affiliations. But these can't be a governing set of convictions on which to build a work. (pause) So, I mean, in a way we're always
building work for ourselves, and I don't mean that in the sense that art is
personal therapy, making work to expunge our own garbage, but I mean it
rather more that we are our own first viewer for our work, we're the lens
through which all those systems of critique get filtered in the studio.

CH: One filter is, of course, the critic, and we just mentioned that you
write—about art—and I'm curious about what would be the motive that
underwrites your writing. Have you assembled an idea of where you come
from as an art critic when you write art criticism?

LH: Not consciously, although I've thought about it a couple of times as
we've been speaking, because I've realized that the ways in which I talk
about my own work are often arrived at tangentially from the way I've
spoken about some else's work. As we discussed at the beginning of the
interview, I am in fact interested in absurdity, I've written about absurdity in that kind of existential Sisyphean model in Jon Sasaki's work, for

instance. It's not something I would have thought about enough to use as a framing device for my own work without having spent the time with somebody else who was clearly working with it as a theme, or thinking about ghosts and haunting and what ghosts mean for how memory works. I was writing about Rebekah Miller's work at Stride a few years ago, and again it's not something I would have arrived at in relationship to my own work without having done that and spent the time thinking about it. So I suppose in that sense I use writing very selfishly (laughs), to work as a sort of incubator for modes of discourse around my own work, as well as for other people's. I'm interested in it as a conversational device too, I ask my students a lot, what kinds of conversations do you want to grow out of your work—if you don't want to define your ideal viewer, or define a set of objectives or a set of takeaways—what kinds of things do you expect people to talk about when they encounter your work? So I guess criticism, in that respect, is a kind of long-form conversation, by which I mean the time frame in which the conversation unfolds. It's not just a morning, writing occupies a much longer period of time, and it's a more public forum for conversation too.

CH: The public forum includes not only criticism, but of course, as well, the collector, whether private or a curator working for a public institution. Where do you situate yourself with the idea of having your work collected?

LH: Because I went to school in western Canada, and because it was the late '90s, there wasn't really a sense that you would be able to sell work if you were making video or performance installations. Not feasible in Canada—you'd have to go Europe. Maybe Asia. I think that's changed over time, the way we handle systems of collecting—what is "the thing" that's being collected—that's opened up. But, at the same time, it's not something I was trained to think about because it was simply off the radar when I was in school. The emphasis was placed on artist-run centres, and if you were going to be making installation art or video or performance, or anything at all that was outside of, you know, paintings of grain elevators—it was Calgary!—then the artist-run centre was where you were going to find venues and sustain a practice. That's where I'm coming from. That said, I'm in the fortunate position of having representation with someone who understands that art's value is liquid and multifaceted and depends on its ability to provide an experience as well as objects. So the space of the commercial gallery is in the process of becoming hybrid, both a project and an object space. Maybe that's a blip, but I don't think so, given how our work and our economies are becoming information-based, intellectual property economies rather than material economies. I mean, Paul Mason gives capitalism fifty years at the outside anyway, so we'll see!

CH: Grain elevators. Now, they seem real. I can see why people would want a painting of a grain elevator, or something of that nature. It seems authentic, solidly in place, you pass it every day possibly. Even if they're disappearing from the landscape, and even if the painting itself is trite, they represent a loss of that solidity or authenticity. What you're describing would seem to be a new kind of authenticity, a new kind of grounding, something much more fluid than a grain elevator. Would you see this as a new articulation of something authentically real?

LH: I'm not sure how new it is. Is it a dematerialization, or is it a re-materialization into semi-material things like light and information? I'm not sure it's that much of a shift—it's a subtle adjustment maybe. Because the things you're talking about with grain elevator paintings, those are abstract values. The reason people like such paintings is not actually because of anything material, it's because of sets of ideas, even more, they are affective responses to belonging, to regional identity, nostalgia, all of these layers of sentiment. We kind of malign sentiment, but that's where all of this comes from. We were talking earlier about the panic around death and that apprehensive fear—that's another way of talking about sentiment (pause). Perhaps I should just start making paintings about grain elevators!

CH: Well, it would seem to be within the finality—or is it the absurdity?—of death.

LH: (laughs) That's true, and so is that Le Corbusier modernist fist raised against the horizon—the middle finger of the grain elevator raised towards death.

Robert Houle

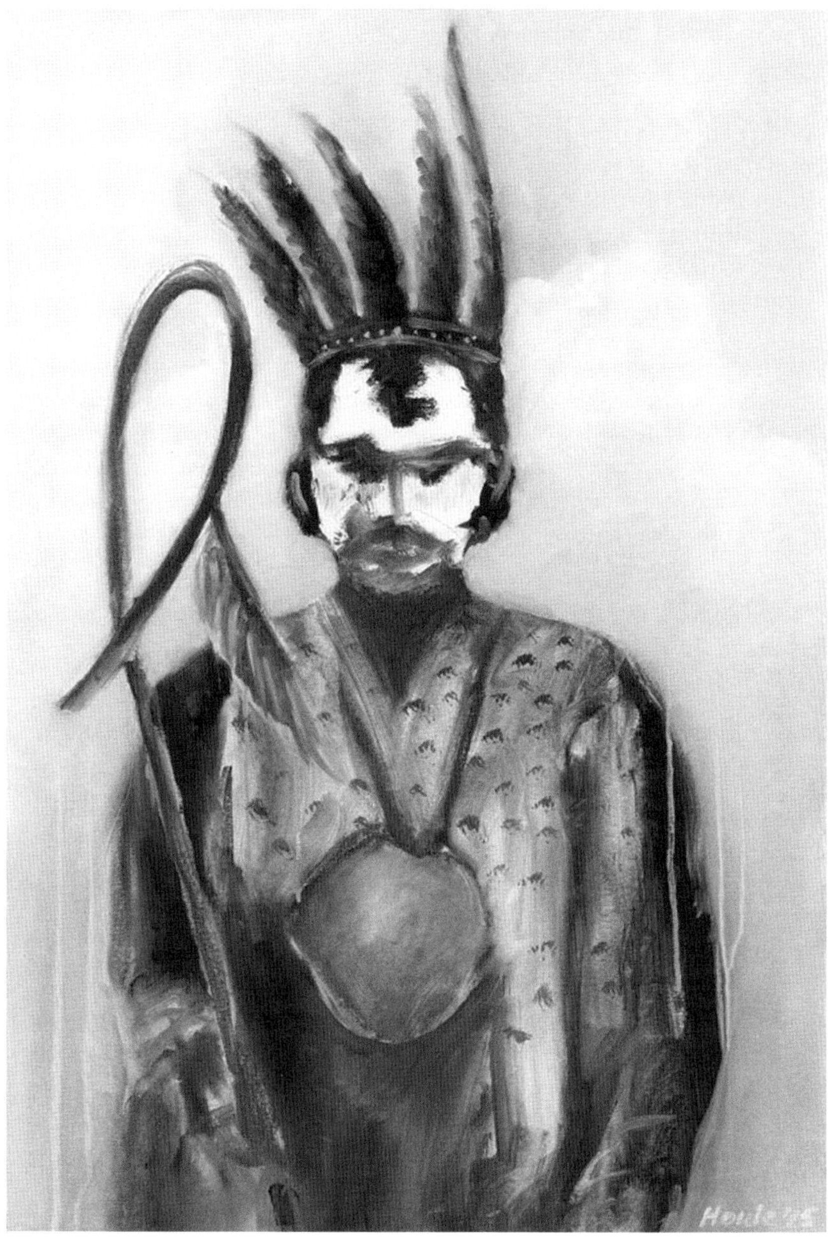

3.14   Robert Houle, *Shaman Dream in Colour*, 2015. Oil on canvas, 91 × 60.96 cm. Collection of Sylvia and Michael Smith. Photo: Michael Cullin, courtesy the Kinsman Robinson Galleries, Toronto.

This interview was recorded on December 5, 2016

Born in St. Boniface, Robert grew up in Sandy Bay First Nation, Manitoba. He has written: "I fundamentally believe that when you bring stories down to bare-bone principles, they become universal."

(Editor's note: The transcription of this interview should be read as an attempt to relate the raw emotional engagement that Robert brought to our meeting. While edited here, his words are at one and the same time chosen with exquisite care and with an explosive, passionate intensity. The hope is that the written word can somehow rise to the challenge that Robert's voice has launched.)

Yvonne Lammerich and Ian Carr-Harris are set up in Robert's house in Toronto, and Yvonne is positioning the two cameras ready to start filming. She will be moving position throughout the session. Robert is sitting on a day couch near the window, and behind him is a large painting against the wall. Ian is sitting on a chair a few feet away facing him with the interview question sheet that Yvonne and Ian have prepared on a small table beside him. It is mid-morning with filtered light filling the room. Yvonne signals and the interview begins.

CH: Robert, we would like to begin with an obvious question perhaps, why or how you began your long career as an artist, and I'm reminded of something you said—that your high school teachers were impressed by your drawing skills. But more than that, perhaps, you were inspired by the Romantic poets—William Blake in particular. Would you talk to that?

RH: Yes, well, it started quite early, when at Christmas time the nuns at elementary school would give me the entire blackboard to draw the Nativity. And that's how it all started—as well as in high school with certain teachers. Now, when I was a student at McGill, I had come there from Manitoba to study art history, and I took a filler painting course—the course lasted from September to April, and one of our assignments was to paint our interpretation of love. I was twenty-two, twenty-three, and I searched high and low to find out what love was about, and of course I didn't find it! I had a lot of, you know—I wouldn't call them affairs, but I had—well, I went to four different graduations for four different girlfriends! Anyway, I thought and thought about it, and what am I going to do?

Funnily enough, I was studying beadwork design with a woman ethnographer hired by the Bureau of Indian Affairs in Washington, and using this book of many, many different quillwork and beadwork designs. I was fascinated by geometry, and of course I was fascinated with Frank Stella's geometric paintings at this time.

I would come to class around November, because by December we were supposed to come up with a plan. And I knew I didn't have a plan in terms of what I thought love was. But I looked at my classmates and, well, Robert Indiana, the Jasper Johns hearts, and all of these people that were dealing with pop culture. I was only a few years away from my reserve, and raised in—well, first of all, in a residential school from grade one to grade eight, on the reserve. I didn't have a TV, we were very poor, and so I was not exposed to urban life at all, or television. I had no idea, so when I saw them, I couldn't react to my classmates' submissions. I came in with some of the sketches that I had done that I had appropriated from some of the geometric designs in the book. It was a start, was my argument, not knowing what it was. But I said I was working on it.

So January comes along and I'm beginning to be anxious because the beginning of April, I have to hand in an assignment. So I started to do at least four acrylic paintings using the same geometric patterns. When I was finished, I submitted them to an exhibition at Hotel Bonaventure in Montreal—the exhibition was organized by the Canadian Guild of Craft—of aboriginal artefacts. And I submitted my paintings—three of them—and they accepted them. I sold one of them, a small one—ninety dollars, it was called *Red is Beautiful*. At that period already I liked colour and I didn't think any-thing of it. The thing is, the ethnologist Ted Brasser at the Museum of Man at that time bought it! So, ninety bucks, I said—WOW, you know, maybe I can make a living out of this! I didn't really think seriously about it, but it was an opening.

And now came April and time to submit work and I really, really thought about it. I submitted what I had—I made one more painting so that would have been four—I submitted them to my professor and then I said—but I had a dream, I had a dream—and he said, don't you know what love is yet? I said no, not really, but I had a dream and I'm telling you truth, I had a dream, I said —because I was getting really, really worked up and getting nervous, I wanted the mark, I wanted a good mark, I had been working at it, you know, conceptually, culturally, even sort of emotionally, trying to find it. I had this dream of canvas, a triptych. It was blue, purple and red. I eventually found out, being interested in colour, that you arrive at purple by mixing those two opposite colours.

So I had a long discussion with the professor, and he gave me a good mark. But he said can you paint it, are you going to submit it, and I said no because I don't really know it, but I'll present a painting—I'll make another one but only with the primary colours and that will take shape. That was in 1974, '75. From that dream, I painted this painting for One Bedford two years ago. I finally painted it—because, well you know, I knew now what love was!

And also, at that time, despite having sold a ninety-dollar painting, I could never really tell anybody that I was an artist or that I wanted to be an artist or was going to be an artist. The idea was there but it wasn't until that dream—and I remember that dream to this day, too—because in my culture dreaming is an important part of an affirmation with things. And from that moment on, after talking with my professor, I was able confidently, without feeling any hesitation, any embarrassment, I could say: I am an artist.

And then what happened after that, a former girlfriend from the University of Manitoba, she's in Winnipeg now, she was then at that time Dean of Women, and I told her about this and she sent me thirteen poems that she'd written—her name is Brenda Grushko, she lives in Vancouver now. I painted twelve of these paintings, still in geometrics, still the quill and beadwork Ojibwa designs, and they're all in pastel colours. So that was the first time that poetry began to play a major role in stimulating an inner emotion—and then once the emotion was activated, I tried to articulate that visually through what I had been working with. But I had a problem with thirteen because one of the poems is only one word—the thirteenth one— and I said, well, I can't really do that. All those paintings, 1975, '76, were bought by Indigenous Affairs at that time and they're all there in Ottawa. They've never been published. A couple of them are in teepee shape, and that shape of the canvas actually came from *Jericho* by Barnett Newman. I was a young artist, you know, and eventually in the late '70s—by the time I left Montreal, 1976, '77—I became aware of Yves Gaucher's work and that's where my pastel colours came about. But by the time I left Montreal I was particularly fascinated with Mondrian because I was getting closer to something—I didn't really like the Plasticiens, it wasn't for me—but I liked De Stijl, there was something idealistic, something pure about it for me. It took me until 1981 when I went to Amsterdam to do a serious study on Mondrian—by that time I had had exhibitions here in Toronto—that I realized I had a problem with Mondrian. It was when I looked at a good volume of his work—I went to The Hague—that I could see the absence of organic line, and as an Indigenous person, organic lines are very, very important— and green, too—and so I left him, of course, and became more and more attracted to Barnett Newman again—that was a result of looking at *Cathedra*. Here I am at The Hague looking at the Mondrians, just fascinated with the way the paint is applied because you can see the brushwork, it's not at all like the Plasticiens with a roller, no. But then I turned around and there's this painting as long as these two rooms—*Cathedra*, by Newman—and I said, ok, fine.

That's how I started, through a dream. And dreaming will continue to take a role in my process as a painter.

CH: That's interesting, Robert. As I hear you speak, do you think that an artist can reveal the imagination through dreams or through the sensitivity that one has to something like love?

RH: Well, I've never really considered myself a romantic, in that sense. I am intellectually drawn because—coming back to your first question about— When I was at the University of Manitoba, I took a course on the Romantic poets. I mean Shelley, Byron, John Donne, Milton, the whole gamut. I read all their poetry, this was a course that was offered. I became really fascinated by what would happen to me if I read—and Blake, William Blake, I was attracted to him as well because he came the closest to where, as I would read the prose, images would manifest themselves in my brain, you know— I really liked that. Whereas with other poets, like John Donne, the imagery wouldn't be as obvious or emotional, but Blake's prose would be more, a lot more emotional, it wouldn't be specific even, it wouldn't be as specific imagistically, but it would be specific emotionally and it would always contain a narrative.

CH: I'm going to suggest something that may be overly generalized, but it occurs to me from the way you speak about the interests you have had that there does seem to be emerging here the sense of a conversation between the Western paradigms that these poets and painters represent and the Saulteaux traditions that, of course, have so much meaning for you. Would a conversation between these seem an adequate way of describing the relationship that you see as one of your core interests or concepts?

RH: It wasn't obvious at that time. I was too busy absorbing everything that was happening to me, I was too busy aligning myself with various aesthetics, with various artists as well, with what they did and what I liked and it wasn't so much what I didn't like, but what didn't trigger a core. And what I've learned over the years now when I go to an exhibition, a group exhibition, a large exhibition, certain works would resonate—they would leave a memory, they would constantly resurface in my mind and in my memory. That work would play a major role and I would think seriously where it came from, what it meant, how I related to it. And, at this time, it was Western aesthetics that was most important to me—but not because I was unfamiliar with the aesthetics on my side—I was raised very traditional. I have a traditional name, I am known as Blue Thunder.

You know, it has taken up until five, six years ago to be able to tell anyone that, because the residential school forbade me to use that name, because—well, my first day at school I even had no idea my name was Robert! (smiles) So it became something I held back—well, I didn't really hold it back, you know, my culture. I would wake up in the morning with my brothers—I am the eldest in the family, it was a large family, and my mother would be at the stove cooking our eggs for everybody. Everybody had different tastes—I like mine sunny-side up! The first she would say as she was cooking, and we were all sitting around and we would try to beat each other to it—because she would ask: "Did you dream?" That was the beginning of the day as a child, so dreaming became an absolutely important part of life, of understanding life, of knowing what was happening—what was happening in your dreams, what you saw in your dreams, who you met in your dreams—it all became really sort of, how should I say, culturally pertinent. Not so much to analyze your dreams, but to see them as narratives, as stories. I've done that all my life, so it's there.

And also being a speaker, in my family when I go home, my siblings, we all speak our maternal language, Saulteaux, so I was never afraid that my identity was—sure, I knew it was under attack, it was being suppressed, but I was never insecure about it—it was always there because at school, every time I went home for the weekend—I went home once a month when I was the University of Manitoba, and in Montreal I went home every Christmas to celebrate with family.

We would go to the Sundance on the Summer Solstice, and that's where things began to be very difficult for me and actually made me very angry for years, and I didn't realize that until 2009 when I did the twenty-four drawings on the Sandy Bay Residential School abuse trauma—again using memory to articulate what had happened to me.

But going back to this particular story: I was sixteen years old, and the family put up a tent at the sacred grounds on our reserve, where the Sundance lodges were built. After the Sundance is over, they only take the outer rims and they leave the poles in place—you see them everywhere and so you know this is sacred ground. Anyway, this particular summer, we all found out there was going to be a ceremony, they were going to have a piercing, so we stayed because they couldn't do that during daylight—the RCMP. It was around five o'clock in the morning just as the sun is coming up and no one's anywhere around except for the participants and the guests. We couldn't go into the lodge, so we peeked through the bushes, poplars that were planted around as a wall for the wigwam, and I saw a piercing, a man that we knew. To make a story short, after that weekend, that Sunday, we went back to residential school—school went until the end of June in those days. And the priests invited us all into the chapel—the boys. "Ok, who went to the Sundance?" I raised my arm, and my cousins too. So we were punished! We were forced to go into the confessional, and the priest gave me a lecture and said, you have worshipped false gods, this is pagan, this is wrong, you are going to do two rosaries—that's 106 Hail Marys. I was flabbergasted! Sixteen! There were trajectories of colonialism like that. It was forced upon me. But it never deterred me from understanding what Western aesthetics was, and I was attracted to it—attracted to it because I was interested in being a good painter.

CH: The Parfleche series of thirteen paintings, *Parfleches for the Last Supper*, is a stunningly beautiful work. Would you be interested in speaking to it, given the story you've just told?

RH: Yes. I'd left the museum in '82, and I came to Toronto, and up to that point, I'd been borrowing from everybody, you know. But before that, when I was at the museum in Ottawa, I'd moved into a haunted house on Hawthorn Avenue—I didn't know it was haunted—when I was a curator, and I was given a show by the Pollock Gallery, so I was doing drawings. I had a research day and I would use it to draw for the show here in Toronto. But back in Ottawa, in my house, I began dreaming again. I would wake up at three o'clock in the morning, wake up sweating, nervous, my eyes would focus and there would be a figure standing at my bedroom door. But as soon as I would focus my eyes it would disappear. And this went on for about a month and it began to wear on my body—everybody that appeared was dying. So I called my mother. Well, she said, you have to come. The shaman who works through dreams that our family goes to, he wants you to come, and he'll heal you.

What he told me, what I was told to do, was put a paper by the bed and draw a face as soon as it happens. So I did, I drew about four of them. And I went home and we went to see him. And of course he had to go to sleep. But when I was there, he put his hands over them—slowly, all of them. I knew I wouldn't get an answer from him that day or night. Two nights later, I'm sleeping at my parents' home, in my room, and I slowly woke up and I realized somebody had penetrated my brain—it was just so obvious! Just woke up slowly. For a second or two, I got really angry and I said, what have I done to myself? I've exposed myself to something I have no idea of—I felt I had submitted myself! And here I am, a very rational person, I've gone to university and just really liking Mondrian (laughs) and stuff like that! I couldn't go back to sleep, so I got up and what am I going to do? Well, I'll get a glass of water. I get out of my room and go to the kitchen and my mother hears me and she comes and sits down and, same thing as at break- fast time: "You're dreaming?" And I said, yes, and she said, sit down. "So what is it." I said I don't know. "Are you scared?" And I said "No, I'm not scared, but I almost got angry." "You're being healed, you're being cured," she said. "And you know who it is." Yes, I said, I know who it is, it's the guy we went to see. I don't want to name him. And he's dead now.

Anyway, I've never had problems with my dreams since that time. And I trusted this man as well, it's a man we always went to see, and he was also a man that taught me medicine and he was married to one of my cousins, part of the family.

But I've got off track here about your original question. So what happens is, I went to Toronto, I had to find my own path, my own way of creating, I was tired of borrowing—it's ok to be inspired, but it was time to, well, get a hold of my culture, where I come from, especially spiritually, and that's beginning to play a very important part in my work. That's when I went and bought handmade paper, from India, brown, at Gwartzman's on Spadina, and took acrylic and porcupine quills and, for the first time, I wanted to marry Indigenous spirituality, my culture, with modern art practice. I folded them to make a square.

I remember, as a child, my mom calling this man to name us. And he would open his parfleche, and inside was this amulet, a rattle, and the windows will be closed and he would go into a trance with his rattle, and he would talk to various people who would be name-givers or the spirit guardians, and then suddenly you could tell by his conversation, by his manner, that somebody was ready to give a name to the child. He would laugh and for the first time he would utter the name of the child, and it would pass around and you would repeat the name of the child.

And this is what inspired my *Parfleches for the Last Supper*. My grandfather and my father raised us to believe that Jesus was a shaman, and so were all the people at the Last Supper—they have each their own powers. I had learned through Barnett Newman's *Stations of the Cross*—he was of Jewish faith, and I was raised by the nuns and priests not to touch that, it was sacred. But I said to myself, well, if he could do it, I can do it, and so I began to craft, to articulate in my brain what it would be. So that's when I made *Parfleches for the Last Supper*—based on the parfleches.

There were two uses for them: one for carrying pemmican on a horse, but there were usually two because that's how many you can make out of one hide. But some of them were made a little differently, for medicine bags, hence my parfleches. And I read the Bible, I read the quotes, because I've always been interested in verse. There were thirteen of them and I had to read about the lives of each of these thirteen people. They all died violently—for example, Bartholomew was flayed in Armenia. It was all very interesting because I didn't know who they were. So I started reading the first four gospels and they became a script because each of those paintings, *Parfleches for the Last Supper* has a quote in them, for example: "If they have hated you, they have hated me before," something like that. It was very cathartic.

But nobody would buy them! That was in 1984 or '85 and it took four years to sell them, because there were thirteen of them—people would want to buy one of them, everyone was superstitious because of the number. But I said, I'm not going to break them up. And eventually somebody bought them and donated them to the Winnipeg Art Gallery. Because it would be close to home, you know.

So, parfleches. I still work on that thing a lot and it has translated lately, in the last ten years, into diptychs. It was the first time I've started to use Indigenous material like quills. I began to find out more and more about the habits of the porcupine, the pricking from the quills. This was all very diffi-cult terrain because of my being a Catholic altar boy! But I did it. It needed to be done. And from that time on, that was essentially the first work that was mine. And I created them here. At Wellesley and Sherbourne.

There is a short break. Yvonne rearranges the cameras. Robert changes position, and is now seated further from the window in an armchair in front of a large crate set against the wall. Ian is facing Robert.

CH: I'd like to pick up on something you said a few minutes ago. I was going to ask what you thought about the difference between material and concepts in your work, and you were talking about the porcupine. Would it be fair to say that when we talk about material and ideas as opposites, perhaps the idea is embodied in the material or the material in the idea, something hard for those in the Western binary paradigm to acknowledge.

RH: That's a very interesting question, Ian. I think in many different ways—well, I'll start off by suggesting a term, "Indigenous materiality," and I can give you an example where dichotomies break down. In terms of Indigenous material, not the quill, but the canoe. Pollution has changed its physicality, its strength. You can't do birch bark biting anymore because its texture has been changed, because of pollution. So we are dealing with this complication as Indigenous artists who use Indigenous material. And it relates to my use of quills as a natural material, because the thing about the *Parfleches* was the combination of acrylic as synthetic and the use of quills as a natural material. And I deliberately put those in use together at the same time because I began to see these not as so much as dichotomies because they're part of the physical world—one is made, one is not made.

In terms of Indigenous material, after the quills, around 1989, I used a cow's skull. I covered it with wax and encaustic and paint and attached things to it, like ribbons—that's when I came the closest to animism. It brought me to a shamanistic creative activity. Now I live here in the studio with a sacred buffalo skull. In terms of material and idea, it's not comfortable, it's been slow to integrate or articulate this shamanistic background that I have, but I'm more and more comfortable with it because I know the other side, the rational, even abstraction. And you know, I'm beginning to articulate abstraction from within my own culture, and that comes from its practice, in the traditional way, practiced more by women than by men. Men are more realistic! They will draw something or paint something that will tell a narrative, a story, for instance, on teepees.

Faye HeavyShield, an artist from Calgary—I went to visit her, we went into an antique store and we saw this set of ten photographs, printed by the Department of Agriculture, of a gathering of Blackfoot people in 1907 in Fort McCloud. Tinted. Beautiful postcards, I couldn't afford them—they were over 200 bucks—good images. And then, as we left the store, she says to me, "Oh I forgot something, could you wait for me here." So I sat on a bench outside the store for a while, and then she comes out and hands me this envelope and says, "Thank you for coming to my territory." And I opened it, and there they were! I used them in my *Premises for Self-Rule*.

One of the first photographs in that package was of medicine lodges. What they are is teepees, four or five of them, and inside of them are medicine bundles—medicine bundles are living things for us. That's one of the reasons why I left the museum. I left the museum—just to go off track a bit, but it accentuates what I'm about to say. The same guy that bought my painting for ninety dollars, he specialized in Plains culture, my backyard, and he would share a lot of information with me. So he shared with me a story of a shaman in Alberta who had this medicine bundle, and his children were hard-core Roman Catholics—his children. He was afraid that this bundle would be molested—so he confided in Ted, and Ted said: "We'll take care of it for you at the National Museum." So he brought it into the acquisition as a permanent loan, and he showed it to me—I didn't open it, of course, he gave me the catalogue number and I looked at a little bit of the notes on the card, and this was about a month before I resigned from the museum. I used to have to walk through the Collections room and there were these big tables where ethnologists and scientists, often other people, curators, would be looking at stuff, it would just be lying there. This time there was one in the corner, a large table, and this young woman was introduced to me as an ethno-chemist. I walked by, said hi, and she'd opened that particular medicine bundle. I looked at the card, the number, I went back to the entries, and sure enough it was that one. She was examining its chemical structure—of things that were in that medicine bundle, a living thing—just sacrilegious! And I said to myself, I have to get out of here! It's not a place for me. I wasn't angry. It was just about the place where I come from. I've got to get out of here. So these kinds of things began to take a very import-ant role in terms of how I place myself within the larger society. It's not easy all the time to work with that.

So, getting back to the photographs of the medicine lodges, one of the most interesting things about them is the skirts—there are no doors, the doors are painted, they are abstract portals. What they do is they lift the skirts and then they bring the tripod with the medicine bundle hanging on it and they follow the sun all around. As they go around, they lift the skirt of the teepee, all of them, there were five or six of them, and there were medicine bundles for each shaman that was present. And I use that to explain these portals of abstraction. And I do the same thing about living things—a medicine bundle being a living thing—as an abstraction. That goes to the notion of the parfleche as well. And that also deals with material, you know, because the material is actually given a redefinition by its shamanistic significance.

CH: Thinking partly about what you've just been saying, and about what's happening in today's contemporary culture, is there something that might be called a prevailing discourse that you find yourself relating to?

RH: Oh, definitely. I think performance art has given a texture to what I'm talking about, because performing is kind of a ritual, you know. Ok, I'll give you a personal example. I don't do it so much here anymore, but when I had a studio on Spadina, I would arrive, I would meditate—I learned it from Norval Morrisseau. He said to me, *neechee*, which means brother, living in a city, all the bombardment, all the stimuli, all the different things, tools, sound, people, languages, you know—philosophies, religions, and not only that, what I learned from Daphne Odjig—wires, telephone wires, they inter-fere with your dreams! And when I went to see Daphne—at the museum, I was sent to go on tours—and this was when I met Morrisseau as well—Daphne said to me: "tell me, I'm curious, what's it like living in Winnipeg." Because she lived on Manitoulin Island. She takes me upstairs to her studio and she points outside her window. She says, I have a lot of problems with my dreaming. And I said, why? "Look at them, all these wires, they interfere with my dreams...and Norval said the same thing, not the same words, but he said to me, "Robert, I have difficulty concentrating because there are so many things, there is too much mental garbage in the city." I said to myself, I wonder what that means? But I soon realized what he meant. Eventually I used that, and when I would go to my studio, I would wonder, how do I clear my mind, how do I put myself on a level of consciousness? I would meditate when I arrived at the studio. I would practice breathing—I learned it in Montreal with Katie Malloch, she used to run the jazz program on CBC radio. I went to McGill with her, and she once introduced me to that. And I put it aside, but as I became more mature in my practice, and I wanted to clear my head so that I could actually paint. And that's how I concentrated to paint *Premises for Self-Rule*.

CH: Yes, it has been suggested that performance, or performativity, is a central element in contemporary art.

RH: I think it's absolutely crucial. And it varies as much as there are various artists. They have different bodies, different experiences, different ideas, different metabolisms—you act out how you mix your paints, how you position things—these are all rituals and I find those secularly very, very important.

CH: I'm reminded of something you've said about the Baumgarten frieze at the AGO, that what he didn't understand was the importance of speech over the written word, that the naming of things is grounded in speech, not in Western written words. Would you see the question of speech as one aspect of this question of performativity?

RH: Absolutely, because speech is an articulation from your body, it's not just movement, it's also sound and I think it's intrinsic, in many ways, to the notion of performance. I'm not a singer, but I talk to myself. An example, in 2006 after my residency in Paris when I created *Paris/Ojibwa*—right here in these crates by the wall behind me—I had begun to draw them, but I couldn't place them. I knew they were ghosts, I knew they were spirits, I knew they were helpers, and I would be in constant conversation with my family because they all speak this kind of thing.

So I had brought them back here from Paris where they had died. And I just could not place them here, where I had I had brought them—they were here, I could feel them! The moment I drew the first drawing I began to weep—I had brought their spirit home. But the question became, where do I place them? So I placed them in a photograph that I had taken when my grandfather—it's next to the cemetery, between the graveyard, the marsh, and Lake Manitoba, facing east. I took a photograph of that and it became my guide. But that was not enough, that physical memory of the place and that connection. It was the sound. I learned to talk to myself, but not in English. I spoke to myself, Anishinaabemowin, and right away I knew what was happening. Some time later as I was finishing the work I began to real-ize that I had *de-colonized* my body, my *voice*. Why? Because up to that point

I was always thinking in English when I was painting. This time I spoke in my mother tongue.

I constantly learn something in trying to do the best I can in creating something. In *Paris/Ojibwa*, in trying to place them, in having created a trans-Atlantic presence here, I said, so what do I do? So I began to speak to myself in my language and sure enough—smooth sailing, confidence, and I also knew I had done the right thing. They were facing east because, well, the Resurrection.

CH: Choosing to speak in your own tongue is also to lay claim to something at the core of the modernist movement—the requirement to be authentic, or real. If I put that question to you, Robert, how would you answer?

RH: I think it's all in what I just immediately said. The fact that I was speaking in my own language, my original language, my first language that I ever spoke—that sound is very, very real. I can describe things much more fully and also penetrate spirituality much more fully, quickly, and much more rewardingly if I am to speak in my maternal language. I think that's my experience of authenticity. And also the memory of actual ritual, but even the daily ritual of going to your studio, opening the door, and deciding what you are going to do, how are you going to use it. I think that, for me, gives me the reality of doing what I do as a painter. If you are articulating the notion of making art, well, for me, I have found it in language. It's a different language from English or French or any European language. And there is a misconception that in Indigenous languages we have no word for art—that's not true—*mazinaakizige*, "Image-Maker." For example, our translation for film is *mazinaatese*, "moving images." To craft something, be it filming, be it making a painting, be it the act of drawing, of *putting together*—now that's actually more rational than the notion of creation, it's making—once in the end something is made, sure, it's a creation, but it has to come *from somewhere*, that's what's important—where it has come *from*—and, well, of course it's come from within your own body.

CH: A last question. Art can be a form of nuance, a form of subtlety, as much as a form of critique or a form of tragedy. With its nuanced subtleties, do you find a place for comedy, perhaps, in your work?

RH: Comedy, for me? Not really. But I can suggest an example, and again, it's the body. In 2008, there was an apology for the residential schools. I spent twelve years in the residential schools—elementary from grade one to grade eight on my reserve, and grade nine to twelve in Winnipeg, a high school. But the elementary one on my reserve—seven years old I get picked up, lined up to get a number. I had a very, very traumatic experience in my elementary school on the reserve—I was bullied, I was abused—in all forms. So were my parents. I didn't know I carried that as well.

2008, the day before I went to Ottawa for the apology of Harper. Ian, I'm walking back and forth here in my house. I'm going to Ottawa the next day. And I had this—I felt dirty, I felt ashamed, somehow I felt something was going to happen, something—I knew it, I could feel it. I could feel it! So I was in Ottawa—I mean I'm glad that I went. It was cathartic in so many different ways, but superficially, too. The next year, I go home to my reserve and I'm at a wake. I shake hands with a woman—she was about five, six years older than me—who goes to all of these things, *only to remember—her husband* was my bully, my abuser. I never knew that!

But that night after I shook hands with her, it all came back. When I got off the plane to come here, I put my luggage down, Paul is sitting over there, my partner. I said, Paul, I've got to tell you something—I found out, this is what happened to me. I said, I'm going to find out more. I'm going to spend the next month—this was the beginning of August. I'm going to spend twenty-four days, each day I'm going to draw, I'm going to remember trauma. I was afraid that every time I would remember an incident, I could feel the trauma—more than trauma, I would actually re-live the fear—twenty-four of them, residential school drawings.

And I said to myself before doing that—I said to myself, how can I do that? But I teach students at OCAD to remember things. I'm going to remember. So what I would do is move the bed. The next day I would put out a brand-new sheet of paper. Move the bed. I would find out who the abuser was, who the person in authority was, who knew what was going on. And I would also remember the little boys that would come into the dormitory in September—little ones, seven years old, eight years old—and my bed is there and they're over there, all in a row of course, weeping at night. I drew that. Weeping! And we were not allowed to go and comfort them.

And so I lived through all of that. I can sleep without the light on now. I had always had this anger, this trauma, this memory locked up. You know what? I'm very happy now. Really—really happy. And I realized that when I shared it with my sisters—because they talk about it now too. And now the men on my reserve are coming out, they're telling their stories. And our father was one of those people that was experimented with—he would get half a glass of milk, they were experimenting with vitamins on children.

But, but am I angry? No. No I'm not. One of the hardest things for me to do was find another word for forgiveness, because it doesn't exist in our language. The only word we could come up with is two words, it's the same root, *bagidinan*, "let it go," and *bagidendan*, "let your mind go of it." That's the closest epistemological thing we have about forgiveness. And therefore also, you don't judge. The Christian law judges, yes. But the Creator only *listens* to you. And these are things now, at my age, I am very, very comfortable to hold. And I feel very *happy* and I'm very *proud* of that, thank God. I'm not ——! I could have been worse, you know. And I'm *so* happy that I have the opportunity to share, to share that *with* you, and—Yes.

CH: Thank you, Robert.

RH: *Miigwech*. Yes. Thank you.

Anique Jordan

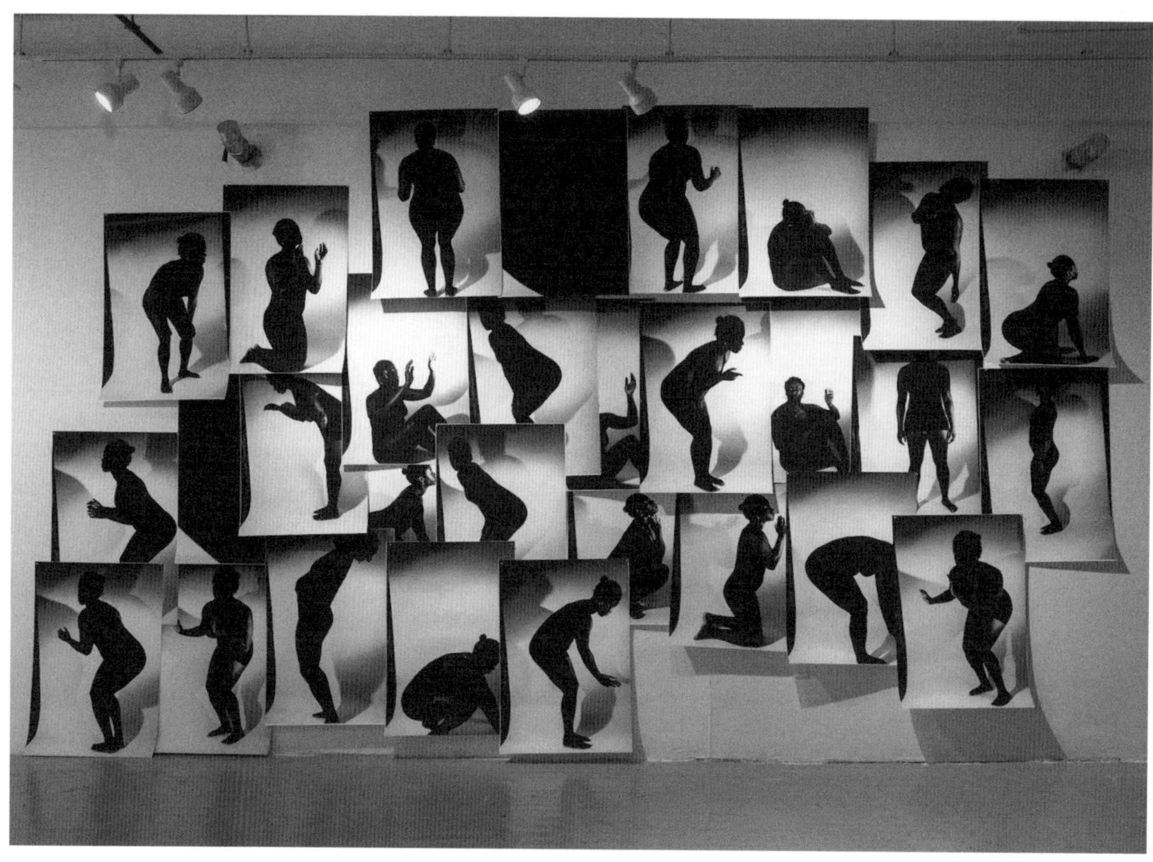

3.15   Anique Jordan, *To Score the Marvelous*, 2022. Photographs, installation variable. Courtesy the artist.

This interview was recorded on June 21, 2017.

Growing up in Toronto's Scarborough district, Anique Jordan's work employs photography, performance, poetry, and installation to draw attention to the body as a site of political resistance and futurist imagining. Her art creation processes are guided by the questions: What stories do we tell that go unchallenged? And in how many ways can we know a thing?

(Editor's note: I would like to emphasize that the transcription of this interview cannot adequately reflect Anique's genuine enthusiasm and generosity of spirit. Her ability to laugh while demanding from us serious reflection on the nature of the Canadian experience as it touches on communities such as her own Trinidadian Black heritage, and that of other communities, makes her comments all the more compelling).

Yvonne Lammerich and Ian Carr-Harris have met with Anique in a friend's borrowed house just off Roncesvalles in Toronto's west end. It's a typical Toronto semi-detached, and the front living room is small. It is evening, and the room is mostly lit by the portable film lights that Yvonne has been positioning. Throughout the filming, she will be changing camera angle several times. Anique is sitting on a wingback armchair by the window. Ian sits on a stool across the small room and to Anique's right. He consults his notes. Yvonne gives the signal to start, and the interview begins.

CH: Anique, you speak about beginning with a question: "how do we survive?" I'm interested in this question and how it bears on where you are now. Would you talk about that a little bit?

AJ: Sure. I grew up as a Black kid in Scarborough, of Caribbean heritage, and had a very distinct immigrant experience since, while I was born in Canada, I always felt like I wasn't from Canada. A lot of those sentiments came, I think, through the education system, where I wasn't taught anything that made me feel a sense of joy or a sense of groundedness in myself. As a child, I learned a lot about the sort of things that still continue to be thought of as the idea of Canada—and because of that, I have always been confused about who I am—what it means to be a Black person. Because the depiction of Blackness, like myself, had always been—on TV, for instance, slavery and these sorts of hyper-extreme versions of a sense of self. There wasn't anything that felt like a family, like my family with its troubles, with its love, all the complexities of a family, and I think, because of that, I had always tried to understand these timelines. So I remember talking to a friend when

I was a lot younger and asking him: let me get this straight, when was Jesus around, when was slavery around, and when were the dinosaurs? (laughs)

Because you were never really taught history in the way that it could be understood by you, and the only idea of who you are was this one particular dramatic, violent experience. So I was really troubled by this as a kid, and because of that I have always been stuck on this very, perhaps naïve, question of how is it that I'm alive, how is it that I survived if we've experienced slavery and all these atrocities and racism—and all of these things still exist? How is it that my mother was able to be born and I was born? Through what choices, what sacrifices, what decision-making processes were we allowed to survive? So this obsession started me going towards economic development with communities across the Americas and communities across Toronto, working on a more material idea of survival. I would think a lot about how we can use what we have to create what we need, and how to do a lot of work in the field of innovation in all these different spaces—just trying to make sense for myself how we survived, how *do* we survive, what are the things that help us to do so. And that really led towards my finding many different ways of answering that question, by asking it as innocently as I possibly could, genuinely seeking: how do we survive?

CH: Thinking about taking ownership, about this trajectory you've just talked about, what do you, with this background, understand as the potential for you of being an artist?

AJ: (laughs) What's beautiful about that question I think is asking about the potential of an artist—period. For me, I have often talked about the artist as having a very particular responsibility within communities. I remember this book my friend had given me a long time ago that talked about that, instead of celebrating birthdays we could celebrate moments of mastery, and it spoke about everyone in the community, no matter who they were, they all had this very specific role, or something specific they could master, like a craftsperson in it, so even down to the person who's able just to keep a secret, the master secret-keeper! (laughs) And they would graduate in their mastery of their craft.

And so I started to think about the role of the artist. One, for me, what becomes really important is that the artist is constantly practicing a type of newness. The artist has the ability to create something that never has existed before, never has been imagined before, except in the magic of bridging conflicting things that one felt should never, could never fit together. The artist brings that together and allows us to see it differently. So, for me, the artist has the responsibility in the community to be thinking these ideas, and if the artist was not doing this work, whose job would it be?

Whose title would it be (laughs) to think about something that's invisible, impossible, unreal, unimagined, if not the artist? So it's a responsibility, something I don't take lightly. A lot of the work that I have been doing has been looking at the Black history of Canada—I almost want to say the history of Canada in general—and it looks at trying to imagine the invisible, the erased, the things that get displaced from these traditional archives, and I start to see, through producing this work, the psychological impact it has on me, the reverberations it has on people that witness it and how they talk about the possibilities through seeing this. I really begin to see how this responsibility becomes actualized and is felt within communities. (pause) Yeah, so it's like that…

CH: I'd like to read you a quote: "Anique's work employs photography, performance, poetry and installation to draw attention to the body as a site of political resistance and futuristic imagining." I especially like that last phrase, "futuristic imagining." Would you see this that as an adequate description of how you see the core of the practice that you've been developing?

AJ: Hmm. I use the word future in a lot of my work, not talking about the future, but in talking about a complete disregard for temporality. I'm quite obsessed with the idea that things that feel like they're on the opposite ends of the spectrum—things that feel like they can conflict—can actually be brought together, and how can we understand two things that feel so different but are the same. How can we break through that idea of the dichotomy, and I really think about that through understanding Time, and through understanding this sort of meshing of Time into this *Now* moment.

For example, or to clarify it, I did a residency recently with Wanda Nanibush at Banff, and she said something that really stuck with me: she said we can understand time as the present being impregnated with the future and the past—and for me that sort of described exactly what it is that I'm trying to understand when I speak about a multiplicity of things or opposite things being true at the same time. How can we hold that together? So when I speak about these futuristic imaginings, I'm speaking about how multiple things can be true at the same time. And why that's so important is that I see that as at the root of everything, really. You have your experience, you have your way and perspective of seeing the world and I do too, and those come together. As opposed to trumping each other in any way, they're both true, whether or not they feel as though they're conflicting.

When I think about that, I think about how, in my own art practice, I can conflate things so that they no longer exist in this realm of the dichotomy—I'm thinking about this liminal space where anything can happen and many things do, and so we can experiment with what is possible. In this space, for me, we see gender as a fluid, changing, malleable thing—and all these things can happen, right? So in thinking about all this, I imagine them in the site of Carnival, and a lot of my work comes from this aesthetic, thinking about the Carnival aesthetic, which for me houses these ideas of multiplicity, because you can have a zombie on the same float as a woman wearing, like, a bikini and bra (laughs) or a political figure like Trump (laughs again), so when I'm practicing art or when I'm creating something that's hopefully asking something different from the viewer or asking the viewer to question their own perspectives, at the same time, I'm practicing a world I'm envisaging, and inviting a viewer to envisage it with me. How they too can disregard temporality, how they too can imagine something we don't feel right now, or challenge that something must exist over something else, as one has always been told. And, to me, it feels like a practice of peace, of social justice, a practice of trying to find a place of some kind of truth— how can we relate to each other differently, how can we start to understand humanity differently, how can we understand land differently—how can we share land differently—what is possible within that? And I think that's what my work is trying to get at.

CH: With that in mind, would you talk about the work *Mas'* that you performed at the AGO?

AJ: Sure. So, the *Mas'* series consists of one large image—actually it's sort of this micro-series that has four parts to it, and then a performance. Well, a performance and then a public performance. The one at the AGO is a ten-foot-long image that shows a central figure, a priest or some such spiritual-guidance figure, centred in the middle and then everyone else is in the background and almost hidden in the darkness of the scene, all wearing Victorian mourning clothing. So that's one.

The other is a set of images called *Mas' for 94 Chestnut at the Crossroads* and that's a series of four images in which you see a woman standing and facing the four cardinal points, and in each image, she's facing forward, then right, then back, then left, and she's in the process of this ritual at the site, 94 Chestnut Street. The performance at the AGO re-enacts this initial image. There's a group of Black actors, artists, activists, community workers, elders and members of my family who walk across the AGO's rotunda in this really slow-paced cadence where it takes them an hour just to cross the small space. And over a mic I'm naming all the different heads of households that lived in this particular area of Toronto during the height of the Black population of the early 1800s. As I'm speaking the names of all these different individuals, their names start to get warped and elongated and distorted, eventually to the point where all the names sound like white noise, just as those who are crossing the space complete their crossing. I'm standing at the mic, but the mic is set up as though it's an altar space, the same type that's also in the image.

This performance was curated by Andrew Hunter, who was doing a show about Lawren Harris, and what he was doing was looking at the history of Toronto's St. John's Ward, which was the area where Harris had spent a lot of time producing work, and where he'd even been a part of the community. It was one of the areas of immigration to Toronto, and had one of the largest Black populations, as well, from 1871 and 1872. So my piece looks at a church that had existed in that area called the British Methodist Episcopal Church. In 2015 it had recently been excavated to make way for a new courthouse, and as long as I had known the area, it had always been a parking lot. But during the excavation they found thousands of artefacts and it is actually considered to be one of the largest archaeological digs in North American history, so it was a huge deal!

When I had first started working with Andrew, and thinking about the space that Harris would have passed through and how busy it would have been and what type of practices would have existed there—the craftspersons and all these different things that would have been in this super-densely populated area—I really started to become interested in these spaces of community, and spaces of worship, particularly since it had just been excavated. So I approached Infrastructure Ontario, which was the official body that was overseeing the project, and asked if I could do this re-enactment of the congregation behind the construction site barrier—which was dormant at that time, with no activity going on. Initially, I was given a yes, and they were really excited and just asked that we wear construction hats and so on. Then someone from Infrastructure Ontario contacted me and asked me what the work was about. Foolishly, I gave them the artist statement, which talked about Black Canadian history, reclaiming the spaces of erasure, talked about how we could understand Canadian history in different ways through reproducing images that don't exist in the archives. And at that time, Black Lives Matter was protesting in front of Police Headquarters—which was just conveniently down the street from this site—and I got a response from Infrastructure Ontario that was basically saying, we feel uncomfortable with the direction you're taking this project.

Well, of course I had to continue what I was doing, and it was really clear to me that it had come to the point, in the world actually, but in this city and in this country that, as a Black person, for me to talk about Canadian history I have to either do it through the sterilized lens of what the state essentially wants the story to be told as, or climb over a fence and break the law and trespass just to tell the story of what I'm connected to! And this connected so many things for me—it reaffirmed how history gets told, how stories get archived, it became this incredibly subjective process of negotiating power—between me, myself, one young Black female artist and the State, right? (laughs) How am I able to tell this story that really belongs to my ancestors, but now I have to go through a bureaucracy and then it becomes some sort of conversation with Canada!—with Ontario!—instead of my being able to have an opportunity to say, hey, this existed!

Anyway, I started to ask questions about how power is housed. What happens when a history is excavated and brought to the forefront and now has to be contended with for people living in this moment now, and how to stage, how to archive this? And who holds this tangible power to have the authority that enables them to be able to maintain these stories? How is it that I now have to come up and negotiate with them, right? There's this story of the lion that will always be told by the hunter—or some version of that—that for me was iconic of that moment. It felt as though, despite how genuine my search was, how open I would have been to even a collaboration, thinking of how we could talk about this moment—all these things—it was threatening for them. It was threatening, one, to the way Canada positions itself as this benevolent saviour of Black people, and threatening, two, because Black Lives Matter's very important work was happening at that very moment. And Infrastructure Ontario—and by arms-length, Ontario— was really afraid to get into a conversation about Blackness, and especially on the terms of a Black person instead of on their terms. Through the grapevine I, in fact, learned that they were really afraid of having someone else telling a story before they got to say it in an apolitical, sterile, happy-go-lucky version of this story. It doubled for me how important it was to get into it on my own and galvanize community support to do this work.

So it went from simply working with friends to re-enact this congregation that would have been on the land where they had excavated to being very deliberate and intentional about who I would involve in the project. I selected one of the founders of Black Lives Matter, I selected one of the founders of the Zero Gun Violence movement, people who had been involved in very strong activist roles in the Black community, I consulted with a lot of Elders to learn more about what I was attempting to do. And I staged it in Holy Trinity Church, which is the only church that still exists from that time, and so created that initial congregation re-enactment. And then, in front of the doors of 94 Chestnut, which is the address of the original church, I re-enacted this ritual where you see the woman standing directly in front of the locked gate—it has a standard danger sign of two hands raised, which also symbolizes for me a lot of the police resistance, police violence, and the innocence of Black lives that have been taken and constantly been made to feel guilty before any sort of process can happen.

And, for me, this woman standing there is not thinking about the viewer, she cares not at all about who is watching, she's doing it for her own self, participating in a ritual that is remembering the lives of the people there, naming the lives of those to come—standing at the crossroads. The crossroads represents this liminal space, a space where many things can exist, can be true at the same time. The re-enactment of *Mas'* as a performance was something that felt very important in order to animate the AGO as an institution and to bring those Black bodies into the museum. So many who I invited to participate said that it was the first time they had ever been inside the AGO and, though they passed by so many times, they never felt they belonged in that space, or that anything there would have significance to them or reflect them in any way. And I'll tell you that creating that space for Black bodies to walk through in this very deliberate way—a way of owning a space you never thought you could even walk into—has such a transformative impact.

After the performance I never felt such a feeling of being protected, of being loved—that sense of belonging that I could feel with this group, this *Mas'*—*Mas'* as in masqueraders—so therefore connecting with the Carnival tradition of a procession, *Mas'* as in this mass body of people moving in synchrony through this space, and *Mas'* as in thinking about the church Mass, a re-enactment of this space, thinking then about the church itself, once buried, that is now being turned into a provincial courthouse! So this space of safety and a space of social justice at the time—a lot of people came north after the enactment of the Fugitive Slave laws in the United States, and bounty hunters from the United States were not allowed in the churches— now this space of the former church is to be a space of cells and a justice that has proven time and time again not to be a space of justice for Black bodies, Indigenous bodies, people of colour, trans—anybody who does not fit within a particular idea of Canada. So I also think about this *Mas'* that happens within the court system—I discovered that the church is set up in the exact same way as a courthouse, and it is actually the same space but in totally different ways. So that comes out in the performance as well.

CH: I was going to ask you to talk about art history, but it seems perhaps more important to talk about history. And you have. There's a quotation here that I'd like to pull up, in which you say: "I'm drawn to the idea of disregarding all temporalities. I consider myself thinking about Time in a sense that there is no time, there's continuum." This continuum, Anique, do you see it in political terms, primarily, or more in existential terms?

AJ: With this show that's coming at the AGO, we've spent a lot of time talking about Time and I would like to clarify what I mean when I speak about it because, as I say, I try to hold two things as true at the same time. I think about Time as this continuum of spirals upon spirals upon spirals, and I think it's important to think of Time the way it would have been understood through spiritual practices, through working with the land, and this is essential to the way I move through the world. At the same time, I think it's vitally important to think of Time in a very deliberately political way with political, social markers. By that I mean we cannot forget that colonization happened, we cannot forget that Indigenous treaties have been broken, that people have been displaced from their territories, that slavery has happened—we cannot forget all that by conflating it into a very broad definition of Time that does not account for things that have happened because of Time. So I don't ever lose my hold on those two things. Because of certain traditions and practices I've been exposed to, I am able to understand Time in broader ways because of my political position, because of who I am, because of my relationship with friends who are Indigenous, because of my need to understand what has happened at particular moments and how that's impacted my life. I need to understand these things as multiple things that will and do exist simultaneously.

All of this helps me to make sure that my work is being accountable to people as a guest on this land, being accountable to my ancestors who have made very particular sacrifices and decisions in order for me and my lineage to have been born. And, at the same time, it allows me to think outside the realm of colonial empire, outside the realm of the New World and to a place that gives me more freedom to think about myself in and of myself, of an entity that does not exist in relationship to whiteness or colonial empire or all that, and, for me, that does something, that says that I own me, I am possessed by my own self, I am my own possession, right? And having that sort of stance, I move through the world differently, I can encourage people to do things through the world differently, I can create works that also are influenced by that idea.

CH: You've just completed a major degree at the university, and I wonder whether theory, or theorizing plays an important role in your practice. Is there a particular theoretical structure that you've found important? Any thoughts?

AJ: Yeah, well I studied theory (laughs) as I guess we all do, going to higher education, and there are theorists that have spoken to me, but I think I'm more interested in—I mean, what is theory other than trying to make sense of the world? And I'm most interested in the way of sense-making that I've seen in my neighbourhood growing up. A lot of my work started off in youth work, in community housing across North America, and some work in the Caribbean—with people who will spend some time with me on the stoop, on the veranda, in hallways, in staircases (laughs), who have, for me, the most astounding perspectives on life. I've learnt so much through people's observation of the world. And I think that, for me, this is a skill that I've been trying to learn for myself, because I think that the theorists who have most inspired me have been people who are just really good at observing and then telling me what it is that they've seen.

I have begun this practice of trying to see something different since I started to realize that I'm only seeing the same thing instead of what I'm *actually* seeing, which also then becomes this holding onto the same perspective. So I have this practice when I'm walking to say out loud the things I'm seeing—like book, chair, blue, purple, or whatever—and I'll just say these things to hear for myself what is it that I'm noticing, I challenge myself to see something different. I look to see what might be that colour blue or that aesthetic or that type of emotion to try to force myself to observe. And I think there is something there that might get lost if the only way you understand the world is by reading about it, as opposed to standing there and interpreting the world yourself, or understanding it through different means. Literature is only one way of processing information—there's processing through touch, or understanding things through colour, what colour and texture can say to us. As somebody who didn't go through art school, for me, these are the ways I sort of teach myself about art and about the world and about what it is that's important—what it is I'm seeing.

CH: We often look at the world through the idea of a Zeitgeist, or way of seeing things that, coming back to theory, is also called a dominant discourse. When you're looking at the world, do you have a sense that there's a way of being in the world that is predominant at the moment?

AJ: Hmm. Maybe if you look at it through the lens of Toronto (laughs) as opposed to, I don't know, the lens of the Caribbean, for example! The Zeitgeist, I think, is an illusion—it's another form of subjective archiving. Whoever is producing it or naming it is seeing it in the same way that I only see certain colours when I'm walking—they only see things through the theories that they're looking for. I think that a Zeitgeist is important for being this thing that, as humans, we love to do—to classify, to taxonomize into species. And that's therefore also a colonial project, right? To be constantly grouping things in "like this" and then saying everything is "like that." So the Zeitgeist is interesting for the sake of interest (laughs), but it's not the type of work I want to do. I want to do work that troubles us, creates complexities and revels in the complexity of things without trying to conflate them into categories of likeness. I think we learn to work across difference in that way instead of trying to make us all similar in some way. Why can't we all be different and still work together? I'm more interested in that.

CH: Nice answer. Somebody asked you what were the six things you couldn't live without, and you mentioned play and humour.

AJ: (laughs) Play and humour are the pillars in my life! Which is interesting, because in my artwork, when I do my own self-portraits, I have no emotion, because I want people to write their own emotion onto the image that they're seeing so they have to do some work, some type of labour in seeing me, right? Or whoever I'm working with, which is primarily Black bodies. Recently some people have said to me: I didn't know you laugh, or I can't imagine you smiling (laughs). I think play is a type of release, a sign that the armour has been released and some vulnerability is available to me and to the people in the room that I share a space with. When I can laugh or joke, that is a moment of freedom, that is a very political place for me, a place that says, I feel safe, which is not a common thing. That moment is such a strong sense of release, like a supernova (laughs) that it means something else is happening, a shift against something else, it helps me realize that I'm wearing an armour—a deadpan expression, or an angry expression, like a "don't talk to me, don't come near me" type of expression—because that is how I've been able to survive, as a woman, as a Black woman, it has been a tool that I've learned—not so much from my family—but from other women around me that this is how you have to behave in order not to be harassed, or taken lightly, for somebody to begin the process of assuming intelligence, which is not something I'm granted if I'm open. So play or joy is not a tool for me, but a signifier that I'm in a place that is safe, and I know that there are very few such spaces for me, so I hold onto it very closely. What is interesting, too, is this one-dimensional view of what a woman experiences, particularly the range of emotion that a Black woman experiences—that there is no depth of emotion that is felt. For me, when I think about emotion on a Black person's body, I also think about the ways in which Black people are seen, as though they can't feel sorrow or joy. You see that on TV or in the movies, and that's perpetuated in the justice system, where it's like, oh well, this person doesn't feel pain so this isn't an act of violence against a human. It feeds into this type of cycle. So I try to understand emotion, I try to understand what it is I'm actually exhibiting to the world about what I'm really feeling because I know that emotion can have an almost life-threatening outcome depending on how it's portrayed on me.

CH: Well, speaking about how others see us, do you have any thoughts, as an artist, about the public, whether the professional public on the one side or the general public on the other?

AJ: To answer that question, a huge component is that I didn't go to art school (laughs). I did not realize how essential an art-school experience is to so many artists and the entire infrastructure that supports artists. I had no idea, because I only started to meet people who went to OCAD last year (laughs), right? So because of that I feel as though I have multiple perspectives on what art is. What it means to be an artist, what the career of an artist looks like and what the infrastructure of it that surrounds an artist looks like. So when I realized how little the general public understands about this infrastructure surrounding artists, a lot of my work has been in trying to create a language that allows people to speak to the art before even the critics or the curators. It allows the art that I'm working on to have a very visceral response to the immediate audience that I'm focusing on. And that immediate visceral response means that anyone can hold some sort of coded language that is able to decode what I'm creating, and that can prompt somebody else. So it's privileging the language that they come from, and these are people who live more in the suburbs than in the town core, for sure. Or have grown up with very particular lived experiences and have never seen themselves reflected in art spaces, are not privileged with opportunities to speak about art in a way that allows your experiences to be just as valid, if not more so, because you helped me, in a way, to create this work. I've really spent a lot of time and labour trying to figure out ways that make art most accessible to the audience that I'm privileging, an audience that typically is not privileged. And I think in doing this in my work that the infrastructure has to catch up, it has to figure out what it is I'm saying, it has to ask questions. And the answers are coming from my mom—right!— it's coming from a little girl, it's coming from people who the work is so immediately for. I think about that, and I think about the ways we can construct an infrastructure to support artists that does not look like the ways it has always looked like in the city. And that means more Black, Indigenous, trans, people of colour curators, art buyers, critics. The entire infrastructure requires some kind of shift, which is now happening in the city, and maybe it needs an acknowledging and a naming of the shift that is changing who is seeing the art, who is deciding what is art. I learned a lot about that studying and doing work in Jamaica, but I think I learned most through having conversations with my mom and my aunts about what they see. I'm more interested in that and I'm more interested in how we shift to what this infrastructure could look like.

CH: In some of the things that you've said, you suggest that somehow we have to get back to something that's essential, something that is close to the body, however one might want to describe that. Making art or being in the world is not a question of fooling around. It's serious business, and the point of that seriousness is to find joy. So the word often used to describe this experience is authenticity, something of value. Do have any thoughts about this sense of something fundamental?

AJ: I studied for about two years under d'bi.young, who's a dub poet, and one of the things that she really instilled in us as students was holding true to integrity and what it means to really find it. I want to say that I don't really know if there's something fundamental that we should be in touch with. I do not know this because I'm seeking many things, and sometimes there's not even the space to think more broadly about oneself when there's so much riding on the Now, on survival, on making it through the day. So I can kind of hold on to this idea of what is integrity to oneself, and then pair it with the question she often asked us, which is, what is urgent to you? I think together those two questions allow me to feel a sense of grounding and a sense of checking in with myself to know if I'm actually making the right decisions, actually using the right words, actually having the type of relationship that I think I'm having with someone, with work, with whatever it is that I'm doing, and that sort of investment in integrity grounds me, it grounds me in the times when I'm not grounded in something greater than myself, it allows me to have something within myself to narrow in on.

And so, for me, I would like to believe that it can really help us in forming relationships that will make for something positive in the world, something that feels like it's centred with love, that feels like the road to hell is not really paved with good intentions but it's a different road (laughs), one that has good intentions that are doing good things—which I know is complicated and mainly untrue in the world that we've created. So I ground myself in that, I ground myself in the idea of integrity and in the trust that I have for myself that I know what integrity means and I know who I am.

Notes, 1982–2018

Fiction (1982)

Published in the catalogue for *Fiction: An Exhibition of Recent Work by Ian Carr-Harris, General Idea, Mary Janitch, Shirley Wiitasalo*, curated by Elke Town, Art Gallery of Ontario, Toronto, April 2 to May 30, 1982. All incomplete sentences are reproduced as they appeared in the original.

and in fact I've never been sure about certainty. Many people seem to be, and occasionally I've felt inadequate that this state escaped me. I often have revelations. They're not the same though.

Partly it's the sense of unity I feel in making connections between events which at first seemed arbitrary. History as a discipline is of course quite structural. But more important for me is the sense of being able to reach out and touch people—real people like myself—who are separated from me in time rather than in space. The intimacy of this fascinates me.

…more than ideas. What is interesting about ideas is the effect they have on people. Ideas come in a variety of sizes. To some extent it's a matter of tailoring. Ideas can be extraordinarily seductive, of course, and I don't mean to denigrate them. Not at all. But personally I've always found them slightly disenchanting. All that promise. Another idea, I say to myself. Sort of like Emily Dickinson's poem about the frog. Ideas are always different, depending on who's trying to deal with them. I like most of all watching people trying to deal with ideas. This is what most contact between people actually comes down to, no doubt.

I like objects. Some people don't, I understand. I expect this means they simply aren't paying attention or aren't thinking about them. It seems strange, to spend all this time surrounded by objects and not think about them. Many people appear to spend a lot of time thinking about themselves; and this seems to be an internal thing. Their own boundaries escape them, so they don't really ever see themselves, they don't see any connections, and they don't give themselves the chance to have a coherent relationship with the context that they are inevitably constructing and actually existing in. I think this is the reason they don't like objects. They don't understand that they are really situations. Perhaps it's just a matter of arrogance.

Quite by chance I was in the AGO the other day, which is very unusual because it hardly ever happens. I was looking at Rodin's sculptures there, and thinking how different they are from what people had done before.

1   This discussion is as old as Plato's dismissal of art in general as a distortion of the ideal state of ideation, but the problem of sculpture is more specifically raised in Leonardo da Vinci's "Paragone" and in Baudelaire's 1846 essay *"Pourquoi la sculpture est ennuyeuse"* ("Why Sculpture is Boring").

Their sexuality is very vulnerable. I like this quality. I think Rodin's sensuality is honest about himself and therefore about all of us. Our sensuality is constant; it's in the way we move, it's in what we say, what we think but don't say, it's in our voices. I like voices especially. Voices reveal a lot, because on the one hand they're used for constructing information of various kinds—rational facts about the world, moral judgements, and more or less objective reporting on states of being—and on the other hand they reveal their tone and pattern, the significance this information has for that person. So there's a lot of built-in "presence," as it were, which is what we are really listening *for* when we listen *to* someone. This complexity intrigues me. It's in language too, of course, and I've frequently looked at language. But with language I find myself dealing with mythology directly, not with individuals. There's the concept of examples here, I guess.

[The following sentence is the continuation of the last sentence at the end of this text.]

...great majority of ordinary people for whom structures are a contingent question of survival rather than of theoretical debate.

Ian Carr-Harris was a student at art college in the late Sixties when Donald Judd was articulating the Minimalist position in opposition to artists like Anthony Caro. In a famous essay by Michael Fried in 1967, the "theatrical" implications of Minimalism were clearly identified as a threat to the modernist concern for the essential nature of discrete experience. Fried was suggesting that the "literal" or theatrical, nature of Minimalism's concept of experience, while an accurate account of the durational nature of general experience, was inadequate to deal with the peculiar awareness, the sense of implosion within a single moment of intuitive clarity or "presentness" which he maintained was the singular experience with which a work of art should be concerned.

Fried's criticism was, of course, a restatement of the idealist insistence on the essentially critical position that a subject occupied in relation to an object, and that the value of the object, and hence its definition as art, lay precisely in the degree to which this moral connection was manifested.

Carr-Harris took this critique—and the broader context of what was, in effect, an historic discussion[1] on the validity of sculpture—as the basis for certain decisions on the possibilities sculpture presented for his own attempts to understand experience. Fried's justifications for moral and pictorial idealism confirmed his own growing conviction that the nature of experience was in fact indiscrete, that the essential relationship between people and phenomena was situational and inescapably durational, as the Minimalists argued, and that this was so however much we—and Michael Fried—might wish otherwise. And this latter point—however much we might wish otherwise—was for Carr-Harris a crucial aspect of the conditions surrounding a work of art.

No work of art—no experience of any kind—could be valid without admitting the extent of its own circumstance, and that circumstance included most specifically the relationship between the audience and the work. For Carr-Harris, Fried's moral framework was a denial of this experience rather than an investigation of it, but the Minimalist aesthetic of primary form and its restriction to considerations of abstract structural problems failed to address the reason why those structural problems had importance. What was interesting, however, was the implication of the Minimalist position for the use of language and the characteristics of organized experience that language implied. This was, of course, an inherent aspect of Minimalism, and quickly became the premise for the Conceptual movement of the 1970s, but Carr-Harris's concern for the relationship between people and structures had developed independently during his earlier study of history at Queen's. What pre-eminently interested him was not so much the often-obscure question of structural origins; rather, it was the manner in which we function within the structures which define our existence and over which typically as individuals we have no extensive control, but on which, nevertheless, we have ideas and degrees of influence.

Clearly, then, the relation between the work of art and its audience was a paradigm for the normal working relationships of ordinary existence. It was obvious that a natural strategy for any work would be to recognize the active and extensive dialectic it held in its relationship with the viewer. These two basic and related conditions—the situational nature of experience and the dialectic potential of the relationship—led Carr-Harris to the conclusion that the most viable mode for addressing questions of experience lay in precisely the direction that Fried had rejected: that is, through a development of the theatrical implications of sculpture.

Why sculpture? Like its more useful alter ego—statuary—sculpture is of all the arts the one that most directly confronts the nature of our physicality and reflects the intimate complexities of the human recognition of the divisions between the self and the non-self. Sculpture, whether statuary or installation, is an insertion of the material embodiment of human constructs into the real space of normal existence. Unlike painting's speculation into a universe of experience beyond the space and experience and time occupied by the viewer, and unlike architecture's construction of a container for experience, sculpture addresses the mirror recognition of the nervous expectancy of human identity.

As a surrogate of human identity, sculpture by virtue of its shared occupation of our space and by virtue of its intentionality as a mental construct

2   This concern with human equivalence is, of course, what separates sculpture from furniture or other objects in the real world. A chair, for example, shares powerful associations with human experience that must be acknowledged as placing its status as an "obdurate object" somewhat in doubt, but it does not pretend to be a surrogate for human value construction.

was, Carr-Harris felt, not an "obdurate object" as the Minimalists had suggested, but a vulnerable situation or event in the same manner in which any human experience is based on the constant construction of situation in order to protect the self against intrusion.

Sculpture, then, through its concern with human equivalence, was essentially theatrical, and the power of theatre's involvement with its audience to include the viewer as a participant in the investigation of ethics must in one way or another be acknowledged.[2] For Carr-Harris, the aggressive syntax of theatre—its natural ability to confront the audience and force a reply from the viewer—was the single most valuable aspect to be gained from this connection.

Given these basic premises, Carr-Harris proceeded to consider the implications involved. Pivotal among these was the question concerning the limits of rational experience. With theatre as a model, he accepted the power of argument (an entity which skirts the boundaries of reason) in the conviction that experience is as much a reflection on circumstance—and thus of conscious desire and calculated expectation—as it might be of supra-rational interjection.

Consequently, if sculpture was seen as a paradigm of experience, it was not merely metaphor—could not in fact be metaphor (though it might legitimately make use of metaphor)—but an actual event, or performance, within the experience it suggested. The work is thus a part of the reality it also discusses, and this inherent ambiguity—distinct on the one hand from art's traditional metaphysical transcendence and on the other from the continuity of normal reality—furnishes Carr-Harris with the means of extending the investigation of experience vertically, into time and the dimension of argument, and horizontally into space and the dimension of presence.

This particular nexus in the work is important enough to require special consideration, since it is one of the most significant formal concerns it addresses. Its premise derives, as we have indicated, from the ambiguous reality occupied by the work, but it derives as well from the larger issue of translational equivalence basic to our attempts to make our reality coherent, and from our recognition—as part of this translation—that ambiguities and incoherencies are a necessary condition of any translation, warping even the most coherent reconstructions of reality. Thus, while the work must reflect an acceptance of the physicality—the constituents of construction—of its own existence, it must also construct a syntax or context, and while it utilizes a carefully constructed vocabulary and grammar to do so, it cannot by virtue of the situational nature of experience be limited by its means. Our desire to know is confronted instead by the limitations and extensions of our own expectations.

This concept can be most easily understood by referring to the nature of memory, a consistent strategy in the work. If human experience is situational, it can only be so with the use of memory to guide it and reflect on it. Since our experience does not exist in the present, but in the past and in the future, the situation we confront durationally is a function of desire and expectation. Desire is our attempt to reconstruct situations as we would like them to have been; expectation is our ambivalence over the consequences. The work reflects these ambiguities through its inherent physical intimacy with the viewer on the one hand, and on the other through its almost photographic—or filmic—and frankly theatrical appeal to the viewer's past and future definitions of their circumstance in the present.

To a considerable degree, then, Carr-Harris's work states categorically that "reality" can be usefully considered a construct—a fiction if you like—for the specific purpose of constructing a coherent reality, and that this "coherent reality" is multidimensional and continuous—a contingency of socialized but individual memory. A work of art—and in particular a work of sculpture—performs not as a moral definition for a singular persuasion (though it will inevitably reflect the artist's perception of the issues), but as a reflector for the viewer's "systolic" act of reconstituting identity through every moment of existence. The implications of this position sets Carr-Harris in sympathy, but apart from, current poststructuralist interest in discovering the nature of structural relations (an extension of Levi-Strauss's ambitious failure) and connects him with the

[This sentence continues above on page 182 with the words "great majority of ordinary people…" The result is that this text coils back on itself, and consequently avoids an identifiable summarizing conclusion.]

Author's note (2023): I wrote this catalogue essay for the exhibition *Fiction* as a thought-experiment in suggesting the fragmentary or "incomplete" quality of an essay in process, and the possibility of its endlessness—to borrow from the Minimalist concept of meaning. Additionally, I was adopting Foucault's idea that the author function was up for grabs. In my essay "An Approach to Criticism" for *Parachute* in 1975 (see page 185 in this volume) I had played with the idea that a published essay could be written in different registers.

Philip Monk: Sentences on Art (1983)

Published as "Philip Monk: Sentences on Art," *Parachute* 30 (March–April–May 1983). The Philip Monk lecture under review took place at Rivoli Tavern, Toronto, November 22, 1982.

I went because I wanted to hear what Philip Monk would have to say about theory. I also went because I could always get a drink, if nothing else, and this was important given the uneven quality of public lectures. I went chiefly because there seems to have been certain changes in Toronto's energy patterns in the last two or three years, changes which require notice.

This is not in itself a review of those changes, because they deserve more attention than I can give them here. I want instead to comment briefly on the Philip Monk talk alone because it seemed an interesting consummation of the basic purpose of two series of public critical lectures sponsored by A Space on the one hand and YYZ on the other. Together they marked an important, if problematic, development in the city's continuing struggle to establish a sense of focus and maturity.

Initially, following on the general pattern of YYZ's series, Monk was matched with another speaker: Benjamin Buchloh. I already knew Buchloh would not be there, and in a way I was disappointed. He has a reputation for being clever and entertaining, and I looked forward to hearing him in a Toronto context. I do not know whether he's ever been in Toronto, but it wouldn't surprise me. That he did not come, however, served to radicalize YYZ's objective. From being a forum to allow Toronto artists and critics equal time to debate general issues with their foreign counterparts, the evening became a unique solo performance by a Toronto critic devoted to the public criticism of a significant member of Toronto's art establishment. And Philip played it for all it was worth.

The Rivoli space is small and cheap, on the north side of Queen Street West, just east of Spadina Avenue. There is a small bar at one end, and a raised stage at the other. The room was packed when we got there. I propped myself at the bar, bought a beer, and counted: there were well over two hundred artists, critics, dealers, students, and assorted others. It was a real party; I wondered how long I would last in the cigarette smoke. About a quarter of an hour after the announced time, Philip made his way politely through the crowd and seated himself on the stage. I was suitably impressed. He had chosen to wear a black leather coat set off by a red rose in the lapel. With his shock of unruly fair red hair falling over one side of his forehead, and his firm features with set jaw and pursed lips, he reflected the slightly nervous self-assurance and moral rectitude of a Presbyterian minister. I sipped my beer and considered how much Anglo-Canadian intellectual history had been written by Presbyterian ministers; I wondered how many of them wore red roses in their lapels; I wondered how deliberately Philip Monk was playing to them.

I filed this away for future research. The microphones had been adjusted, the slide projector fine-tuned against the screen at the right back of the stage, and the moderator was explaining Buchloh's absence. Philip began, his soft voice reading with calculated deliberation and pausing from a prepared text with slide accompaniment which he made clear would take an hour and a half before questions would be considered. It did take an hour and a half, and I want now to leave Philip talking, and consider what he had to say.

The substance was simple, and its focus was political. Taking as his departure two quotations from Nietzsche and Brecht respectively, Philip raised the question of trust and the degree to which language may be seen as vehicle for dissimulation or vehicle for truth. In order to raise this question at all, he proceeded to launch an attack on structural critique, with its basic assumption that language—and hence reality as we know it—is a closed self-referential system independent of any referent. Philip's question was: "When things are not taken at their word, what type of aesthetic system does that signify, and more importantly perhaps, what type of social place for art?"

Having linked the problem of social relevance to the critical use of language (or, we could say: having asked what price we pay for action by limiting ourselves to intention), he proceeded to isolate the strategy of "inhabitation" or "appropriation"—a strategy he in turn linked to the 1970s and a decadent and even moribund social dilettantism (he suggested that the 1980 election of Ronald Reagan held a resemblance to the 1933 emergence of Adolf Hitler in terms of the effectiveness of such strategies) and their use by artists to find a "social place for art." For Philip, this represented a delusion that he then used as a fulcrum for addressing the general problem of judgement, a problem which is of course central to any process of criticism. If this strategy of inhabitation could be seen to paralyze judgement by claiming through structuralism's self-referential critique of reality that the only—or all—reality lies within the boundaries set by the work, then Philip could state with some confidence that such strategies were dissimulative rather than truthful, and consequently suspect as a vehicle for addressing questions of social engagement. The freedom to judge is, after all, the cornerstone of all freedom: the test of truth. It is the basis of what is real for us.

To examine this phenomenon, Philip chose General Idea as a model for analysis. The balance of the lecture became a lengthy critique of their work, in which he noted the "fascist" nature of their attempt to appropriate at once all meaning and all challenge to that meaning, and their flirtation with mega-capitalism; and he painstakingly elaborated their rhetorical appropriation of French textual theory, a.k.a. structuralism. Despite their rhetoric—indeed, because of their rhetoric—Philip questioned whether General Idea simply accommodated itself to the realities it pretended to critique. In the end, he asked, is General Idea simply form, "that in mirroring mirrors, General Idea has discovered its tautology, its image and fetish in capitalism?"

What seemed curious and puzzling about Philip's analysis was his failure to define his terms for dissimulation and truth, beyond linking them to a vague reference to political action. It appeared more or less clear from his context that in taking things at their word he hoped to return artmaking to a concern with the enduring questions of justice and truth, and their moral and social dimensions. After all, his presentation was Presbyterian. But if his objective was to free art from syntactical self-absorptions such as appropriation and modernism itself, it seems even more curious that he chose to couch his thesis in such a way as to depend on audience understanding of structural and semiotic vocabulary in order to "take things at their word." Philip intentionally chose to adopt an inhabitation of his own: the black leather coat and rose in the lapel echoed the style of General Idea itself. But irony is a two-edged sword; whether directed at General Idea or at Derrida, if taking things at their word implies a desire to cut through style to the "thing itself," irony is a dubious choice of weapon: the audience is left wondering whether the sword cut Philip or General Idea. And when all's said and done, does the final irony belong to Derrida?

I do not want to dismiss this issue simply because the intricacies of attempting to understand what is real require more subtle analysis than Philip was able or willing to devote to it in his lecture. We all wish to confront what we conceive of as the basic purpose of our existence, however complex and formidable the barriers to that confrontation may appear. Indeed, Philip was addressing what most artists now have been turning to for several years, and perhaps he's right that 1980 marks that point: If in the 1970s we found that the structures of existence do not by themselves clarify what they represent, how can one find what lies beyond them? Is it hopeless? Is it even a validly formulated question? And what of the audience? I could go on; what is clear is only that the answers are not.

Critical direction, however, was not the principal element at issue for me: In openly challenging the members of General Idea by seeking to take them at their word in a public forum of their peers, Philip accomplished his real—and stated—objective: to return critical debate in this city to its realities. Criticism in Toronto, and no doubt mostly everywhere else, has been dominated by French and American values to such an extent that their proper attachments have remained largely hidden. It would be naive to accept the few desperate remarks by Philip Monk that evening at the Rivoli as a coherent and defensible formulation of a native criticism; but as a brave and honest bid for one it cannot be ignored. Philip threw down a challenge, and if it is ignored, Toronto's art institutions—and its artists and critics—cannot complain that no one is interested: Over two hundred people were witness.

New City of Sculpture (1984)

Published as "The New City of Sculpture," *Parachute* 37 (December–January–February 1984–85). The exhibitions under review took place at Mercer Union, YYZ, A.R.C., Studio 620, Grunwald Gallery, and Gallery 76, Toronto, August 25 to September 22, 1984.

1   The catalogue for the *New City of Sculpture* appears as a special section in issue no. 3 of *C Magazine*, complete with illustrations of the work. The exhibition was curated by David Clarkson and Robert Wiens, sponsored by YYZ and Mercer Union, and exhibited at six galleries.

The *New City of Sculpture* is not new. I will spend some time addressing this judgement, and consequently—and reluctantly—this review is bound to fail in an important respect: it will not address the actual artists and work included under the *New City*'s umbrella. My embarrassment in this is genuine, but it is mitigated by a conviction that I am forced to play Bull to the New City's Red Flag; forced, that is, to address its critical dimension first and foremost. Having said that, however, I do intend to at least refer to some of the works in this *New City*.[1]

Why, one might ask, should I do something for which I feel I must apologize? The issue is one of context, and of critical validity, and I take such things seriously. Otherwise I wouldn't bother writing reviews. I believe others take these things seriously as well, otherwise you wouldn't be reading this, and the organizers of the *New City of Sculpture* would have been content to call their exhibition *Some Toronto Sculptors*. We simply do require context because context constructs meaning.

With any attempt to establish meaning, however, there comes a fair degree of responsibility. My concern is going to be focused on what I detect to be a certain irresponsibility—both defensible and indefensible—in the naming of the *New City*, and in the attempt of its founders to construct meaning from it. I will assume that by "New" they do not mean merely young, and that by "City" they do not simply mean neighbourhood. And since I have been unable to detect in their remarks or in their published statements any indication that the term is meant ironically, I will assume that the *New City of Sculpture* is meant to define a new sensibility, a new direction for sculpture, if not—apparently—a new way of seeing. There is a subtle alternative to this final assumption: that the "New City" does not actually exist, and that it remains—for its curators and artists—an ideal beyond the exhibition. I will not concern myself directly with this alternative because idealism of that kind is impossible to discuss or conceptualize effectively.

To construct the character of the New City we must begin with the essay by Bruce Grenville that introduces the exhibition. Grenville defines the works' desires as revolving around a question of discourse which "does not represent a new way of seeing, but must be understood as a critique of the illusion of full presence" in Western metaphysics. Grenville suggests that by "giving primacy to the indeterminacy of moments, the uncertainty of effort, the oppressiveness of choice," the exhibition indicates that the artists it represents seek to construct "a 'surface' which escapes the determinations that the viewer tries to give to it." And finally, he suggests that the artists are in fact constructing a form of allegory, a "sculptural allegory," which by exhibiting the look of fragmentation, of uncertainty, thereby exposes the fragile nature of knowledge, and of existence. Why? To quote Barthes, as Grenville does, "to fissure the very representation of meaning." Summarized more briefly, Grenville attempts to construct the *New City of Sculpture* as a "reaction to the modernist and late modernist desire for purity and presence," and a "frustrating, but necessary step towards the production of a new position for art and culture."

I have difficulty with Grenville's offhand characterization of modernism's "purity," and I see it as the source of the intellectual problems that arise with the *New City*. But first one must confront Grenville's statement concerning "a 'surface' which escapes the determinations that the viewer tries to give to it." Unless he refers to simple ambiguity, I do not believe he actually means this, since what it would amount to would be a sheer indecipherable presence that would exclude the viewer from the work. It's conceivable that this is what Barthes had in mind as a radical act to disrupt representation itself, but Grenville is not Barthes, and Barthes's nihilism would be irrelevant to any City that called itself by anything so stolidly traditional as Sculpture. The tenor of Grenville's remarks—and certainly the artists' works—seems more involved with questions of metaphor or, as Grenville calls it, sculptural allegory.

Let's get back to the question of modernism that seems to underlie the *New City*. Modernism has a complex history, and a complex and even contradictory character; but from its inception as an idea—as Baudelaire's idea if you want—it has held at its core the concept of "the transitory, the fugitive, the contingent." And it has held that in return for being Modern, modernism could not be more than "presentness"; it could not aspire to the condition of an historical authoritarianism. To quote Stephen Spender writing in 1963, modernism "is the art of observers conscious of the action of the conditions observed upon their sensibility. Their critical awareness includes ironic self-criticism."[2] What Grenville sets up in opposition to, and therefore defining for, his claims to a New City is a historicist

2   See Stephen Spender, *The Struggle of the Modern* (Berkeley and Los Angeles: University of California Press, 1963), 72. Quoted in Matei Calinescu, *Faces of Modernity* (Bloomington: Indiana University Press, 1977), 89.

Presence which modernism had already rejected as rationalist, idealist, and authoritarian.

Now it is a fact that any coherent venture is ipso facto going to suggest a presence, or purity. Modernism's purity was—is—a self-conscious and self-critical dialectic between the idea of history and the idea of presentness. It is also arguably a fact that a venture of this kind is often distorted among its practitioners; and it is certainly true that the venture itself cannot be easily described, cannot be rendered as accessible as a lollipop, given its internal instabilities. Grenville may therefore be forgiven for his apparent misunderstanding of modernism, but that doesn't rescue his thesis, just as incoherence for the sake of destroying or deconstructing, Presence cannot avoid the issue of coherence. Modernism was, and is, at its core deeply critical of Presence, including its own.

Critical, but not dismissive. I have trouble with Grenville's quotation of Barthes. I have no idea of the context from which the quotation comes, but in Grenville's context Barthes's demand rings as a hollow frustration with the entire process and methodology by which we construct experience. We all indulge in daydreams of total renewal, of total annihilation and rebirth. They are the basis of all ventures, of all change, and to the extent that they are flashes of impatience rather than programmes, they are as indispensable as they are predictable. Elevating them to an agenda, however, is to construct nihilism, a different kettle of fish entirely, and one I will return to.

The obscurities of modernism aside, there are two phrases Grenville uses in describing the character of the New City which tickled my interest: "the uncertainty of effort" and "the oppressiveness of choice." There's nothing wrong with these characterizations because they are familiar aspects of human experience.

What is wrong is to suggest that the mere illustration of these experiences—an implied surrender to them—is valid. Effort and choice are states of Being around which we exercise what free will we have. It has become axiomatic for human experience that we exert effort, make choices, in order first to survive, and second to wish to survive. Even in California. That they are uncertain and oppressive is inherent in our interest in them—in survival—at all. The question is not about their qualities, but about our response to them. What response does the *New City*'s rhetoric construct? Barthes's?

If Grenville is unwilling to go further than to quote a fragment of Barthes, Clarkson and Wiens are unwilling to do much more than quote fragments of Grenville. And this they do reluctantly. For them, the *New City* becomes apparently a chance to compare their own work with their contemporaries in Toronto. And who could object to that? The problem, however, is that they continue to insist that the exhibition, as a whole, reveals an anti-monumental, anti-presence intention on the part of the artists. And by insisting on this without further elaboration, they imply that this is their distinguishing, their New accomplishment. In so doing, they insist upon precisely the conviction that has characterized sculpture in Toronto—indeed, sculpture internationally—for at least a decade, a conviction which has in fact characterized the broad basis of Modern art and literature since the mid-nineteenth century: the conviction that in uncertainty, in irony, in "shuffling grace" lies the only hope of constructing an understanding of personal meaning. If Clarkson and Wiens are serious, the *New City of Sculpture* is the current city of sculpture, with only one difference: its builders think it is new. Why?

Part of the problem lies in an understanding of Presence. The obvious historical foil for the *New City* would seem to be heroic sculpture, or religious sculpture; that is to say the various classical (and, I suspect, even romantic) traditions which date back to the beginnings of civilization, whether Egypt, Greece, or Easter Island. While the enduring attraction of these traditions for the modern middle class certainly provides a rationale for the New City to attack them, this would not construct a New City. As I have said, modernism already did that, still does that. Perhaps the natural foil, then, for the New City in recent art would seem to be not the work of the 1970s—despite Grenville's attempt to suggest an unexplained difference of issues and circumstance—but the minimalist work of the 1960s: Donald Judd, Tony Smith, Robert Morris. But minimalist, or to use Fried's term, *literalist* Presence, based its reductivism on a dialectic struggle with what its leaders saw as European historical Presence, a struggle against an incurably corrupted formal pictorialism deriving from idealist notions of harmony which amounted to an intricate and monumental labyrinth of history. They sought to construct an American presence derived from American material pragmatism: things-as-they-are-encountered, actual experiential—theatrical—Presence. As is obvious from Grenville's essay and the curators' remarks, this sense of actual presence, theatrical presence, is precisely what the *New City* embraces. Where does this leave the notion of Presence and the New City? Both modernism and minimalism pre-empt any claim of novelty in addressing the issue of Presence as such. There is one other possibility: Fried himself.

Fried, in rejecting the term minimalism and referring to it as *literalism*, presents us with a clue, and perhaps most aptly locates the New City as a radically focused form of literalism. Inescapably one finds in the *New City*'s rhetoric the tactic of "fragmentation" referred to time and again. In an interview, Clarkson and Wiens singled out Robert McNealy's work as a key to the exhibition in this fashion: "His work is very open-ended and runs the gamut of styles and materials in a single piece. It's very fragmented and accessible." It becomes clear that the formal attribute of fragmentation, or appropriation of different styles, modes of construction, and so on, is seen to construct this New City. What is "new," one realizes then, is not so much an intention to subvert Presence, which would require more than formal devices, as an intention to appropriate styles, to appropriate historical, literary, or mythological references, to mix and match materials; to construct, if not a new Presence, then to construct a new *Look*. What we have, in fact, is not a critical direction based on the deconstruction of Presence, but a desire for a formal change or difference from the immediate past. Fragmentation—dismantling the sentence into its separate words or letters—is the most immediate form of establishing difference. What is possibly "new" about the *New City* becomes its intentional ignorance about the past as anything more than Look, as anything more than letters in a line, an ignorance which is inevitably an ignorance about the dynamics of the history which constructs not only the *New City*'s precursors, but more significantly its own inhabitants: Fried's Formalism Revisited.

I do not think I am being flippant or dismissive in this. Ignorance is a vice as much as it is a misfortune, and it has an unfortunately familiar as well as profound consequence for the *New City*. I believe that the *New City* is grounded in the romantic ennui of the historical avant-garde and its nihilistic—wilfully ignorant—impatience with history and process. The unfortunately familiar consequence of their ignorance is that the founders of the *New City* are simply playing out the historical, and one might say discredited, role of the European avant-garde without having the grace to realize it. The profound consequence of their playing out that role is that their *New City* has nowhere to go, nothing to do, except to fuss about in the fragments of old art and old history. Their nihilism, founded on superficial appearance as an alternative to historical dialectic, ensures this. The *New City* is simply another failure to realize that nihilism is not deconstructive, but simply narcissistic. And narcissism reconstructs the emptiest of formalisms.

I have been hard on the *New City* because their lack of responsibility in articulating their position concerns me. Is there anything to be said in their defence? I think there is. The *New City* may not be new, but it is important. The instability of our understanding of modernist (that is, *our*) notion of "presentness," the requirement that what we do be constantly scrutinized and challenged, the importance of periodic nihilism in the history of culture all indicate that we cannot sustain our own convictions without some sort of suspension of disbelief in the complexities of what is "new." The *New City* must be respected—cautiously—for having the audacity to call itself new.

On the other hand, and fortunately, many of the artists in the *New City* were there for reasons other than the founders' defining intentions. They were there for the most natural reason: Clarkson and Wiens knew

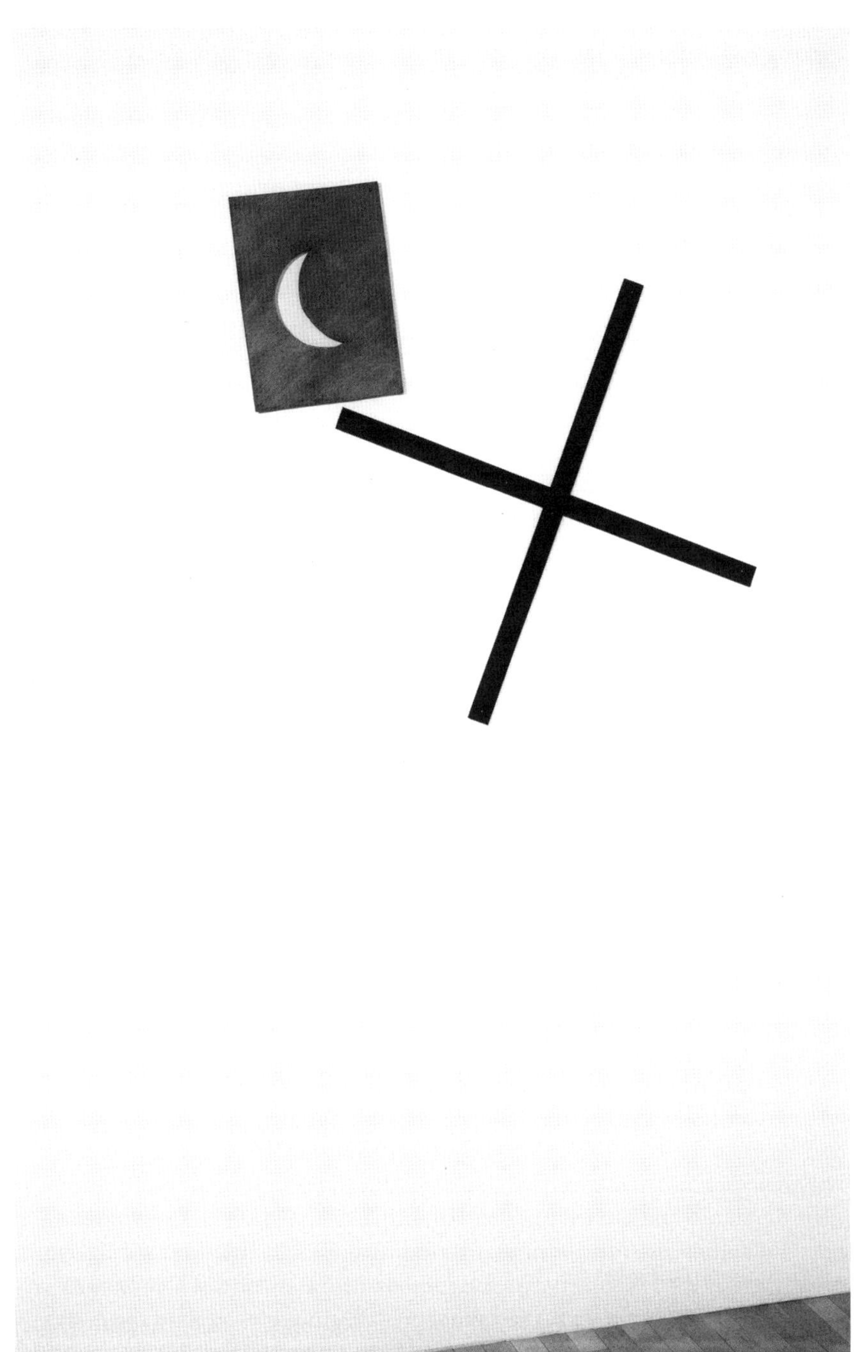

4.1   Brian Groombridge, *Balance and Power*, 1984. Copper and steel, 91.4 × 96.5 cm. Courtesy of the artist. Photo: Peter MacCallum.

and respected their work, and were finally not so concerned about the apocalyptic character of the *New City* as they were about its generation and location: young artists in downtown Toronto. It would be trite to attempt to characterize current young Toronto sculpture, because generally stated its concerns are those of current contemporary sculpture throughout the modern Western world: varied. And no, there is nothing particularly Toronto, or even Canadian, about those concerns, though in at least one case Toronto was a site. Personally, I am critical of that as a cumulative refusal to engage with, or even locate, an aspect of actual experience. However, that refusal, or perhaps simple unconscious "un-occurrence," is itself deeply embedded in our culture. I am more interested in characterizing the work I personally found exciting, and four artists—Louise Noguchi, Magdalen Celestino, Peter Cosco, and Brian Groombridge—did excite me, though they were not the only ones I found that did so. Since I cannot consider individual artists in depth here, I will use Brian Groombridge's piece *Balance and Power* to summarize what I consider to be the concerns and abilities of the best art in the *New City*. The gestural simplicity and epigrammatic clarity of this work acts like an arrow—or better, a laser—speeding simultaneously into and out of history and culture, its carefully chosen symbolic materiality crossing in a dialectic with the codes of its imagery in reverberations of ironic reference not only to the broader dialectics of civilizations and gender, but to all that we know and only partially comprehend about the complexities of our own individual place in the world.

These same characteristics of irony, coded materiality, and historical self-consciousness are reflected in Cosco's mock-monumental papier mâché architectural cartoon, Celestino's seductive *Noli me tangere*, with its intimate obliqueness and ironically titled inventory of cultural histories and fascinations, and Noguchi's elliptical yet straightforward construction of moral narrative and metaphoric physicality.

Irony, coded materiality, historic self-consciousness: the presence of intimate relations with the "Presentness of the Other's Presence in our own," and the history and projection of that presence. Baudelaire called it "the transitory, the fugitive, the contingent." I have suggested that the best work in the *New City of Sculpture*, if it shows any coherence, continues a historic process firmly rooted in the modernist programme, and I have also suggested that the rhetoric surrounding the *New City* acknowledges that. To defend the title of his exhibition, Bruce Grenville's introduction suggests that the "New City" is founded on a new address which is concerned not with the "meaning of an utterance," but instead with the codes or language of sculpture itself. I view this as a logical fallacy; Grenville's thesis, or rather, his appropriation of Barthes, is merely the flip side of Michael Fried's defence of Greenbergian formalism, whose "purity" he finds so hard. But Fried is just another tree in the forest. The fact is that the main priorities of intellectual history in the modern era have been directed towards the complexity inherent in the relationship between form and content; towards the "meaning of an utterance" through an attack on the "representation of meaning" as part of an over-all critique of all authoritative assumptions, even its own. If the work in the *New City of Sculpture*—all of it, not just what I like—pursues the same purposes as work done in the 1970s, is this unfortunate, or anti-climactic? Of course not. The *New City*— its name and its artists—occupies an essential position in the dialectic of our culture. It would be the suspension of that dialectic which would put us at peril. The culture of societies is always at risk from those who stand to gain from entropy, or vapidity.

Sex and Representation (1984)

Published as "Sex & Representation," *Vanguard* 13, no. 9 (November 1984).

1   I am aware of broadly held suspicion about terms such as "essential" or "Being," and hostility towards ontological thinking in general. I am sympathetic. But the interpretation of ourselves as constructs of culture, as products of a web of knowledge, seems to differ from my understanding of Being only in that it consults the process of construction without dwelling on the product which results.

> The purpose of a man is to love a woman/and
> The purpose of a woman is to love a man
> —Clint Ballard Jr., "Game of Love" (1965)
>
> I wish they wouldn't make women into ash trays.
> —remark overheard in a tourist shop, Amalfi, 1984
>
> "And what is culture, Boys and Girls?"
> (children in chorus): "It's what we do, and how we do it!"
> —from *The Radio Educational Broadcast to Schools*,
> Radio St. Lucia, recorded February 16, 1984

What we do, and how we do it. Sex and representation. The issue is representation; but the smell in our nostrils is, sex. And since smells are invariably more powerful than issues, the real subject of this article is sex.

I want to be plain about these priorities, and consequently about what constitutes our real subject. Certainly nowhere is this more the case than with something at once so generally shared and so privately experienced as sex. But let's not beat about the bush. Sex is our subject; how and why we make representations is an issue—an extremely important one for us as human beings—in defining the conditions we attach to the fact of our sex.

I must therefore also be plain about why I wish to clarify the reason for insisting on this priority. Representations, or artworks in the vocabulary of the visual arts, are ontological structures that challenge or confirm our sense of Being. Our sense of Being is a function of our sense of sex. Discussions about sex are therefore usefully not about sex, but about Being.[1] But while discussions about representations must also be about Being, they have become, fashionably, either formalist discussions about Kantian derived notions of ideal harmonic tension, or more recently (and sometimes more entertainingly) Marxian discussions about power relations. They have become, that is, warnings about correct strategy and—equally problematically—externalized discussions about questions of knowledge and appropriation.[2] Such discussions are inevitably interesting, sometimes radical, and usually irrelevant to my main concern here: what actually holds power over us; what constructs our complicity in an engagement; what, finally, is the power that we are willing to share in? The answer to these questions lies less in a discussion about representation than in the preconditions for those representations.

We comprehend the world through similarity and difference. Experimental psychology has shown that when we seek to identify another human being, we instinctively seek first to identify their sex. That is, we seek to begin the process of constructing their similarities and differences with respect to our own Being, and their sex, whether similar to or different from our own, will form the continuing basis for that construction. While social role definition places a demand on us from a very early age, and therefore conditions us to authorized patterns of behaviour and expectation, it is clear from psychoanalytical studies concerning the so-called mirror phase of human childhood development (between the ages of six and eight months) that the basis for the identification of self and non-self, subject and object, the identification of similarity and difference, begins well before social roles have meaning. And this process appears to be a function of our biology. The language centre of the brain occupies one section of the left hemisphere. The corresponding section on the right hemisphere seems less definable, but the indications are that it enables us to move in the world as we enter it. That is, it enables us to construct an abstract three-dimensional map of the conditions we encounter, and relate our movements through those conditions to that map.[3] In other words, it constructs the knowledge of difference and similarity required to be rational. Language—symbolic representation—is simply a sophisticated extension of that basic tool of knowledge.

Identification of sex, then, is not primarily a question of power relations in society, but of self-identification: what is like us, and what is not like us. The discovery that we embark on earliest is the discovery of our own bodies, including the active processes of eating, touching, or grasping, and so on, and the classification of ourselves as human beings through the visual "mirror" identification of a concept of objectified self. Sooner or later, we make the most significant and astounding discovery of all: that physical size and sophistication of knowledge, the relation between child and adult or between children of different ages, is not the primary distinction between human beings, between ourselves and others; that there is a far more confounding distinction. We call that distinction sex, and it is confounding for us at the point of discovery precisely because it exists despite an otherwise structurally similar identity, an identity hitherto conceived of as defining our Being.

2   As an apposite example, Kate Linker's article "Representations and Sexuality" in *Parachute* 32 (Fall 1983) is a valuable if somewhat understandably ideological feminist review of Lacanian analysis applied to patriarchal power structures. The Linker article is typical of the degree to which the tool of psychoanalysis, and particularly French poststructural or semiotic theory, has been brought to bear on the problems of knowledge and power. In some degree what I am going to be saying may be seen as a response to her article. I am not concerned, however, with agreeing or disagreeing with her remarks; I am concerned with what she does not deal with.

3   Jacob Bronowski, *The Ascent of Man* (Toronto: Little, Brown, & Co., 1973), 421.

4   The deeply entrenched, though in the current context, perverse, veneration of Mary Mother of God in the Catholic religion is such an instance of female power, and it is interesting to note that the older Roman religion, as opposed to the modern and northern protestant ones, retains a dual Godhead encompassing both male and female principles. It is, of course, also clear that the conditions of a male-dominated society have ordered that duality to its own advantage. Nevertheless, it bears enduring witness to an experience of difference transcending mere phallic indulgence.

5   Kate Linker, "Representation and Sexuality," *Parachute* 32 (Fall 1983), 17.

I want to dwell on this for a bit because this speculation is simply an attempt to analyze my own experience in my memory. I am, of course, aware that I run the risks associated with generalizing from the Particular and Un-provable. What is vitally significant here is the confusion of similarity and difference. Now, much has been written, at the very least beginning with Freud, on the phallus and the phallocentricity of European culture especially. Adoration of the phallus—the obvious emblem of specifically male sexual power is as old as the hills, as is also adoration of female sexual power expressed equally obviously through the signs of fertility.[4] Lacan, according to Kate Linker anyway, is simply the latest restatement of the Freudian interpretation that male "possession" of the penis and female "lack" of that possession determines a primal comprehension of ourselves as positive "whole" on the one hand or negative "hole" on the other; singular producer or consumable consumer. I can't deny that our culture is phallocentric in its dominant institutions. But what has always struck me as dubious in Freud's concentrated focus on the phallus, is that this focus seems very much a male bias. That the confusion over the existence of the penis on the one hand and the existence of the vulva on the other should be ascribed entirely to the female I find unconvincing, and I find myself tacitly supported in this, at least, by something Linker reports in her summary of Lacan's position:

> Given the arbitrary construction of sexual identity; given the intersubjective network on which it rests; and given the unavailability of the phallus to all, any speaking being, regardless of sex, is entitled to assume the phallus, to position itself on either side of its divide.[5]

Stripped of its male-dominated viewpoint, Lacan is simply saying that real men and women, real male and female children, are not bound by the symbols of phallic authority, and one's sex as male or female does not in itself determine one's value of self and others in the world. But Lacan reinterprets Freud using the research and theories we have since developed in the role that language plays in construction of reality. As one would expect, therefore, he rejects notions of "essentialist" or necessary determinants outside of language as ideological, and insists on the arbitrary and certainly relativistic nature of language as sole producer of meaning. I do not have to be an essentialist to disagree with him. I am convinced that it is in the discovery of sexual difference; that is, of structural difference between ourselves and others like us, on an immediate level, in our right hemisphere map, that we must look for the primal confusion that constructs our subsequent comprehension of the world, whether we are males possessing a penis, or females possessing a vulva: a confusion of similarity and difference irrespective of genitalia. And what this confusion fundamentally constructs is a frozen fascination in disbelief that is suspended throughout our entire existence. That is, that we literally cannot believe our eyes, and that inherent in our actions, whether in rational or irrational situations, whether in direct behavioural stances or in the representations we construct to act as maps for those actions, there is at play an almost obsessive desire to resolve this confusion, to exorcise a disbelief which is, after all, an affront to our instinctive need to survive through Knowing. Our recognition of sex difference, therefore, is our recognition of the limitations of the generality—the similarity—of Being, and of course our recognition consequently of the limitations of knowledge.[6]

Kate Linker makes a tantalizing, if undeveloped reference to the "masculine dream of symmetry" as a key aspect of patriarchal power. Let me develop it, because it is a key, and Linker confuses a sense of loss for an imposition of will. Not that I blame her: the dominant and semi-independent authorities within the social power structure such as the advertising and film industries as corporate capitalism, and the major religious institutions as conservative traditionalists, propagate the illusion of that dream either directly or indirectly. My caution lies in her implication that what is, to put it differently, a desire for completion is simply male and political, and that women do not share in such a desire; that is, that women find that completeness within themselves. I cannot, obviously, speak from the experience of a female perspective. But from my own, male perspective, I find the polemical terms of her reference disappointing. The "dream of symmetry" is in my experience hardly a dream, but an intuition based on physical evidence, an intuition of extreme asymmetric tension, of terrifying liberation and magnificent disbelief faced with the shocking comprehension of incompleteness; an intuition that there can be no such thing as "completeness," and that we are forever fated to speculate on what the Other is, on what the Other feels; on what constitutes the unimaginable dangers and shattered Form of our own—now male—inadequacy. And I see no structural reason for this to be any different for female experience.[7] I cannot, of course, prove this myself. But I find evidence for it in such works as Adrienne Trent's piece *Priapus* in the *Alter Eros* show at A Space, and constant evidence for it in the work of Renée Van Halm; and these are but two artists, although certainly among the best, in what could be a very long list.

In developing Kate Linker's phrase, I am not avoiding the political dimension that Linker poses. I am saying that it fails to consider the origins, the true character, of that dimension, and in that failure misunderstands and underestimates the power of sex. And there is one further elaboration which is fundamentally important in our confusion of the self through the dissonant similarity of sex recognition: once we have confronted

6   All very well, but what about pornography? For me the problem of pornography is its pathological obsessiveness with limitation, and consequently power. This is not to dismiss it; pathological obsessiveness is a structural social problem of immense danger. I mean simply that it is a distortion of the inherent natural fact I am describing, a distortion arising most likely out of power struggles in the society, but perhaps a function, as well, of specific individual body chemistry. The theoretical key to controlling pornography, therefore, would seem to be in deciding when and why fascination becomes obsession.

7   Male inadequacy (and I assume female inadequacy) is easily converted into unuseful forms of rejection and destruction. But the knowledge *in itself*, I am insisting, is not the familiar consequence. The primary consequence is that sexual self-consciousness becomes the ordering factor for existence in the world, ultimately becoming indistinguishable and inseparable from our entire range of experiences, embracing simultaneously love and hatred, compassion and cruelty.

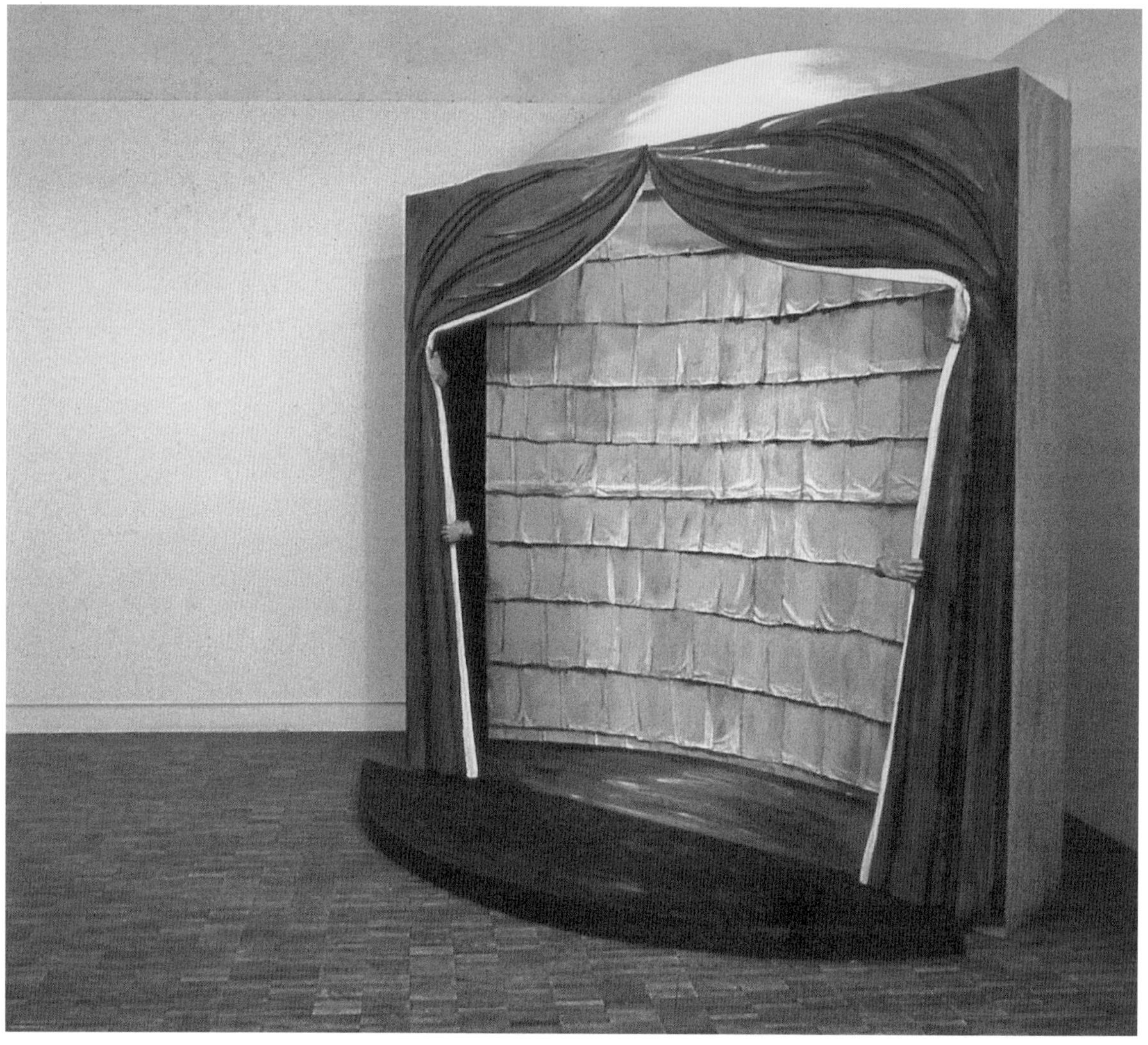

4.2/4.3 (above and opposite)   Renée Van Halm, *Anticipating the Eventual Emergence of Form, Part 1 and 2*, 1983. Plywood, plaster, and cloth with acrylic, 244 × 305 × 61 cm, assembled. Collection National Gallery of Canada. Photo: Ian Carr-Harris.

our recognition of the unbelievable possibility of irretrievable structural dissimilarity at the core of Being, that recognition is extendable in all directions. Sex almost simultaneously has nothing to do with specific gender difference. Sex is the Pandora's box from which all recognition of "Being-in-the-World" derives. Our own sex, our own physicality, is a property of that recognition. This is what the tale of the Garden of Eden is

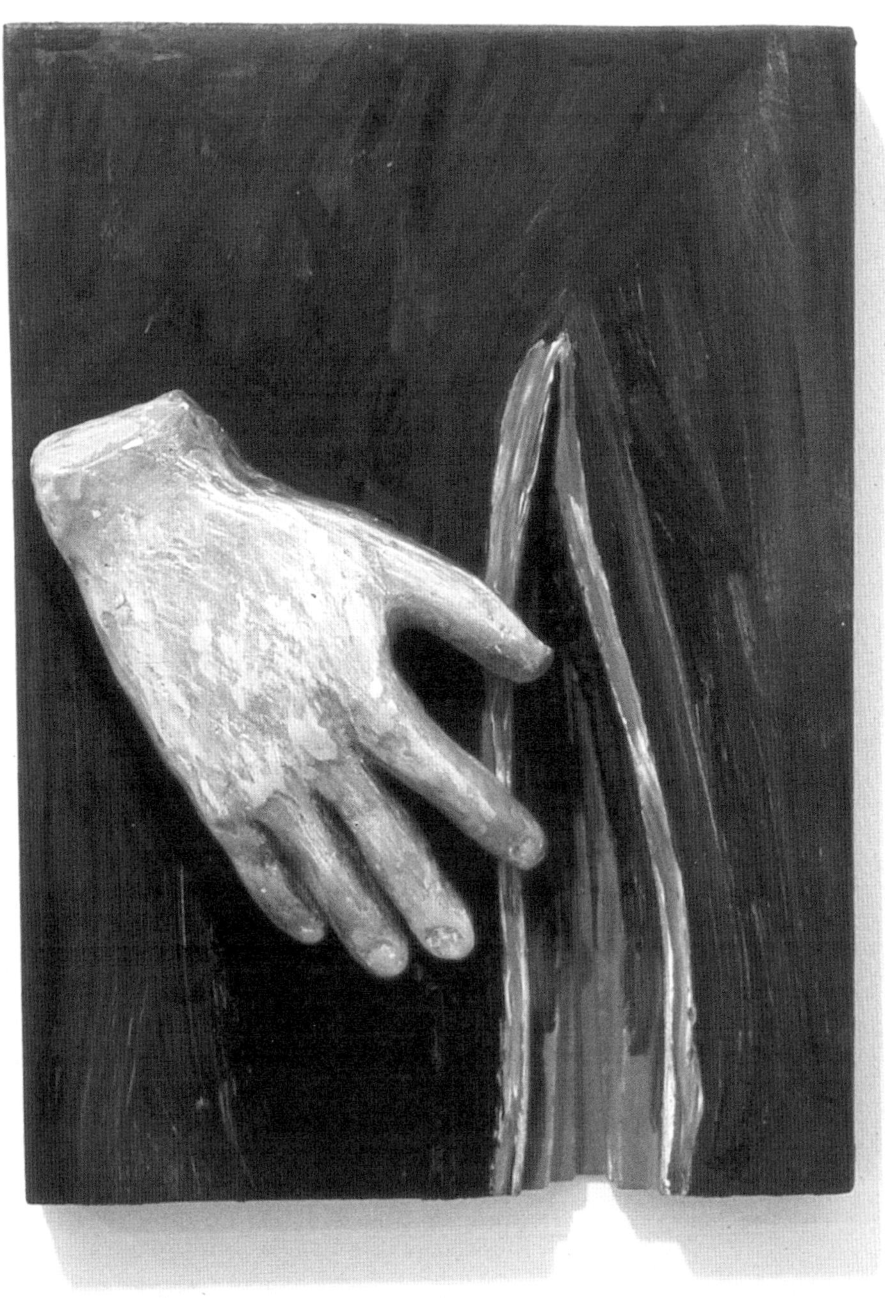

8   Studies of different cultures, and the history of our own, would indicate that cultural positioning can be strong enough to override most of the individual's attempts to position themselves in a separable meaning. I am not concerned here, however, with the complex developments that construct the edifices on the foundations of difference.

about: knowledge cast not between men and women, but in the confounding experience of being caught between a discredited singular absolute Being and a new and fearful recognition of a very present and material—and partial—Being. The Garden of Eden is about the destruction of the dream of completeness, and it is no whim that it is cast in sexual terms of recognition.

So what about representations? After all, myths such as those I have mentioned are representations. We all know that they are not just pretty pictures. They are attempts to order meaning, and to embody it. Our construction of meaning is central to our frustrated instinctive necessity to know the world. Where does it arise, then? Situating it in language, or in any apparatus of conscious manipulation in the world, for that matter, is to miss the point. To suggest, for instance, that meaning exists only in the codes of language, and can therefore be used to manipulate us, or to correct us, is a well-intentioned over-simplification, bound to fail, which begs the question of language and culture: at what point is the individual separate from cultural positioning? At what point does the individual position itself? At what point does meaning—that is, the significance of choice—arise? Where could it arise, but at the point of structured difference between like beings, at the point of sexual recognition; at the cataclysmic point of personal confusion, when the individual begins to construct out of necessity the basic conditions for meaning (evidence and doubt, questioning and speculation), the conditions necessary to make judgements about their validity in the face of difference. The development of meaning, then the development of the individual within culture, is a function of sexual difference. Culture, and representations, are attempts to construct order out of sex.[8]

I would like, at this point, to take the liberty of quoting from one of my own artworks, something I would normally avoid in an article. But this is a very personal article, and I want to secure my comments within my own art practice. So, rightly or wrongly, it's important to me. The quotation is from an installation—*5 Explanations*—which I did in 1983, and it forms one entire segment of that work. It begins with a woman's voice in chant that fades out to a male voice, my own, addressed directly to the viewer. Here it is:

With visible breath I am walking.
A voice I am sending as I walk.
In a sacred manner I am walking.
With visible tracks I am walking.
In a sacred manner I walk.

There is a story told by Black Elk, warrior and medicine man of the Oglala Sioux, of the way the sacred pipe first came to his people. And I want to read it to you, because it has something to do with what you see in front of you now.

A very long time ago, they say, two scouts were looking for bison, and when they came to the top of a high hill and looked north, they saw something a long way off; and when it came closer, they cried out: "It is a woman!" And it was.

Then one of the scouts, being foolish, had bad thoughts and spoke them; but the other said: "That is a sacred woman, throw all bad thoughts away." When she came still closer, they saw that she wore a fine white buckskin dress, that her hair was very long, and that she was young and beautiful. And she knew their thoughts and said in a voice that was like singing: "You do not know me; but if you want to do as you think, you may come." And the foolish one went; but just as he stood there before her, there was a white cloud that came and covered them. And the beautiful young woman came out of the cloud; and when it blew away, the foolish man was a skeleton covered with worms.

Now, I am not telling you this story because it is well told, or because it is interesting as myth; or even because it can be read as a moral.

Instead, examine yourself closely. Consider the image I've constructed in front of you as roughly analogous to a photograph. It is a photograph then, of a woman holding something—it doesn't matter now just what it is—for you to see. It could just as well be a man walking down the street for that matter, but this particular image is—I think—appropriately dramatic. Now imagine that that woman is real, and that she is showing you something. As she talks, you are aware of many things that have little or nothing to do with what she is saying—the tone of her voice; the smell of her sweat; the muscles moving in her arms; the warmth of her body; you can see the blood in her veins. You fight against her physicality, against her womanness, as you attempt to register what she says. Above all, you fight to maintain that illusion you must both uphold that your entire response to her is contained in the logic of her information.

You will notice, however, an odd aspect to her physicality. If you think carefully, you will realize that it has as much to do with yours as it does with hers. There is, you might say, a photographic quality to it, as though while acknowledging her independent status, you nevertheless simultaneously impose on her the condition of projected and incestuous desire, and like a photograph, she ceases to be independent and becomes instead a reflection of your own body and will.

You will recall that the wise scout in Black Elk's story resisted the seduction of that reflection in the knowledge that to violate the sacred woman—to violate the photograph—would be to destroy himself.

And that—not pious stories or moral rhetoric—is how things are.

What actually holds power over us, then? What constructs our complicity in an engagement? What is the power we are willing to share in? To understand what that power is we have to understand what we mean by sex. And what we mean by sex is the recognition of incompleteness; that is to say, the recognition that we cannot know ourselves by simple self-reference but must complete that knowledge by outside reference to similar yet different beings. And that the natural process of that reference—inherent in the necessity to map our world—creates our own self-conscious sexuality, and in so doing constitutes our sense of Being, a sense which is ultimately characterized by a confounding confusion. And it is this sense of confusion that actually holds power over us and constitutes the power we have to share in.

With this understanding in mind, it is interesting to consider the Paul Wong tapes not shown last year at the Vancouver Art Gallery. The work was titled *Confused: Sexual Views*, and consisted of twenty-seven colour video interviews, each on separate cassettes, each identified by the name (or in a few cases by the names) of the person or persons interviewed. The interviews themselves were constructed as disarmingly clumsy "community TV" encounters with the people-next-door, using a static camera and hidden interviewer. The frame of reference included only a face-on stance of the upper part of the subject. The refusal to engage with the whole figure was brutally emphasized by a cutting technique that fragmented each interview into a series of obsessive revelations concerning the respondents' sexual activities and ambitions, or views, and in the process revealed the predictable triteness, as reportage, of the subject.

I felt ambivalent about the tapes at the time I saw them. There is naturally something absorbing about watching real people address issues as private as sexual desire. But the fragmentation of the individual through placement and cutting interfered at precisely those moments when they began to express what they felt rather than what they had accomplished, would like to accomplish, or had failed to accomplish. And while under other circumstances I might find sociological value in this information, I saw it within this context as arrogance on the part of Paul Wong; as evidence that what Wong wanted was not to discover what constitutes our understanding of sex and Being, but to reveal the obvious delusions and failures we all encounter in mechanical performance. The cutting then became, for me, a metaphor as well as interjection, with Wong's own *a priori* notion of sex as mechanical advantage applied as a tool of power to divorce the individual from their own history; a product rather than an aspect of their confusion.

It therefore seemed clear to me that the title, *Confused: Sexual Views*, referred only to the obvious confusion arising from power and convenience, and therefore that the tapes were, as Michael Fried would say, merely interesting. However, the term "confused" nevertheless intrigued me, and I found myself unable to dismiss them as easily as I might have. Moreover, their significance had been established by the importance placed on them by the Director of the Vancouver Art Gallery in denying them exhibition. What interested me was how something so banal could exert such power. And the reason was obvious, once I stopped to consider it. What the interviews discuss, in fact, is the question of sexually centered confusion that, as I have said, is the central point of meaning in the construction of our lifelong encounter with ourselves. Paul Wong and his subjects are no more confused than the rest of us. Nor does Wong indicate that he is any clearer about the source of that confusion. His intended audience, certainly the apprehension of that audience that prompted Luke Rombout to adopt the role of institutional scapegoat, differed only in that it would not publicly tolerate even a hint of that confusion. Intolerance is always revealing, and what Paul Wong could or did not complete, was done for him. They are now joint authors.

It is evident, at least to me, that representations—whether honest investigations of Being, or cynical manipulations of introverted obsession—are dispositions arising out of our recognition of the consequence of sexual difference. There is therefore nothing strange about the recent appearance of sex in representation either at the production or at the consumer level; either in Paul Wong or Renée Van Halm, or in the curious inversion of Luke Rombout's curatorial decision. Sex always has been central to representations, and it's just a matter of what property of that Being we are able to express or consider at particular historical moments.

I have not written, I must confess, an article, and certainly not the article I anticipated writing, but a personal speculation which constitutes an appeal to understand why we seek to represent things. To borrow and apply Noel Harding's useful phrase: we attempt, surely, to represent conditions of "original experience." I have set forth a reasonably examined account of what I feel constitutes the organizing factor for that experience. I have placed that factor in our knowledge of sex. I may be wrong; but if I am right, it is hardly a surprise: it is simply a reminder. I started the article with three quotations. In their different ways they serve as authority for this reminder—for better and for worse.

Author's note (2023): In an exceptionally detailed and impressively critical letter to the editor following this article, Liz Magor took me to task primarily for occupying a form of biological essentialism in ignoring my own privileged male subjectivity and its status as a dominant experience in power relations that operate on the level of gender identification. While I responded in defence of my suggestions—or perhaps speculations is a better characterization—about the play of similarity and difference in sexual construction, I accepted the letter's criticisms as both important and useful. To quote briefly from my letter in reply: "How do I feel about this article now? In discussing it with women…I have been struck by the degree to which… my speculation as peculiarly male may hold true. Or rather, I should say, by the degree to which any such speculation is rendered, shall we say, 'merely interesting' in light of the urgent political problems in reconstructing women's power. The urgency of the problem [outlined in the letter] comes as no surprise; it is the sheer passionate commitment to a solution that commands my respect."

Serious Art in Toronto: Tracing Curatorial Imperatives (1988)

Published as "Serious Art in Toronto: Tracing Curatorial Imperatives," *Canadian Art* (Spring 1988).

It's a common belief that artworks can speak for themselves. People also believe that we should be able to understand what artworks are saying. Since this is rarely the case for anything but kitsch, most art, it can be assumed, is either fraudulent or pretentious.

Needless to say, this is somewhat dismissive. It is possible that art deserves more sustained attention. To hint at this, the term "serious art" has become a sort of riposte to popular suspicion. Misleading or not, it immediately begs the question: how are we to address art seriously? Such questioning leads inevitably to discussions of "critical perspective," or criticism, for short.

A bit of background is important here. In its assertion that artworks can and should speak for themselves, the public reveals its acceptance of a critical tradition based on positivist philosophy: facts are objective and clear, and common-sense observation is both rational and correct. The question of identity is simple: it is to identify. This is an old tradition, though not an ancient one, and its roots are most secure in North America. So much so that it has become an amusing Anglo-Saxonism to dismiss as "French" the challenges to this authorized view. These conflicting ideas are not just French, however, they reflect instead the twentieth century's general discovery of relative positioning and the complexities of interaction between a viewer and an artwork, for instance. "Serious" art is serious because it is concerned with these complexities, and with their implications for both art and social experience.

Toronto has a history of being serious. This has recently been applied to culture. Already the leading centre for artists in Canada, Toronto is also becoming the centre for criticism as well. A growing number of influential critics interconnected with artists, artist-run centres, commercial dealers, public institutions, and the art magazines constitute a powerful network of advocacies. Most visible among them at the moment are Philip Monk, the Art Gallery of Ontario's curator of contemporary Canadian art, *C Magazine* editor Richard Rhodes, and independent critics and sometimes curators Elke Town, Dot Tuer, Jeanne Randolph, and Bruce Grenville. Each holds a somewhat different position, but they share overlapping allegiances. Bruce Grenville has moved into the foreground in the last three months with two exhibitions he curated: *At the Threshold: representation and identity* for the S.L. Simpson Gallery, a leading commercial dealer, and *Active Surplus: the economy of the object* for the Power Plant, currently the most prestigious public space for contemporary art in the city. Grenville's critical justifications for these exhibitions are the very embodiment of those "French" theories opposed to our popular tradition, and the shows provided an opportunity to illustrate how art—serious art—functions in this city now.

Let's start with an ingenuous question: what is Bruce Grenville saying, and how does this relate to the art works? In asking this, we have already discarded any notion about the art speaking for itself. It is Bruce Grenville who speaks for it, through the two catalogue essays that effectively bound these exhibitions together. Grenville comes at his position from slightly different directions. In the S.L. Simpson catalogue he concentrates on the

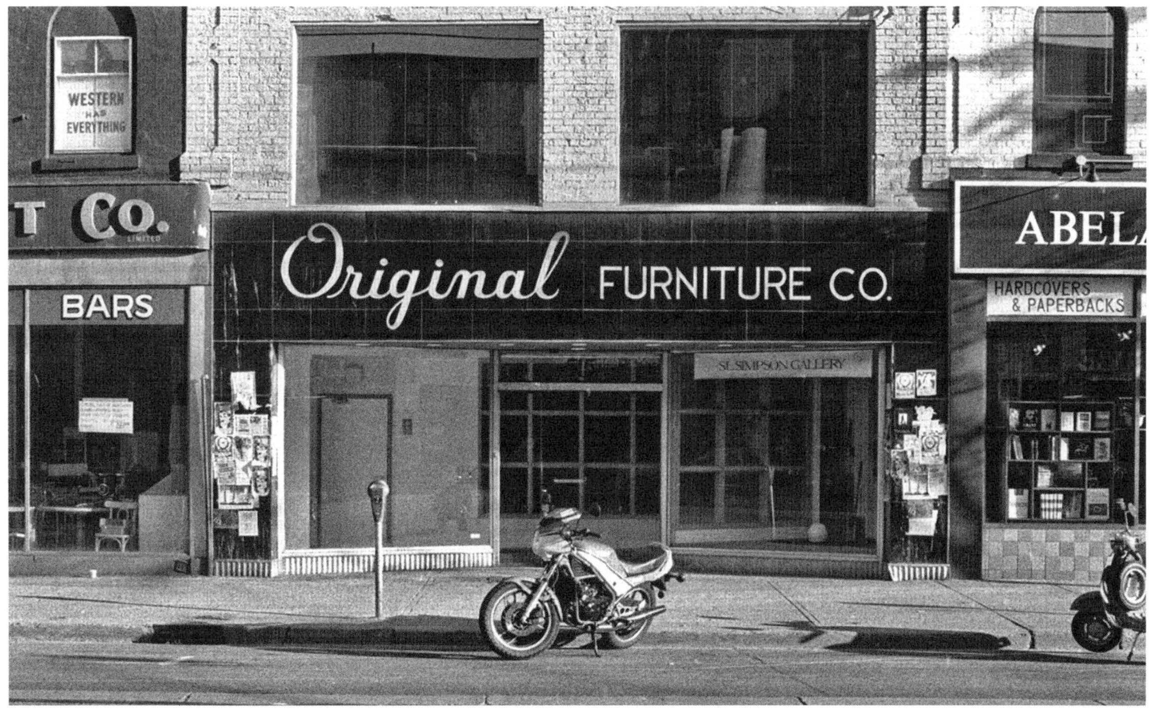

4.4   S.L. Simpson Gallery, 515 Queen Street West, Toronto, ca. 1980. Photo: Ian Carr-Harris.

basic problem of representation and identity. He attacks the idea that in representing—that is, re-presenting—reality we can arrive at a valid identity for ourselves. As he puts it, "The sense of identity which is created within this process is one which is predicated on an absence of the real and a repetition of the Same." When we copy, or "represent," something, we find ourselves representing only previous representations, since our relations with the "something" we seek to represent are far more complicit than can be defined by simple observation. He rejects the notion of an original experience, and with it the notion of "good or bad" copies of it, although he points out that "the pervasive presence of the good copy/bad copy axis is such that it has become virtually impossible for us to think outside of this structure."

Grenville thus throws into question our whole qualitative system for judging art works. The intent of this exhibition, and of these artworks, is therefore "to pervert the configuration of this axis," "to breach the threshold of representation and to create within that breach a process of identity." The quaint coding of Grenville's writing, and its emphasis on the collapse of representation, is more or less borrowed straight from poststructuralist discourse. We could simplify it a bit by saying that Grenville is examining what we are doing when we represent our reality to ourselves, and how much our sense of identity can be reconstructed by questioning traditional forms of representation.

The value of Grenville's approach is obvious when applied to an artist like Robert Fones, whose work has often been seen as simply eccentrically sensitive, the result of an exquisitely subtle appreciation of formal entities. Bruce Grenville argues instead that Fones is demonstrating the *oppression* of those forms and our subservience to the powerful definition of our identities. Whether that involves this artist's scientific maps of North American tree ranges in the fifteenth century, or his simple landscape photographs with highway signs, Grenville's thesis "that there is no identity in the work other than that produced by the apparatus of representation" enables him to situate Fones within a crisis of identity, a crisis arising from our unwitting failure to recognize the ways in which we construct ourselves. Fones may or may not have a subtle appreciation of forms, but his work gains significantly from an existential reading. This show was an opportunity for Grenville to pull together some concerns—appropriation, authenticity, repetition—common to some fairly disparate artists. As well as Fones, the S.L. Simpson show included Arlene Stamp, Janice Gurney, Robert Flack, and Douglas Walker.

In the catalogue for his exhibition at the Power Plant, Grenville builds on the groundwork laid out at S.L. Simpson. If our identity, or our perception of reality if you prefer, is not secured in any original validity, then what are the forces bearing on it? In *Active Surplus*, he supplies an answer derived largely from Jean Baudrillard's political version of post-structuralism. A central concern here is "the pervasiveness of the current post-industrial state," by which is meant mass consumer culture. The crux of that concern is this "pervasive nature" of the culture, and consequently its power to manipulate meaning in our unsecured reality: in consumer culture, the materialist reduction of social values produces simple exchange value alone. This, in turn, produces stasis, an endlessly circulating economy of fashion in which no moral development or social progression can take place. The post-industrial state has no room for complex relations. It is this endgame scenario that Grenville attacks here in an attempt to demonstrate that objects in our culture do in fact have their own economies, or social and political dimensions, and that the apparent indifference of mass consumer culture disguises a self-interested politics of the status quo. In the Power Plant show, Grenville included seventeen artists, demonstrating through his critical position links between the work of New York artists such as Louise Lawler and Allan McCollum and Canadians Robin Collyer, Liz Magor, and Bernie Miller.

The reduction of social value to exchange value has been a concern in Liz Magor's work for a long time, and it is clearly evident in the "double" theme of her *Baker's Showcase*. There is a charming wand-like flourish in the way Magor collapses the processes of production and distribution associated with her own bookwork *Four Notable Bakers* of 1983 into a single palpable image locked inside an old-fashioned display cabinet. But as Grenville points out, behind this charm lies a truth shared by all fairy tales, a determined reminder that culture is *produced*, that it does not merely *exist*, and Magor is reminding us that this is as true of *Baker's Showcase* as it is of the ordinary objects we consume.

Grenville's exhibitions can be seen as distillations of the current critical concern that our representations *of* reality are politically important to our identification *with* reality. Few artists can resist the seduction of suddenly discovering that what they make is significant after all, that how artists colour the world is how others may lead better lives. Artists have always felt this was true in some sense, although the validity of the claim has had a rocky row to hoe. Poststructuralist discourse, with its roots in Marxism, constitutes a powerful justification for those claims. Do the artists in these exhibitions therefore illustrate this discourse in some self-serving manner? Grenville's selection of work favours no particular group of artists, no movement. His selection is undeniably concentrated on younger artists, who quite clearly are more political than many older artists; they are for the most part not only familiar with his terms, but they also subscribe to his view that ideology is the basis for representation. But this is all they really have in common, and that describes many more artists than are included here.

In fact, Grenville's selection is as significant in showing how serious art is *introduced* as it is to a discussion of what it seeks to state. The fulcrum here is the S.L. Simpson exhibition. Sandra Simpson is a commercial dealer with her own slate of artists; the gallery is a business in competition with other galleries. Yet of the five artists Grenville selected for this exhibition, only one is represented by Simpson; the remainder are represented by other commercial dealers. Clearly, this is not garden-variety business competition. What Grenville does—for Simpson, of course, but also for the other commercial dealers noted in the catalogue—is to establish the *serious* nature of her gallery, its distance from mere market economy. S.L. Simpson becomes, that is, as seriously engaged as our public institutions—the Power Plant, for instance. The message is easily read: work shown here is already within the public domain; it is already valid.

This may seem cynical and manipulative, and if it were simply that it would fail. The particular advocacy and international credentials of Grenville's theoretical framework are essential. The archaeological character of his critique insists that this work directly addresses both the philosophical and the social conditions of our existence; that this is no aesthete's withdrawal from the real world, but is, rather, as close to the real world as you're going to get. This validation is urgent news—irresistible to anyone who is, well, serious.

While I generally share Grenville's theoretical approach—and his remarks on individual artists are well worth reading—I find the academic abstraction of this "writing" of it unconvincing. That is all the more disappointing since the force of poststructuralist analysis is directed toward cultural artifacts and the turbulent world of flesh and blood they bear witness to. I catch myself supplying the contexts of historical struggle and personal disaster, which alone can justify Grenville's appropriation of social purpose. That this curatorial thesis, and these art works, are serious cannot be in doubt. The context for that seriousness, however, remains to be explored.

Standing on the Mezzanine: Ewen, Wiitasalo, Monk, and the AGO (1988)

Published as "Standing on the Mezzanine: Ewen, Wiitasalo, Monk, and the AGO," *Vanguard* 17, no. 6 (December 1988–January 1989): 10–15.

I want to talk about Pat and Shirley and Philip, about my viewing of them from a mezzanine in the Art Gallery of Ontario—not as a voyeur, but as, perhaps, a lover. I find myself writing this hesitantly, with even a mild surprise and distrust, as I search for the necessity. It would seem, it *has* seemed, so easy to acknowledge that there is no necessity, that there never is, or that it exists somewhere else. But Necessity is the Daughter of my Passion, and standing on that mezzanine, at that single (rather banal) spot at which Shirley and Pat met for a moment in Philip's determined History, yes, I felt a passion. And I want to talk about it.

If revealing passion is art, talking about it is inevitably criticism; and central to criticism is critical theory. I have a theory in mind: that the internationalist assumptions and longings of the historical political avant-garde were as utopian as anything Sir Thomas More could have imagined. The political and cultural realities we face involve the continuance of a specific national culture as the arena within which we must formulate our actions; the alternative is not international perspective, but regional self-interest on the one hand, and imperial demands on the other. For purely practical purposes it is time to bury the idol of this idealist internationalism, to cease singing false praises, and to recognize the significance of cultural context, of a pragmatic internationalism. This theory is not particularly original, but it is generally under-appreciated. Andreas Huyssen has stated it for the Americans: "The cultural politics of [European] twentieth-century avant-gardism would have been meaningless (if not regressive) in the United States [of the 1920s] where 'high art' was still struggling hard to gain wider legitimacy and to be taken seriously by the public."[1] Philip Monk states it for *our* context: "It is necessary to develop a theory adequate to a community of interest; it is time for a theory of locality which is our place here in Canada. Necessarily this must become a history."[2]

1 Andreas Huyssen, *After the Great Divide* (Bloomington: Indiana University Press, 1986), 167.

2 Philip Monk, "In Retrospect: Presenting Events," *Parachute* 46 (March–April–May 1987), 11.

Let's imagine this article, then, as that moment after passionate embrace when we sit back to smoke that famous cigarette, to insert an embrace into the fabric of our lives, to order the intentions of our reason. The site is the art museum.

It has become common lately to dismiss the institution of the museum. I believe this is misconceived, and it is important to address this misconception if we are to understand the conditions under which our voice can be heard, and if we are to understand, really, why these two exhibitions are important for us.

How then, are we to judge the museum? Certainly not against imaginary ideals of "pure" access. We must ask: what does the museum represent—what "class" now represents the culture of our society as we experience it? The history of culture is a history of succeeding authorities—village elders, priests, kings, aristocrats, and so on. The dominant class in the world today, and successor to the European bourgeoisie, is the mass middle class. It is a mark of this class that in appropriating the tool by which the bourgeoisie itself originally attained power—free speech and public debate—the middle class has institutionalized that tool as mass culture. What is most striking about mass culture, and what distinguishes it from previous cultures, is its inherently archaeological eclecticism. It is important to bear this in mind when we turn to the role of the art museum as a site of meaning within this culture. That it is a site is a consequence of its evolution from princely demonstrations of wealth to public demonstrations of debate. It has remained, that is, a central institution for public education and power, a site of validation. Let's be clear about what this validation now serves: to demonstrate the *physical* power of the dominant class, to guarantee its security; to declare the *intellectual* power to make discriminating, not merely self-serving, judgements; and to know what is valid and what is not within a culture that has no fixed boundaries and no consensual absolutes. It is consequently, and crucially, the critical *independence* of the artwork, its ability to represent *difference*—the criterion by which we judge debate and free speech in a mass society—that will convincingly signal the strength of a class founded upon these tools; just as, internationally, a nation's strength lies in its different voice. The problem of the museum, then, is a problem of class consciousness, the consciousness of the mass middle class concerning its own complex necessities for validation.

The obvious problem that emerges, and the one we face in this country, is a crisis arising from the failure of a local middle class to understand the importance of self-validation, or when it settles for a validation from elsewhere, becomes colonial or branch-plant. Abdication of cultural self-interest always has the same consequence—invalidation of the culture and voice of the class it represents. It is, in fact, a self-betrayal. In Canada, this betrayal has been fairly genial, and disguised by the difficulties of disentangling the cultural and political concerns that distinguish an evolving culture from its British and American colonial attachments. But geniality cannot disguise the confusion that results within our society, and the barely concealed contempt—expressed as patronizing ignorance—that others reveal towards that confusion. The consequence is further erosion of energetic action within our culture. This is tragic. Not just for our culture, but much more significantly because it serves to further restrict the possibility, internationally, for *alternative* views and actions to those followed by imperial middle classes bent on imposing their structures outside the range of debate, outside legitimate context. Legitimacy is the crux of value, and before considering how *our* legitimacy can be recuperated as a history—the project Philip Monk now represents at the museum—I want to look at what Paterson Ewen and Shirley Wiitasalo represent individually within that possible history, what *they* see as forms of legitimate experience.

"I observe, contemplate and then attack."[3]

I want to construct an intersection between Ewen and Shirley Wiitasalo that begins with Paterson Ewen. I believe we first have to approach Ewen's *position* because a recognition of our ambivalence towards the seductive assumptions upon which Ewen builds his "phenomascapes" is necessary in order to appreciate the ambivalences we find in Wiitasalo's paintings.

The term "phenomenon" means something we perceive directly, though we generally reserve it to single out something curious or striking. While Ewen's phenomascapes are about striking phenomena, it becomes clear from his discussions about the work that he intends more nearly the idea of perceiving directly, of *comprehension.* Ewen's earliest paintings dealing with phenomena, *Artesian Well* for instance, are interesting for their scientific demonstrations. They reveal an interest not in simple visual experience, but in diagrammatic perception, in the ability to perceive the imperceptible, to *anticipate* phenomena. Anticipation is at the heart of one of the most influential philosophical theories of this century, and curiously Ewen's description of the uncertainties through which he came to recognize his need to concentrate on phenomena parallels on a personal level the social conditions of the 1920s within which Edmund Husserl developed his phenomenology. Following the First World War, Europe was a society in ruins, and the dislocations which produced Dada produced, as well a desire for something to stand on, some certainty in a world of uncertainty. In insisting that anything beyond immediate experience must be ignored, or "bracketed," and that the external world is reducible to the contents of our

3   Philip Monk, *Paterson Ewen: Phenomena; Paintings 1971–1987* (Toronto: Art Gallery of Ontario, 1987), 21.

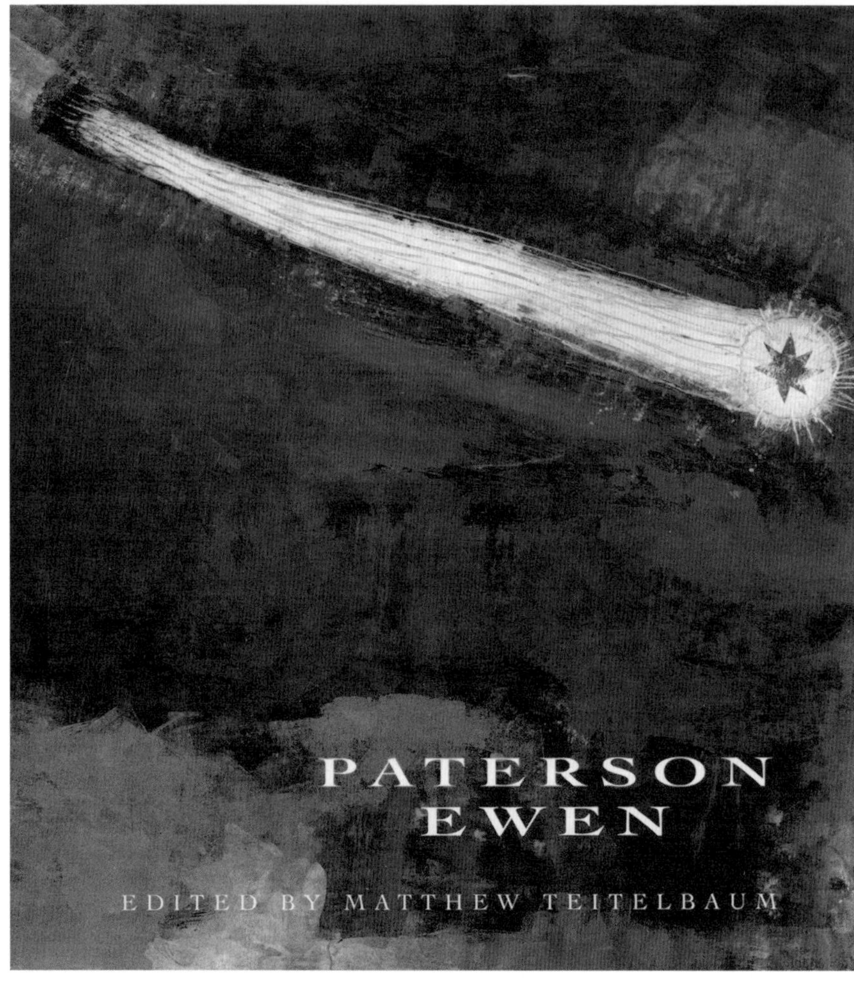

4.5   Paterson Ewen, *Halley's Comet as Seen by Giotto*, 1979. Cover illustration for Paterson Ewen, exh. cat., ed. Matthew Teitelbaum (Toronto: Art Gallery of Ontario, 1996). Photo: Ian Carr-Harris.

consciousness alone, phenomenology provided grounds for certainty. This reductivism was not meant to serve a random flux of disparate phenomena; rather, it was intended to isolate universal essences—to grasp what is invariable about specific experience, what can be anticipated. This implicit understanding that the world is both unplanned and yet knowable marks a critical secular triumph over earlier theological explanations. It is this secularized position that Ewen holds. Some time ago, in contrasting Ewen's *Rocks Moving in the Current of a Stream* with work by the Group of Seven,

I suggested that "Ewen's moving rocks are intentionally neither perceived—nor even perceivable as such—but are, rather, theoretical reconstructions comprehended by a knowing self-critical subject conditioned and armed with language,"[4] and that "in re-constructing Nature as a force having its own laws and powers, [this painting] clears the deck for a discussion about how our relationship to those forces may be seen."[5]

In spite of its strengths, phenomenology has certain problems. It is one thing to insist on the significance of immediate experience, but it is another to insist that we can intuit, irresistibly, invariable essentials on the basis of that alone. Husserl's knowable world was secured at the cost of enclosing that world within the centrality of a universal subject unmarked by difference. While Ewen's apprehended phenomenological nature owes much to the use of language, and Philip Monk concentrates on this use, Ewen sees language simply, as a way of providing *evidence*: a tool, like a router.[6] Ewen speaks of his practice in appropriate terms: "I observe, contemplate and then attack." It may not seem contemporary, but we all know it sounds good, and I believe it is Ewen's very inconsistency that we share and enjoy. Ultimately, however, we *do* recognize that if we understand how nature works, we must surely also understand that the metaphor of the martial arts can only be a local tactic, not a guiding strategy. For all his intellectual awareness, and *because* he accepts implicitly the notion of a universal subject, Ewen stops short of applying his self-critical knowledge to the *condition* of his subject, to "a discussion about how our relations to those forces may be seen."

By trying to face subjects that had resistance for me (like my own identity and how I felt about my art) I learned something, and my paintings came out stronger. Some things really are corny and still close to the truth at the same time.[7]

Haunted by the comment someone made to her when she was a student: "Why not be the model instead of the artist?" she made note of the differences.[8]

At the time when the death of the author has seen authors become extraordinarily articulate on that death, Shirley Wiitasalo's silence is all the more tantalizing—and effective. That silence becomes appropriate ground for viewing Wiitasalo's project as a modern Dance of Death, a witness to the stages of our ungainly passage through the world, our "corny" passion. I want to examine this passage Wiitasalo describes.

It seems clear that through all the elements of the work in this exhibition—the ambiguous images, the surfaces, the maskings, and the screens—there is a single pervasive purpose: to deny the possibility of that certainty we so enjoy in Ewen, and to demonstrate the implausibility

4   Ian Carr-Harris, *How We See/What We Say*, exh. cat. (Toronto: Art Gallery at Harbourfront, 1986), 16.

5   Carr-Harris, 18.

6   Carr-Harris, 18.

7   Shirley Wiitasalo, "Myths," in *Some Canadian Women Artists*, ed. Mayo Graham (Ottawa: National Gallery of Canada, 1975), 104.

8   Angela Leach, *Shirley Wiitasalo* (unpublished paper, Ontario College of Art, 1988), 1.

of direct perception. An inventory of Wiitasalo's history is useful: in her early "lakes, birds, and plants" we encounter not views of the natural world, but "signs"—maps and diagrams, an "unravelling," to quote the title of one painting—that seem analogous to Ewen's practice at the same period. In the work of the late 1970s, Wiitasalo used disjointed imagery to elaborate the degree to which dreams *become* models or simulations through which we *interpret* reality. In the work that forms Philip Monk's exhibition and reflects her position since the early 1980s, Wiitasalo turns to the maskings, or surfaces, which separate us from each other and screen even this interpreted reality from view. It is *this* step which most eloquently takes Wiitasalo beyond Ewen's anticipated nature. In effect, she has abandoned even the remote illusion that we could somehow rationally penetrate experience—not because we cannot act in the world, and most certainly not, if I understand her, because we *shouldn't* act in the world—but because to apply such an understanding is to *mi*sunderstand the possibilities for action within a reality of shifting, shadowy, "insubstantial" echoes, as Gary Michael Dault put it. Nowhere is this more clearly addressed than in Wiitasalo's use of

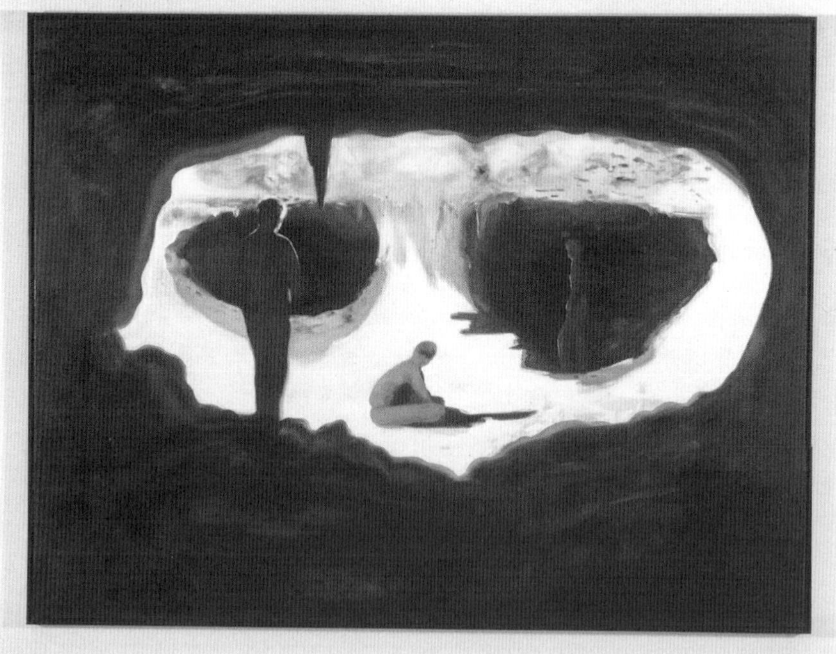

4.6   Shirley Wiitasalo, *Black & White*, 1986. Oil on canvas, 167.6 × 213.4 cm. Collection the Art Gallery of Ontario. Photo: Clinton Ashton.

the cave image, an image that poses a direct challenge to Plato's famous allegory. For Wiitasalo, Plato missed the point: cruel deception lies not in shadowy images, which are at least perceivable, but in the fantasy that there exists an external world of objective, substantial truths. Wiitasalo's nature unmasked is simply the mask revealed.

I believe Wiitasalo views this screened reality with some regret. The evidence for this regret exists, it seems to me, in the very diversity of images through which Wiitasalo depicts the interruptions and distortions that intercept our desire to view directly and establish secured conditions. The fractured television figures, the ghost reflections in the glass, the mirrored spaces, the landforms that, cloud-like, reveal ambiguous other forms—this lingering reflects a complex desire, it operates as a substitute connection, a dance *with* death not unlike the quite opposite tactic we see in Ewen's practice. It permeates the work with a haunting power that informs it with a politics broader than partisan advocacy, a political regret that comes from finally recognizing an ideal or longing—a *fantasy*—for what it is, as when a child puts away her toys and stops believing in Puff the Magic Dragon. It is tempting, and useful, to cast Wiitasalo's recognition in feminist terms, to view "Puff" as the phallus laid to rest ("unpuffed" as it were), and I would argue this as a legitimate reading for this work. But we must remember that within the logic of Wiitasalo's position—a logic for which Ewen's engaging "attack" is misconstrued—such a reading must recognize the necessity for this politics to proceed through complex mediations, mediations which inevitably produce surfaces and can never engage those anticipations we imagine could magically eliminate or settle difference. There is, of course, a central paradox in this position: surfaces can suffocate, and it is the acceptance of this paradox, forged across these paintings, that I believe constructs Wiitasalo's "deep regret," her recognition of failure. Such a recognition, on the other hand, is also pragmatic, and within this pragmatism the lingering shadows of patriarchy become no more nor less absurd than all the other shadows we encounter and must resolve. The death here is not an advocated killing of this or that illusion; it is, instead, a wistful insistence on the death of that noble embodiment that gives Ewen his heroic stature.

If phemomena can be recognized as a type of sign, their transcription in art is a further semiotic interpretation.[9]

[I]t is what the work leads to *that is the important question. It is a matter of how they function rather than what they mean.*[10]

The issue Philip Monk has most forcefully and publicly addressed is the matter of our specific, or local historical condition: how can our

9   Monk, *Paterson Ewen*, 11.

10   Philip Monk, "Axes of Difference," *Vanguard* 13, no. 4 (May 1984), 12.

11 Monk, "In Retrospect," 11.

12 Monk, "Axes of Difference," 11.

13 Monk, *Paterson Ewen,* 27.

14 Philip Monk, "Colony, Commodity and Copyright," *Vanguard* 12, no. 5/6 (1983), 14.

legitimacy be constituted? How indeed, and can Philip helps? To understand his position, it is necessary to grasp the notion of what we could call first principles. We must put aside for the moment the question of how Ewen and Wiitasalo, for instance, contribute their individual experience to our systems of value, and concentrate instead on the nature of proof. Or, as Monk himself puts it: "Starting from a theory, and not a history, theory must prove this history—the necessity of its facts, theory's conjecture of a concrete reality. (But how to demonstrate this 'concrete' 'reality'?)"[11] This focus on proof requires that, for Monk, the question of our relationship to the real, or we could say the "referent," is a secondary question that can be satisfied by evidence of a recognition of the *significance* of the referent, by signs of a struggle to define a "sense of the possibility of action."[12] What therefore becomes most essential in Ewen's art is what establishes the break in his practice that led him to work on plywood, to move from "mimesis to semiosis," to talk about how "a length of wire becomes rain, a piece of link fence becomes fog and so on."[13] Behind Monk's focus on this break, and his definition of the exhibition through it, lies his determination not only to *not* "mount a retrospective," but more significantly to question the very *notion* of the retrospective and its "narrative pull of a history." There are trade-offs: while depriving us of the personal bonding that we can derive from such a narrative, Monk is anxious to forestall the personal in favour of the social; to prove the necessity of *this* work as "having the power to signify by profoundly material means" *our* history, a History independent of its producer's *personal* narrative, which is merely *a* history. In exercising this point, Monk aligns himself against those tendencies which work to remove the artist from their culture, to privilege the individual with a merely personal narrative. Instead he aligns us with the construction of a social history which ties the production of the artist to a cultural context shared by artist and viewer: a context most efficiently legitimized as *our* necessity in the site of the museum. As he asked in 1983: "Why has the artist, or the index of the artist, become the subject of this art? What does it displace? What reference does self-reference replace?"[14] For Monk, the reference replaced is a "lack," "an absence of reality"—the consequence of self-betrayal. An extensive self-referentiality in Canadian art must therefore be recognized as an assertion against that absence.

In refusing the notion of a retrospective, Monk extends his critical argument curatorially against the desperation of this assertion and argues instead for an evidence of socially constituted signs—of things which "become" in a shared language of imagination. Centrally important to his project, this austere logic acts to restore the site of the museum—in opposition to the free-floating validation of the artist's name—as the site of art's construction of social meaning, and of *this* culture's *history.* It is easy to see why Monk insists on a semiotic analysis in both these exhibitions. Signs—language—represent social cohesion; they are meaningless otherwise. By denying the significance of simple biography, by using semiotics, by asserting the significance of the museum, by "giving a group of objects somewhat of the character of an event,"[15] Monk hopes to restore to a culture in distraction a focused comprehension of its coherent, collective value.

While Philip Monk demonstrates how Ewen's work can be read as a sign system of "materials and methods," his analysis of Ewen is less detailed than the one he constructs for Wiitasalo. In 1983 he organized her work around the "dynamic interplay between interior and exterior, 'subjective' and 'objective,' public and private," where the subject—constituted in the split between the frame of the painting and the frame *within* the painting—vacillates "uneasily between constraint and catastrophe."[16] In his catalogue essay, Monk pursues this further: "We know there is only surface in Wiitasalo's paintings." "Her paintings ultimately deal with the relations between the image and subjectivity: how the latter receives or registers the former; how the image helps form the individual; what is seen in representation and what is not seen and left out."[17] For Monk, Wiitasalo's work *leads to* a recognition of the *mediating signs* which construct consciousness, the distortions and *mirage*s that characterize the surfaces which, in *effect,* constitute our sole knowable reality—the reality, after all—of an illusionist.

Monk's presence at the institution-museum of the Art Gallery of Ontario represents his opportunity to answer the question of Canadian culture he posed as critic: "How to demonstrate this 'concrete' 'reality'?" In the process required to establish the proof for a theory that would permit a history, control over the museum means control over the process of demonstration necessary to complete that proof. In Monk's semiotically determined demonstration, Paterson Ewen's representational practice is progressive in its detailed attempt to look like, or to become an external referent—the forces of nature—avoiding in the process the self-referentiality of received signs that Monk sees as a disruption of the social and a threat to a history. He emphasizes Ewen's lack of interest in "professional" meteorology and its enclosed sign systems and focuses on his greater interest in the sheer act of making—"to signify by profoundly material means." And if Ewen's intense commitment to action forms one pole of Monk's purpose, Wiitasalo's recognition of the complex mediations of the surface as the only referent accessible to our actions forms the other. It is important to remember here that for purposes of proving a theory, Monk is not concerned with whether the referent is "real" or not, accessible or inaccessible; he is concerned only with the significance of signs as they operate in the work of these artists, and whether through these signs a sense exists "of the possibility of action." Wiitasalo's work, for Monk, must be seen as a struggle

15   Monk, "In Retrospect," 12.

16   Monk, "Axes of Difference," 13.

17   Philip Monk, *Shirley Wiitasalo* (Toronto: Art Gallery of Ontario, 1987), 17.

18 Monk, "In Retrospect," 12.

against the surface of the sign, a struggle marvellously recorded in *Famous Face*, a struggle to construct the subject's identity that is every bit as compelling, as heroic, after all, as Paterson Ewen's "direct act of making."

Is Philip Monk convincing? It is unfortunately not enough, however welcome, "to make objects appear."[18] Monk knows this. Yet beyond the objects in these exhibitions, we are required here to read his call for our own history as satisfied by a demonstration of linguistic functions which *imply* a possibility for action and the establishment of value. I do not dispute Monk's logic; it follows from his conviction that we must begin by recognizing the necessity of theory—and the consequent necessity of the museum as collective site of meaning—before involving ourselves in the meaning or intentionality of artworks. I *am* unsure that the cautiousness of this logic is necessary, and whether in fact it really indeed *is* time for us to consider the dimension of those "intentional voices" in our current historical context. I would be curious whether Monk believes *any* action is sufficient—and this seems highly unlikely—or whether there are *particular* actions that would seem more necessary than others, actions which are very much in debate within the work of these artists. After all, Paterson Ewen's work witnesses a generation for whom survival on the frontier within the natural forces he depicts was still an issue, if only as a memory. Shirley Wiitasalo, on the other hand, represents a young urban generation informed both theoretically and practically about the relative naivety of that memory, and the greater threat to survival posed by the problematics of social identity. I attempted earlier to suggest an evaluation of those differing viewpoints— simply to insist on the necessity of registering the *character* of our social condition within the "absence" that Philip Monk quite rightly describes. It is Monk's silence concerning that character, an absence in his theoretical approach to a history, that marks his project, and *his* intersection of these two exhibitions, as curiously suspended and incomplete: an awkward desiring—like a nervous lover left standing on the mezzanine.

Postscript

I think it is important for me to acknowledge that through a coincidence in timing this article appears in *Vanguard* at the same time that Philip Monk is curating an exhibition of certain early works of mine at the Art Gallery of Ontario. A complicating factor might also be that both artists discussed in the article are represented by my own dealer—Carmen Lamanna.

For some, this may cast the article into an appropriative role reflecting a strategic intent. While one option to avoid such a misconstruction would be simply to delay or cancel publication of my essay, such a solution seems to me—and to the editors of *Vanguard*—both unnecessary and highly problematic. Unnecessary, because appropriative strategies are always read for what they are, and their effects nullified by an aware audience; highly problematic, because the logic of such a solution accepts that our actions must be so singularly focused, and reductive, that contradictions and alliances cannot occur. Common sense tells us that this leads to inaction, or at best to a painful scrutinizing that would suspend useful debate in a community as intricate as the visual arts. More precisely to the point, however, is a recognition within current criticism and artmaking that the "autonomies" which have come to mark specific investigations must be dismantled in order to clarify the obligations and responsibilities that those investigations carry in common. Within this context, it is inevitable, and appropriate, that the complexion of the authors of these investigations will intersect. The publication of this essay, and this postscript, illustrates the applications of this fact of life to my own case, and serves to emphasize my view that we must both speak, and know who speaks.

On Footnotes (1990)

Published in *The Readymade Boomerang: Certain Relations in 20th Century Art*, exh. cat., ed. René Block, Lynne Cooke, Bernice Murphy, and Anne-Marie Freybourg (Sydney: Biennale of Sydney Ltd., 1990), 288–89.

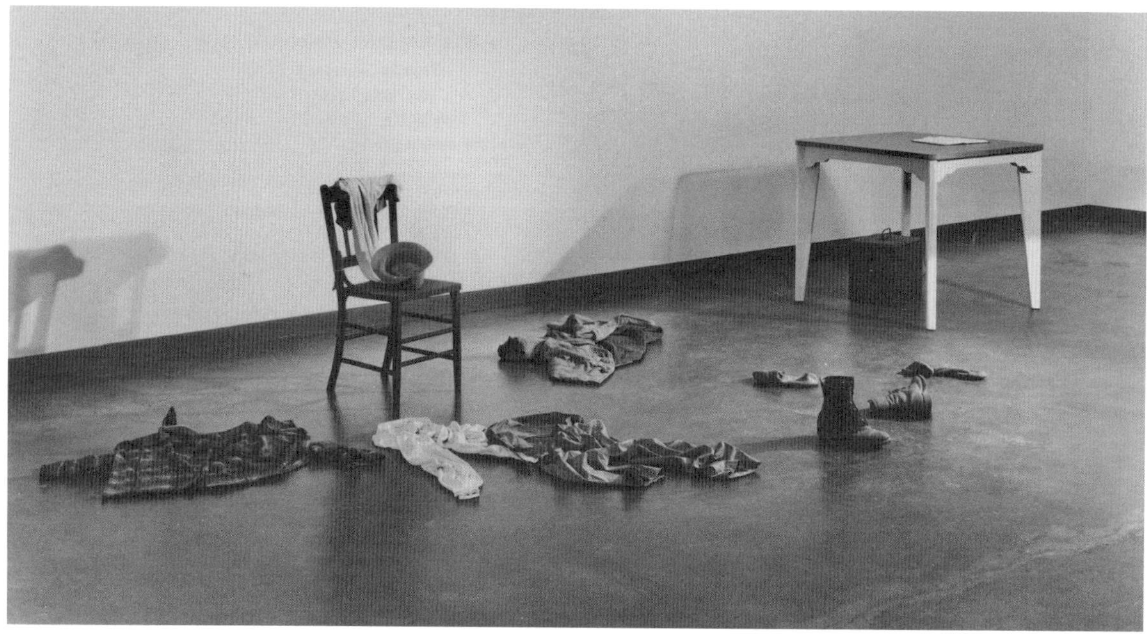

4.7   Ian Carr-Harris, *Nellie L. McClung. Clearing in the West; my own story (Toronto, 1965), 286*, 1988. Painted wood and fiberglass-resin-impregnated clothing and boots, wooden chair painted black, painted wood table with 12-volt lighting supplied by automobile battery in housing, fabricated book with backlit section. Installation at Carmen Lamanna Gallery, Toronto. Courtesy the artist.

About two years ago I found enough time to take a quick look at an exhibition of medieval manuscripts and Renaissance books at the Art Gallery of Ontario. I was probably there no longer than twenty minutes, but it was long enough to be reminded of something I had almost forgotten—the power of illustration or "illumination" as text.

To state this might seem merely quaint: after all, we are surrounded by a mass media whose semiotically based marketing strategies apparently assume this very recognition. In common with many artists, I have myself from the beginning worked with image and text as a model by which to sort out the definitions and authorizations that construct identity, and consequently meaning in our culture. Why, then, would seeing these manuscripts and books affect me? Simply Walter Benjamin's "aura"?

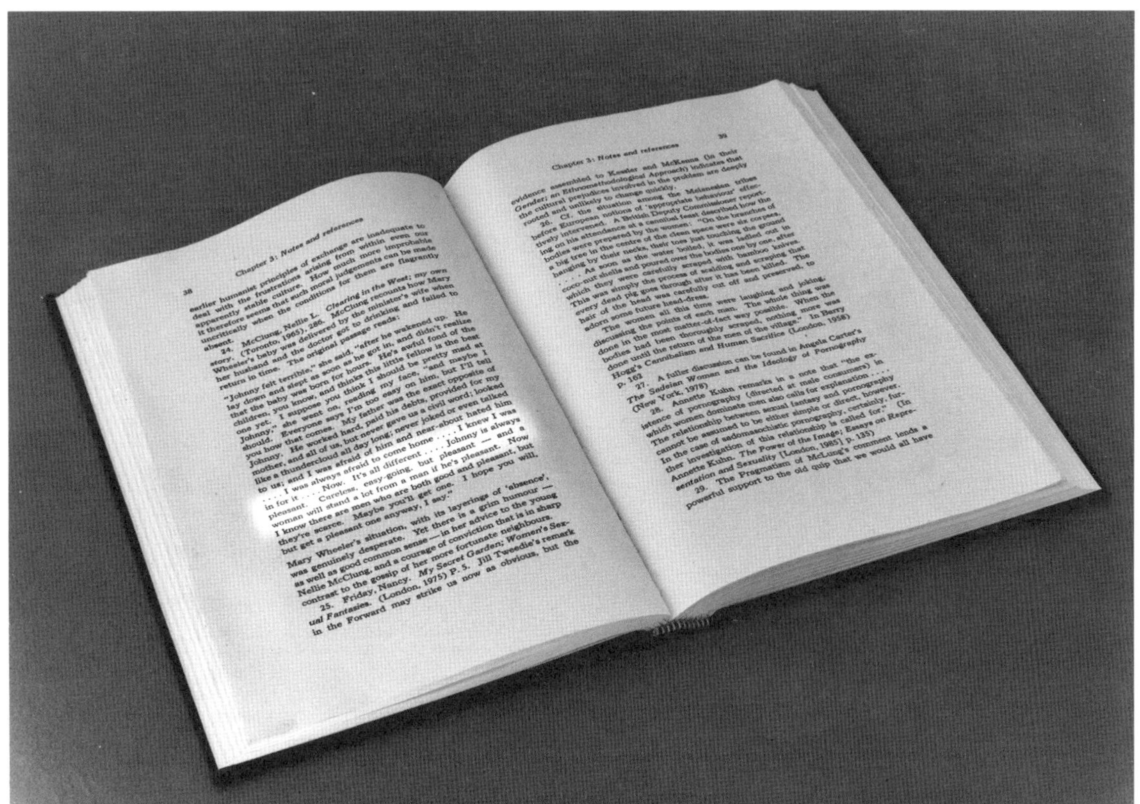

4.8   Ian Carr-Harris, *Nellie L. McClung. Clearing in the West; my own story (Toronto, 1965), 286*, 1988. Detail of book. Courtesy the artist.

It involves footnotes. What struck me most forcibly about what I experienced in those twenty minutes was the sheer tenaciousness of text—the indelible power of "having said that." I was reminded, that is, of the dialectical quality—I could say rather the contingent quality—of every single moment: the constant shift of recognition from its moment to another. But just how "other"?

Dialectic has of course a progressive agenda. To note this is not to deny notions of progress, but instead to beg what may constitute a procedure for progress, and its expectations. In considering those books and manuscripts, it was not so much a sense of their distance from me that I found impressive, but rather a sense of their inherent validity, their "right" to say what they did, the necessity for me—half a millennium away or not—that they had. What does this have to do with footnotes?

Footnotes, like Letters to the Editor, are the significant arena in texts for challenge and response. They are the means by which we accept argumentation as fundamental to legitimate experience. And what is argument, but our recognition of an illuminated moment, a moment which will be—begs to be—obliterated by a new illumination, though never quite: a series of originals that never were, as series of moments never known, moments which seem, nonetheless, as though they could have been.

Statement Concerning the Work (1991)

Author's note (2023): This text was written following my exhibition *The Merlin Manufacturing Co. Ltd.* at the Carmen Lamanna Gallery, May 6–24, 1991. This exhibition ended the day following Carmen Lamanna's unexpected death on May 23, 1991.

How do we *know* something? How can we say what we know? And *what* is this something that we say we know: what are its expressed convictions? In the end, *what is persuasion*?

These are primary questions in any philosophical sense, and they are inherent in any work of art. But the traditional approaches to such questions, and their inherences in art practice, are today experiencing a crisis in which persuasion is seen as not only impossible, but nonsensical. Yet we persist in persuasions; clearly, we have a crisis in the comprehension of coherence.

I have for some time been concerned with how we understand something to be identical, or more precisely *not* identical, to our own defined experience. This question of comprehending identity is complicated by the fluidity of comprehension itself, its collusions between desire and history. In this dialectic of the subject, its split into parallel others, identity becomes a matter of invoked limitation; and if the consequent dichotomies are indeed the primary literary within which we work, the problem of being literate—by which I mean *persuasive*—becomes a problem of maintaining coherence while simultaneously tracking the contradictions, or *in*coherences, of that literacy.

If "maintain coherence" requires close attention to the various critiques of culture advanced in the last thirty years or so, it requires also a historical consciousness and a skeptical reserve. Irony and dissonance seem more appropriate to our time than metaphors of *ravissement*, though pleasure is essential for any claim of literacy. Pleasure, after all, is a form of disclosure, of intimacy, and any program of persuasion seems necessarily grounded in a certain frankness of demonstration. Brecht may have misjudged the limits of rational analysis, as Duchamp and Benjamin misjudged the deconstructive power of technological *éclat*, but grasped ironically their work remains not only historically instructive, but methodologically useful.

My work has therefore involved the construction of theatres or "models" of circumstance within which to explore our capacity for unsecured presence; it is only by finding this capacity within a critical culture that we can use, rather than abuse, our apparent incoherences. History, irony, complex allusions, and a pervasively elusive yet highly readable reality invest the work's direct address to the viewer. Because this address *is* direct, these models have been constructed so as to form points of *encounter* for an event completed by the presence of the viewer, a presence rendered all the more noticeable, and accountable, for its apprehension through language; and it is *apprehension*, as both closure and deferral, which binds viewer to model in a self-critical *re-enactment* of conviction and the possibilities of persuasion.

A Far Country: Viewing the Isaacs Gallery (1992)

Commissioned by the Art Gallery of Hamilton in 1992, unpublished.

I am in vaguely familiar territory: the public opening of an exhibition in a modern art museum, or at least what an architect thought a few years ago a modern art museum should look like, and it is Hamilton, Ontario. It's a Thursday evening—September 17, 1992, to be exact—and with just a slight sense of perversity I am standing eight feet from the floor on a rented industrial scaffolding in the middle of a large gallery. It's 8:53, and familiarity is suddenly focused not on *this* place and time, but on another through a single object displayed in front of me: a 1960s portable record player on which a scratchy LP is belting out—in a just barely audible whisper—a lively cut from that symbol of early '60s Toronto, the Artist's Jazz Band.

It is the uncomfortable intimacy of this other place and time I feel compelled to dissect: the place and time of the Isaacs Gallery. Of course, the opening I have just described, and to which I will briefly return, was in recognition of the immense contribution that gallery—its artists and most certainly Avrom Isaacs himself—has made to the history of culture in this country. But what intrigues me is just what I understand that contribution to be, and I am writing this now because I find I must address this through my own history of recognitions rather than through the documentary record.

For now, however, we are at the opening, just to pause a while. Not out of sentiment necessarily, nor even out of respect, though perhaps that is a given. This pause is more like a silence, a sort of suspended moment—the sort where you watch others talk and gesture but hear no focused sound. It's a moment of examination that is not so much analysis of something present, as it is an experience of history, an episodic space in which fragments of known things merge in patterns of elusive meaning. That is why I found myself oddly caught by the Artists Jazz Band in 33 ⅓ rpm at close to zero volume whispering: "we were here." It is why I found myself struck, in another room not far away, by a disturbing sense of, well, *removal*, where that whisper becomes a frozen exclamation of exaggerated images merging quickly into one—the image of "the Isaacs artist": young, or at least virile;

1   An interesting discussion of these changing conditions can be examined more fully in Maria Tippett's *Making Culture: English Canadian Institutions and the Arts before the Massey Commission* (Toronto: University of Toronto Press, 1990).

handsome, or at least imposing; tragic, or at least touched by apparent tragedy; male, or at least trying to be. Perhaps it's time we leave this opening, time to view this history.

My view is a late one. I reminded myself of this by dusting off an old issue of *artscanada* from October 1967, the year I enrolled in the Ontario College of Art. Isaacs had been in business already eleven years, Dorothy Cameron had lost her gallery over the "eroticism show," and Carmen Lamanna had opened his gallery in her old space in the summer of 1966. I had then lived in Toronto since 1964. David Mirvish Gallery, the Artist's Workshop on Bloor, the Art Gallery of Toronto, Pollock Gallery, Jerrold Morris Gallery, not to mention *artscanada*, Barry Lord, and the *Globe & Mail*'s Kay Kritzweiser: these were the local elements that defined in large part the institutional context for my interests. It was a world of Michael Snow versus Henry Moore, of Clement Greenberg versus Harold Rosenberg, of New York City and the Canada Council. It was Canada's centennial, and for me it was a complicated world of determined disbelief. Too late, then, for me to fully appreciate the frontier world that Isaacs entered into in 1956. It is important to remember that the Canada Council only came into existence in 1957, and this watershed in our history marked a fundamental shift in expectations that I believe separates my generation from Av Isaacs and the artists he came to represent. By 1967 the Council was a central assumption of our culture: its jury structure and procedures supported immensely diverse claims to national significance that extended into every region and cut across age and gender boundaries. Most significantly, the Council represented an idea of literacy and mobility. Unlike a gallery or a patron, its support was always contingent—artists were required to defend their position and to compete with one another. This demand alone, however much it was and is resented by many artists, constructed a climate of skepticism, some would say professionalism, radically different from the more adventurous, perhaps romantic, and certainly patron-centred conditions of 1956.[1]

In any case, the Isaacs that I encountered in 1967 was settled, and impressive: Coughtry, Rayner, Redinger, Burton, Curnoe, Mark Prent, John MacGregor, and of course the famous couple: Joyce Wieland and Michael Snow. Isaacs was national; indeed, Isaacs was international. But Isaacs remained for me and for others at the time curiously foreign, and if that perception seems curious, it lies at the heart of my response to the gallery and to its moment in Canada's culture. This is what needs some explaining.

It seems to me that the period 1965 to 1970, let us say, represents the maturing into consciousness of a massive new generation, people born after the war into prosperity, TV, constant news programming, Vietnam hysteria,

and irony. Irony is a powerful, although duplicitous force in political awareness, but in 1967 its duplicity was not evident. Indeed, in the figure of Pierre
Trudeau's famous shrug, irony seemed the ultimate test of truth. Applied to
the truths of modern art, or at least that art which had become synonymous
with austere form and its alter ego, expressive or idiosyncratic gesture, what
seemed most evident was that artists had failed to grasp a changed condition, one in which identity could no longer be played out in the privacy of
the individual as a legitimate model for public contemplation. This failure
was itself ironic. Modern art, after all, described itself as "avant-garde," as
a Tradition of the New, in Rosenberg's words. For a young culture like
English Canada's, that tradition would seem to have been tailor-made
to represent its interests, both as historically "new," and as generation-
ally "emerging." Puzzling, that it didn't; that when seen at Isaacs such art
seemed oddly colonized instead, whatever the nationality of the artist, and
this despite the obvious fact that Isaacs had with every justification become
identified with, and clearly believed in, an independent "Canadian art."

The problem lay in the values involved. Modern art, as I then perceived
it within the model presented by the Isaacs Gallery, constituted an appeal to
humanity. If I think of Coughtry, Rayner, Mark Prent, even Michael Snow
and Joyce Wieland, what connected these artists was a strong belief in the
presence of the artist as lightning rod to a lost cohesion. Perhaps Kurelek
most obviously and obliviously recorded this longing, but we can in fact
trace this presence to the origins of modern art itself. I'll be brief since this
is not intended as a primer on the avant-garde. It has been suggested that
aesthetic modernity is a product of the French Enlightenment and its belief
in the "infinite progress of knowledge and in the infinite advance towards
social and moral betterment."[2] It has further been suggested that the culture
of modernity, of which modern art is a category, is characterized by values
derived from a collapse of difference and diversity, of identity, into the
trans-personal embodiment of the single authorial voice, a voice based
upon a male-centred notion of the heroic individual as both caught within
and in struggle against Nature, a kind of living Laocoon.[3] To note these
points is not to dismiss modernity, but rather to recognize certain formulations within it. What was becoming a point of disenchantment in 1967
for myself, and for others, was that these formulations no longer produced
what the philosopher Jürgen Habermas has called "an emancipatory effect."
The "liberal" tradition of modern art seemed more and more the problem,
not the solution, to the question: what should I believe, how should I act?
Skepticism concerning the viability of this liberal humanism was undoubtedly hastened by the contradictions of Vietnam. But Vietnam only pointed
to the obvious: that coherence and truth are subjects of power and force,
and that identity is not necessarily portable.

2   Jurgen Habermas,
"Modernity—An Incomplete
Project," in *The Anti-Aesthetic:
Essays on Postmodern Culture*, ed.
Hal Foster (Port Townsend,
WA: Bay Press, 1983), 4.

3   For example, see Andreas
Huyssen, "Mass Culture
as Woman: Modernism's
Other," in *After the Great
Divide: Modernism, Mass Culture,
Postmodernism* (Bloomington:
Indiana University Press, 1986).

4   Elsewhere in this catalogue there is printed the text of Isaacs's opening "manifesto" from 1956. In that message, Isaacs speaks very straightforwardly, and I would say endearingly, of his objective: "In choosing this exhibition to mark the opening of the Greenwich Gallery I have endeavoured to present a visual statement of the gallery's aims for the future. While these five young painters represent diverse directions in painting, their work suggests, I believe, a common standard of artistic integrity and it is my earnest intention to adopt this standard and grow with it as it grows, rather than trying to adjust to any mythical 'level of public taste.'" I am conscious that my characterization of this purpose as "abstract heroics or connoisseurship" may seem facile and ungenerous. Since I don't intend this, it is important to stress that this characterization is not directed at Isaacs himself, but at the institution of modern art which held authority for so long, and which Isaacs internalized and championed. On the question of the appropriateness of such a position, it is interesting to read Andreas Huyssen's remarks concerning modern art in the United States at an earlier stage. See *After the Great Divide*, 167.

5   Although A Space was the first such centre, founded in 1971, it in turn grew out of Chris Young's Nightingale Gallery, whose exhibition *Concept '70* focused on a thematic rather than individualized approach towards issues of identity, structure, and power.

6   Carmen Lamanna was another exception. Lamanna's choices perhaps reflected

The failure of "classical" modern art to address these questions adequately was therefore a fundamental problem facing any artist, or gallery, and had become by 1967 unavoidable. Intelligent and passionate though Isaacs artists were, it seemed to me that they continued to avoid this issue. This avoidance was only exacerbated by the pluralistic approach that Av Isaacs had established from the beginning. It can be argued that modern art has many intensities within it, intensities that can be focused into specific critiques which establish a *ground* for difference even when they do not themselves acknowledge it. The emphasis that the Isaacs Gallery placed on a multiplicity of voices made it difficult, I felt, to detect such critiques. Instead, the Gallery appeared to sponsor a congeniality and a celebration of the artist which did not appear justifiable, however "tough" or honest the work remained. Grand, perhaps, especially if you were male; utopian, certainly. But believable? Not really. There was no room in 1967 for such lack of irony; and in a colonial culture like Canada's, abstract heroics or connoisseurship seemed beside the point.[4]

The point was that such celebration, despite its clear and heartfelt intention to liberate the culture, led back to the New York School, to Clement Greenberg even, rather than to the more socially critical environment, which was becoming the hallmark of contemporary art internationally, as much in New York as in Europe. Or Canada; there were many reasons why conditions here in the late sixties, in Toronto, at least, required a shift which became explicit as the newly founded "parallel galleries," or artist-run centres, re-wrote the agenda for serious art.[5] Admittedly one powerful motivation lay in the lack of private commercial galleries interested in contemporary Canadian art. Isaacs was exceptional, but the gallery represented a full complement of artists whose reputations and lineage effectively excluded the emerging artists of this generation.[6] Nonetheless, a more fundamental motivation than the obvious need for representation lay in the fact that an increasingly critical culture required an arena in which to question the role of the individual versus the institution, the politics of gender privilege, and the utopian vision of progress itself. These, after all, were the issues which had become dominant for a generation which had grown up on the graphic inhumanities of Vietnam, suburban alienation, and the excesses of fifties stereotyping. For this generation, there was nothing to celebrate. On the contrary, there was work to do: a whole culture needed dismantling. What was needed was not artistic vision, but cultural critique. It was not that Av Isaacs had no interest in this critique; after all, he came from a background of "prairie socialism" and remained committed throughout his gallery's history to the core issues of social liberation—freedom from censorship, due process in the public arena, and protest against totalitarian regimes. Rather, it was a question of methodology: neither the tradition of art he sponsored, nor the pluralistic approach he adopted, could take into account the problem of ideology. For Isaacs, the route to "social and moral betterment" lay through the individualized voice and in a faith that this progress was an inevitable effect of freedom and independence. For younger artists, there seemed no evidence that progress was an effect of freedom, or of independence, nor that the individual was the key; such betterment as might be attainable lay through investigations of conflict and the recognition of politicized difference. It lay through close scrutiny of the individual as an institution. And indeed that is what this "history of recognitions" amounts to: a scrutiny of Avrom Isaacs as an institution with quite particular characteristics. The Isaacs Gallery, it could be said, represented a moment of liberal democracy in the evolving culture of this country. This liberalism seems distant now, as it seemed already "foreign," or "out of place," in 1967.[7] But, naive though it seems in hindsight, utopian though it intentionally was, and gender-privileged as its claims to universal value clearly were, Isaacs represented a determined faith in freedom, a belief in the spirit, in the body politic, that I think was absolutely essential in the evolution of late sixties irony into a self-conscious politics. Isaacs was palpable, and tough-minded. It was precisely for this reason that a legitimate refusal was possible, that a distinction could be made, and that a different voice—indeed, many different voices—could be raised. It is not just important, but only truthful, to insist that we were—I was—an inheritor of a vision; and if I opposed it, I was not so much its opponent as its product. That is why, straining to hear the Artists' Jazz Band scratching away on an old portable in the Hamilton Art Gallery, I can whisper back, with gratitude: "yes, you were there."

more emphasis towards a "critical" role for the artist, but again there was little room for expanding the gallery's representation. Perhaps it is appropriate to note here that while Lamanna's position was different from Isaacs's, this does not mean that it was somehow less debatable, or more "informed." It is especially important for me to clarify this, since I am aware that the fact that Carmen represented my own work could easily be seen as itself positioning me in a historical or even professional bias against the Isaacs Gallery. In fact, the Lamanna Gallery is just as susceptible to critique as Isaacs: personality and presence, and sheer commitment, were centrally significant for Lamanna, and constituted both a productive and self-limiting ideology.

7   I recently read Sartre's *Why Write* (1949), and I was struck by the degree to which this position describes the theoretical foundation for Isaacs's own understanding of the centrality of freedom in the relations between writer and reader, artist and viewer, or between an institution and its public.

Rozenstraat 8 (1995)

Written for *Furnishing the Office*, a project for Proton ICA, Amsterdam, 1995. Unpublished.

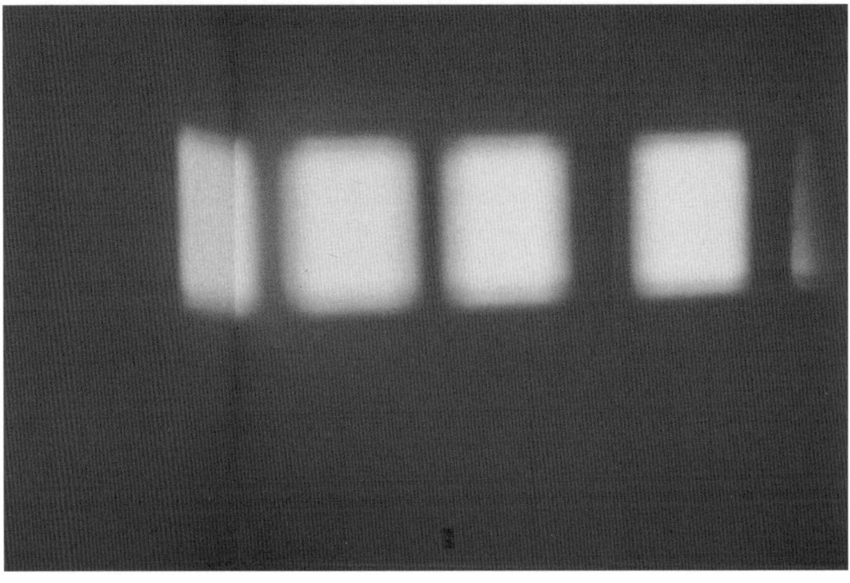

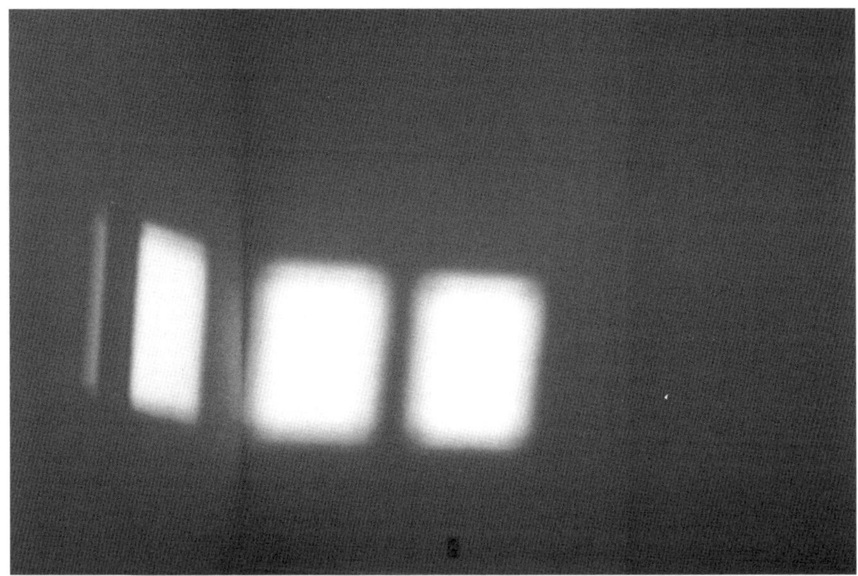

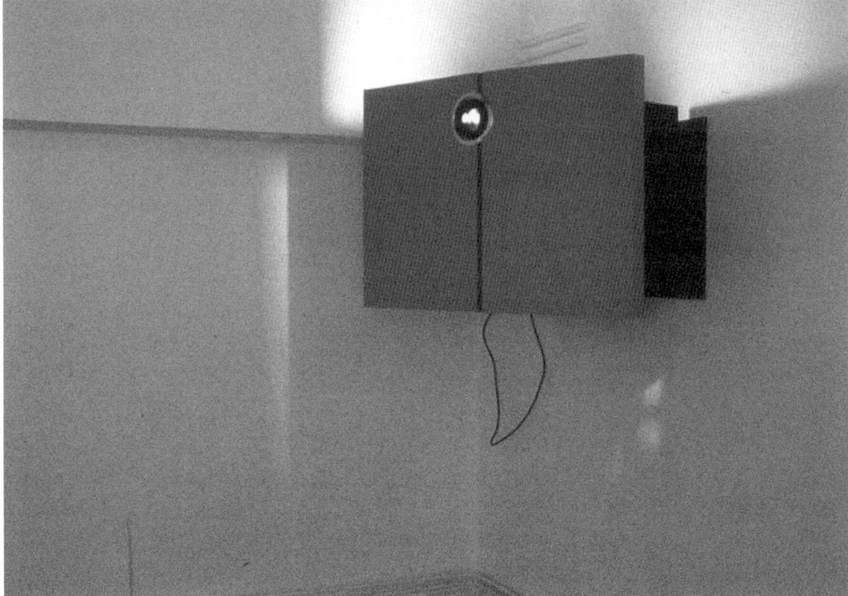

4.9/4.10 (opposite) and 4.11 (top)   Ian Carr-Harris, *Rozenstraat 8, Part 1*, 1995. Details of projection installation at Proton ICA, Amsterdam; time of projection cycle, about 20 mins., on continuous repeat. Installation dimension varies depending on the space. Courtesy the artist.

4.12 (bottom)   Ian Carr-Harris, *Rozenstraat 8, Part 1*, 1995. Wall-mounted projection unit of plywood construction with front faced with plastic laminate, geared motor on dead-slow speed, laser-cut metal disk, theater projection lamp system, 90 × 81 × 56 cm. Courtesy the artist.

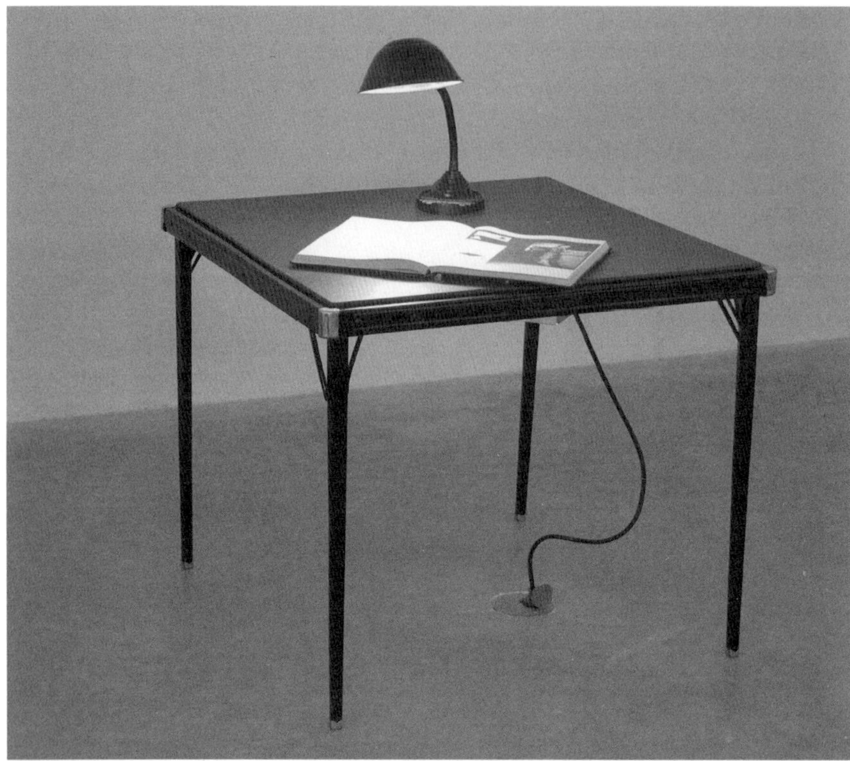

4.13   Ian Carr-Harris, *Rozenstraat 8, Part 2*, 1995. Metal card-table with vinyl surface, reading lamp, fabricated book with backlit illumination; table, 100 × 75 × 75 cm. Installation dimension varies. Courtesy the artist.

4.14   Ian Carr-Harris, *Rozenstraat 8, Part 2*, 1995. Detail of book. Courtesy the artist.

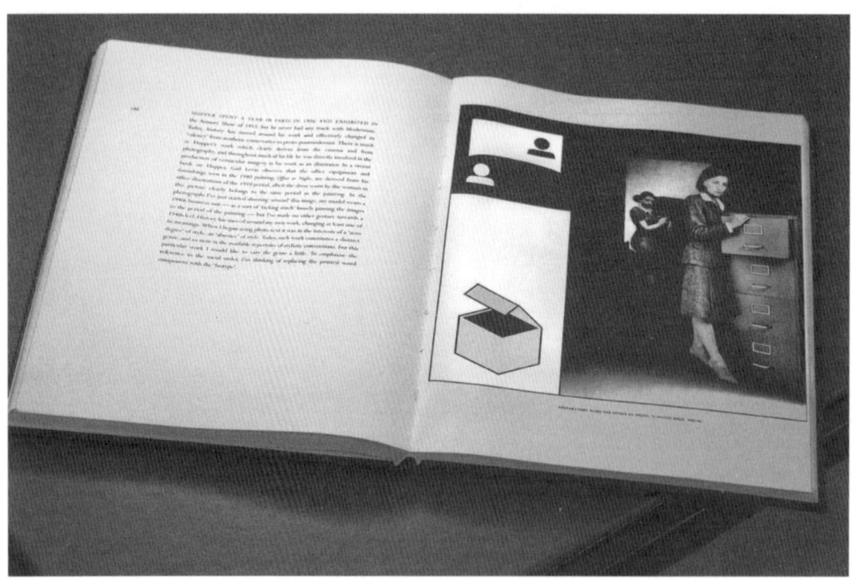

Description

Part 1 consists of a projection system (light source a 750-watt Quartz lamp)
which sends a moving shaft of sunlight "through" the five windows onto the
far walls of the main space at Rozenstraat 8.

The sunlight appears and disappears over approximately a twenty
minute cycle and descends laterally to the left from near the ceiling on the
right to near the floor on the left wall; only at midpoint are all the windows
represented; otherwise, the projection always begins as a small sliver
of light high up and to the right, and ends as a disappearing trace low on the
left wall. The room is otherwise empty except for the projection unit itself,
a geared motorized assembly housed and partially hidden behind a precise
rectangular grey laminated façade; the unit is mounted on the wall beside
and just below the windows of the space and emits a low hum. The light
from the windows is filtered daylight, leaving the room generally dark.

Part 2 is installed in a small adjoining room next to the administrative
office of Proton ICA; a small collapsible table (a black card table with red
oilcloth surface whose design dates from the 1940s) supports a goose-
necked desk lamp from the same era under whose pool of light is placed
a book, possibly an art textbook or museum catalogue, opened and fixed
to two facing pages. On the left-hand page, a short text discusses Edward
Hopper's painting *Office at Night* (1940) as the basis for another work—
not attributed within the text but known to be Victor Burgin's 1985 *The
Office at Night*, a remake of and commentary on Hopper's painting. On the
right-hand page there is an illustration of Burgin's work in one of its initial
versions. This illustration has been modified in *Rozenstraat 8, Part 2*, by
backlighting its content in two areas: in the one, Burgin's projection from
the original Hopper painting of the office girl standing at the filing cabinet
has been "re-lit" so as to place the office girl herself—as an opaque figure—
against a glowing wall, as though interrupting the projection that Burgin
has engineered; similarly in the other, backlighting picks out the interior of
the blank vertical panel Burgin introduces to the left of his restaged "office
girl," a panel in which floats what Burgin describes as an "isotype" of an
opening box—a formal sign which references the "real" filing cabinet whose
top drawer has been opened by the woman—and which now rests opaque
against its lit panel, lifting it—in effect—into contiguity with the opaque
figure of Hopper's office worker.

Commentary

The project has as its subject the site—the offices of Proton ICA at
Rozenstraat 8—and the potential the site offers for a discourse on address.

Situated in and for a public space, one that offers itself in fact specifically as a site of remembrances, the work constructs a linked particularity of place—the real second floor at number 8, Rozenstraat—with the representational space of Burgin's work within a sense of particular time—the circular and repetitive passage of light over a twenty minute period—while the real, constant light from the lamp illuminates the false book. Fact and fiction are brought together in a text that merges presence and absence, real and duplicate.

Part 1 rehearses the nature of address, the address addressed to itself. The representation of real sunlight (re-presenting the actual sunlight from the now sealed-up windows) modified or formatted by the street address (the shape of the windows at Rozenstraat 8), constructs for us our sense of the real. To this reality we can apply with some assuredness a name: Rozenstraat 8. Yet the name itself is a mirror, as the projected light is a representation, both standing for that textual identity we call Nature.

Part 2 extends this text through commentary, or rather commentary on a commentary, Victor Burgin's, returning us to Hopper's painting and his represented "text"—an office at night. In *Rozenstraat 8, Part 2*, the focal point is an equivalence set up between Burgin's open box and Hopper's woman. In this address, the address of one signifier to another, the work appears to assimilate the myth of Pandora into the figure of the secretary. While Burgin's original work—the previous commentary—was indeed intended to problematize Hopper's work in its social politics, the commentary here, with its "shedding of light" onto the process of mirroring reality, directs attention to the act of projection—addressing—itself. In *Part 2*, as in *Part 1*, the play of lighting is the mirror which reflects our own image, our own address, as a flickering oscillation between where and who we "are," and where and who we thought we were. If we see that Pandora's box is open, it is open at an address where seeing is no longer distinguishable from being seen.

Tracing Reading Writing (2002)

Presented as "Tracing Reading Writing," The Joan Carlisle-Irving Lectures, University of British Columbia, February 7, 2002. An earlier version of this lecture, titled "Tracings: Writing, Art, and Architecture," was presented at the University of Waterloo's School of Architecture Arriscraft Lecture Series on January 29, 1998.

Introductory Remarks

I was asked to address the question: Why do I do what I do? Why do I make art—what process leads me to it, has led me to it, in determining the narrative of my production?

This is therefore not a lecture on art, but on my participation in it. The subject presents two intricacies: how to define those interests from among many that may be seen to connect the diversities of a production; and how to legitimate that interest within the constantly evolving discourse and politicized landscape of art.

This address may set the stage for a discussion of those intricacies. But one point I would like to make as a preface is that when I speak of the trace, or tracing, I mean it rather specifically as an apprehension of the resistant and the tangible. The relation that this may have to a dematerialized simulacrum or an infinity of codes is worth investigation, but that is for now suspended. I am concerned here with how, in the history that is my work, the relationship between the trace of the given, its artifactuality, and the concept of origination has been an establishing argument.

Tracing Reading Writing

The engraving: art being born of imitation, only belongs to the work proper as far as it can be retained in an engraving, in the reproductive impression of its outline. If the beautiful loses nothing by being reproduced, if one recognizes it in its sign, in the sign of the sign that a copy must be, then in the "first time" of its production there was already a reproductive essence. The engraving, which copies the models of art, is nonetheless the model for art. And thus we say "writing" for all that gives rise to an inscription in general, whether it is literal or not and even if what it distributes in space is alien to the order of the voice: cinematography, choreography, of course, but also pictorial, musical, sculptural "writing."

Jacques Derrida, *Of Grammatology*[1]

1 Jacques Derrida, *Of Grammatology*, rev. ed., trans. G.C. Spivak (Baltimore: Johns Hopkins University Press, 1997), 9.

2   Author's note (2003):
I was influenced in deciding
on this personal approach to
the lecture through my earlier
readings of Jeanne Randolph's
ficto-criticism. But I had also
recently read and been struck
by Eunice Lipton's *Alias
Olympia: A Woman's Search for
Manet's Notorious Model & Her
Own Desire* (Ithaca and London:
Cornell University Press,
1992). Together, they seemed
to offer a counterpoint to the
more objective voice of the
commentator.

I'd like to begin by telling a story. A personal story.[2]

I am seven years old—I know this partly because we had recently moved into the big Victorian house on Blackburn Avenue, and partly because, after considerable resistance, I had only just learned to read.

I'm excited because I have just realized that by exercising great care, and using a sharp pencil against the sunlit window of the dining-room, I can cause to appear on a blank sheet of paper, as if by magic, the exact outlines of the imperilled boat, tossed blindly in a convincingly foaming sea, that carries the plot—let alone Donald Duck and his nephews—in the comic book I have been reading with nothing less than spellbound absorption.

Still excited, I remember racing into the drawing room to show this— what shall we call it? A transcription? An embodiment? Just a copy? Yet for me it was an invention!—to my mother. To which she calmly replied: "Yes, dear. It's very nice. But you copied it, didn't you? It's so much better if you make it yourself." What shall we call what I felt? Tragedy? Humiliation? Confusion? Strong emotions, to be the consequence of so seemingly inconsequential a remark.

Now, I don't doubt the wisdom of my mother's response. And I dedicated the next twenty-five years or so to that wisdom. Curiously perhaps, it was only when I finally went to art school and dedicated myself to making art that I came to question the grounds of that wisdom, and to reconsider— to revisit—that moment of excitement I had experienced when I was seven. What I came to realize was that no subsequent experience, no amount of exercising "originality," no amount of making "something new" had ever touched me so deeply, excited me as much, as that discovery of the "trace."

It is not my intention to pursue the anecdote in its personal dimension. I do, however, want to explore its possibilities as a model for what we experience in the linked domains of tracing, reading, and writing as they relate to artmaking. What I want to accomplish in this short lecture is quite simple and unambitious. I would like to introduce one or two thoughts about tracing and writing, and to demonstrate, if that's the word, how I see these operating in my own practice. I am not a theoretician, and since whatever passing acquaintanceship with theory I may possess does not amount to any claim of expertise, I must frame my thoughts in a largely intuitive manner. And therefore, since intuition can benefit enormously from commentary, I hope that you will all feel free to open up anything I say to further discussion.

When I traced that "comic boat," what could we imagine I meant to do? What can we imagine a tracing to be: a form of writing? And what does it mean to write: what is writing?

It would seem that we are situated to a great degree by tense—past, present, and future. We think in terms of historical modality. It matters

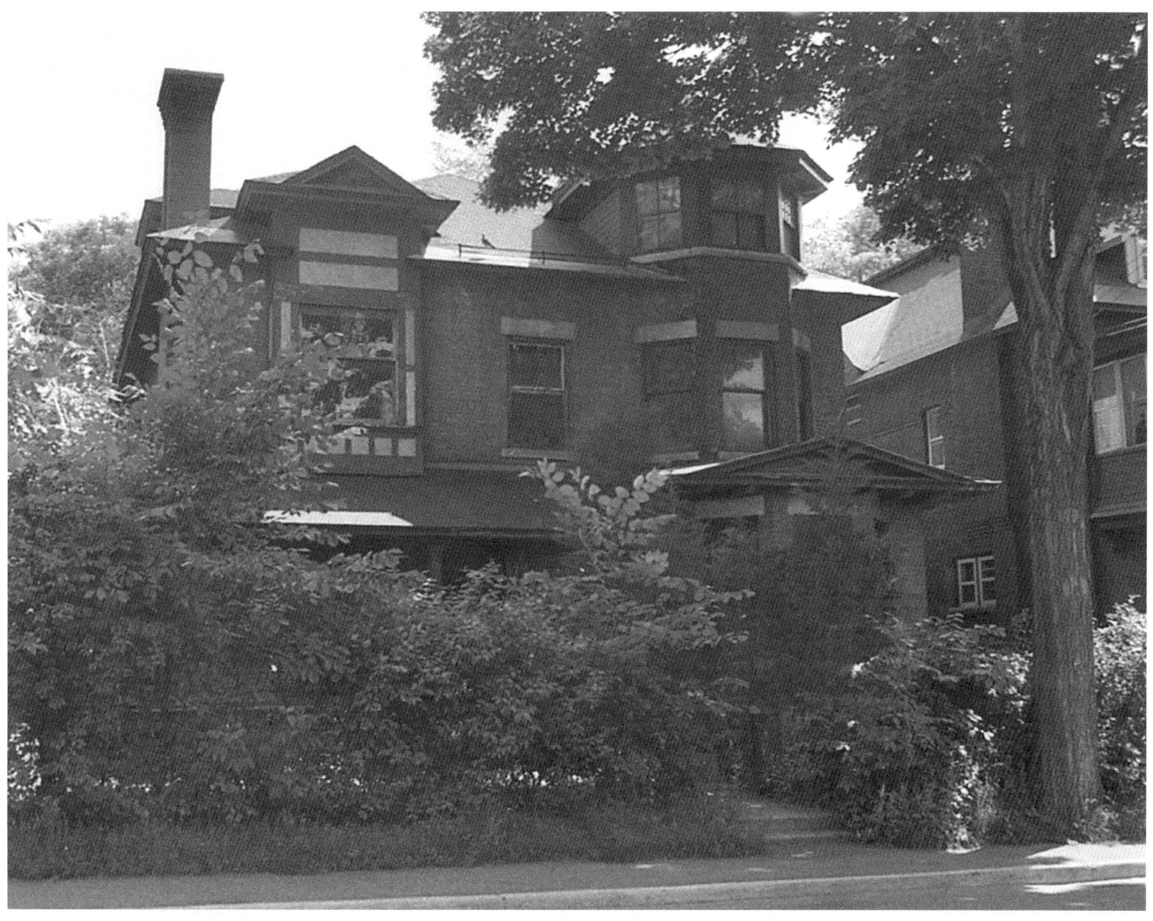

4.15   11 Blackburn Avenue, Ottawa, ca. 1975. Photo courtesy of the artist.

what tense I am in. This might not seem so difficult. We tend to imagine ourselves as acting in the Present, while having a memory of having been in the Past, and looking vaguely forward to being in the Future. Mostly, that is, we are absorbed by the present. An autographic gesture, an invention, an original intuition—all these insist on the stability, the primacy of the present tense, and through it, on what Michael Fried has termed "presentness," the trans-historical implosive experience of an eternal present. Art, for many, and in many different configurations, exists in just this "present" Present, and it is for us to cohere ourselves within it, to stabilize ourselves long enough in order to align ourselves with that perpetual moment.

But the past and the future are not so simply displaced—and neither is art, nor are we, so stable that the present is uninflected. What, then, can we imagine a tracing to be? In Derrida's reference to an engraving, I note the insistence in the trace on the instability, the contingency of the present, on the fluidity of the tense—under tension—in which the past and the future merge in the determination of "that which is to have been traced." Further, this instability, it seems, precludes the possibility of singularity. Why? Because under the sign of trace there is an expectation, a logic of momentum or mobility which draws us, we could say, to trace that which we anticipate having revealed not once, but a thousand times—an insistence that is even infinite in its proportions or quantifiability—as completely invested in the necessity of repetition as it is disinvested in the possibility of singularity. Our alignment is therefore not with a perpetual moment, but with a moment in perpetual transcription. Not with the absolute and perfect stability of presentness, but with the shifts, the minute failures—the history—of variance.

This insistence on disclosure carries, we could therefore also say, a vertiginous quality of divestment, a verge to the body, to the intimacy of the body experienced as the nakedness of touch. To trace is to touch the other in the extension of the self, reaching out to trace, to make a tracing, of that which exists (already) to be traced. To trace is to experience the *jouissance* of touch. To trace is to re-experience the feminine.

I suggested earlier that tracing, the act of touching the traceable, of delineating its form, might be a form of writing. Perhaps it would be more accurate to say instead that it is a form *for* writing. Derrida's suggestion that "we say 'writing' for all that gives rise to an inscription in general" is, I believe, a conflation. When I rushed to show that tracing to my mother, I had already shifted, at the point of completing the tracing, from tracing to writing, from "that which will have been written" to writing as "that which will have been read." I had shifted from a paradigm of touching—touching the sign—to a paradigm of demonstration—demonstrating that sign which we will recognize as a consequence of the demonstration. I shifted, we could say, from the Future Past of writing to the Future Past of reading, from a practice—tracing—to be undertaken in a Present with only a future, to a theory to be comprehended in a Future with only a past.

Unfortunately, as is so often the case, this theory that lay dormant in the tracing I showed my mother was in that instance swiftly rejected. But rejection is no cause for resignation, and I suspect that my subsequent curiosity, if not actual fascination, with grammar in school was a continuation of my concern with how things are to be placed in the world. What leads to a value distinction between a copy and an original, between things with a past and things with a future? In the course of time this leads to entertaining such arcane interests as the suggestion, in the quotation I have taken from Derrida, that the trace is the principal agency through which we establish meaning, that meaning is therefore always both relational and deferred, and that under the sign of writing we can therefore discern the sign of trace. Writing, then, is in particular an effect of the trace; it is the trace as "that which will have been desired" projected onto reading as "that which we were desiring, now revealed as that which we will have desired." What in the act of tracing is potential becomes in the act of writing a form of exhaustion.

This insistence on exhaustion carries, in my experience, a divestment as well, though one that is not so much vertiginous as analytical. Rather, it is the divestment of touch—and the materiality of the sign—in favour of virtuality and the sign's meaning-effects. Writing, as against tracing, produces not the intimate interactivity of potential, but the separateness of coherence, however multivalent and deferred it may prove to be. To write is to anticipate the completion of comprehension. To write is to experience the *jouissance* of finality. To write is to re-experience the masculine.

At this point, I'd like to remind ourselves that what I have just expressed as difference—tracing and writing—cannot be maintained as difference. To reiterate—inherent in writing is the trace; without the trace there is no writing. Yet equally the trace cannot be traced without becoming an inscription—that is to say, writing. Implicit, then, in my remarks has been the suggestion that artmaking is inevitably inscribed within acts of touching and virtuality, materiality and infinity, intimacy and separation—experiences that we can also assemble, I have implied, under the general sign of gender and sexuality.

If I am then talking about "writing art" as a linkage between tracing and reading, I am addressing art as an event-structure, an engagement inevitably caught up in the relation of one to another. I have sketched out an idea of how I picture this in terms of tense, or narrative, and the mobility of time. There is another essential dimension of mobility which I'd like now to frame, and that involves the dimension of space. It is this which allows me to employ the term architecture, and I would like to apply it in terms of "passage," which is also for me the question of sculpture.

The Victorian house on Blackburn Avenue was a study in interlocking separations. To a small child, it represented spatially the experience of time—the possibility of being here and there, now and then, caught in ever-shifting and delightfully surprising, perhaps even erotic, recognitions. Doors opened and closed, worlds disappeared, only to return. Doors defined the house, and it is the door, it occurs to me, that represents the fulcrum for our concept of architecture. With a certain insouciant exuberance almost twenty years ago I remarked in a catalogue entry for an exhibition,

3   Terry Eagleton, *Literary Theory: An Introduction* (London: Blackwell Publishers Ltd., 1983), 185.

personal image for social space, that "buildings as objects are simply design problems; buildings as internal space are complexities of human history." It is our passage through space, which is also a passage through time, that sets the terms of experience in architecture and sculpture. More critically, it is the provision of a passage of return, an entry and exit, that describes the spatial narrative we require. Architecture's power lies in its allegorical replication of the maze, and Ariadne's thread is the key to architecture as a redemptive process of self-identification. Our narrative demands on sculpture are no different. We seek out what we know we must find: our point of return. For just this reason, Baudelaire wrote his famous 1846 essay on why he found sculpture "boring." His point was that sculpture provides no fixed reference and is consequently passive and subject to the whim of a viewer's intentions. I believe he was too resistant to sculpture's form to discern sculpture's logic. Of course, we, the viewer, will indeed inevitably provide our own vantage point—it may in fact be multiple—the one we will use to define the work and thereby fix its forms for us. But those forms only mark the elements of a journey and the furthest reach from which we can and must return. As with architecture, sculpture's power rests not in its forms but in the passage of return it forms. It is the assurance of that return which motivates sculpture's point of reference in the narrative of desire we set out to seek. And it is the rehearsal of this narrative, not a fixation on the forms themselves, that we act out in every coffee-table art book and art history textbook we treasure.

At the risk of being entirely speculative, I have an idea about this derived from Freud's description of the fort/da game. Again, we probably all know this one, but to be brief let me simply quote Terry Eagleton's summary in his book *Literary Theory*:

> Watching his grandson playing in his pram one day, Freud observed him throwing a toy out of the pram and exclaiming *fort* (gone away), then hauling it in again on a string to the cry of *da!* (here). This, the famous fort-da game, Freud interpreted in *Beyond the Pleasure Principle* as the infant's symbolic mastery of his mother's absence; but it can also be read as the first glimmerings of narrative…In Lacanian theory, it is an original lost object—the mother's body—which drives forward the narrative of our lives, impelling us to pursue substitutes for this lost paradise in the endless metonymic movement of desire. For Freud, it is a desire to scramble back to a place where we cannot be harmed.[3]

I am suggesting that our passage through space—in architecture or sculpture—provides us with the passage of fort to da, or to be more exact, da to fort to da (here to there to here), as a necessary spatial resolution of our narrative of desire. In the case of sculpture, whether object-based or installational, this passage adheres in its free availability to access which allows us as viewer to assert our own unconscious requirement to, as Lewis Carroll helpfully put it, "begin at the beginning and work towards the end"—which will, of course, always be where we began, though never quite.

We have, therefore, a structure that exhibits characteristics both of sexuality (understood as the play of desire) and of writing (understood as the play of narrative)—which is perhaps to say that in fact these terms embrace a commonality—certainly a position we could connect with Lacan's observation, as I understand it, that in the unconscious, our sexuality is structured as a language. In this we can read the outlines of that other temporal "space" I have previously discussed in terms of tense. In its writing, art, like architecture, betrays the narrative trace of our desire. In its reading, art provides us a rehearsal of that play that returns us, through its variations and its instabilities, to the trace.

Why, you might ask, should I be concerned with all this? It may have seemed that a lot is being made of rather fine arguments whose validity may therefore seem specious. It may be, in fact it probably is the case, that the argument I have made here is faulty. However, I can say that my purpose has been to attempt an understanding for myself that would integrate our so-called aesthetic experience—our intuition that there is something specific about the experience—with other experiences that many might consider to be irrelevant to it. There is always unease that aesthetic experience becomes too much subsumed, even contaminated, by such superfluous discourse. We know that contemporary theory has supported an intertextuality linking discourses. I have found this, even to the limited degree of my familiarity, enormously productive in its significant reflection of, and contribution to, how I find myself in the world. These short notes today represent a preliminary personal application of such linkage by looking once again at the specificity of my experience—returning to my own history for a defining anecdote—through which to unwrap, if not a "deep structure," then perhaps a motivating mechanism that may suggest at least a genealogical commonality between aesthetic production and the formulations of identity. Like my anecdote, it may of course only be a story. In practice, only a theory.

Partners (2004)

Written as a review of Ydessa Hendeles's exhibition *Partners* at
Haus der Kunst, Munich, November 7, 2003 to February 15, 2004.
Unpublished.

> Baby, let me be
> Your lovin' teddy bear
> Put a chain around my neck.
> And lead me anywhere
> Oh, let me be
> Your teddy bear.
> Elvis Presley, "Teddy Bear" (1957)

Imagine this. It is evening in Munich on November 5 at Haus der Kunst,
Adolf Hitler's former Haus der *Deutschen* Kunst, whose opening exhibition
in 1937 notoriously sought to discredit modern art as *Entartete Kunst*, the
title of Hitler's now infinitely more memorable *salon des refusés*. You are here
at the preview opening of the exhibition *Partners*, work collected by and
curated for this very particular place by Ydessa Hendeles, the internationally respected collector-curator of international contemporary art based in
Toronto, Canada. Ydessa Hendeles, born Jewish in 1948 in Marburg, the
only child of Holocaust survivors who left shortly after for Canada.

Standing for over an hour, you have listened patiently through the
introductory addresses whose claims have sought to reclaim the history
of this place. Suddenly a surprise guest is announced, and onto the stage
bounds none other than Elvis himself to sing three—exactly three—of his
classic songs. Within seconds, as you look around, the entire room is moving to the rhythms, and ahead, past three women who have linked arms and
are singing to the lyrics, you watch Ydessa dancing to Elvis in the arms of
his impersonator.

It is not possible in the space of this very short review to even begin
to delineate the intricate complexities of Ydessa Hendeles's astonishingly
conceived and executed response to the history of the twentieth century.
With implacable precision, Hendeles tracks that history through implications to be found in works by sixteen artists, including Jeff Wall, Maurizio
Cattelan, Giulio Paolini, James Coleman, Hanne Darboven, and Bruce
Nauman, to name a few, and through two remarkable projects of Ydessa's
own, one of which lends its title to the exhibition. *Partners (The Teddy Bear*

Project) occupies two galleries transformed into a "teddy bear museum" of historical photographs—hundreds on hundreds of them—each a depiction of a child or adult with their "teddies." Collectively they overwhelm with their pathos and the sheer weight of their unspoken human stories. And

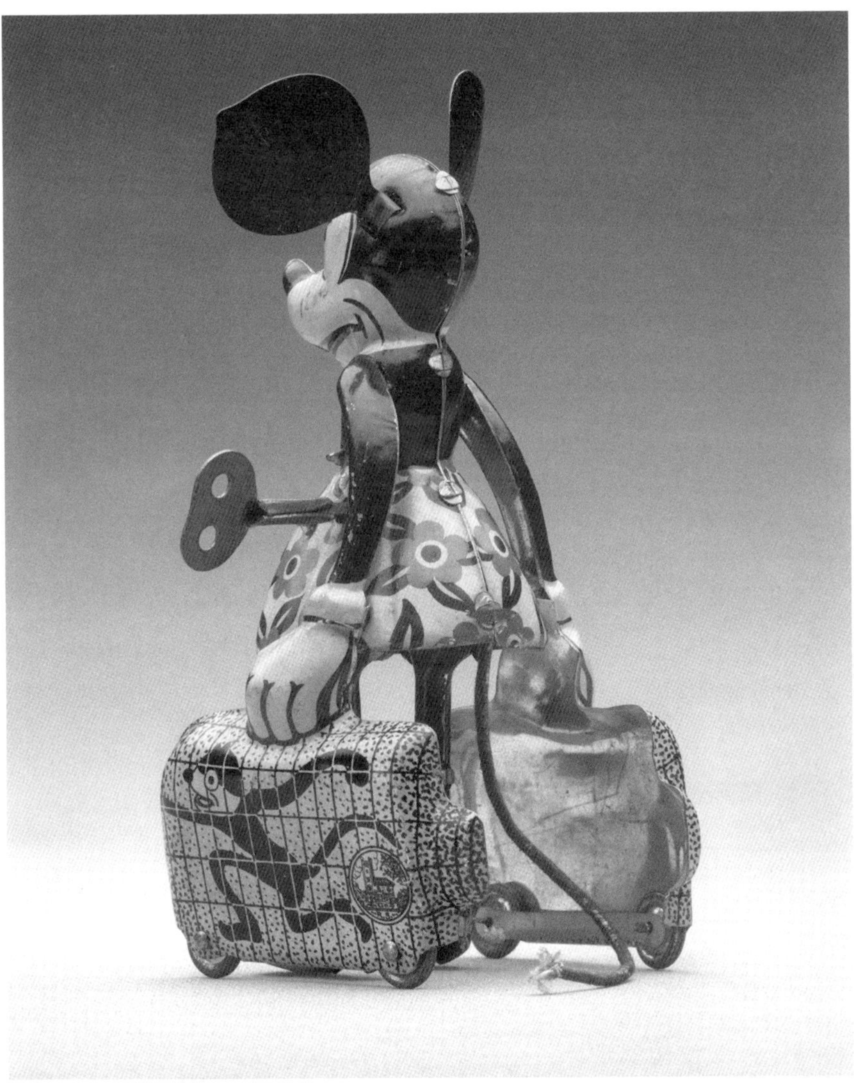

4.16 *Minnie Mouse Carrying Felix in Cages*, R.S. (La Isla Toys), Spain, ca. 1926–36. Lithographed tin plate, key-wind clockwork toy, 17.8 cm in height. From the exhibition *Partners*, Haus der Kunst, Munich, November 7, 2003 to February 15, 2004. Photo: Robert Keziere, © Ydessa Hendeles Art Foundation.

in resonance with this reminder of those other unspoken stories, *Partners* holds a sting: beyond its galleries of once-living children and their teddies, facing away from us in solitary isolation within a gallery from which one can only return, kneels the winsomely slight figure of a strange boy whose old-fashioned Sunday-best manner of dress and supplicating gesture recalls an effort at redemption, but whose face, when you discover it, is the face of Hitler himself, caught in a timeless grimace of grim determination. A grimace whose intensity, framed against the images of human longing and compassion behind him, casts him here as none other than Lucifer, God's repudiated Other.

I have not yet even mentioned the vintage toy figure of Minnie Mouse we first encountered as we entered. Minnie, almost literally brushing past us with Felix the cat safely captured in the suitcases she grips firmly in her two hands. But unfortunately it must suffice here to record only two thoughts that occurred to me that night. The first is that the exhibition must be viewed as a map. Ydessa speaks about her exhibition in terms of "passages"—three, to be exact. Passage: to book a passage; to follow a passage; to find a passage—there are many "passages" to define. And that triggers the second thought: this exhibition is constructed as not simply a map, but more significantly as a maze—*a trap*, even—with but a single possibility for escape: to retrace one's steps, *to double back*. Three passages, but only one return.

And the impersonator? He is, after all, Elvis's only chance at that return. His only chance to escape—and once again to sing and dance.

Notes on a Potato, Grade Nine Physics Class, 1954 (2006)

Presented at Big Talk Conference, "Rethinking Boundaries in Art and Design Education," Ontario College of Art and Design (now OCAD University), April 28, 2006.

Grade nine physics class, 1954. The teacher has set a hollowed-out potato in a dish of water, and I'm astonished as I watch the water vanish from the dish and reappear in the potato. I'm told this magic act is called osmosis, and I have to tell you, it became a great comfort to me as I struggled through my schooling and the admonitions of teachers that I seemed inattentive. Something must surely be gained, I told myself. Call it osmosis. I treasured my possession of the word. I still do.

I didn't set out to teach art. I am in fact trained as a library cataloguer. I always liked libraries. While studying modern history at Queen's University, I looked forward to sitting—standing, even—for hours in the dimly lit stacks of the Douglas Library, a wintry daylight barely penetrating the gothic windows. That's where I discovered *Lolita*. Nabokov lent a certain extra dimension to my determination that libraries were the place to be.

I did set out to make art. I didn't really know what art was, but I knew how to draw. Much follows from knowing how to draw.

Why am I telling you this? I have, a bit to my surprise, now taught at this college for longer than I normally count, but let's just say since 1975. While I do not consider myself expert in the pedagogical discourse that is increasingly a central concern of contemporary college life, I am also aware that the demands on postsecondary education now are increasingly complex and run the risk of overwhelming that sense of larger accomplishment without which no activity can provide the satisfaction of a confident contribution. I would therefore like to reflect on a personal trajectory, employing it as one person's witness to those demands and the responses that seemed to pose choices that, however contingently, have assisted me in working out criteria that got me through the day.

Of course, every art librarian's favourite Duchamp quotation is that he enjoyed working in the library, in his case the Bibliotheque nationale in Paris. Mentally placing Duchamp's encouragement on my desk as a cataloguer working in the bowels of the University of Toronto library system, my first criterion for getting through the day was not to look at the clock. Instead, I immersed myself in the esotericisms locked within disintegrating nineteenth-century German doctoral dissertations, and how to make cataloguing sense of them so all that ingenuity and desperate individual effort would continue to find a dedicated mind. I wasn't thinking about art, but I was thinking about commitment.

Later I did think about art, because I committed myself to its study here at OCA, as OCAD was then known. But before I detail some main threads of that experience, I want to pause and note the significance of one of this conference discussion points, the matter of interdisciplinary permeability. I enjoyed both my studies in modern history and my studies in library science (as it was then somewhat modestly called—it is now more ambitiously referred to as information science). And I have become used to declaring myself an artist, though I'm suspicious of nouns and would prefer to say I like to re-present things in the world. This usually just confuses people, however. But the idea of an artist is for me inseparable from the idea of history and of the classification systems that define the internal boundaries of knowledge. It is the very permeability of this network that provides the possibility for me to be "an artist." And, I would add the obvious footnote, those particular permeabilities are only the beginning. Permeability breeds curiosity, and curiosity knows no bounds.

Most of you probably know that in the early 1970s OCA had a madcap moment of interdisciplinarity in the brief regime of Roy Ascott, the first named president of the college (before Ascott, OCA was run by a principal). That disaster delayed things, and permeability was largely redefined as a game of musical chairs for disaffected faculty groups. But some several years later another President, David Hall-Humpherson, initiated a rethinking of the college's structure that in due course substituted programs for the existing departments. The results were mixed—departments and faculty familiarities die hard—but the principle inserted an important linguistic premise: that the college was a single entity and its courses were available to all, at least theoretically. Programs, unlike departments, are built on constellations of interest, not on ownership. An example of what this made possible can be found in both the Sculpture/Installation program and the Criticism and Curatorial program, neither of which were possible so long as courses were owned by departments since neither program could overnight claim sufficient registration to fund the courses they would have required. As programs they didn't have to: those courses were for the most part already taught in the college.

Let's linger on that phrase "constellations of interest." As one of the panels implied, the studio as a teaching concept has been radically redefined over the last several years. In its original form, it occupied central place in the art school; in fact it was the art school, and the art school was primarily artisanal in complexion. A student in the studio learned to make things, traditionally under the tutelage of a "master artist" and for the purpose of learning "how it was done." In its later, more modern configuration, it became a sort of drop-in centre of experimentation leading to, at least hopefully, a laboratory of the avant-garde. In either case, the studio was directed almost exclusively at the *making* of art. The discussion of what this making was all about was not the province of the artist, but that of the critic or curator, art historian, collector, or dedicated public. This is no longer an adequate definition of the studio. Why? we can ask.

On the theoretical level, the literature is enormous, but perhaps it can be summed up by a cultural retreat from the individual as the locus of authority, and we have seen the concept of original authorship as a *deus ex machina* fade to a teasing smile reminiscent of Lewis Carroll's Cheshire cat. If the studio has remained the primary site of art's discourse, it is because the studio now only makes sense if it is the site of critical discussion and debate, a debate in which the student must now answer not simply to their technical or formal skill, nor only to their individualistically determined path, but to how both of those qualities intersect with history itself. The studio, in other words, is the pedagogical crucible in which debate is centred, and out of which a practice is forged.

About this word "practice." I mean by it that the studio is not a place simply to make individual works of art any more than this is how we would understand the career of a professional artist or designer. Rather, it is the platform for a student's insertion into—and contribution to—the discourses of contemporary art and design. It is a place in which to evolve a methodology that will define the student's contributions to her or his field. Yes, students are expected to bring their individual histories and abilities to the studio and its productions. But the studio, whose teaching model we might describe as a discriminating practice of discursivity embracing both the instructor and the student collective, brings context and an interrogation of definition to bear on those productions. No production without a function. No function without a direction.

Consequently, while I am suggesting that the contemporary studio is central within this constellation of interest, as I have called it, that constellation involves realms of equivalence each of which is charged with bringing certain crucial recognitions to bear on the various facets of intellectual experience that coalesce in the student's evolving direction. The charge is a serious one, and for it to work the key issues must be both the institution's supervision of the individual student's particular interests and the instructor's sensitivity to those interests in the subject delivery. Only then do these constellations cohere for the student.

It would be foolhardy to legislate frameworks for others. I can say for myself, however accidentally they emerged, that the study of history and of library science provided dual mechanisms by which, on the one hand, to guard against my own cultural biases, and on the other hand, to recognize the degree to which knowledge and experience are contingently defined forms. Those forms are both boundaries and opportunities. The conference panels have considered some, and roughly speaking, they are four: cultural, disciplinary, perceptual, and responsive. Whether boundary or opportunity becomes a matter of presentation—and apprehension.

Nor have I forgotten about a certain potato in grade nine physics class in 1954.

On Authenticity (2006)

Presented at the Art Gallery of Alberta, Edmonton, October 5, 2006.

My practice is not as a photographer, though I have—as you will see—deployed photographic and filmic images, and the discourse of photography (insofar as it merges with the discourse of art in general) has impacted considerably on my work.

This impact has reflected the fact that the photographic image has normally been seen as true or "real" (as opposed to, for instance, a drawn or painted image) and therefore a form of documentary. This relationship with photography reflects my own studies in history—a discourse based upon the document—which I pursued previous to the decision to train and practice as an artist.

In both photography and history, the question of authenticity arises as a central dilemma of judgment: how can we judge the "truth" or value of something if we cannot be sure of the authentic nature of the statement, whether one of origin or one of commentary?

This question immediately produces another: what, in fact, is authenticity? It's a question that lies at the heart of much of the critical discussion concerning cultural transformations over the last half-century or more.

In my own work, one component of authenticity has been of particular interest. That is the matter of authority—or we might say the status of the "author"—and the larger issues of identity and identification. A corollary and centrally important question, to which I will return, is to ask by what routes do we produce or adhere to the authority of an image?

Earlier I noted that judgments of value depend themselves on judgments of authenticity, and that photography's contribution to judgment formation has traditionally reflected the expectation that it delivers a true representation of lived reality; that it is, as it were, a document of history. But the fact that we also know—have known from the beginning (playful misrepresentations using the photographic image go back to the very invention of the medium)—that the fact that this document can be falsified represents a paradox in our conceptual framework.

It is consequently the paradoxical nature of the photographic image's authority—its problematic authenticity—that strikes me as central to our relationship with it. It is, in fact, paradox that we must examine.

The French cultural critic Roland Barthes reminds us that paradox literally means a set of parallel documents—parallel because they do not meet or combine, or are contradictory even, yet nevertheless are linked in the common apprehension of a truth. We both believe in, and reject, the photograph as "real"—and through this we define our relationship to what is real.

If this describes paradox, a natural question arises concerning the functioning of language. The term language, it should be noted, includes all coherent forms of sign systems, including photographic images. To see how language functions, we can turn to the influential semiotic system proposed by the American philosopher C.S. Pierce.

Pierce's system is triadic in that he suggests that the meaning of a sign—an image, for instance—operates on three levels.

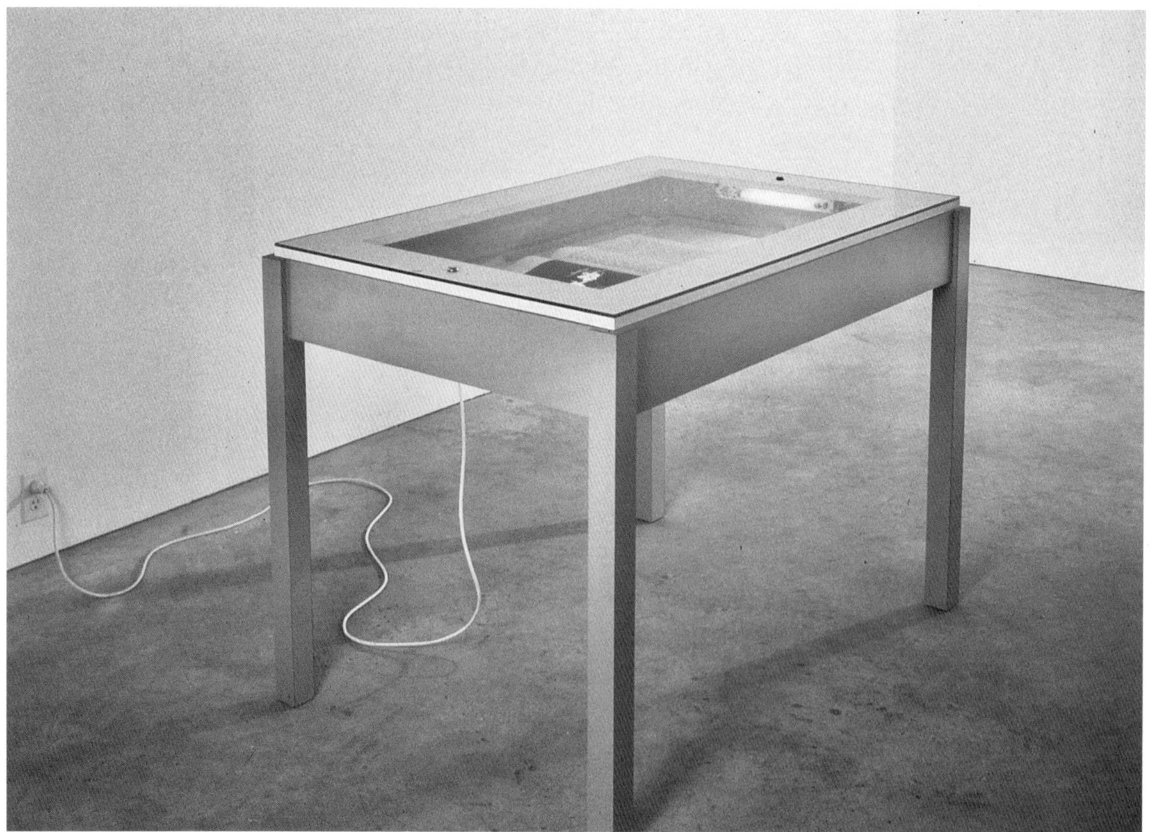

4.17   Ian Carr-Harris, *Narcissus*, 1994. Wood construction vitrine faced with grey plastic laminate, plate glass, 110 vac-light source, fabricated copy of encyclopedia with backlit illustration of Narcissus flower, 123.5 × 100 × 83 cm; book, 68.5 × 47 × 6.5 cm. Installation, Susan Hobbs Gallery, Toronto. Photo: Isaac Applebaum.

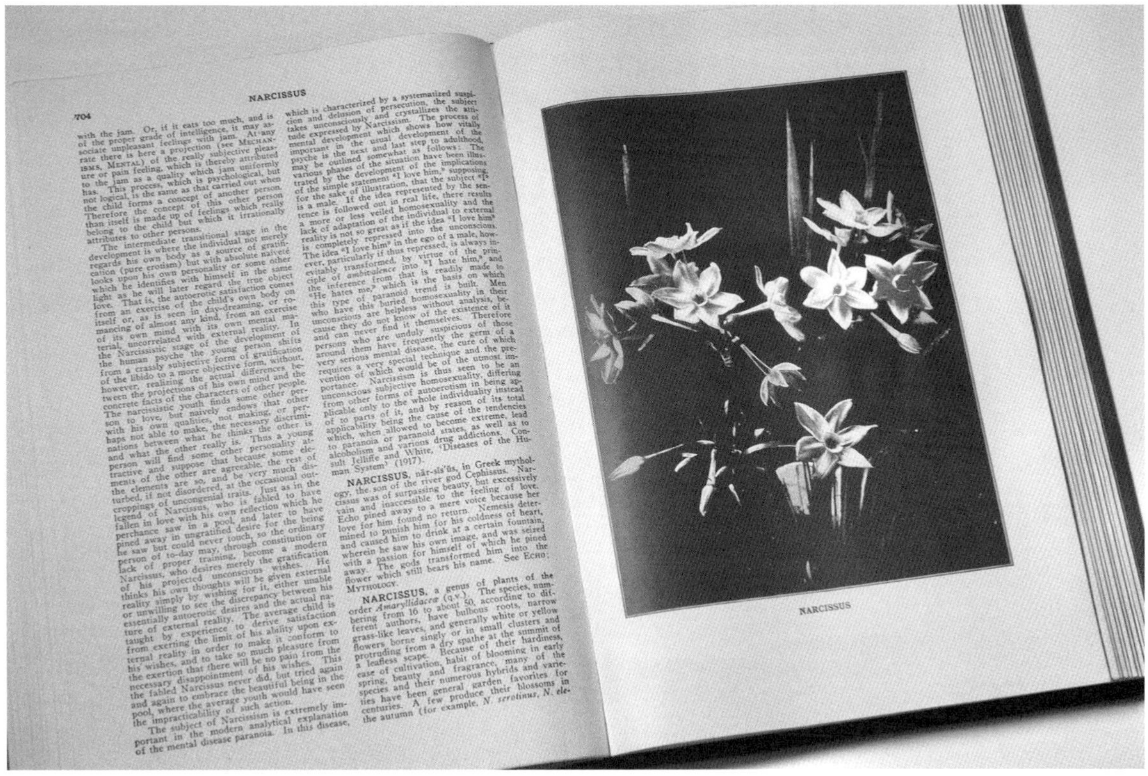

4.18   Ian Carr-Harris, *Narcissus*, 1944. Detail of backlit book. Courtesy the artist.

Let's take the image of the narcissus flower I used in my work of the same name.

The image is clear and whether or not we identify it as a narcissus flower we identify it as a flower, a plant at least. In other words, it's status as a resemblance to something we "know" in the lived world is effortless. In the language of semiotics, it is an *iconic sign*: it acts as an iconic image, or icon for short, and our relationship to this two-dimensional image is drawn from whatever relationships we have to it as a flower.

But we can also have another relationship with the image, not as simply a resemblance to a flower, but in addition as an analogy to something the flower image can signify or index. For instance, as an image on a product, say, it can signify something natural, or pure. It can index, that is, an idea of normal unencumbered or transparent expectation, unsullied as it were. In this mode of the triadic signification, the image of the flower can act *as an index*, indexing "appropriate" or desired decorum.

Yet a third relationship with this image is constituted by convention, including cultural and historical references that are likely to be particular to a given culture or subculture. In the case of the narcissus flower it can be generally assumed that most people in Europe and North America would know that the name of this flower refers to a Greek myth concerning self-involvement, and that the term narcissism is derived from that myth. In this mode of the triadic sign, the image of the flower—underscored by the symbolic written language used to describe it—is purely symbolic. The image of the flower now acts *as a symbol*, and its role as such is entirely dependent on being recognized for its symbolic reference.

For myself, it is precisely this linkage of three modes inherent within the sign system of the photograph that has suggested its authority. More generally, it is within this linkage that the authority of the image retains an appropriate expectation of authenticity in artworks. How do I mean this?

If I were to assume that only the iconic or resemblance mode of the photographic sign underwrote authenticity—truth—I would soon be disenchanted. Resemblance is a trap, since as we know appearances can be deceptive and since as well a literal reference satisfies little besides an acknowledgment of visual recognition. If, however, the photograph's authenticity is not exhausted in its role as an icon but has an extended existence as both index and symbol, then its productivity as a sign is multivalent or layered and can be employed to suggest complexities in our experience that exceed its apparent reference. The authority and authenticity of the image consequently escapes closure.

I want to introduce a second and final reference, this time directed not to linguistic operations only, but to an extended field of meaning production—the matter of how we produce "authentic" meaning—specifically through works of art. The reference is to Roland Barthes's discussion of meaning in Eisenstein's famous film, *Ivan the Terrible* (1944).

Barthes's task is to consider what defines an artwork. Again, he suggests a triadic structure for how meaning coheres. The three levels of meaning-production for Barthes are comprised of:

1. The *literal or communicative level* by which is stated what is referenced. This correlates to Pierce's icon, and in the case of Eisenstein's film the stated reference is the figure of Ivan the Terrible and the plot that represents him to us. We can watch the film confident that we know it is somehow about Ivan the Terrible.

2. The *symbolic level*, by which is implied or demonstrated what is meant in employing the literal reference. This level concentrates on—it questions or interrogates—the content or subject of the work, and this is therefore the level of meaning required for various forms of social instruction or critique. To this extent, the symbolic level is a closed system, closing in on its intended subject.

3 Finally, and crucially, because this is in fact the special arena of the artwork, Barthes defines a third level of meaning he names the *obtuse level*. By this he means that at this level it is not the content of the artwork that is in question, or under interrogation, but the very system or formal means by which the work approaches meaning. This level is an open system, it does not close on anything (it is not a critique of something external to its means of production) but rather it opens the artwork up to a production outside itself (that is, its apparently intended subject) and to this extent it opens itself up to the reader or viewer in whose experience the artwork can be, again, multivalent. It is characteristically produced through fragments, disguises, discontinuations or interruptions, insertions (akin to marginalia in texts or asides in a play), emphases of one kind or another. In a word, it is performative, playful, even audacious or mischievous in its determination to make assertions outside of the formal language of the artwork's production.

Another way of describing this third level by which meaning is constituted in the artwork is to return to Barthes's definition of a paradox—the parallel and contestable or interrogative relationships between two different "documents" or logics operating in the work. The operation is no recent phenomenon. An example can be found in Shakespeare's plays in the form of "comic relief" scenes and peripheral characters (Falstaff or Rosencrantz and Guildenstern) that have little or nothing to do with the plot's advancement or the ideological framing of the play. These scenes and characters embedded within the work consequently produce in the viewer a "paradoxical engagement" that both deepens and frustrates (another word for interrogation) the play's impact upon us.

To summarize these points, two things are notable:

1. The photographic image may be seen as both a triadic sign system and a document comprising three levels of meaning. On both counts, it can be read or experienced paradoxically as operating simultaneously with different and contradictory logics.

2.   Since the image is doubly paradoxical, its authority or authenticity occupies several modes and is produced through a multiplicity of productions. It cannot fail in its authority *precisely because it is paradoxical*. In the end, the authenticity of the photographic image need not be—paradoxically—"photographic."

To conclude, Marcus Miller, by whose invitation I am here this evening, argued in a piece he wrote a while back that, in my work, I cover my tracks like a criminal. In accepting Marcus's invitation to speak in this series, I thought I'd expand on this and admit to the description, admit to the "criminality" exposed in framing paradox.

Theoris: a paradox (2018)

Theoris: a paradox—A User's Guide was published online to accompany the exhibition *Theoris: a paradox* at Susan Hobbs Gallery, Toronto, November 29, 2018 to February 2, 2019. See http://susanhobbs.com/exhibits/1441-theoris-a-paradox.

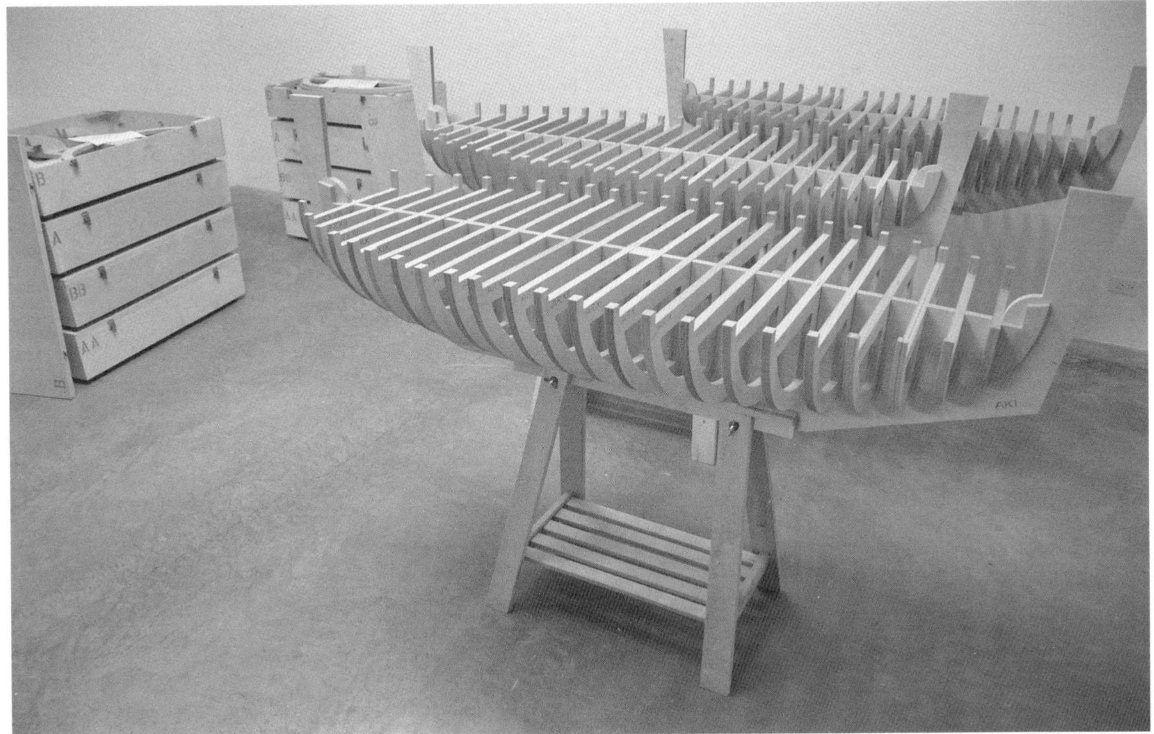

4.19   Ian Carr-Harris, *Theoris: a paradox*, 2018. Four boxes with three ship constructions in laser-cut plywood (as ribs only); boxes in 2 sizes: box #1, 99 × 68.5 × 20.3 cm; box #2, 83.8 × 33 × 24 cm; boxes include the ship constructions, a user's guide, an IKEA Finngard trestle, hardware. Installation dimensions variable. Studio installation image by the artist.

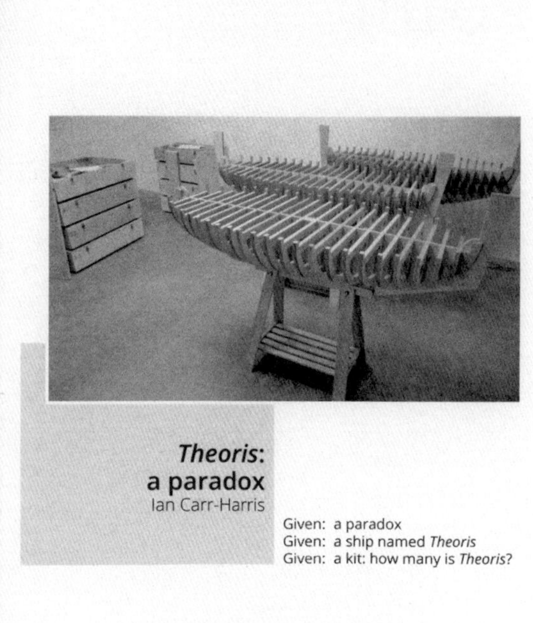

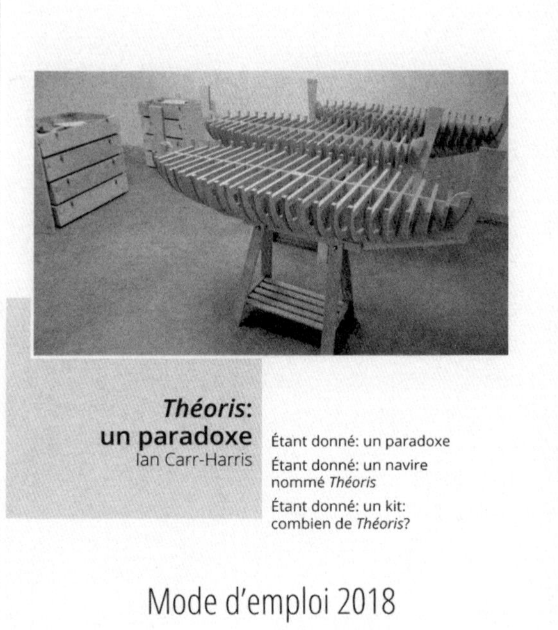

4.20   Ian Carr-Harris, *Theoris: a paradox, User's Guide*, 2018. English and French text, 18 pp., b&w illus., 21.5 × 14 cm. Courtesy the artist.

An introduction to *Theoris*: a paradox

Theseus and the Minotaur
In the mythic telling of Athens's history, King Minos of Crete, in order to avenge the death of his son at the hands of King Aegeas of Athens, extracted a regular tribute of fourteen young men and women to be fed to the Minotaur (the Bull of Minos) in the famous Labyrinth. Eventually, Aegeas's son, Theseus, elects to join the latest tribute in order to slay the Minotaur, sailing with the doomed victims on a ship with black sails. Aided by Ariadne, King Minos's daughter, he succeeds in negotiating the labyrinth and killing the Minotaur. Returning to his ship, the *Theoris* (θεωρίς), he forgets to substitute a white sail for the black as a signal to his father of his success. Seeing the black sail, King Aegeas throws himself into the sea, thus named the Aegean Sea, leaving Theseus to now become King of Athens, free of the fearful tributes to the King of Crete.

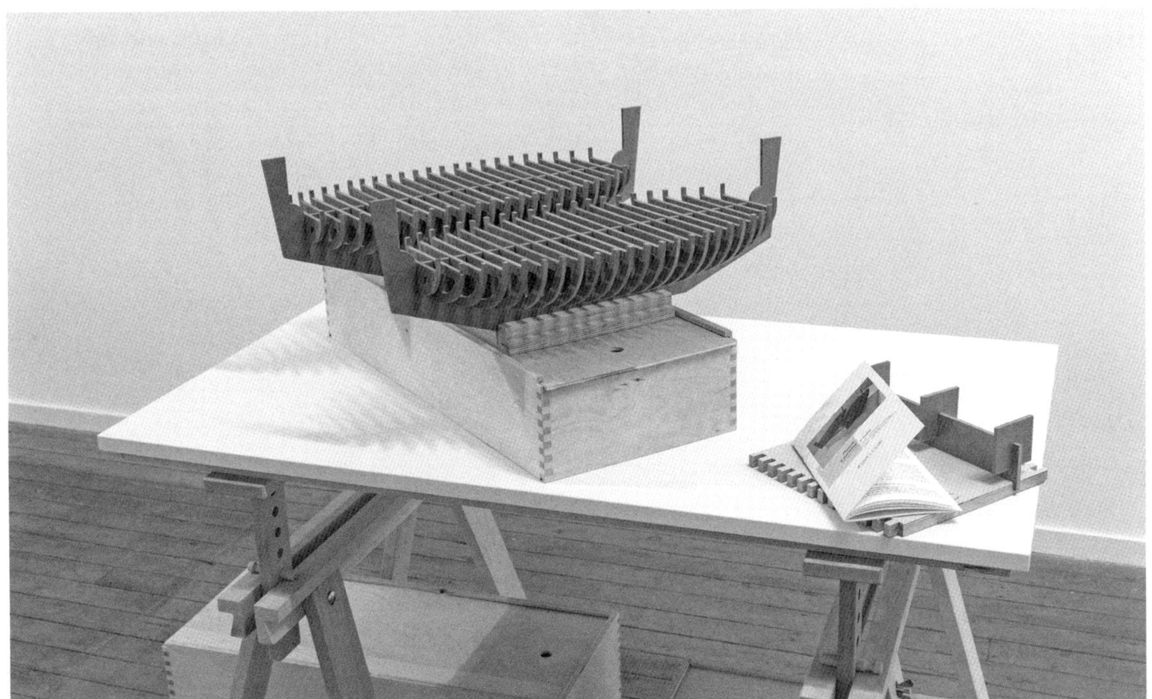

4.21   Ian Carr-Harris, *Theoris: a paradox; a game*, 2018. Two complete models of the ship (ribs only) with stand, each ship in pieces to be assembled to 61 × 20.3 × 5.4 cm, of .5 cm hardboard in a plywood box with sliding lid, user's guide included; box dimensions, 68.6 × 29.2 × 16.5 cm. Installation of assembled game on IKEA Finngard trestle table at Susan Hobbs Gallery, Toronto. Photo: Toni Hafkenscheid.

Athens and the Theorists

Athens had from ancient times participated in annual games to celebrate the god Apollo on the island of Delos, Apollo's birthplace. To honour the memory and celebrate Theseus's victory over the Minotaur, the Athenians had preserved and maintained Theseus's ship, and it was the *Theoris* that carried the embassy each year to Delos. Notably, during the ship's absence from Athens, the city was purified and no execution could be performed. According to the first-century biographer, Plutarch, the *Theoris* remained in service until the time of Aristotle. As can be imagined, the ship—constructed of wood—required constant repairs, to the point that sooner or later not a single scrap of its original fabric remained on the *Theoris*.

Theoris *and the paradox of identity*

Plutarch is credited with reporting on a puzzle discussed by the Greek philosophers Heraclitus and Plato with respect to the identity of Theseus's ship, a puzzle arising from the constant replacement of parts in order to maintain the ship. Is the *Theoris*, in the course of time, still the *Theoris*, or is it no longer? Is it the same ship that Theseus sailed, or something else? At what point could it be said that the ship was—or was not—the same ship?

To this question, the English philosopher Thomas Hobbes added another and related question, or thought experiment. Hobbes speculates that the workers, instead of discarding the material they removed from the *Theoris*, carefully placed it in another area and part by part put the old material together in exactly the same positions as on the ship under repair. At a certain point, *Theoris* would exist in its repaired state as well as in its original unrepaired state. There would therefore be two ships with a legitimate claim to being the *Theoris*. Or, to put it another way, which ship is the *Theoris*, which is Theseus's ship?

Description for *Theoris*: a paradox (2018)

Theoris: a paradox is an artwork designed to offer a material and historical engagement with problems of identity and the nature of our own selfhood. This is further elaborated later in the guide.

Conceived as a paradigm or exemplar for situations in which an appeal to some originating thing or entity runs into complications, the work builds on Plutarch and Hobbes to suggest a further reference to the Infinite Regress, the familiar phenomenon in which one thing leads to another ad infinitum or, as in the case of the mirror, the image that repeats itself to infinity.

Paradigms are examples serving as a model or pattern that coheres the idea of a thing in such a way that it can be used to effect action. Paradigms are what we learn in school as models of definition, articulation, and even moral behaviour. Paradigms are what we buy when we go to a toy store and we pick up a plastic model of the Titanic, a Harley Davidson motorcycle, or some such iconic object. We usually call such a paradigm a kit.

Simply put, the work is structured as a kit comprising the parts required to build a model of the ship that would answer to its evasion of a stable entity. The kit consists of four individual models contained in eight boxes. Each model requires two boxes in order to distribute the weight of the ship and the IKEA trestle that supports the ship in the installation. The few tools needed to assemble the models are also included.

A Brief Guide to Paradoxes

We are all drawn to magic, and a paradox is like a magic act. When the rabbit is triumphantly pulled from the hat, we applaud the spectacle precisely because there is a trick. And that trick has made us think or question how it was performed. The rabbit's appearance appears to be a simple act of being pulled from the hat. And the hat appears to be just a hat. But the conclusion that there was a rabbit lurking in the magician's hat seems preposterous. Unacceptably absurd. Hilarious, of course.

More soberly, Mark Sainsbury, a philosopher of language, has remarked that a paradox can be defined "as an apparently unacceptable conclusion derived by apparently acceptable reasoning from apparently acceptable premises,"[1] and the analytical philosopher Willard Quine adds that "a paradox is just any conclusion that at first sounds absurd, but that has an argument to sustain it."[2] The tired rabbit has launched the search for a compelling argument for its surprising appearance.

But we are not finished with our unfortunate rabbit. Related to the paradox is the concept of antinomy, which the eighteenth-century philosopher Immanuel Kant employed to identify limitations to reasoning, and when claims to truth are justified or not justified. Examples of antinomy can be readily found. The frequently used phrase "There is no absolute truth" can be considered an antinomy due to its suggestion that there is indeed an absolute truth since it simultaneously proclaims to be one itself. There is an ancient Greek paradox that similarly engages this antinomy: "I am a rabbit. All rabbits are liars. Therefore I am a liar." There is no way of trusting the speaker's statements—for the sentence to be true, it must be false, and vice versa. Do we in fact have here a rabbit? Is this rabbit for real?

The magician's greatest feat is to investigate the degree to which we can trust our senses when what our eyes see appears to defy their logic. The magic performed intercedes with our normal ability to trust cause

1   R.M. Sainsbury, *Paradoxes*, 3rd ed. (Cambridge: Cambridge University Press, 2009), 1.

2   W.V. Quine, *The Ways of Paradox and Other Essays*, rev. and enlarged ed. (Cambridge, MA: Harvard University Press, 1976), 1.

and effect, to trust our power to reason. We are induced into a realm of doubt. We are forced to depend on a form of faith—that somehow there is a rational explanation, an obscure cause-effect relationship that remains for the time being at any rate inexplicable. While eventually an explanation may be provided, in the moment of the performance and the paradox of a live rabbit pulled from a hat, what we have experienced we call art.

The French writer and critic Roland Barthes, in discussing the film stills of Russian filmmaker Sergei Eisenstein, makes a distinction between three levels of meaning. The first and second have to do, respectively, with simple or informational meaning on the one side, and symbolic or referential meaning on the other. But it is the third level of meaning that produces the experience we can associate with magic, and with art. This level he calls "obtuse" for the fact that it defies obvious analysis—it is the level at which the representation cannot be represented. This, Barthes suggests, is where meaning interrogates itself, is open to masquerade, disguise and derision, the level of discontinuity, of the erotic, of operating between the suture and the fissure of meaning. It is performative, often comedic. Its operation is paradox, informed by the root meanings of the word: from the Greek prefix *para-* (beside, against) and *doxa* (knowledge, especially common knowledge). In effect, "unexpected" or "incredible." Like a magic act.

An equation of sorts could be constructed that links together doubt and paradox through a series of terms that invite the consequences of both. This equation might look like this:

Doubt—uncertainty—ambiguity—ambivalence—resistance—critique—transgression—comedy—*Paradox*—uncertainty—ambiguity—comedy—ambivalence—resistance—critique—transgression—*Doubt*

A particular example of a paradox that centres on doubt is the concept of the Infinite Regress. We are familiar with its visual phenomenon, the receding image in opposed mirrors. But it is easiest to appreciate the problem it poses by using a simple example. In an infinite chain of the same ship, let us say, the question must be which is the "first or original ship"? But there is no first ship in an infinite chain. Consequently, there is no chain based on a first ship—the chain is an illusion and does not in fact exist. The very existence of the ship is in doubt to the point that it is impossible to conceive. It remains paradoxical in the sense that despite our belief in its existence, it cannot exist.

The example is of course the Ship of Theseus itself, a ship lost in the mists of myth and storytelling. The question of the ship's real existence, that is the "original" ship Theseus is said to have sailed, remains in doubt. That there was a ship historically ascribed to the mythical hero is not in doubt. But the reality of the ship must be deemed suspect. If both Theseus and his ship are imaginary, the ship that was brought into port to be fixed must have been brought into port in an infinity of time. Taken at the level of the Infinite Regress, it must be concluded that there never was a *Theoris*, and that no image or structure purporting to be the *Theoris* can exist.

But of course the ship does exist as an idea, and here it runs into the paradox of its materiality. It must be repaired to be able to exist. But in the thought experiment, the *Theoris* starts to multiply. How many times need it be repaired, and how many identical *Theorises* must result? There are compelling arguments for two different conclusions: that both ships are one and the same—the original ship *Theoris*—or that they are not the same, or that in fact it doesn't even exist at all! We are left therefore with a dilemma.

Dilemmas are products of identification and the attempt to assign fixed identity to things, whether objects or ourselves. In the case of the Ship of Theseus paradox, there is an opposition between identities—the identities of the two ships. In the paradox, the attempt to assign identity is frustrated by the dichotomous character of the arguments: that there can be a resolution of the confusion based on an "is/is not" structure. One resolution proposed—the so-called Four-Dimensionalist position—argues that with the element of time built into the paradox, the ship remains numerically identical to itself despite the fact that the ship's individual moments-in-time, or time-slices of itself, differ from each other. The ship remains numerically identical to itself across time.

A further argument takes the position that the two ships can trace their identity to an original and are as such identical with one another—they are a single ship existing in two locations at the same time. This argument is based in the transitive relations of equivalence: A (the original ship) = B (the repaired ship) and A (the original ship) = C (the unrepaired ship) such that B (the repaired ship) = C (the unrepaired ship). Then again, a counter argument against this position is that while both ships are identical to the original ship that came into dry dock, they are not identical to one another. This argument, however, is complicated by its denial of a key logical concept—transitive relations.

As these arguments may suggest, paradoxes produce arguments. A paradox like the Ship of Theseus produces arguments that produce arguments—which is to say that a resolution that would produce a winning argument does not arise. While an unresolved paradox might clearly threaten our trust in reason, this would be a mistaken assumption. Like our failure to understand why the magician was able to pull a rabbit from the hat, our failure to resolve the paradox incites a curiosity about meaning and its construction. The Ship of Theseus conundrum reveals much about how we understand the identity of a physical object, but more broadly it invites us into the realm of argument and the search for justified belief. There have been many coherent attempts to resolve the paradox, both commonsensical and philosophical. None have ended the debate, and this is the tantalizing value of a paradox: what is achieved is the realization that there are many ways in which to view a problem—the problem is in effect a mirror to ourselves.

Another interesting venture into the paradox of identity is Jorge Luis Borges's story "Pierre Menard, Author of the *Quixote*." In Borges's story, the fictional writer, Pierre Menard, sets out to rewrite Cervantes's famous novel line by line, to "translate" it into a contemporary mode. After a lifetime of labour, he succeeds only in finishing a part of his project. But what is notable to those who read his draft is the fact that it is line by line identical to the Cervantes. We are assured, however, that it is indeed a new and exciting version of Cervantes book. Why? Because Menard's rewriting came with his greater experience of world events subsequent to Cervantes writing in the seventeenth century. The new "Don Quixote," while identical to the original in every respect, nonetheless is different for the fact that its rewriting occurs centuries later. To the reader of Menard's rewriting, the novel would be infused with allusions not available to Cervantes. So, two books, each an "original," both one and the same—and different.

Harvard psychologist Daniel Gilbert has remarked that "human beings are works in progress that mistakenly think they are finished." The mistake in question arises from language itself, specifically the verb "to be." When I say, "It is" or "I am," I freeze that entity—an object, or my selfhood—in time. All the processes that engage the object or myself are eliminated and a false version of identity is constructed. Is the Cervantes I experience today the same Cervantes I experienced a decade ago? Who am I at any one time, and am I different at another time? What would constitute an original me, and how do my present and future selves relate to that original, if indeed I could ever hope to recapture it? If I am a copy of that original, how many copies have constructed my present self? Paradoxes, positioned not on the verb "to be," but on the verb "to become," direct us to consider not ourselves, but ourselves in transition. The *Theoris* not as it is but as it is in its becoming.

Where does an artwork come from? Does it have an origin or some influential event or model by which its identity can be traced? Can it be registered on a scale of productions that suggest a pattern or trajectory?

The work for which this guide is made can be seen as part of a history of works that investigate knowledge—how we come to it, what it is we find within it, what we do with it. In the course of examining that history, we could isolate a number of elements that have become principal strategies for individual productions. The blackboard, for instance, directs our attention to the acquisition of language and the complexity of linguistic structures:

the alphabet, the building block of articulation, tenses, which open up time, nouns and verbs, which enable the subject's active relationship to the world of things and other subjects, and speech—the means by which to communicate meaning.

Other works, such as a series of pop-up pieces, have examined the mechanics of surprise and delight and their ability to reinterpret classic works through an engagement with the physicality of the text. The structures of theatre and its relationship to issues of time and the world of objects through which we move have also surfaced in work that has constructed an equivalence between the space of the work and the space of the viewer.

But rather than search for such a history, perhaps it is better to consider two particular aspects of how we come to know the world and our placement in it. We are all familiar with models, or what are called paradigms in philosophy. A paradigm is an example or pattern that is typical of a given structure, in a sense an archetype. It forms the basis for assembling the architecture of our world. Paradigms, or models, lay the groundwork of certainty that permits us to act confidently and purposefully. Armed with models for action or argument, we enact structures that command authority derived from those models.

Paradigms in themselves, however, lack an essential dimension. A model can describe or inform, but it cannot challenge that information or counter its description. It cannot represent itself to itself. This calls for another dimension of thought, and that requires that a conflictual relationship exist between equally admissible paradigms. That relationship we can call paradoxical, and paradox is a key structure that provides the critical relationship we need by which to interrogate the models or arguments we use and to build a more secure foundation for what we think we know. Unlike the paradigm in itself, the paradox confuses the question of truth, calls it into question, even subjects it to parody and derision. It calls into question what appear to be even the most obvious truths we unquestioningly assume on an everyday basis.

Theoris: a paradox offers a playful introduction to the complicated business of determining the dynamics of truth. Conceived as a kind of kit, something that can be trotted out and put up whenever convenient, *Theoris*: a paradox addresses the questions: what is an object, who am I, and how did I get here?

Postscript for an Anthology

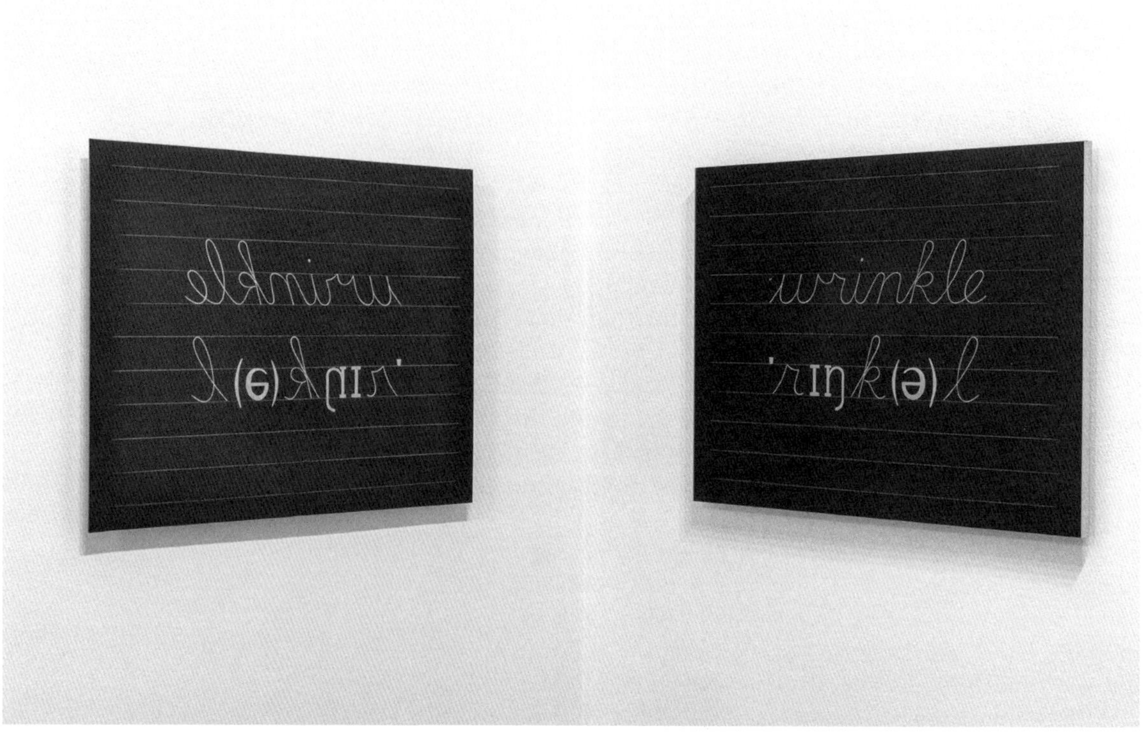

4.22   Ian Carr-Harris, *Wrinkle*, 2022. Blackboard material on 1.9 cm MDF, oil stick, 76.5 × 58.5 × 3.5 cm. Installation, Susan Hobbs Gallery, Toronto. Photo: Toni Hafkenscheid.

When all is said and done, I find myself asking what meaning attaches to an anthology of an artist's writings on art when that body of writing, rather than the individual texts themselves, reveals itself as a form. Particularly since it aligns with another body of work, the practice of art itself.

Ekphrasis is a Greek word applied to the description of a work of art for the purpose of expanding its meaning, and we could assume that this word would nicely summarize the practice of writing about art. But does it? In the preface I cite Borges's Pierre Menard story to raise the issue of the *palimpsest*, another Greek word. That concept, referring to the incomplete erasure of one text in order to apply another in its place, would seem to more truly clarify my relationship between the work of art and the discussion that must follow. I find that in the act of writing there is a moment when the writing itself erases its subject, the work of art, though clearly that work remains as a trace. To use Heidegger's invention, it remains "under erasure," present and necessary but for that moment set aside or overwritten. In its place are the words, and it is now the authority of the words that determines the work.

I write this with some trepidation since undeniably it is the work of art that enables the writing. But there is no contradiction, or rather there would only be a contradiction if both the work and the word were simultaneously to occupy the same space. It is the very absence of the one in the space of the other that enables their dialectical relationship to engage the viewer in a space that neither the work nor the words can themselves occupy. Hovering over the pages of the text, and Magritte-like over the work itself, is the inchoate shape of possibility that remains greater than either.

What then is this text that rests on the page? What relationship does it hold for the absent work, this work that is now under erasure? It is not the work; it is not even a semblance of the work. It has become a working-out-in-itself, an un-concealing, to use another Heideggerian term, that is not so much about the truth of its subject, but about the text as an opening up of what could be of value in the possibilities that the work has either intentionally or inadvertently called into existence.

And I have asked myself, how does this text function if it is to call into existence these possibilities? The text is writing, and must it not be its writeability, its allure—the sound of the word that will ring true to the work, like that invitation to a dance—that is key to its obligation to interrogate and if possible persuade. Because it is that which lies outside the frame, the reading viewer, to whom the palimpsest is dedicated.

As an artist, when I reflect on my own work it occurs to me that something of Alice passing through the looking-glass lingers in the history of my practice. Perhaps for that reason I have been fascinated by the simple childhood pop-up book. With its conflation of image, text, and passage, it rehearses that significance of discovery and loss that is inherent in our attempt to hold onto meaning. When I retrace the work through the text, I trace the capacity of the text to touch a memory of the work—for a moment only before it slips away, folding back on itself, becoming once again the text.

Ian Carr-Harris, January 2023

Index